ARCHAEOLOGIES
OF VIOLENCE
AND PRIVILEGE

Archaeologies of Violence and Privilege

EDITED BY CHRISTOPHER N. MATTHEWS
AND BRADLEY D. PHILLIPPI

University of New Mexico Press Albuquerque

ISBN 978-0-8263-6184-4 (cloth)
ISBN 978-0-8263-6185-1 (e-book)

Library of Congress Control Number: 2020945294

COVER ILLUSTRATIONS

"Block 60, 7/18/43." Historic photograph of Block 60, Butte Camp,
Gila River, taken from a nearby butte. Courtesy Ozawa
Family Collection; photographer unknown.

Detail of a Franklin Survey Company plate showing the location
of the "colored" YMCA along Oakwood Avenue in Orange, 1932.
The YWCA was part of a complex in the small building south
of Charles Saver Inc. Downloaded from Historic Map Works,
Rare Historic Maps Collection, http://www.historicmapworks.com.

DESIGNED BY Mindy Basinger Hill   COMPOSED IN Parkinson Electra

CONTENTS

ILLUSTRATIONS

TABLES

ARCHAEOLOGIES

OF VIOLENCE

AND PRIVILEGE

ONE

An Introduction to Archaeologies of Violence and Privilege

CHRISTOPHER N. MATTHEWS & BRADLEY D. PHILLIPPI

> While certain kinds of suffering are readily observable—and the subject
> of countless films, novels, and poems—structural violence all too
> often defeats those who would describe it.
>
> *Paul Farmer*

Violence rides rampant in contemporary society, though it is arguably an essential part of what makes modernity (and some say humanity) distinct (e.g., Baumann 1989; Sussman 1997; Wrangham and Peterson 1996). From state violence to the violence of war and genocide, from interpersonal violence to the way social lives are structured and symbolized by and through violence, we confront people doing terrible things to others almost every day and across almost every field of inter-action. As archaeologists, we are additionally exposed to forms of violence that occurred in past decades, centuries, and millennia, adding the depth of time to our understanding of human cruelty. Archaeological evidence of past violence emerges in the surviving remains of broken bodies, destroyed homes, hallowed battlefields, vacated and polluted places, as well as erased pasts. We also see violence when we work to understand why people commit atrocities, hoping to see beyond their rationalizations for injustice to what lies closer to their obscured hearts and minds. This effort forces confrontations at the intersections of past and present as well as conservative and progressive agendas that can easily erupt in new forms of violence in defense of a worldview or, at times, lead to painful transcendence as a former way of life is abandoned. Regardless, exposing the suppressed struggles of structural violence that drive some to cruelty reveals quite a lot about how persons, communities, nations, and cultures exist and intersect. The problem, as Paul Farmer describes in the epigraph, is that getting at the violence resident in the hearts and minds of those we study can be quite difficult. For

Farmer, one solution lies in documenting suffering, especially as it is embodied in individual lives. We think archaeologists are equally empowered to do the work of documenting the materiality and embodiment of suffering (also see Pollock 2016).

This book presents a series of archaeological studies of the early and late modern eras that document in specific times and places how past social formations rested on violent acts and reproduced violent social and cultural structures. The authors bring to light—through an interpretation of material objects, spaces, and their relations—how past communities perpetrated and faced modern forms of violence. A thread connecting the individual case studies is a focus on less observable structural and symbolic violence in addition to more direct evidence of violent acts. This is captured in our title, *Archaeologies of Violence and Privilege*, which ties the social and cultural advantages bestowed upon some to the way violence was unevenly distributed and experienced in past societies. The premise is simple: for privilege to exist, there must also be forms of violence that sustain and defend it.

Robert Kennedy captured this understanding of violence in a concise speech following the assassination of Martin Luther King Jr. As riots erupted across the United States, Kennedy said the following:

> Too often we honor swagger and bluster and the wielders of force; too often we excuse those who are willing to build their own lives on the shattered dreams of others. Some Americans who preach nonviolence abroad fail to practice it here at home. Some who accuse others of inciting riots have by their own conduct invited them. Some look for scapegoats, others look for conspiracies, but this much is clear; violence breeds violence, repression brings retaliation, and only a cleaning of our whole society can remove this sickness from our soul. For there is another kind of violence, slower but just as deadly, destructive as the shot or the bomb in the night. This is the violence of institutions; indifference and inaction and slow decay. This is the violence that afflicts the poor, that poisons relations between men because their skin has different colors. This is a slow destruction of a child by hunger, and schools without books and homes without heat in the winter. (Kennedy 1968)

The potency of the statement is evident as Kennedy shows that the interconnections that bind Americans are infused with violence, repression, resistance, and retaliation. He also identifies that this violence is found not only in what we see in riots but also in the institutions, indifference, and inaction that sustain and characterize the majority. What is more, this very same speech could have been given dozens more times by other public figures in the fifty-plus years since 1968. Similar sentiments, in fact, have been shared in responses to other devastating public executions. In response to the police shooting of Michael Brown in Ferguson, Missouri, in 2014, the Reverend Jesse Jackson said that Brown's death was part of "a pattern around the country of a black man being shot by white police, [falsely] arrested, stop and frisk, excessive jailing. This is a kind of lynching in 2014" (BBC News 2014). In 2013 the Malcom X Grassroots Movement published a report stating that killings of black Americans by "'law enforcement, security guards and stand-your-ground vigilantes' have increased from one every 36 hours, in the first half of 2012, to one every 28 hours by the end of that year" (Ragland 2014). Massive public protests around the world following Michael Brown's death, and again following subsequent police killings of young black men in Baltimore, Charlotte, Minneapolis, New York, Pittsburgh, and other places, make us aware that the experience and acknowledgment of institutional violence are widespread.

Also writing in response to the shooting of Michael Brown, legal scholar Lynda Sheryl Greene (2015:4) argues that "individual instances of police deadly force against unarmed Black men are enabled by a legal jurisprudence of structural violence which provides no accountability for the societal marginalization and stigmatization of young Black men, as well as by a jurisprudence of actual violence, which permits police officers to decide whom to target and whom to kill with virtually no threat of criminal sanction or institutional civil liability." She notes as well that there are significant disparities between whites and people of color in terms of being victims of a crime and having their cases addressed and resolved by the police. Greene is stating effectively that police violence and killings are not incidents solely related to the events and the people involved. Rather they reflect institutional structures within police departments and society at large that support racism, segregation, and unequal jurisprudence. That is, they are examples of structural violence that position people, because of race, class, and other markers, into different and hierarchically ranked categories of humanity. Forms of structural violence are found not only in law enforcement but also in employment, housing, education, and health care discrimination. Moreover, the violence experienced across these arenas together produces radically unequal life chances among American and global citizens.

Many readers will know the Black Lives Matter movement founded by Alicia Garza, Patrisse Cullors, and Opal Tometi in 2013 in response to the shooting of Trayvon Martin, an unarmed teenager, by a neighborhood watch vigilante. The organization gained national attention following the Michael Brown killing a year later. Black Lives Matter is a grassroots network of organizations advocating for reform in criminal justice as well as other arenas where "Black lives are systematically and intentionally targeted for demise." Its leadership of protests in Ferguson, Missouri, and elsewhere brought an understanding of structural violence in ways not seen before. It focuses on affirming "Black folks' humanity, our contributions to this society, and our resilience in the face of deadly oppression" (Black Lives Matter 2019).

The purpose and voice of Black Lives Matter have inspired a wide range of responses, including negative ones, such as organizations framed by mottoes such as "All Lives Matter" and "Blue Lives Matter," but for many, acknowledgment of the reality of structural violence in American society is something new and important to understand. Since 2014 professional and academic communities have looked with more clarity at their own positions to identify ways they perpetrate and benefit from racial, gender, sexual, class, and ability inequalities. Archaeologists, for example, have recently examined the issue of sexual harassment in the field, lab, and classroom, especially in light of the #MeToo movement (White 2017). This concern stands with a long acknowledged but poorly addressed fact that professional archaeologists are overwhelmingly white (Franklin 2001) and that most archaeologists in senior and supervisory positions are white men (White 2017).

It was in the spirit of Black Lives Matter and its consciousness-raising effects that Brad Phillippi and I chose to organize a session on archaeologies of violence and privilege at the 2016 conference of the Society for Historical Archaeology in Washington, DC. Our goal was to bring together colleagues with a shared interest in the archaeology of violence. However, we asked contributors to think specifically about the relationship between violence visible in the archaeological record and the sources of power and privilege that were imposed and sustained through these violent acts. The session was very successful, and we are pleased that many of the original participants have contributed chapters to this book. We are of course also pleased that the authors in this collection have carried forward the same spirit that led Brad and I to put together that session. In sum, we think this book presents a compilation of diverse case studies that show how archaeology can identify and interpret structural violence in the recent past. We hope these studies inspire future research in this field of study and support the global effort now under way to reform the institutions and cultural traditions that perpetuate social injustice against vulnerable people. In the following section I provide a brief review of related research in anthropology and other social sciences on the topic of structural violence. I then discuss the chapters that follow.

Studying Structural Violence

Nancy Scheper-Hughes and Philippe Bourgois (2003:20) write that "everyday forms of state violence make a certain kind of domestic peace [that is, privilege] possible." Slavoj Žižek (2008:2) identifies structural violence as "invisible" and "objective," such that it is the "background" or the "'normal' peaceful state of things." It is, in reality, "'the dark matter' ... that has to be taken into account if one is to make sense of what otherwise seem to be 'irrational' explosions of subjective violence." In other words, the idea of "senseless" violence is only possible when we also have a simultaneous conception that violent acts, speech, and indifference play out on (or explode from) a presumed field of nonviolence. The problem, as Žižek observes, is that the visible acts and agents of subjective violence are just the tip of a vast field of structural violence that is essential to the cultivation of objectivity and normalcy at the outset. Thus the subjectivity of violence—its explosive character and seeming senselessness—founders when it is understood to be simply a manifestation of what Pierre Bourdieu and Loïc Wacquant (2004:272) call "the order of things."[1]

Paul Farmer (2004a:281–82) sees this sort of violence as the process through which "various large-scale social forces [such as racism and poverty] come to be translated into personal distress and disease" or "the hard surfaces of individual suffering." Farmer's (2004b:307–8) goal is "to inform the study of the social machinery of oppression," and he sees this machinery based in the "materiality of the social order." Archaeologists gain from Farmer a sense of materiality that is at root social and cultural since he insists that, as anthropologists, we are trained to work hard to understand the historical and political economic contexts of those people and events we study. While other disciplines have generalized or "desocialized" their approaches to suffering, Farmer argues that anthropology (and we include archaeology) remains committed to recognizing that bodies, objects, places, acts, and ideas do not exist (or at least do not *matter*) in the abstract but emerge, suffer, succeed, and expand solely in concrete material conditions that we must understand. Moreover, as these conditions are primarily social, they tell us about the actual relations between people and groups that inflict violence and sustain privilege. This is why his appeal (Farmer 2004a:287) to consider the insights of liberation theology—or the restorative work that "moves immediately to the structural analyses of [oppressive] forces and denounces systems, structures, and mechanisms that 'create a situation where the rich get richer at the expense of the poor, who get even poorer'"—makes sense. We simply add that Farmer's interest in understanding both the rich and the poor in liberation theology is reflected here in our interest in understanding the archaeology of privilege and violence.

Sustaining privilege also requires various forms of defense. In modern society, based on the establishment of far-flung colonial and postcolonial networks and the development later of economies based on mass production and consumption, and complex and enormous urban centers, there is a premium placed on strategies and tactics of social control. Direct physical violence can be an effective defense of privilege, but it is costly and atomized. It is also constrained, since only individuals or small groups can be physically violated, coerced, or contained. Structural violence such as racism—the way communities and cultures are designed and operate through the exclusion of some as foreign, lesser, and disposable—or poverty, such as when prosperity and perceived success are made visible through conspicuous consumption and when failure, in turn, is designated as the result of personal deficiencies or decisions, provides a farther-reaching and more efficient way to establish and preserve privilege. In fact, according to Hannah Arendt (1969), direct physical violence lacks the legitimacy of structural violence since the perpetrators must waste effort in demonstrating their authority rather than being able take it for granted (Scheper-Hughes and Bourgois 2003:21). The use of symbols (in both discursive and material forms) to cohere the privileged to one another, despite other often obvious material differences among them, is thus a relatively inexpensive and more efficient way to sustain social advantage. Again, race can be used as an example, such as in Du Bois's notion of the "wages of whiteness," which explains that working-class American whites earn a psychological wage from being white that affords them greater security and privilege in the United States than nonwhites, regardless of their levels of education, social status, or wealth.

Another part of defending privilege is how structural violence constructs a range of violent acts, from the symbolic to the physical, as "expected, routine, even justified" by those who commit them *as well as* by their victims (Scheper-Hughes and Bourgois 2003:22). As opposed to instances of shocking corporeal violence (such as mass shootings) that can trigger official reactions, structural violence desensitizes populations to its effects, most clearly evidenced in the lack of any social response to violence at all. So, for example, the mass incarceration of young men of color remains tolerable in the United States even as increasingly visible police violence against this community is called out (Alexander 2010). It is thus imperative for researchers to interrogate the violence of social structures and symbols as well to consider how these are related to more overt and less socially acceptable forms of violence also witnessed in modern society.

An important method for this kind of research derives from Bourdieu's conceptualization of symbolic violence, which rests on a process of "misrecognition." Symbolic violence is "the violence which is exercised upon a social agent with his or her complicity" (Bourdieu 2004:272). Misrecognition sustains symbolic violence in the way people fail to see or deny the "economic and political interests present in a set of practices." Instead, these interests are "misrecognized as representing disinterested forms of activities and resources" (Schwartz 1997:43). Researchers often attribute misrecognition, which is sometimes glossed as a form of Marxian false consciousness, to working-class and marginal people who buy into dominant ideologies, such as individualism and the American Dream in the United States. In this case, the violence of a false egalitarian ideology is in part perpetrated by its victims on themselves. The concept of misrecognition also works in the reverse, such that those who commit violence against others may misrecognize their actions as disinterested, unrelated, or even good works. Misrecognition in this direction leads to a failure to recognize most of all a position of privilege. Bourdieu calls this privileged position "symbolic capital" or the benefits gained "from the transformation of self-interest into disinterest" (Schwartz 1997:43) that allow violent offenders to remain out of sight and inculpable.

THE CHAPTERS

The following chapters elaborate on these themes and illustrate how material objects, spaces, and practices represent the results of violent acts and have been arranged to support the misrecognition of economic and political interests and thus the reproduction and defense of privilege. As a collective, we recognize that there are topics and themes not covered herein. For example, none of the authors considers the relationship between routine corporeal violence against enslaved laborers and the quietude of the master's home. Nor is there a study of the massacre of indigenous people for the sake of opening lands to new settlers. These themes are essential to understanding the ways violence and privilege have been entwined to make the modern world, and many archaeologists have explored these topics (e.g., Blakey 1998; Gonzalez-Tennant 2018; Liebmann and Murphy 2011; Weik 2012; Wilcox 2009a). Rather, the chapters that follow examine somewhat less dramatic (if not less studied) though no less powerful moments and processes in the American past and its archaeological interpretations.

Reinhard Bernbeck's chapter considers privilege inherent to archaeology and related historical research. He outlines an approach framed by the concept of recognition, or the way human subjectivity is at play in the documentation of violent acts. While both victims and perpetrators of violence are present at the time of the act, it is not uncommon that one or both are absent, ignored, forgotten, or downplayed in the specific frameworks employed to document the events. Drawing on Axel Honneth (2008), Bernbeck argues that violence is the result of forgetting the original nature of intersubjectivity—or "the recognition of the other as a subject"—by those involved as well as by those reporting on violent acts to others. Forgetting intersubjectivity leads to objectification and in more extreme cases to reification, such that those who suffer or perpetrate are no longer seen as "one of us." Speaking directly to archaeological and historical practice, Bernbeck cautions strongly against the "scholarly reification" of the violence of past people and events through photography, materiality, and narrative. He quotes novelist Peter Weiss, who writes regarding a group viewing the graphically violent third-century Pergamon Altar in a Berlin museum, "The work gave pleasure to the privileged; the others sensed a segregation under a draconian law of hierarchy." The point is that the archaeologists in this example "solidarize with powerful," but also that all that is preserved, displayed, interpreted, and valued reflects the subjectivities of multiple persons both past and present who have engaged with artifacts. At no point are objects fully mute, but, as with Žižek, their presumed objectivity is the result of definitive social subjectivities that have created and deployed them for various, sometimes violent purposes.

Guido Pezzarossi's chapter on "Discursive Violence and Archaeological Ruptures" examines the sharp external conceptual divide between ancient and modern Maya communities. While the ancient Maya are well-known archaeological subjects, famous for their ceremonial centers in southern Mexico and Central America, the contemporary Maya are considered a fallen population whose existence can be juxtaposed to modernity. Pezzarossi points to a variety of factors for this impression, including the cultural changes and violence of colonialism, a prized ideology of mixed heritage or *mestizaje,* and the collusion of archaeologists who typically work in the Maya region without the consent of the descendent community. Clearly, separating the living Maya people from their past is a powerful form of symbolic violence. Yet Pezzarossi notes that a great deal of Mayan archaeology highlights the idea that the ancient Maya themselves were violent, a discourse that fuels a popular theory of cultural collapse that has underwritten the career success and privilege (that is, symbolic capital) of many archaeologists and other experts. To counter this trend, Pezzarossi researches colonial-period archaeological data showing that Maya people not only survived their supposed ancient collapse but also developed successful strategies to persist as a distinct people despite well-documented and objectively violent colonial-era efforts to control and destroy them. Sadly, even this persistence is discounted since their survival strategies imply a lack of a "cultural continuity" preferred by archaeologists and the Guatemalan state.

Kathryn Sampeck also considers the violence of colonialism in her chapter on "Spanish Colonialism and Spatial Violence." She engages the spatial theories of Michel Foucault to propose an approach to place as not just the location of violence but as a tactic of violence itself. Her focus is the spatial actions of Spanish colonial authorities over indigenous communities in both Central America and the North American Southeast. She examines in particular the Spanish practices of *congregación*, *reducción*, and *policía*, which moved indigenous populations into nucleated communities where they could be more easily surveilled and habituated into a colonial way of living. A firm basis of Spanish authority derived from an imposed morality, which was made evident in such spatial urban forms as racial segregation and the centrality and prominence of the church building. It was also revealed in the use of the public space for corporeal punishment of Indians. Less visible structural tactics of violence were also place-based, such as high rents and fees for public festivals that drained the wealth of indigenous people. Sampeck closes her chapter with a discussion of widowed landscapes—former indigenous territories that, due to ravages of warfare, disease, and dispossession, have since lost an association with their original inhabitants, especially after they were claimed by new settlers. This practice of "unseeing" Indians dates to the colonial era, when even places richly used and inhabited were identified as wilderness. Sampeck cites examples of Indian resistance, such as the destruction of colonial buildings of the Spanish in the Southeast. She interprets this as "a native act of undoing those who did not see them" and encourages archaeologists to address similar indigenous invisibilities by returning "place to the placeless" in their own research.

Examining the "incurable evil" of mercury poisoning in colonial Peru, Douglas Smit and Terren Proctor expose the direct and structural forces of colonial violence on indigenous people at *la mina de la muerte*, or "the mine of death." Skeletal evidence of several former mine workers supports Smit and Proctor's observations of the trauma of everyday direct violence associated with being compelled to labor as well as the long-term bodily effects from the repetitive motion and hard work of using pickaxes and hauling in the mines. Three fetal burials also suggest that miscarriage and stillbirths were regularities, a fact resulting from exposure to heavy metals associated with mining. While Smit and Proctor identify high levels of mercury poisoning in most individuals, they also refer to colonial records that suggest that miners developed ways to mitigate mercury poisoning, confirming that exposure to toxins was a normal experience. These various causes of suffering in the colonial past shed light on the physical horrors of colonial subjugation, but Smit and Proctor also remind us that poisonous industries leave a legacy for others to deal with. In this case, the descendant community of the colonial miners continues to struggle with mercury-contaminated soil and homes as part of daily life.

Michael Roller discusses multiple layers of violence related to the Lattimer Massacre, which occurred in Hazleton, Pennsylvania, in 1897. The massacre itself resulted in the death of nineteen striking coal miners, most of whom were "new immigrants" from eastern and southern Europe. Clearly exhibiting the connections between violence and privilege, the posse assembled to stop the strikers consisted of white, middle-class men with ties to the coal industry. Thus the violent killing of miners was perpetrated in defense of capital against labor. Roller sees the massacre as a form of subjective violence tied to other factors in the mining community's material world that reflect pervasive forms of systemic and symbolic violence committed by the mine owners and their community. Systemically, the landscape of Lattimer worker housing reinforced the distinctions between old and new immigrants through their segregation into separate sections of company housing as well as through the renting of land on the edge of settlements to the vulnerable newcomers, who had to build their own homes. Research and excavation at one of these marginal "shanty" communities revealed that it was densely packed with forty-two tiny homes and contained abundant evidence that the residents had to deal the ill effects of living in homes without the sanitation, space, and infrastructure found in the formal company housing. These physical attributes were subsequently deployed to racialize the residents as an inferior people, a social fact used not only to explain why they live in squalor but also to explain their labor activism. Of course, those explaining the lives and actions of laborers were middle-class people speaking to others in the middle class in order to symbolize and defend their mutual privilege.

Working with a combination oral history, documentary sources, and archaeology, Koji Lau-Ozawa discusses the violence of incarceration and erasure experienced by Japanese American detainees during World War II. Ten incarceration camps were constructed during the war to house more than 120,000 mostly

American citizens, who, because of race, were considered threats to American national security. Lau-Ozawa's focus is the Gila River Incarceration Camp in Arizona. In addition to illustrating the physical and emotional violence of forced mass removal, exclusion, incarceration, and surviving in harsh environmental conditions, he details three other subtle forms of violence evidenced at the camp. The first is the fact that the establishment of the camp on the reserved lands of the Gila River Indian community was a direct violation of Native American sovereignty. The second is a dominant narrative that emphasizes a false cultural homogeneity among the detainees. The third is that the evidence of gardens constructed by inmates reflects a way to create a sense of home and community under dire conditions but also a longer history of racism that pushed Japanese immigrants out of independent farming and other laboring professions. The fact that many Japanese people worked as gardeners was in large part the result of forces that denied them access to other work, so the gardens discovered at the incarceration camps reveal more than just their role in those sites. Lau-Ozawa's study is reminder to be cautious in our assessment of evidence without understanding the proper cultural and political economic contexts. He closes the chapter in turn by recognizing that the general ignorance among Americans of the incarceration camps is part of the privilege of being in the mainstream, a process that forces those who suffered to internalize their struggle but also presents the archaeological responsibility to bring attention to this history.

Paul Mullins, Kyle Huskins, and Susan Hyatt consider the role of structural violence and racism tied to polluted waterways in Indianapolis, Indiana. They document the clear associations between polluted waters in the city, especially the White River, and the predominantly African American Near Westside neighborhood that runs along the riverbank. As an example, nineteenth-and early twentieth-century plans to create a river-based urban park system were abandoned so they would not have to include the Near Westside. While some pointed to the fact that the White River was a "malodorous, septic stream," this character was also transferred to the nearby African American residents, who were cast as "bringing with them the lowest standard of housing and sanitary conveniences." Such assessments reflect the racialization of urban space while ignoring that most of the impurities in the water derived from riverside industries as well as the failure to expand sewer systems to poor and African American neighborhoods. Mullins, Huskins, and Hyatt further document that the city's effort to offer sanitary swimming options reinforced Jim Crow racial segregation and thus failed to provide for African Americans. The city never built a municipal pool in the Near Westside, citing its proximity to the White River, which was reassessed to be safe for black swimmers. Efforts by well-off African Americans to provide access to sanitary swimming for themselves by building a country club were also denied by racist residents living near the proposed club site. Mullins, Huskins, and Hyatt conclude their chapter noting that recent efforts to once again rehabilitate the White River shoreline for public recreational use reflect a stark ignorance of the racist and structurally violent history tied to waterways in Indianapolis. They urge instead that any such public land use be cognizant of the harm the city's neglect of its water has done to its vulnerable communities as way to foster a more socially aware understanding of how infrastructure, race, and privilege are entangled.

The final substantive chapter, by Chris Matthews, examines another example of how urban infrastructure enacts structural violence on marginal communities. His study is of the impact of Interstate 280 on the small city of Orange, New Jersey. Constructed in the late 1960s, I-280 is a depressed highway that was cut through the center of Orange, paving a path from the city of Newark and other major highways to new suburban developments to the west. In Orange, I-280 cut through the historic African American and Italian American working-class neighborhoods, removing from each dozens of homes and small family-owned businesses as well as key social institutions such as YMCAS, churches, and community centers. Matthews argues that the highway was one facet of a broad effort to build a racially segregated carceral landscape that contained a heavily policed and violent urban core populated predominantly by people of color. This core is surrounded by majority white suburbs that enjoy comparatively low crime rates and were untouched by highway construction. The point of the highway in this case was to provide easy and safe access to the urban center for suburbanites, yet its effect in Orange and surrounding cities has been to create a desolate and dangerous local landscape that further devalues local communities. Furthermore, as Matthews shows, travel along I-280 and similar urban freeways provides the opportunity for privileged motorists to be unaware of the communities they pass through even as the speed, fumes, and sounds of their vehicles leave behind streams of pollution and other ill effects.

The final chapter in the book is a commentary on the chapters by LouAnn Wurst. Wurst offers insights on many common themes found throughout the chapters, such as challenging dominant narratives about the past and revealing ties between past violent events and persistent and present consequences. She also highlights a shared focus on the resilience of actors in the face of violence as well as the way violence informs how people past and present are made visible and invisible to contemporary communities. Wurst imparts a very clear concern that the study of violence itself is problematic. Following Žižek, she cautions that archaeologists be wary of a "cold analysis" of past violence that dehumanizes and classifies violent acts. She offers a corrective to this concern by encouraging archaeologists to maintain a focus on the perpetrators as well as their victims. Especially in the study of structural violence, where perpetrators are sometimes faceless or obscured, Wurst demands that we work hard to identify those who hold the strings of power. Whether this be specific individuals or those who directly benefit from the violence suffered by others, the perpetrators of violence need to be named and to remain in view.

FORUM

Following the commentary, we put together a forum among the contributors, who were given the chance to reflect on Wurst's observations as well as the broader conceptions embodied by this book. Each contributor prepared a short statement on how their work presents a view on the archaeology of violence as something not yet examined by other research on past inequalities. Authors were also asked to comment on the value of considering the dialectic of violence and privilege as a means of understanding the nuances of unequal social relations.

Archaeology as Witness

One final component of privilege is latent in most of these chapters, yet it is essential to their individual and collective success. This is the act of being a witness to violence. Unlike ethnographic accounts of violence that often derive from firsthand engagements with perpetrators and victims, archaeologists document violence retroactively through what has survived or been left behind in the form of objects that can be excavated and analyzed, memories that can be recorded, and documents that can be reviewed. Nevertheless, we would be remiss to think that temporal distance relieves us of the responsibility to be an engaged witness for those who suffered. Like most archaeology, the work included here is framed by a goal of recognition and recovery, but what is recovered in these pages is also tied to an additional commitment "to eschew the privileges of neutrality" (Scheper-Hughes and Bourgois 2004:26) typical of scientific research. Rather the authors in this book employ archaeological research to reassess what we know about the past so that we can change what we know about the present. This process of "diachronic recognition" (Bernbeck, this volume) allows victims of violence from decades and centuries ago to play a role in the modern communities that inherited the legacies of that violence in various forms. Framing the following research as a form of recognition and recovery leads to cultural critique. This critique is of course of the inherited privilege of the majority, who know almost nothing at all about the violence caused by the construction of their own ways of life or, of course, that the normalcy of their ignorance could be seen in what Giorgio Agamben (2004:441) describes as "the true horror of the camp." Scheper-Hughes and Bourgois (2004:26) urge that we recover and write these stories so that we might inform those distanced or blinded by privilege and resensitize them to the violence that surrounds them and that the defense of their way of life continues to cause.

Note

1. Defining symbolic violence, Bourdieu and Wacquant (2004:272) write, "Being born in a social world, we accept a whole range of postulates, axioms, which go without saying and require no inculcating. This is why the analysis of the doxic acceptance of the world, due to the immediate agreement of objective structures and cognitive structures, is the true foundation of a realistic theory of domination and politics. Of all forms of 'hidden persuasion,' the most implacable is the one exerted, quite simply, by the *order of things*."

TWO

Violence in Archaeology
and the Violence of Archaeology

REINHARD BERNBECK

In the spring of 1991, I worked for a humanitarian organization in the western Afghan city of Herat. One day, when driving a pickup through Herat's colorful bazaar, my car suddenly jumped forward, and I heard a loud noise somewhere behind me. A bomb had gone off not too far away. Bystanders quickly ran to the spot and helped bloodstained people into the back of the pickup, which I then drove to a nearby hospital.

This is a standard scenario that fits general imaginations of "violence." During my time in Herat, the communist military forces in the castle above the city were regularly using their artillery to aim at mujahedin-occupied areas. The mujahedin, already in the western suburbs, fired their Kalashnikovs without any apparent strategy from the rubble of ruined buildings into east-west streets. On many days it became impossible to set foot outside of the walled compound in which I lived. Still, life had a strangely normal feel: an environment rife with quotidian physical violence produces adjustments to these conditions by changing one's expectations about the immediate future.

In 2016 I met a Syrian family on a regular basis. The father and two sons had fled to Berlin some eighteen months before from a place in eastern Syria ruled nowadays by the Islamic State (IS). The father worked as a nurse in Syria and had a small village pharmacy. One day members of IS came to his house and tried to force him to work for them; at that point he decided to flee. Another reason was that one of the sons was—and still is—in need of special medical treatment of a kind that became unavailable under IS. The mother and three smaller children stayed behind but were later also able to flee Syria and take refuge in the city of Urfa in southeastern Turkey. However, despite the dire situation of the whole family and the severe health condition of one of the sons, the German refugee administration did not grant the family the right to be reunited. From a bureaucratic point of view, this may be seen as a simple decision taken according to current law. However, from other perspectives, such a verdict amounts to "structural violence."

The contrast between these two forms of violence is striking. The one in Afghanistan was direct, physical, and immediately life-threatening. In all likelihood, the perpetrators behind the bombing were mujahedin. The case of the Syrian refugees in Berlin is about faceless perpetrators. It is the structures and rules set up by the German state that keep people in a condition of desperation—and decidedly not just the warring parties in Syria. While there is a vast array of different forms of violence, any attempt to give an account of them—or even of a single incident—must also reflect on the position from which they are analyzed and interpreted.

In this paper I am concerned with hidden forms of violence that structure our archaeological forms of knowledge production. I analyze these through a consideration of different kinds of sources, including photographic, material, and narrative ones. Before delving into specific cases, I discuss a recognition-theoretical approach to these issues that is based on the writings of Louis Althusser, Judith Butler, and Axel Honneth. As the reader will realize, I have no easy solutions to offer for problems encountered. Rather my goal is to sharpen our sense for the aporias and logical impasses in this sphere of human life and death.

What Is Violence?

In daily life, we talk about violence as brutalities that impinge on people's physical integrity. Media reports constantly feed this understanding. Violence boils down to acts characterized as emotional outbursts of individuals who have lost self-control, a mode of action that has been foregrounded in sociology as well (e.g., Collins 2008). Or we envision torturers as particularly unusual and evil characters who expertly devise and inflict suffering on others in cold blood. In the present moment, the most immediate association may be the scenario of the proverbial terrorist: an individual or a small group imagined as intent on wreaking havoc on targets that consist of random groups of people in public spaces who are maimed or killed. The means for such actions range from large amounts of explosives to the use of everyday things such as cars and trucks.

The ways in which violence is carried out seem to be endless. But if we want to grasp this multifariousness, a few preliminary issues need to be clarified. First, violence differs from other social relations because there is no other possibility to account for it than as a post hoc assessment or coincidental witnessing. "Testing" reactions to violence would amount to committing it. And trying to involve oneself in acts of violence with the goal of observing the outcome cannot but contribute to carrying out violence and is thus deeply enmeshed in what it pretends to observe. Second, because of these particularities, social and academic discourses about violence do not normally start from an insider's position. Therefore it is important to investigate discursive constructions of violence and what they represent as its most basic features. Third, research on different kinds of violence, as well as the definition of the term, is fast expanding, leading to a need to assess its outer boundaries.

To start with archaeology: a search on the internet for the keywords *archaeology* and *violence* turns up mostly reports on prehistoric massacres, mass graves, and trepanation, as well as references to the works of Azar Gat (2008), Steven Pinker (2011), and Ian Morris (2014). These latter works, large-scale, ultra-long-term accounts of the evolution of human societies, all claim that we can be glad to live in the present, as the overall trend in human history is marked by a global waning of violence. They share this conviction with Norbert Elias (1969) and Lawrence Keeley (1996). Common to such treatises is a notion of violence as physical and leading to death. With the exception of Elias, who focuses on inner repression as a mechanism to tame human subjects, the main grounds for an argument of long-term evolutionary pacification of the human species are demographic statistics, measured in terms of the number of violent deaths per one hundred thousand people (Lawler 2012).

Now that the thesis of decreasing violence has become dominant, every new piece of evidence for physical violence in prehistory is inserted into this narrative as proof. A particular role in current discourse is played by Neolithic *Linearbandkeramik* sites in central Europe. Evidence for bodily violence was recently discovered at sites such as Talheim, Asparn/Schletz, Jungfernhöhle, Menneville, and Herxheim, and it has been turned into support for the brutality of our ancestors (e.g., Golitko and Keeley 2007). However, such evidence also lends itself to different interpretations, a prominent one being "ritualistic violence" (Zeeb-Lanz and Haack 2016; for a Maya case, see Duncan and Schwarz 2015). There were, according to the latter scholars, rules about how to carry out violent acts, and triggers for physical aggression that were part of past people's set of cultural values.

These archaeological discussions display patterns that can also be found in controversies over violence in modern times. In the social sciences, we find a divide between research based on a notion of violence as rational and calculated, and a phenomenological-psychological approach that focuses on its emotional and irrational aspects. Often, those working with a rationalist definition also consider violence to be primarily a collective phenomenon. We encounter notions such as an "economy of violence" (Münkler 2005:74–98).[1] Because it is backed by or at the core of an institution, whether the state or a military apparatus, the temporality of violence is conceptualized as enduring, managed, and open to a planned future. In such a framework, a range of specific questions emerge: an institution that commits violence may provoke counterviolence, from banditry to open revolt, insurgency, and revolution. Within this discursive field there is a strong tendency to discuss violence in terms of its legitimacy, provoking ethical questions about who has the moral authority to attack an Other. Walter Benjamin's *Critique of Violence* (1986 [1921]) revolves around the general right to counterviolence, while Frantz Fanon's *Wretched of the Earth* (1963) can be read as a legitimation of the right to take up arms in anticolonial struggles.

In contrast, since the 1990s there have been more investigations of the emotional sides of violence. This research focuses on violence as an act of embodied cruelty, zeroing in on the instant of brutality. There is a tendency to limit analyses to small scales and the quintessential vulnerability of human bodies (e.g., Knüsel and Smith 2013; Martin, Harrod, and Pérez 2013), with reference to Merleau-Ponty's notion of "intercorporeality" (Merleau-Ponty 1968; see also Moran 2016). Such reflections argue that a search for causes of violence does nothing to explain it, as these causes remain conditions external to actual practices, leaving the perpetrators as pawns incapable of taking responsibility for their own actions. Such scholars also criticize the objectivist statistical basis of larger-scale research, preferring an approach they liken to Clifford Geertz's "thick description." The result is a move away from the "why" of violence to the "how" (Staudigl 2013:47–50), from institutions and collectivities to relations that are characterized by intersubjective proximity. Historical as well as sociological writings on the Nazi period have deeply influenced this approach. Christopher Browning's *Ordinary Men* (1992) is an extraordinarily impressive (and nauseating) account of how "normal" members of a Hamburg police battalion transformed into bloodthirsty murderers who killed tens of thousands of people. The narrative is mainly based on court documents of the battalion's members—most of whom were acquitted in their 1968 trial. The power of Browning's approach is exactly the close description of the scenes of mass murder, of individual perpetrators and their reasons for contributing (and, for very few, not contributing) to merciless atrocities. The village of Józefów, with its small streets and marketplace, and the individual Jewish victims—their names and relatives, ages and health—appear in front of the readers' eyes, only then to be annihilated. Wolfgang Sofsky (1999) takes a different phenomenological approach to the Holocaust. He describes an idealized concentration camp's elements in great detail, sometimes including references to concrete places but mostly staying on an abstract level. This text is especially relevant for anyone interested in material culture, as it exposes the relation between the material frames of camp spaces, temporalities, and functional elements, and the actions of the SS and other perpetrators in the camps.

The examples of Nazi Germany and other genocidal occurrences (Hinton 2002; Kotek and Rigoulet 2000; Scheper-Hughes and Bourgois 2003) may be considered cases of violence that are all too obvious to serve as a background for an exploration of violence in archaeology. The contributions to this book are based on a much broader notion of violence that includes spatial order, narratives, race relations, and privilege. These go beyond the usual quotidian understanding of our subject and require some considerations that transcend thick descriptions of brutal acts.

Recognition and Violence

I start this section from the premise that all violence is based on relations of power—mostly but not always political power. However, not all power relations are violent. This is nothing new. Johan Galtung's well-known "structural violence," amended later by "cultural violence" (Galtung 1969, 1985; Schroer 2000), Pierre Bourdieu's writings on "symbolic violence" (Bourdieu and Passeron 1990), and ideas about "slow violence" (Ahmann 2018; Nixon 2011) have set the stage for other work in a similar vein. There are also numerous critiques of these expansive understandings of violence, mainly objecting to a terminological extension that makes it hard to distinguish between such "abstract" forms of violence on the one hand and inequality and power on the other. Such disputes date back several decades and have to be read in the intellectual context of movements against the French occupation of Algeria and the Vietnam War, and in the late 1960s and 1970s student protests. Questions about the legitimacy of counterviolence were part of daily life.

More importantly, they were coupled with a deeper inquiry into the functioning of political power. Louis Althusser's (1971) influential treatise on ideology, published in 1970 in La Pensée, frames many of those arguments. For him, power is political and is always constituted by two elements: a "repressive state apparatus" (RSA), which includes military, police, and other state institutions, and an "ideological state apparatuses (ISA). The RSA "functions 'by violence,' whereas the Ideological State Apparatuses 'function' 'by ideology'" (Althusser 1971:145). Apart from the tautology—which he elaborates later in the essay—Althusser's vocabulary already shows his focus on the state as a repressive and potentially violent actor. However, the discussion implicitly also harks back to Max Weber's oft-cited definition of the state, which is also centered on the role of violence: "A compulsory political association with continuous organization will be called a 'state' if and insofar as its administrative staff successfully upholds a claim to the monopoly of the legitimate use of physical force in the enforcement of its order" (Weber 1978:54).[2] This kind of approach is based on the idea that states organize an absence of violence by appropriating for themselves the sole right to exercise it, as outlined already by Hobbes in his *Leviathan* (Hobbes 2010 [1651]). Althusser's questioning, however, does not concern the state's seizure of a right to violence but rather the citizenry's submission under such circumstances. Contrary to Hobbes's assertion that any rational person would give up rights in order to join the security umbrella of states, Althusser asks what the conditions are for establishing the possibility of such submissive, nonviolent relations.

While Althusser's wording may appear problematic and overly state-focused, his general idea about relations of dominance in the production of subjects continues to be widely discussed (e.g., Charim 2009; Lock 1996; Močnik 1993; Montag 2013:118–40; Ricoeur 1994). As he outlines, the notion of a subject contains both the meaning of a freely choosing and acting individual as well as the status indicated by the original Latin meaning, a *sub-iectum*, or a "subjugated" person. Althusser also claims that even the cruelest political regimes do not rely on repression alone. They always include the ideological apparatuses that convince the dominated about the usefulness of their submission. Every single repressive apparatus incorporates ideological components and vice versa (Althusser 1971:145).

Another part of Althusser's reflections has led to more intense scrutiny. Most of the discussions after the publication of his 1971 essay are centered on his description of "interpellation," sometimes rendered in English as "hailing." In his view, political power interpellates people through various kinds of institutions. He lists family, church, union, school and university, media and advertisement, among others. Interpellation is a particular kind of relationship between an institution or its representatives and those it addresses. The core of Althusser's essay is a simple sentence: "Ideology hails or interpellates individuals as subjects." A few sentences later he adds that *"individuals are always-already subjects"* (Althusser 1971:175–76; emphasis in original). Ideology has the paradoxical capacity to constitute subjects who consider themselves as both acting autonomously and as being subjugated. The simple scene of a policeman calling on someone—"Hey, you there!"—is Althusser's "little theoretical theatre" (Althusser 1971:174), which enables him to explain hailing. Hearing a call, we often suspect that we are called upon no matter who is meant, and we respond accordingly. Advertisements are the most obvious and all-pervasive examples of such mechanisms in our contemporary world. The point is not whether we misinterpret the hailing; rather it is our general willingness to respond to it. It is this willingness that leads to our submission, the simple fact of responding. At the same time, this response is perceived as one's free choice and produces the impression of autonomy, leading to the fundamentally split structure of all subjectivity. Name-giving and responding to it are primary experiences that contribute fundamentally to this effect. In this particular instance, an argument closely resembling Althusser's can be found in Foucault's notion of "subjectivation" (Distelhorst 2007:255–67; Foucault 2000:331).[3]

According to Althusser, the praxis of repressive apparatuses is violence, while ideology works through interpellation. However, he never claims explicitly that interpellation is a nonviolent intervention. This can only be extracted from the firm coupling of the RSA with violence as its prominent praxis. One can deduce that the nonviolent nature of ideological interventions is defined by the recognition of a subject on the side of its addressees. Ideology "supposes" a subject and in addition one that is supposed to believe in an interpellation's content (Močnik 1994), while violence functions without such a supposition. In several contributions to this debate, Judith Butler (1997:106–31; 2009:165–84) has argued against such an interpretation. She claims that interpellation is itself of a violent nature, since hailing is responsible for the constitutive split of all subjectivity. Hailing turns the interpellated person into a true subject with the choice to respond and become subjected or to stay outside the world of subjects and of recognition as a social human being altogether. The violent structure of interpellation is that it leaves no real choice and that it subjugates those called upon under the rules of the institutions and discourses that have the power to interpellate. There is no individual autonomy without its opposite, the caging of a subject into predefined criteria . The two facets are co-constitutive. The violence of interpellation as a subjectivation process goes further, as hailing transforms people not just into abstract subjects but into specific ones with a racialized, gendered, and culturalized internal structure, all against our will and from which there is no complete escape (Butler 2009:167). Butler claims that we cannot escape being subjugated but that this paradoxical assent still provides us with a small space to act autonomously. Furthermore, as already mentioned by Althusser, ideological interpellation consists of a constant reproduction of the primordial contradictory unity of subjection and autonomy. According to Butler, the unending process of a split subjectivation is therefore a constant infliction of violence.

Contrary to Butler's reading of Althusser, I wish to pursue a line of thinking that considers relations between individuals as nonviolent when they are based on a mutual recognition as subjects, even when such relations include stark power differences. (Obviously, this differentiation excludes all cases of direct or physical violence.) It is the lack of recognition in intersubjective encounters that amounts to violence. If we follow this reasoning, we can also distinguish symbolic, structural, or cultural violence from other, nonviolent relations, once we have agreed upon how recognition works. For that, I turn to writings by critical theorist Axel Honneth (2008). Out of a close reading of Georg Lukács's preoccupation with *Verdinglichung*, or "reification" (Lukács 1971), Honneth distills the process of reification in mutual relations as a loss of care for others due to an attitude that sees them at best as a means to other ends or at worst as pure objects. Based on readings of Hegel and Marx but also of the developmental psychologist Michael Tomasello's (2009) work, Honneth claims that human beings establish first and foremost intersubjective relations, while subject–object relations are of a secondary nature. Beyond respect and mutuality, sympathetic engagement—that is, the ability to take over the perspective of those we communicate with—is at the core of human existence and the capacity to interact symbolically. The basic human relation to the world is not an instrumentalist relation of "making" or of a cognition of others as objects external to oneself (Honneth 2008:37). To put it succinctly, "recognition comes before cognition." The detached knowledge of others as exteriorities is preceded by perceiving them as on a par, of the same kind as us.

An ideal of recognition as an attitude toward one's counterparts as subjects of equal value and composition is contrasted with reification, the complete dismissal of all personal traits of others, a positioning that knows neither care nor respect. However, Honneth inserts a third possibility between the two extremes of full recognition and complete reification. He calls this relationship to others one of "objectification." It is by no means always and everywhere necessary to display an attitude of recognition in relations between humans, he claims. An epistemic position of "knowing others," of seeing in them more an object than a subject, is acceptable under the precondition of being conscient of the primacy of a recognitional position. In contrast, central to reification processes is a forgetting of the original nature of intersubjective relations, the recognition of the other as a subject, and a historically changing one at that. I propose that this "forgetfulness of recognition," or what Honneth calls *Anerkennungsvergessenheit*, is typical of violent relations.

In violent relations, the dominating side does not recognize the subjugated one as a subject in the sense of a freely acting individual but only as an object, a sub-iectum. No effort is made in such relations to convince an Other of the usefulness or appropriateness of a power relationship. That is, violence is a power relation without an interpellative aspect. From the perspective of an institution and those in power, the subordinate Other turns into a reified thing. For example, when people are arrested, the mug shots taken by the police constitute a form of violence, since the face of the suspect is not captured by the camera with an interest in a human being with his or her own childhood, traces of joy and sorrow, but is captured as an object that identifies someone suspected to be a dangerous criminal. It is a means to reify a person in order to control and dominate them, not as subject but as object. Many administrative practices work the same way. Employee ID numbers, Social Security numbers, or letters from banks to people who hold accounts with them all have tendencies towards de-subjectivation. Of course, the capitalist logic of abstract exchange is the major force behind our capacity to reify almost anyone. However, there is a fine line between objectification, a cognitional relation to others that remains mindful of their subjectivity, and reification that forgets the latter. For any specific historical case, this boundary must be evaluated carefully.

Again, the Nazi regime provides some of the most extreme examples. Primo Levi's account of his arrest near Carpi includes an episode before he was carted off to the train station where captives were loaded onto the infamous cattle cars that transported them to Auschwitz: "With the absurd precision to which we later had to accustom ourselves, the Germans held a roll-call. At the end the officer asked 'Wieviel Stück?' The corporal saluted smartly and replied that there were six hundred and fifty 'pieces' and that all was in order" (Levi 2007:7). Language itself turns into heinous violence here, presaging the numbers that would be burnt into Levi's and others' skins, a cruel attempt at lifelong withdrawal of subjectivity. But many seemingly innocent persons who enabled the train to depart or who freed up cattle cars had their share in this massive violence. The historian Raul Hilberg sums it up: "In the totality of the administrative process, the destruction of the Jews presented itself as an additional task to a bureaucratic machine that was already straining to fulfill the requirements of the battlefronts. . . . Notwithstanding these priorities, no Jew was left alive for lack of transport to a killing center" (Hilberg 2003:1076).

Violence is not just a loss of physical integrity. The many relations between humans that we can characterize as violent have one element in common: a lack of recognition of the subjectivity of the Other. If our imagination associates physical infringement with the word *violence*, other power relations that are driven by reification can be equally brutal. "You can kill a person with an apartment just as well as with an axe," the Berlin graphic artist Heinrich Zille once said. The hidden ways of causing humiliation, distress, and suffering require our close attention, not only due to their silent, largely undetectable dynamics but also because we ourselves may mobilize them in our research. In the following sections, I discuss three issues of importance to historical archaeology: photographs (and imagery in general), materiality, and the construction of narratives about the past.

Historical Photography as Violence

In his well-known book *Hitler's Willing Executioners*, Daniel Goldhagen writes: "Photographs . . . remind us to question the prevailing views that hold these Germans to have been frightened, coerced, unwilling, disapproving, or horrified killers of people whom they considered to be innocent. Indeed, some of the photos capture men who are looking tranquil and happy, and others show them in poses of pride and joy as they undertake their dealings with their Jewish victims" (Goldhagen 1996:247). The main point for Goldhagen is that the pictures counter the standard historical narrative of German soldiers having been forced into support for a war of aggression against the Soviet Union and an involuntary complicity with SS murderers.

Around the time Goldhagen's book appeared, hundreds of similarly harrowing photos of war crimes were shown in Germany in the so-called *Wehrmachtsausstellung*, an exhibit curated by Hannes Heer for the Hamburg Institute for Social Research. Heer's goal was to reveal the German military's deep involvement in war crimes, particularly during the war against the Soviet Union. From the end of the Nazi regime on, public discourse had upheld the myth of the Wehrmacht as one of the few entities in German society that stayed morally above the fray by adhering to internationally recognized rules of war. If anyone in the Nazi military was guilty, it was only the upper echelons of generals around Hitler himself. The means to dismantle this myth consisted in simply showing a massive amount of mostly private photographs from normal soldiers, the so-called *Landser*. These images display soldiers humiliating Jews, Jewish civilians begging for mercy or shoveling their own graves, mass shootings, hangings, desecration of cemeteries, and other crimes. Often, the perpetrators' faces display gratification and smiles. No one visiting the exhibit could eschew the strange emotional power of these images due to the simultaneity of cruelty and joy. But the exhibit was fiercely attacked by former soldiers and right-wing politicians. Claims of false attribution of photographs led to a scientific inquiry, which concluded that among 1,433 photos, ten captions contained mistakes, such as identifying perpetrators as Nazi military when they were in fact Soviet soldiers (Wiegel 2002). As a consequence, the Hamburg Institute ended the traveling exhibit in 1999.

If we analyze the dispute in the framework of violence as outlined above, several different dimensions emerge. Physical violence is immediately evident as the primary content of the imagery. But what about the photographers? Because they were present during the execution of war crimes, do they not serve an important function as witnesses? The imagery itself rules out such a reading. A photo that shows a handful of grinning men in uniform around makeshift gallows with three dangling bodies and other victims preparing for the same fate reveals its own violent origin.[4] Countless similar scenes make it obvious that these photographers were absolutely incapable of seeing in the captured victims subjects like themselves.

As for the exhibition—organized fifty years after World War II—one could claim that the curators around Hannes Heer had no interest in comprehending the individual stories of the perpetrators as subjects. The exhibition team did not follow historian Browning's strategy of a "thick description" to track the slow brutalization of the perpetrators but rather saw in the uniformed amateur photographers and their motifs a political issue of and for the present. One could even suggest that the few mistakes in their research on the origins of the photographs were the result of what Honneth calls "forgetfulness of recognition." But another, more immediate kind of violence also accompanied the presentation of the photographs. Neo-Nazis marched against the exhibit in many cities. On March 9, 1999, a bomb attack devastated the building in Saarbrücken that housed the exhibit. The perpetrators remain unknown up to today.

When the director of the Hamburg Institute stopped the first exhibit, he announced a revised version with a new curator, Ulrike Jureit. In this second exhibition, the Landser photos of torture, hanging, and other cruelties, along with the smirking Wehrmacht soldiers, were largely removed. The inner logic shifted to the accustomed discourse, mainly blaming a small elite of Nazi generals rather than normal soldiers for the war crimes (Heer 2004:12–45). This amounts to a shift from the display of direct violence to its dissolution into structures of command. The Holocaust and war of annihilation against the Soviet Union turned again into a "pictureless act of faceless perpetrators" (Heer 2004:38). The whole affair is revealing for the multiplicity of forms of violence that crossed one another. Even in the last years of the twentieth century, it was impossible to openly admit that Germans in military uniform were massively and conscientiously involved in violent war crimes and the Holocaust (which took place not only in concentration camps).

However, the angry German debate, the verbal and physical attacks on the exhibit, left a gap. While the curators of the first exhibit, right-wing politicians, and officials in cultural institutions fought over the historical truthfulness of photographs and their representativeness for the overall events in war, it did not occur to them that the display of cruelties, murder, and violence might first and foremost require reflections about the victims' rights to refuse the public display of these photos. Couldn't the circulation of these photographs be considered a case of symbolic violence? Just because most of the images capture victims shortly before or during their violent deaths does not mean that their opinions about being shown in humiliating poses are irrelevant. Recognition as an intersubjective relationship of mutual respect may seem a paradox when one side in such relations is no longer alive. "The slain are really slain," is Max Horkheimer's apodictic comment (in a letter to Walter Benjamin; see Benjamin 1999:471), and "the suffering of past generations receives no compensation" (Horkheimer 2002:26). But does this amount to a license to do with the pictorial, bodily, written, and other remains of the slain whatever we please? Or is there perhaps a need for "diachronic recognition?"

At this juncture, Honneth's differentiation between objectivation and reification seems to me eminently relevant: reification implies the complete forgetting of an Other's subjectivity, while objectivation is a process that stays aware of an Other's subjectivity even when the relationship itself has the trappings of reification. One could therefore argue that the victims in the exhibition's photographs could be shown as long as each sufferer and killed person was perceived not just as a means to prove the criminality of the perpetrators. An overfocus on that goal forgets the victims' suffering, and so the dispute over the first *Wehrmachtsausstellung* was a process of reification on both sides of the debate that amounted to a second, postmortem act of symbolic violence. Referring in general to photographs from the Holocaust and World War II, Susan Crane writes that the shame of victims is prolonged into eternity when such photos of ruthless atrocities are shown in exhibitions or on the internet: "We ought to respond to an ethical injunction to find out more about [an image of atrocity] before we use it, recirculate it, or attempt [to] pass it off as 'representative' of humanity or of history" (Crane 2008:311).

This idea was already expressed by Susan Sontag (1977:14–15) in her well-known essay *On Photography*: "There is something predatory in the act of taking a picture. To photograph people is to violate them, by seeing them as they never see themselves. . . . It turns people into objects that can be symbolically possessed. Just as a camera is a sublimation of the gun, to photograph someone is a sublimated murder—a soft murder, appropriate to a sad, frightened time."

Historical archaeology that investigates sites of violence and terror is confronted with similar issues. Excavations of mass graves, of camps and battlefields, may be justified and needed, as shown so well by Eyal Weizman and his team pursuing what they call "new forensis" (Keenan and Weizman 2012; Weizman 2014). But is it necessary to depict anonymous skeletons from World War I mass graves or the Spanish Civil War (e.g., illustrations in Boura 2017; Renshaw 2011; Theune 2014)?[5] Is this not an act of utter reification, even when or exactly because such photographs are meant to support claims about a historical narrative that tries to address past injustice? There is no exit from this paradoxic situation.

This violent nature of photography overshadows its use in archaeology. Recent discussions about archaeological photography focus on colonial and orientalist attitudes: the omission of local workers but also of women, of tools as indices of labor, of items of everyday use. In these respects, archaeological photographs obscure instead of document (Baird 2011; Bohrer 2011:73–81; Hamilakis, Anagnostopoulos, and Ifantidis 2009;). These critiques are well taken, as photographic practice in archaeology erases subjective elements: the variable feelings of drudgery and sweat, expectations and disappointments of those cooperating in a project are hidden behind a sterile representation of excavated material, with the goal of bringing the past to light again. However, the diagnosis remains incomplete as it questions the photographically visible and ultimately argues simply for the inclusion of a human and material present in the representations of an archaeological past.

There is a more profound layer of distortion. Contexts and objects are rarely photographed as encountered during excavations, mostly because it would be difficult to recognize what is displayed. Photography, often understood as a means to document what we already know, is instead an important means to *produce* epistemic objects in the first place (Daston and Galison 1992). To do so implies not just the removal of all reminders of presentness but also the presence of a clinical cleanliness. Excavation photos deprive reality of two aspects: they delete present practices, and the sterility of clean trenches silences the flux of past life, leading to a double temporal arrest.

In places of terror and violence, the life of victims was precarious and threatened. The removal of all such signs of life from the pictures also empties out a potential representation of former danger, threats to life and the vulnerability associated with these places. Professional excavation photography turns into an act of objectification in Honneth's sense and can easily slide further into a complete loss of recognition of past suffering. Such photographic aesthetics produce a strong contrast between form and content, with far-reaching consequences that run counter to Sontag's contention that "narratives can make us understand. Photographs do something else: they haunt us" (Sontag 2003:89). Reifying archaeological photoaesthetics silences past misery and ordeals by satisfying the present professional gaze. In such cases, Sontag's sentence is to be reformulated: "Photographs should haunt us, instead of limiting us to mere explanation." Otherwise, archaeological photography becomes part of a violent apparatus.

Is there a way out of the dilemma of a need to produce epistemic things in order to approach past subjects and of reifying them by the means available? Can archaeological photographs reach beyond the status of archival material to somehow become witnesses? One could argue that the view of empty excavation sites and fragments of objects leads to a desire to know more. This desire, however, does not necessarily direct itself to persons who once lived at such sites but all too often ends up in the eagerness to obtain more of the same—that is, to discover more material traces through continued excavation. Judith Butler's discussion of Sontag's essay provides a potential solution to this problem. For Butler, photographs are arguments that do not need a verbal dimension. "Framing becomes part of the story; unless there is a way to photograph the frame itself. At that point, the photograph that yields its frame to interpretation thereby opens up to critical scrutiny the restrictions on interpreting reality" (Butler 2009:71–72). The peculiarity of archaeological photography is the withdrawal of all life in it. The task then is a visualization of withdrawal, a sort of reverse alienation effect that draws attention to the artificial, objective character of the professional imagery, at the same time stimulating reflections on the inadequateness of such aesthetics.

I take the example of object photography from excavations at a Nazi forced labor camp in Berlin, where laborers from mainly eastern Europe were forced to produce bombers that would then attack their countries of origin (Bernbeck and Pollock 2018; Pollock and Bernbeck 2015). The photographer, Jessica Meyer, employed a de-alienating approach, transferring many of the objects back to their human dimension by holding them in her hand when taking the pictures. Compared to standard documentation, such photographic representations take on a denotation far beyond the solitude of a technical photograph. A comparison of two photographs of a comb (Figures 2.1a and 2.1b) illustrates this. The object was made from the remains of a thin pane of plexiglass by painstakingly sawing each tine singly. The gesture of holding this object in the photographer's hand reveals not just the delicateness of the fragment but also the care necessary to use it, and even perhaps the frustration at the breaking of the tines. This should be compared to a technical photograph of the comb, which indicates its size, the irregularity of its making, and scratches. The technical image affords an analytical, cold, and abstract gaze, induced by the isolation of the thing from its former and/or present human environment. Such standardized archaeological photoaesthetics have to be bypassed with unconventional means to evoke past human subjects at sites of terror and humiliation. Such evocative means should not be confused with recognition in Honneth's sense, as there is no possibility to reach beyond anonymous characters. However, this particular kind of framing serves as a reminder that things are to be thought of as connected to subjects, and therefore it prevents reification.

Materiality as Violence

Photography is surely something material even though the image content is often so central that the material means of representation are often forgotten (Edwards 2012). In the case of other archaeological image carriers such as reliefs, wall paintings, or sculpture, interpretations of these two elements—the content and the material—tend to be more balanced. However, placing more attention on the materials that serve to depict something includes a dangerous penchant toward reification. Nowhere is this more obvious than in the cruel war scenes of the Assyrian Empire of the early first millennium BCE, recently rendered famous

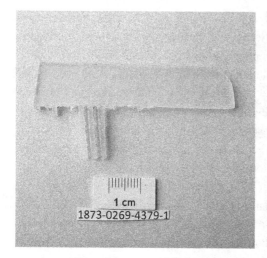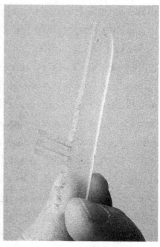

FIGURE 2.1 Two perspectives of a broken plexiglass comb made by a forced laborer. Findspot: Tempelhof Airport, Richthofen-Gemeinschaftslager of Weser Flugzeugbau and Lufthansa. Courtesy Landesdenkmalamt Berlin and Jessica Meyer.

because some of them were destroyed by the Islamic State in northern Iraq. A lot of ink has been spilled over their chronology and their stylistic development (e.g., Collins 2008; Crawford, Harper, and Pittman 1980; Hrouda 1965). Similarly, the kinds of wars, regions, cities, and events depicted in this imagery have received intense scrutiny, as have details such as gardens, architectural forms, and hairdos (e.g., Bleibtreu 1980; Magen 1986; Ussishkin 1980). The astonishingly open displays of cruel violence, including the cutting up of bodies, skinning, and impaling, are often given merely descriptive treatment (e.g., De Backer 2009). Academic discourse does not need to take such a reifying stance, however, as a small number of exceptions to the descriptive and typological approaches show. Some psychologically oriented art historians have discussed whether the Assyrians had a particularly brutal culture (Bahrani 2008; Bersani and Dutoit 1985; Davis 1996). Interestingly, even these discussions about violence center on the state of mind of the perpetrators rather than the victims.

Academic discourse sometimes makes an attempt to re-subjectivize ancient individuals, for example Assyrian kings (Brereton 2018). However, if we stay with this example, any re-subjectivation of the victims meets a particularly complex challenge, as such a procedure must first unveil the triple de-subjectivation inflicted on their enemies by the Assyrians themselves. People became a phalanx of objectivized bodies to be killed in an actual past war. That war then became the object of a set of images for wall reliefs. Finally, the depiction of the war proceeded by standardizing each foreign territory's enemies by taking all individuality out of their faces, hairdos, and clothing, leaving nothing but an endless number of identical figures (Wäfler 1975).

If forgetfulness of recognition is the grounds for violent relations, can this process of *past* de-subjectivation be reversed in the present, and if so, how? Peter Weiss shows us a possible way in the opening pages of his novel *Aesthetics of Resistance* (2005), drawing on the Hellenistic-style Pergamon Altar from the third century CE. In his book, set in 1937, three antifascist workers visit the Berlin Pergamon Museum and gaze at the high-relief frieze of the altar. They discuss the subjects represented, the fight of the victorious Olympian gods against the losing Giants (Kunze 1995). Weiss's detailed rendering of the Giants, including the ruination of the sculptures as an effect of struggle, imbues them with pain and desperation, leaving no doubt that the Gigantomachy is to be read as violent class struggle (Figure 2.2):

> [The demoness of the earth] had given birth to the Giants, the Titans, the Cyclopes, and the Furies. This was our race. We evaluated the history of the earthly beings. We looked up at her again, the demoness stretching out of the ground. . . . The start of the lips, begging for mercy, was discernible in the raw facial plane, which veered sideways and upward. A gash gaped from her chin to her larynx. Alcyoneus, her favorite son, slanted away from her while dropping on his knees. The stump of his left hand groped toward her. She was still touching his left foot, which dangled from his stretched and shattered leg. . . . The pain of death radiated from the small wound inflicted between his ribs by the venomous reptile. (Weiss 2005:6)

"This was our race" is a central sentence of recognition, extending the demise in a depicted past struggle to the three visitors at the museum themselves.

There is also no better description of scholarly reification and aloofness than Weiss's (2005:5) own words in an earlier text passage: "The initiates, the specialists talked about art, praising the harmony of movement, the coordination of gestures; the others, however, who were not even familiar with the concept of 'cultured,' stared furtively into the gaping maws, felt the swoop of the paw in their own flesh. The work gave pleasure to the privileged; the others sensed a segregation under a draconian law of hierarchy."

According to the three antifascists, the reliefs are meant to be misread by most viewers: they are supposed to instill deference in front of the triumphant gods,

FIGURE 2.2 Relief of the battle between Giants and Olympian gods, showing Athena and an unknown Giant figure. Frieze of the Pergamon Altar, Pergamon Museum, Berlin. Courtesy Wikimedia Commons.

and more generally those in power. However, even if these monuments to struggle leave no doubt about the ruling groups and their ideas as the ruling ones, they at least display the subalterns, the slaves and the victims. They interpellate subordinate people as subjects in the word's double meaning, and it is revealing that archaeologists' reading is conventionally driven by a deity-focused interpretation of the struggle rather than the point of view of the giants, implying that archaeology solidarizes with the powerful.

More often than not, past relations of violent inequality must be deciphered from flimsy material remains of practices alone. I will not venture into any detail about the methods used to unravel them. Instead, I am concerned with a problem of preservation, since material remains refer us to past human subjects, a fact that is all too often forgotten in recent discussions about materiality and assemblages. Past subjects are potentially present in enduring objects, so that endurance is a crucial issue for diachronic recognition. I have elsewhere briefly described problems associated with this very basic archaeological issue as "political taphonomy" (Bernbeck 2005:113). Preservation is obviously a matter not just of care for specific material remains but also of other elements, such as the hardness and perishability of matter, size, the quality of production, positioning in a context, and the processes intruding on such materials, as studies of decay—taphonomy—have made abundantly clear. But in all archaeological research, taphonomy must reach beyond a study of the chemistry or physics of decomposition. Human contributions to taphonomy are complex because they include the dialectics of willful differential preservation (letting some things decay while conserving others) and wanton acceleration of disintegration up to outright destruction. But there is more. Obviously, past ability to produce enduring materiality is itself a factor in the potential survival of traces (Brunke et al. 2016). While it may be a truism that the monumental, whether as architecture, sculpture, or other forms, has a better chance of survival than smaller, more delicate and fragile items, one of the fundamental problems of material production and preservation is the boundary between recoverability of ancient *subjects* and their unredeemable loss and silence.

The ultimate end of the subject is reached when it can no longer be reified because no trace is left. In that sense, archaeology has developed paradoxical methods that irrevocably destroy past subjects' traces in an act of trying to reveal them. It is as if one translates a text from another language by erasing each transcribed word. And since all translation is an interpretation (Eco 2008), the result of such activity is by necessity different from the original and would amount to the destruction of evidence and of conditions for the possibility of revealing such evidence—and therefore past subjects. This means that microarchaeological research, involving slow, painstaking discovery, is always to be preferred over a rash and fast excavation (often due to external pressures) because traces of past subjects are at stake, not just some sources for the reconstruction of a past material world. On the other hand, not pursuing excavations in the face of the destruction of an archaeological site would also amount to an act of silencing and thus a form of violence. At a minimum, such reflections mean that no excavations other than salvage work should be done at all and that all excavation borders on or is symbolic violence.

Material objects and their contexts should be seen as signposts toward past subjects. But materiality can also become a serious issue of silencing itself, even in the most unexpected circumstance. The relation between material presences and past absences, as well as between past presences and present absence, should not be taken at face value. For example, Adrian Myers (2011) discusses archaeology at Auschwitz, describing some items from the site museum and buildings. He opines in his conclusion that the "theory and method of historical archaeology, a discipline devoted to the interaction of texts and objects—two manifestations of material culture—offer one way forward in the pursuit of better understanding of concentration camp Auschwitz" (Myers 2011:87), and he argues that "the end of the age of living survivors of the Auschwitz of 1939–1945" (Myers 2011:86) will lead to an increasingly important role of materiality in Holocaust research. This may well be so. But despite the many objects that have been found and will in the future be discovered in concentration camps, surviving victims have left us testimony of a form of violence that puts these things into their place of primary irrelevance: "Who of you can imagine having no one and nothing, absolutely nothing? You are standing in the Appellplatz, naked. There is nothing, nothing in the world that belongs to you. What belongs to a human being at all, what makes a human being? The radiance of one's personality, one's moral stance anchored in the unconscious? At this moment, there is only the hope that what is may pass quickly. It is only important to get five more sips of muck [*Plörre*] and then be selected to the right side. That's my fate" (Fahidi 2011:11; my translation).

No amount of material things is ever able to recover such a situation, since the SS thugs deployed the *absence of any materiality* as a means of utter and complete domination and de-subjectivation (see also Agamben 1999:104–17). Archaeology as the discipline of materiality is unable to reach these extremes of a violence that leaves no traces. Even a badly needed method to document absences and open them up as interpretive non-places will only partly mitigate this fundamental disciplinary weakness (Bernbeck 2013; Starzmann 2014).

Narrative Violence

In his well-known book *Time and the Other*, Johannes Fabian (1983) criticizes the work of anthropology as a "denial of coevalness." Cultural anthropological field-work involves a situation of co-presence and participant observation. But with the return from the proverbial field and the process of writing, observed subjects transmute into objects of knowledge. Fabian analyzes how a shared lifeworld turns into a strict division between observer and observed that is also conceptually categorized into different temporal planes. This is an excellent example of what Honneth describes as "forgetfulness of recognition": an erstwhile situation of practical commonality between the ethnographer and those he or she lived with is destroyed in the production of standardized research procedures of writing. Taken this way, almost all anthropological writing is reification and therefore violent.

To what extent do archaeological narrations display similar tendencies? Mostly, we do not deal with live subjects and cannot forget subjects we never

knew. However, specific kinds of paradigmatic traditions that underlie archaeological research and writing imply that we never even attempt to reconcile this
structural imbalance through attempts at a re-subjectification. An obvious problem of this kind is scale. A focus on the long term, mentioned at the beginning
of this chapter, as well as an exclusive focus on social, economic, political, or
other kinds of structures at the expense of those who acted in and through such
structures, "leaves little scope for considering perspectives other than those of
history's 'winners'" and thus unavoidably produces a forgetting of many past subjects (Pollock 2013:146).

A second issue is the relation between archaeologists and a larger group of
other "stakeholders" who have their own interests in the past. The urge to come
to terms with such relations is particularly important where projects and research
concern times close to the present (Dalglish 2013) as well as in (post)colonial contexts. This led to the development of "public archaeology" and "community archaeology." An awareness that a lot of writing is in fact a silencing developed after
the publication of Gayatri C. Spivak's article "Can the Subaltern Speak?" (1988),
in which she demonstrates that a supposed giving of voice to others through one's
own speech or narration is in fact a silencing. Out of such concerns developed
a "multivocal" archaeology that tries to integrate non-archaeologists into professional narratives (Habu, Fawcett, and Matsunaga 2008). For example, in a
discussion about multivocality's role in the excavations at Çatal Höyük in Turkey,
Ian Hodder (2003:24) lists "government officials at national and regional levels,
Turkish archaeologists, sponsors, carpet sellers, Turkish students, other international archaeologists, Goddess worshippers, artists and musicians." Echoing
Hodder, Stephen Silliman claims that the integration of multiple voices in our
accounts decolonizes archaeology because it blurs the lines between experts and
others, leading to a healthy hybridity not only of voices but of knowledge itself
that is constituted by archaeologists, descendants of those whom archaeology
investigates, and others (Silliman 2009a).

Multivocality did not remain unchallenged. Some scholars differentiate between a "critical" and a "celebratory" multivocality (Colwell and Joy 2015:121–22),
the former including non-archaeological voices that may stand in opposition to
one another. But sharper rejections come from other sides: those who see objectivity and factuality endangered (P. E. L. Kohl in Smith 2004:21), a perspective not
without merit considering the fact that "postfactuality" has become a hallmark
of the present. From the opposite side, objections against multivocality point out
that the inclusion into academic discourse of voices of indigenous peoples, or of

descendants of past subaltern or victimized groups, is a co-optation that cannot undo a narrative order created by archaeology that is tantamount to structural violence: "On the ground, 'having a voice' and 'having control over' are radically different positions" (Starzmann 2010:127).

Interestingly, these disputes over silencing produce another dimension of silencing: past people become a mere function of so-called stakeholder interests in the present. The more the ills of nonrecognition of subalterns' relations to their own past are foregrounded, the more rigorously past subjects are cut off from any participation in the present. In other words, concerns with relations of violence in the present engender a high level of diachronic violence. Some scholars try to mitigate this by relying on interpretive potentials of materiality itself. They suggest that different kinds of archaeological remains are themselves "multivocal," of course on a metaphorical plane (e.g., Greenberg 2009; Inomata 2006; Ylimaunu et al. 2014). Schmidt and Munene (2010:221) sternly rebuke such efforts: "[The trope of multivocality] bundles together a host of different sources, such as the materiality of archaeology, evidence from ethnoarchaeology, and ecological evidence. . . . [These sources] are dead, passive, and inarticulate." This perspective mirrors Horkheimer's quote about the slain cited above. In my view, to castigate the invocation of material multivocality as completely misleading is itself an act of (willful) forgetting, in this case of past subjects. When archaeological things are thought about in their potential relation with past subjects, the possibility of an intersubjective encounter is evoked, a bridging of non-coevalness, to use Fabian's terminology.

Still, the simple attribution of multivocality to objects and ruins as a way of awakening sensibilities toward the multifariousness of past subjects remains general and somewhat simplistic. Another attempt to invoke past subjects consists of their outright invention. In such narrations, named or anonymous figures populate sites and landscapes, with a writing style mobilized to prevent a total reification of the past (e.g., Gibb 2015; Tringham 1991; Van Dyke 2015). This strategy has been criticized as a break of the historiographic taboo of source invention and the abandonment of a silent contract with readers about truthfulness in academia (Pollock 2015). I permit myself here to avoid a clear position. Some time ago, I myself argued against such approaches (Bernbeck 2015), but since then, I have come to the conclusion that the evocational power of things from the past should not simply be suppressed (Bernbeck 2017). At the same time, there is a need for utmost care when resorting to such "methods." An invented person or even whole group must not become a pawn of one's own present desires and imaginations, a problem I see in some of Tringham's explicitly feminist writings (e.g., Tringham 1991). Such a displacement of past individuals by those one wishes had existed risks becoming itself a case of symbolic violence toward past subjects.

Conclusion

Violence as a term is by definition bound to human will. A natural catastrophe may have violent effects but is not a perpetrator. The epistemic framework within which we talk about violence is therefore based on a clear division of acting human subjects and their ("objective") environment, a precondition for this collection of papers that has come under critique elsewhere. Here I have tried to sketch a notion of violence that starts from a recognition-theoretical framework and ends up with a fairly broad understanding of the term. When the term is applied to the past, we may end up with a dense network of violent relations, a sobering thought already voiced by Walter Benjamin (1968:256) in his seventh thesis on the philosophy of history: "The historical materialist views [cultural treasures] with cautious detachment. For without exception the cultural treasures he surveys have an origin which he cannot contemplate without horror. . . . There is no document of civilization which is not at the same time a document of barbarism."

Discursive arguments for a terminological widening always entail an urge to point out the limits of such a broadened notion. A question might come up: Isn't all knowledge production, archaeology included, an act of violence? Indeed, postcolonial theorist Linda Tuhiwai Smith (1999:1) opens her well-known book on decolonizing methodologies by suggesting that "the word itself, 'research,' is probably one of the dirtiest words in the indigenous contexts, it stirs up silence, it conjures up bad memories, it raises a smile that is knowing and distrustful. . . . It appalls us that the West can desire, extract and claim ownership of our ways of knowing, our imagery, the things we create and produce, and then simultaneously reject the people who created and developed those ideas." The relationship between past subjects and archaeologists (or historians) is equally one-sided, if not more so. We almost always start out from "a subject–object relationship between the historian [and archaeologist] and the evidence. In this gesture, the past remains genuinely dead" (Chakrabarty 2000:108). However, Chakrabarty remains confident that with some effort, past subjects can become more active members of our own disruptive and disrupted present. As I tried to show here, they may well be objectified, in a relation of knowledge rather than (mutual) acknowledgment. The point is not to forget their own subjectivity. I remain pessimistic about the prospects for a significant reduction of the violent structures of our discipline. Excavation practices, academic narratives, and their pictorial illustrations all contain strong inbuilt reificatory tendencies. Considerable efforts are needed to break through this disciplinary carapace and recognize the lives of past subjects.

Acknowledgments

I thank Susan Pollock for trenchant critique and insightful comments on an earlier version of this paper. Many people contributed inadvertently to the thoughts that lie behind this text via encounters during my work with a humanitarian organization.

Notes

1. The English translation inappropriately refers to *Gewaltökonomie* as "economy of force." Münkler describes this "economy" as being built up from inexpensive weaponry, underpaid mercenaries, and the rational need to raid and plunder conquered territory for one's own subsistence.

2. Languages categorize practices and conditions connected to violence in different ways. The German *Gewalt*, for example, includes notions of "force," "power," and "violence." Bourdieu's *violence symbolique* is also often translated as "symbolic force."

3. Both write of *assujettissement*, but the translation of Althusser's text renders this as "subjection" (Althusser 1971:133), while in translations of Foucault's writings, it is mostly turned into "subjectivation" (Chambers 2013:98-102).

4. Limit cases are war journalists who witness violent encounters. Whether they contribute to violence or prevent it is likely to depend on each specific situation (Gall and Izard 1986; Kim 2012).

5. Obviously, in terms of recognition theory, all Native American resistance against the excavation of cemeteries and the public display of human remains can be legitimized as a fight against such violence of de-subjectivation.

THREE

Discursive Violence and Archaeological Ruptures

Archaeologies of Colonialism and Narrative Privilege in Highland Guatemala

GUIDO PEZZAROSSI

In this chapter, I explore the entanglements between two distinct types of violence: the violence of colonization in Guatemala, and the enduring legacies of racialized discursive violence that have skewed narratives of Maya history and variously impacted modern descendants of the Maya—a diverse set of ethnolinguistic communities that have inhabited Guatemala, Belize, and parts of Mexico, Honduras, and El Salvador from at least the Preclassic period (2000 BCE–250 CE). The violence of Spanish colonization, and the disruptions it catalyzed, contributed to a redefinition of diverse Native communities into a singular ethnolinguistic identity category and a subject(ed) position as Indios. Later, archaeological interest in the untouched alterity of the Indio past built upon these material and discursive violences to produce "the Maya" as an object of study confined to the ancient past (Joyce 2005b). Such discourses have afforded violent ruptures that juxtapose Maya people from modernity with "authentic" Maya, who, via cultural freezing and temporal marooning, are seen to exist solely in the deep past. The notion that "true Maya culture consists of those features surviving from the pre-contact period" (Fischer and Brown 1996:13) has cast modern Maya populations as either "docile descendants or illegitimate heirs" of the "true" Classic-period Maya (250–1000 CE) (Breglia 2006:209) and thus either fully "without culture or with a dying, residual and oppressed culture" (Cojtí Cuxil 1996:19).

This disassociation of the contemporary Maya from those in the past has played out predominantly through a set of problematic historiographies informed by legacies of archaeological research and knowledge production—in particular:

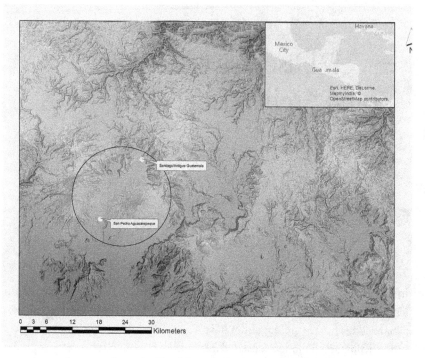

FIGURE 3.1 Locational map, highland Guatemala. (The circle shows the Antigua and Alotenango Valleys.)

(1) the trope of "collapse" that has become a mainstay of popular conceptions of the Maya and archaeological interpretations of the Classic-period Maya abandonment of the large urban settlements in the Petén region (Borgestede and Yaeger 2008:99); (2) archaeological interpretations of Maya precolonial migrations; (3) the assumed "rupture" of colonization, including the demographic collapse caused by disease (as per Dobyns 1991; Dunnell 1991) and assimilationist strategies of the Spanish (see Haber 2007) that rendered the colonial Maya past and present as fundamentally different (and disconnected) from what came before; and (4) the overwhelming archaeological bias for Preclassic and Classic Maya sites in Guatemala to the exclusion of the colonial period from archaeological histories of the Maya.

Beyond this critique, and considering that archaeology has contributed to the emergence of these dispossessing narratives, I argue that the discipline and its practitioners have a responsibility to address these temporal investigative biases and historical erasures. Moreover, historical or colonial archaeology in highland

Guatemala is especially well positioned to productively intervene and to contribute new insights and perspectives that push back against the discourses of colonial rupture, disappearance, and inauthenticity that continue to haunt popular Maya histories and descendant communities. To this end, postcolonial and indigenous archaeological frameworks draw attention to the presence and nature of links between present and past Maya communities, albeit not as rote unchanging "continuity" between pre- and post- "contact" baselines but as the persistence of communities through change (see Panich 2013; Silliman 2009b). In this chapter I work from longue durée settlement pattern analyses from highland Guatemala to provide tangible evidence of the resilience and persistence of highland Maya communities, through both the Classic-period "collapse" and the violence of colonization in all its forms (enslavement, forced resettlement, conversion, labor/tribute impositions, counterinsurgency, and so on). In addition, I draw on excavations and artifact analyses at multicomponent archaeological sites in the highlands to demonstrate long-term persistence of Maya communities on the landscape via the resilience of communities of potters, exchange networks, and knowledge associated with pottery technology and style from the Early Classic into the later colonial periods. All told, the colonial-era focus of the archaeological research presented demonstrates the potential of this work to intervene and push back against dominant historical narratives of modern Maya "rupture" by demonstrating how despite the violence Maya communities and individuals were subjected to, they remained connected to their pasts while emerging as integral and dynamic participants in, and residents of, the colonial and modern world.

Colonial Violence and the Coloniality of Discursive Violence

The disruptive and violent forces brought to bear on Maya populations by Spanish colonists were manifold, be they disease, warfare, conversion/assimilation practices, or the acculturative process of Hispanicization. As a result, a common refrain in popular culture and even in some archaeological literature, particularly that suited for large undergraduate audiences, focuses on the "devastation" of colonization and the "crushed" and "shattered remnants" of the Maya left in its wake (Sharer and Traxler 2006:4-6), a discursive pattern that is also present in talk of the "pathetic" and "miserable" remnants of Maya society after the Classic-period "collapse" (Coe 1993:24-26, 159, cited in Normark 2004:117). Disease was obviously an important factor in Native demographic decline in colonial contexts across the New World, including in highland Guatemala (Lovell 1992; Lovell et al. 2013). The drastic loss of life, potentially reaching near 80 to 90 percent, is argued to have constituted a bottleneck that left descendent populations "stripped down" of much cultural knowledge and memory, and essentially unrelated/unrelatable to ancestral populations (see Dobyns 1991; Dunnell 1991). While these points have been used to make important arguments against the use of ethnographic and ethnohistoric analogy, they problematically posit the colonial period as a point of insurmountable rupture between past and present Maya populations.

Other arguments for the rupturing of modern Maya communities from their pasts emphasize sixteenth-century Spanish colonial conversion and *reducción* practices and the imposition of hierarchical taxonomies of colonial populations. Such violence, both discursive and symbolic, laid the groundwork for later claims of Maya disconnection from an authentic Maya past through enforced changes in dress, language, daily practices, religious observances, and worldview that saw them "reordered" and Christianized (see Hanks 2010 but see also Gosner 1992 for Maya resistance and unexpected productions emerging from these practices). Haber (2007:218) notes how Spanish colonial strategies purposefully and violently attempted to sever Native people from their pasts through harsh punishments leveled on individuals who deviated from (or supplemented) Christian teachings and conversion programs by continuing to practice traditional rituals and religious observances and engaging their sacred landscapes. (See also Frühsorge 2007.)

Spanish colonial taxonomies laid the groundwork for the emergence of "the Maya" through their homogenous ethnoracial categorization of all Native people in Guatemala as Indios (Frühsorge 2007:50). Something close to "Maya" as an assumed identity category may have emerged from the dislocation of Native individuals from their communities and social groupings that served as central loci of identification. As people were displaced into new congregated towns and urban areas, and found themselves in multiethnic settings, possibly intermarrying or reproducing with non-Native individuals, new lines would have been drawn along coarser, Spanish colonial caste categories that demarcated the Native Other as the singular Indio that approximated the Maya category familiar today (Restall 2004:77). However, while Maya people would have been knowledgeable of—and forced to work within—Spanish colonial constructions of a singular Indio ethnicity/subjectivity due to their positioning within broader colonial society, this did not correspond to an "overt" identification as a single community or ethnicity, past or present (Restall 2004). The persistence of the Indio/Maya as an identity category "reflects not a continuity or profundity of Maya ethnic consciousness. Instead, it reflects the racist constraints of a colonial [caste] system that *imposed such a consciousness*" (Normark 2004:136; emphasis mine) to both define and massify the laboring Other. However, while the Spanish colonial caste system sought to maintain these hierarchical divides, it also had the effect of "paradoxically enforcing its weakness by offering partial social mobility to those who collaborated economically or biologically with the colonizers" (Normark 2004:136).

The latter part of Normark's quote points to the role that colonial- and republican-era miscegenation, and narratives of intermarriage, played in the disavowal of Maya persistence, connections to the prehistoric past, and claims of sovereignty. The common, frequently coerced, but by no means normative or homogenizing biological/cultural *mestizaje* became central to the criticisms of claims of Maya alterity and continuity in Guatemala. As Joyce (2004:33) notes, the notion of intermarriage and the subsequent offspring produced by unions between Spanish men and Native women undergirds the "mestizaje ideologies" of critical importance to nineteenth- and twentieth-century Mesoamerican nationalism. These ideologies "represented the future of the region as one of inevitable cultural [and biological] mixture, as if the distinct native peoples were disappearing and being assimilated" (Joyce 2004:33).

For the Guatemalan nation, the pursuit of a multicultural democratic society has profited from the advancement of such a discourse of mestizaje in that it has sought to suppress Maya claims to alterity, sovereignty, and heritage in the interest of building national cohesion through the vehicle of assimilation discourse (Warren 1998:6). Guatemalan critics have in some cases drawn on postcolonial theories of cultural hybridity (such as Bhabha 1985) to argue for the alleged inauthenticity of modern Maya identities due to their hybridization with and adoption of Western cultural and material practices at the expense of pre-Hispanic Maya practices. (See Fischer 1999; Warren 1998 for discussion.) The violence of such discourse is obvious to Maya scholars, who state that it "prescribes the Maya's death in [the melting pot] in order to solve the Indian Problem" (Cojtí Cuxil 1996:21). The "Indian problem" in this case is the remnant colonial anxiety that continues to permeate Guatemalan society, which is in no small part due to the Maya population's demographic majority status within the country (Watanabe 1995:30). The above have in turn facilitated the white Ladino population's appropriation of the pre-Hispanic past of the region as a rallying point for national identity and unity under the auspices of common descent from and hybridization with a past society that wields considerable "global cultural capital" (Chinchilla

2012:56–57; Watanabe 1995:32; Warren 1998:49–50; see also Joyce 2004:32–33; Pagden 1987).

Archaeology Colludes

The "invention" of the Maya as an identity category is also rooted in the introduction of the Maya label by nineteenth-century archaeologists. Based on previous colonial-era essentialisms, archaeologists accepted the classificatory consolidation of a heterogeneous mix of people in the past and present on the basis of a taken-for-granted notion of cultural, ethnic, material, and linguistic unity (Joyce 2004). They helped solidify the Maya as a regional archaeological culture on the basis of these assumed shared material practices, style, and iconographic elements. (See Restall 2004:81.) Working from the delimitation of the Maya as an archaeological culture, archaeologists, historians, anthropologists, and the public have projected this modern, archaeological notion of Maya identity into the past and produced a sense of Maya timelessness, reified through the use of an ethnographic and colonial ethnohistoric analogy that operates from the assumption of a normative static continuity between the Maya through time and space (Joyce 2004, 2005b; see also Meskell 2005). Normark (2006:9) has argued that archaeologists have come to rely on analogy to fill in the interpretive gaps between things and people in the past, which in the process has contributed to the formulation of dichotomous notions of continuity and change that conflate the persistence (or distribution) of material practices with static/unchanging continuity in, or diffusion of, culture/ethnicity/identity. However, the assumption of continuity is a situational one, as claims of continuity are refuted or diminished when this discourse becomes politically charged and potentially a threat to the nation and property (Normark 2004:118). Archaeologists have also exploited and reproduced this paradox by assuming discontinuity to justify excavations and analysis of past remains without the consent or participation of modern descendants while drawing on notions of continuity to facilitate the heavy lifting of archaeological interpretation through the use of ethnographic and historic analogies (Normark 2004:130).

Twentieth-century archaeological narratives of Postclassic "Mexican invasions" of Guatemala (Fox 1980; see also Borgestede and Robinson 2012 for critiques of this model) further entrench discourses of rupture by recasting modern Maya populations as the descendants of nonlocal invaders taking advantage of the vacuum caused by the Terminal Classic Maya "collapse." This "illegitimate heir" status (per Breglia 2006), and the subsequent distancing of Maya populations from their pasts, is derived in part from the discursive violence perpetuated by dominant historical narratives that emphasize only the disruption, absorption, and/or "pollution" of Spanish colonization and the rupture of the Terminal Classic collapse. In other forms, the focus on collapse and colonization as rupture relies on the physical and cultural disappearance of Maya people from the landscape, producing a Mesoamerican alloy of the trope of the "vanishing Indian." (See Gould 2014; McGuire 1992; Mrozowski et al. 2009; Oland and Palka 2016:472; Restall 2003; Wilcox 2009b for North American contexts.) The discourses of rupture and disappearance derived from colonial practices and legacies parallel diffusionist arguments articulated in the seventeenth and eighteenth centuries. Such diffusionist perspectives speculated on the links between extant Maya populations and the monumental pre-Hispanic ruins that dotted the landscape (Chinchilla 2012:56–57; Joyce 2004:32; Yaeger and Borgstede 2004:235; see also Milner 2005 for parallels to North American Mound Builder myths).

Moreover, an element of these discourses of Maya discontinuity focuses on the pre-Hispanic past, specifically the Postclassic, as an already "fallen past" in relation to the apex of civilization that the Classic period represents (Joyce 2004:33). The discourse of collapse and rupture from Classic to Postclassic is seen as spurred by political strife leading to warfare, ecological catastrophes caused by deforestation and other environmental mishandlings, and/or the influence of climatic variables (such as droughts) (Normark 2004:145). McAnany and Negrón (2010) have been particularly critical of explanations for collapse that cast the Maya as cautionary tales for the present. Claims that the Maya "chose" (Diamond 2005) to fail through a series of shortsighted actions, driven by rapacious instincts that ended in cultural and societal extinction, may be politically salient and useful in the present. However, such narratives do violence to descendant Maya populations by discursively severing ties to ancestral communities *and* conveniently undermining their claims to Classic Maya heritage and the lucrative tourist industry it supports (McAnany and Negrón 2010:165). This "collapse" has alternatively been spun as de-evolution or cultural rupture and has thus set the precedent that surviving Maya were merely the "highly degraded descendants" (Joyce 2004:33) of Classic-period Maya who continued to "dwell in the ruined house of their ancestors" (Redfield 1962:152). The complicity of archaeologists and anthropologists was acknowledged early on, as Redfield noted: "It is the archaeologist, not the Indian, who sees [the Maya] living in the broken shell of |their| grandfather's house."

In addition, academic and popular fixation on violence in Maya ritual and sacrificial practices, and the cosmological significance of blood, has provided an added justification for violence and/or dispossession by casting the Maya in the past/present (again playing with continuity and rupture simultaneously) as "fallen," savage, and "deserving" of subjugation (see Montejo 1999). The trope of New World cannibalism served a similar purpose in other colonial contexts (for example, the American Southwest, Mesoamerica), where it operated as a marker of savage otherness that justified oppression and even execution (Carrasco 1995:429-35; McGuire and Van Dyke 2008:8-10). Indeed, Schele and Miller's (1986) argument that "blood was the mortar of ancient Maya ... life," and other such arguments for the "natural" propensity of Maya for violence, served to provide a legitimizing discourse to justify repressive counterinsurgency violence against Maya communities during the Guatemalan civil war (Fisher and Brown 1996:3; Fischer and Hendrikson 2003; Frühsorge 2007:42; Normark 2004:144, 2007). Ever more troubling is the percolation of these academic discourses into more widely disseminated media such as Mel Gibson's *Apocalypto* (2006), which regurgitates and sensationalizes the violence and moral bankruptcy of the Maya in the past (Ardren 2006). In keeping with the "inverted temporal logic of fantasy" that fuels an "imagined nostalgia" of colonialism (Appadurai 1996:77; Hall and Bombardella 2007), the serene arrival of Spanish conquistadores and clergy at the end of the film (juxtaposed with the frenetic chase and violence of the entire film) implies that the Maya "deserve[ed], in fact they needed rescue" from themselves at the hands of the Spanish, reproducing the paternalistic posturing used to justify violence against in the Maya in the twentieth century (Ardren 2006).

Such "social lives" of academic discourse serve to emphatically stress the political volatility of academic—namely archaeological and epigraphic—representations of the Maya past (see Montejo 1999). Castañeda (1996:108), intersecting with Said's critique of orientalism (1979), argues that what has been defined as "Maya culture" is in this light a product of "discursive practices in which Maya alterity has been appropriated for use in Western constructions of what it is to be 'civilized' as measured against non-European derived social forms" (see also Normark 2004:117; Wainwright 2011). There is no question that archaeology has played a role in the construction of potentially marginalizing and exclusionary discourses in the present that may be appropriated as justifying foundations for both physical and conceptual/discursive violence (as per Borgestde and Yaeger 2008:106; Joyce 2005a:269; Meskell 1998.3–4).

Despite the archaeological community's acknowledgment of the connections between modern and ancient Maya populations in Guatemala, the archaeological focus on precolonial contexts, particularly the Classic-period fluorescence, has fallen victim to, as well as perpetrated, these same discourses of disconnection by ignoring the Maya in the colonial period. This differentiation and discursive rupture between Classic, Postclassic, and colonial Maya is an important one that enabled "the Ladino elite of the country to use the heritage of the classical era in constructing a national identity as a mixture of Indigenous and European culture, while at the same time discriminating against the contemporary Indigenous population and leaving them no right to proclaim themselves authentic Maya" (Frühsorge 2007:42). In this light, archaeological heritage became the property of the state as national patrimony that represented the Ladino (ruling) population in all its "hybrid vigor" (Joyce 2004:33), achieved by "grafting" onto the tree of Maya civilization. (See Bahrani 1998; Pagden 1987 for a similar example from Mesopotamia.) Such appropriation would come to serve as justification/legitimation of colonial occupation of the New World, modern-day Maya exclusion, and the production of "distinctive national identities rooted in the region" and separate from the colonial metropole (Joyce 2004:33; see also Chinchilla 2012 for an example from Guatemala).

Archaeology Intrudes

It is here that archaeology can productively intervene in helping tell histories of Maya persistence and participation in the colonial world that can undermine (in some form) the violence done by dominant narratives. An attempt to make archaeology relevant to the goals and questions of connected communities represents an avenue for addressing the "coloniality" (Quijano 2000) of archaeological practice in Guatemala and the historical silences/omissions it has helped produce (see Joyce and Sheptak 2014:180). The production of alternative histories to dominant narratives of colonization in Guatemala are of great promise to Colop (1996:112) for their potential to undermine the process by which "the Other is interpreted, imagined and represented and his future is prescribed" through the appropriation of history to foretell the inevitable Maya demise. This is not an unprecedented proposal, as Latin American "social archaeology" has long sought to contribute to "the construction of an alternative to official history by creating real, historical consciousness" critical of and disconnected from dominant historical narratives that continue to underwrite violence and marginalization of subaltern communities (Vargas 1995:62).

At the same time, the social archaeology movement in Latin America has sought to minimize "ruptures" in history by explicitly bridging prehistoric and historical archaeologies into the type of longue durée framework that, I argue, is necessary for undermining the allochronistic marooning of the "true" Maya in the Classic period. (See Palka 2009:302; Vargas 1995:62; see also Lightfoot 1995; Schmidt and Mrozowski 2014.) While the appeal of the "ancient Maya" in Maya identity formation is found in the desire to root self-representation outside of racist characterizations born of colonial legacies (Warren 1998), archaeological research into colonial Maya experiences in the vein of Latin American social archaeology may provide new or alternative histories of resistance, florescence, survival, and persistence outside of the Classic period and in the more recent past for Maya identity and community formation processes in the present.

In recent years, a more abundant and visible archaeological literature on the persistence of colonial Maya communities has emerged (Palka 2009). This work, predominantly focused in the lowland Petén, Yucatan, and Belize, has provided a check to the Classic-period focus and is providing insights into continuities and changes that characterized Maya colonial persistence. This growing body of work has taken off in part due "to the realization that culture process over more than 400 years—almost as long as the Classic period—has been basically ignored by archaeologists" (Palka 2009:299). As argued above, this blind spot in archaeological investigation has helped foster discourses of rupture and served as an obstacle to the articulation of longue durée Maya histories that better account for persistence and the creative refashioning of Maya people, communities, culture, and practices that have made modern Maya populations who they are. While this upsurge in interest and work is encouraging. At the same time, colonial Maya archaeology is still in its infancy, particularly in highland Guatemala, where the bulk of work carried out is at Spanish colonial heritage sites such as Antigua.

Oland and Palka (2016) recently provided an important summary of the current archaeology of colonialism in the Maya region, albeit with a critical eye toward the enduring tropes of collapse and rupture that haunt Maya archaeology. Working from the concept of the "perduring Maya," Oland and Palka argue that archaeological research into colonial Maya sites provides a way to better grasp the diverse effects and experiences of colonization and the creative ways Maya people navigated and survived the changing and violent colonial world. In turn (dovetailing with my argument in this chapter), these studies help shift "the narrative of the Maya people from one of collapse and conquest, to a more continuous story in which change is understood within a much longer framework of Maya life" (Oland and Palka 2016:484).

Within the expanding archaeological work on colonization in the Maya region, highland Guatemala, where millions of descendant Maya populations reside, has remained only minimally investigated (but see Aparicio 1997; Robinson 1997; Sharer, Ashmore, and Hill 1970). Archaeology of the colonial Maya presence in this region holds great promise in highlighting the persistence of Maya communities during and after the colonial period, despite claims for the Hispanicization (and thus discontinuity) of Maya communities living in such proximity to the capital of the kingdom of Guatemala: Santiago de Guatemala (today Antigua). (See Komisaruk 2010:44.) The goal of this work is not to find evidence of static cultural continuity, despite the importance of "unbroken" continuity to Maya movement scholars. (See Armstrong Fumero 2011; Normark 2004 for critique.) Rather I flesh out evidence of the persistence and prevalence (and changing experiences) of Maya people, practices, and communities and their interconnections in the colonial world. I argue that this subtle shift, away from looking for continuity with a precolonial, "authentic" baseline and toward tracing the complex paths communities took to persist (see Panich 2013 and below for discussion), enables empirical archaeological evidence to undermine notions of collapse and rupture in the colonial period by highlighting linked practices—across space and through time—that continued to connect Maya people into communities of shared practice as they had in the past, albeit in new and different ways.

Continuous Occupations:
Central Highland Guatemala Diachronic
Settlement Patterns

Colonial Maya archaeology in the central highlands owes its existence in part to the work of Eugenia Robinson, one of the pioneers of highland Maya archaeology in and around Antigua, Guatemala. As part of the Proyecto Arqueólogico Area Kaqchikel (PAAK), Robinson (1990, 1997) directed comprehensive surveys in the Antigua Valley, as well as farther south in Alotenango. These surveys recorded all sites encountered—single component or multicomponent, from Preclassic to colonial—based on surface collections and recording of visible features and architecture.

In the Antigua Valley, centered on Antigua, the survey identified sixty-five "protohistoric," or Late Postclassic, sites based on ceramic types present on the surface. A total of thirty-eight colonial-period sites were identified by Spanish colonial material culture (majolica, lead-glazed wares, and so on), indicating a reduction in settlements coinciding with disruptions of colonization (such as disease, violence, and *congregación* resettlement). Of note, many of the protohistoric sites identified cannot be easily dated to either the protohistoric or colonial periods due to the absence of diagnostic ceramics, as nine of eleven ceramic types in the region persist from Postclassic to colonial (Robinson 1997:62; Sharer, Ashmore, and Hill 1970), a common issue in Mesoamerican and Maya colonial archaeology. (See Joyce and Sheptak 2014; Palka 2009.)

In these contexts, the persistence of ceramic craft practice, and disengagement from colonial goods, serves to elide many colonial sites due to their material resemblance to Postclassic sites, allowing colonial Maya sites to be identified only when they exhibit some form of difference or disconnection from the precolonial past. This difference is always defined in terms of the acquisition and use of Spanish traditional material culture rather than on differences within extant Maya material practices as a result of changing conditions of the colonial world (but see Blaisdell-Sloan 2006; Joyce and Sheptak 2014).

Of the protohistoric sites in the region, twenty-four yielded Alotenango Crema type diagnostics sherds. This protohistoric ceramic type is one of only two that do not persist in any known colonial-period sites in the region, indicating that sites where it is found are assuredly precolonial in date (Robinson 1997:62; Sharer, Ashmore, and Hill 1970; but see Pezzarossi 2014:241–42). Of these twenty-four sites, nineteen also showed evidence of colonial components, highlighting the continuity of Maya communities in place, despite colonial resettlement practices, and providing a check to overzealous notions of Maya community attrition in the colonial period. Robinson (1997:70) notes that sites at higher elevations, in more defensive positions, were more commonly abandoned in the colonial period. This observation is supported by 1549 documents from the region that tell of clergy resettling Indios from the hills into towns (Vázquez and Lamadrid 1944:111). However, it appears that people residing at higher elevations were likely resettled piecemeal in extant towns in the region, such as Aguacatepeque (Pezzarossi

2014:75–79), thus adding to and creating new composite communities. (See Hill 1989 for an example from highland Guatemala.)

Immediately to the south of the Antigua Valley, Robinson (1990) surveyed the Alotenango Valley, nestled between the Volcan de Agua and the Volcan de Fuego, and identified 133 sites with Postclassic components. Of note, these sites are not confirmed Postclassic sites by the presence of Alotenango Crema, as in the Antigua Valley survey, and thus some may well be Late Postclassic and colonial settlements. A total of twenty-one colonial-period sites were identified (again with the caveat that many colonial sites were missed due to a lack of diagnostic colonial material culture), and of these, a majority (sixteen) contained a Postclassic component. While this is a more dramatic reduction of sites from Postclassic to colonial than in the Antigua Valley (potentially indicating a more aggressive resettlement program meant to draw laborers to communities in the vicinity of the capital of the *audiencia* to the north, or a greater impact of disease due to location within a modern-day malarial zone), nevertheless, the bulk of colonial settlements in the region were Late Postclassic communities that persisted through the initial encounter.

Of note, the Alotenango survey also reported 108 Late Classic sites within the valley and permits insight into the Late Classic "collapse" in this part of the highlands. Considering the greater number of Postclassic sites/site components (133 total), there appears little room for arguing for collapse in the Alotenango Valley. In addition, of the 108 Late Classic sites, 78 yielded Postclassic components, speaking directly to the continuity and indeed expansion of settlements in the region from Late Classic to Postclassic and continuity from Postclassic to Colonial, insights that undermine normative models of Maya Classic collapse and colonial rupture for this region of highland Guatemala.

San Pedro Aguacatepeque

While the broad-scale survey data is helpful for establishing overall patterns of persistence and continuity through moments/processes of collapse and rupture, intensive excavations and analysis at individual sites provide detailed insight into the (admittedly diverse) dynamics of persistence over the longue durée. Since 2009 I have investigated the colonial-period presence and experiences of Maya communities in highland Guatemala and carried out excavations and analyses at San Pedro Aguacatepeque, a multicomponent site in the Alotenango Valley with occupations dated from the Early Classic (500 CE) to the late colonial period (1814). Excavations carried out in 2011–2012 identified widespread stratified community midden deposits associated with household refuse. Early and Late Classic components were identified and AMS carbon dated and were found underlying possible Postclassic components, which were severely impacted by colonial occupations.

Scholars in highland Guatemala have used ceramic analysis to track community and cultural continuity or rupture within and between chronological periods, with the ceramic continuity exhibited by central highland sites across the Classic to the Postclassic serving as an index of "continuity" or at least persistence of Maya communities through moments of distress or broader transformations associated with events of around 900 CE (see Borgstede and Robinson 2012; Hatch 2002). This point is key, as detailed ceramic attribute analyses carried out at Aguacatepeque have provided evidence of both persistence and change across time periods, as well as a diversity of ceramic types between the Alotenango and Antigua regions through time (indicating the variability of the highland region), thus puncturing notions of a normative Maya culture or material tradition across subregions of the highlands. Ceramic analysis from Aguacatepeque began with a detailed paste analysis of 3,323 sherds (see Orton, Tyers, and Vince 1993), designed to split out sherds on the basis of similar clays type, inclusions, manufacturing, firing practices, and so on. (See Pezzarossi 2014:235–37 for a detailed explanation of ceramic analysis methodology.) This mode of analysis enabled a tracking of ceramic persistence in terms of technology and craft practices, as well as surface treatments, style, and decoration, rather than just a focus on ceramic types and variants that persisted (or not). (See Robinson 1997.) The goal is to evaluate and identify continuity of ceramic potting practices through time that would indicate the continued activity of potting communities. Informing this analytical tack was a concern that rapid changes in ceramic decorative styles, perhaps targeted by colonists and their conversion programs or shifting ideologies, would create a false image of the curtailing and "collapse" of Maya ceramic craft production, distribution, and consumption.

Importantly, many of the ceramics do not fit into other highland Maya ceramic typologies and chronologies, both colonial and precolonial (see Rodriguez Giron 2008; Sharer, Ashmore, and Hill 1970), indicating important variability in ceramic exchange spheres and material practices within, not just between, regions. Indeed, this diversity is an important check to the continued reliance on the

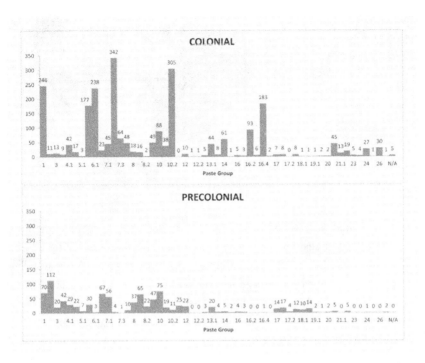

FIGURE 3.2 Ceramic paste groups persisting from precolonial to colonial contexts at San Pedro Aguacatepeque.

homogeneity of the Maya and Maya regions to buttress regional ceramic typologies and chronologies, wherein chronologies elaborated at one site stand in for all sites in a region. Moreover, this heterogeneity in ceramic-producing communities and exchange networks in highland Guatemala may have lent resilience to the broader assemblage of ceramic producers, distribution networks, and consumers, such that while some nodes of production, distribution, and consumption may have ceased to function, others persisted and/or took on greater importance.

In total, twenty-six distinct ceramic paste types were identified. These include everything from Classic-period Amatle wares and Postclassic-period Alotenango Cream and Chinautla wares to colonial-period lead-glazed redwares, Mexican majolicas, and Chinese porcelains. These twenty-six paste types were further refined into a total of fifty-four paste variants, of which a full forty-three were found in precolonial contexts while fifty-two were found in colonial contexts at the site. Only two ceramic types present in precolonial contexts completely disappeared in the colonial period, although many others see a drastic decline in frequency.

FIGURE 3.3
The most common vessel
type associated with
Paste Type 6.1, unique to
the colonial deposits at
Aguacatepeque.

These shared paste types speak to the persistence of Maya ceramic traditions and potting practices, an observation that parallels that observed by Sharer, Ashmore, and Hill (1970) in colonial-period occupations in the Antigua Valley. However, the colonial assemblage sees the presence of an additional nine paste types, many of which are related to Spanish-tradition ceramic wares, such as lead-glazed jars and majolica bowls and cups, as well as imported wares such as Mexican majolica and Chinese porcelain. Rather than showing some form of "acculturation" or loss of Maya practice/identity, these ceramic vessels indicate an expansion of previous networks of exchange that connected Aguacatepeque to new communities and producers of ceramic vessels, such as majolica potters in the capital at Santiago.

Similarly, Paste Type 6.1, restricted mainly to cooking vessels, is found only in colonial contexts and thus may represent a colonial innovation. (See below.) However, ceramics assigned to this paste group strongly resemble the Yepocapa Red type identified by Sharer, Ashmore, and Hill (1970) for both Postclassic and colonial contexts in Antigua, Guatemala, indicating some precolonial precedent. As a result, the sudden appearance of this ceramic type during the colonial occupation of Aguacatepeque potentially speaks to the establishment of new commercial ties between previously unconnected Maya communities in the colonial period and to the new circulation of "old" ceramic types in highland Guatemala. In both cases, recasting colonial-era consumption as productive of new relationships and entanglements critical to persistence, rather than as a decline or discontinuity with "authentic" Maya practice, is key to loosening the hold of acculturative frameworks that cast the true Maya as Classic or even Postclassic fossils, unable to grow by changing or transforming practices in later periods.

Perhaps more important are ceramic paste types (for example, 6.1 and 21.1) present only in colonial contexts that are not a product of Spanish colonial potting traditions but instead represent new Maya ceramic paste types that circulated in this region of the highlands. The assumption that all material culture present at a colonial Maya site would necessarily be either Spanish derived or recognizable precolonial Maya is telling of the continued sway of the "cold" and static cultural perspectives within which the colonial (and modern) Maya are framed, and it ignores the "internal dynamics" of Maya colonial cultural practices. (See Panich 2013.) Rather than supporting the notion that Native technologies could only persist or decline, the ceramic types from Aguacatepeque tell of creative colonial-period innovations by Maya potters in the highlands, especially in light of the specificity and distinctiveness of very thick-walled vessels associated with Paste Type 21.1. I have argued elsewhere that these vessels were likely used as large boiling vats in sugar production at the site. (See Pezzarossi 2014:224–26 for discussion of sugar production and associated ceramics at Aguacatepeque.) This point is key, as this paste group represents the emergence of a new ceramic type, executed in traditional Maya ceramic technologies and materials (clays, tempers, and so on), likely produced in the traditional potting community of Mixco (determined by instrumental neutron activation analysis [INAA]; see Pezzarossi 2014:273–82), albeit for use in a distinctly colonial practice: boiling down sugarcane juice for the production of *rapadura* (coarse sugar) for sale at market.

Finally, an intensive INAA provenance analysis of all ceramic paste groups has helped identify the potential source of various ceramic paste types from both precolonial and colonial occupations of the site (Pezzarossi 2014). The results of this analysis indicate that traditional potting communities, such as those at Chinaulta, Mixco, and the Chimaltenango regions in Guatemala, persisted in their craft production during the colonial period. Moreover, the variety of exchange networks and markets used to acquire ceramics from such disparate potting communities similarly persisted, despite the disruptions set in motion by colonization.

In summary, the analysis of ceramic artifacts from Aguacatepeque reveals the persistence of ceramic paste recipes, and thus ceramic potting communities, and ceramic production and technological practices from the Postclassic to the colonial period, as well as Aguacatepeque's continuing access to and acquisition of such ceramic goods. In addition, new ceramic types and pastes executed in Maya ceramic technologies and practices that appear in colonial-period occupations at Aguacatepeque speak to Maya potters' innovation in creating new ceramic pastes and types to meet emerging needs, demands, and desires, albeit through knowledge and practices rooted in precolonial and colonial teachings, and/or through Aguacatepeque's new connections to potting communities they were previously disconnected from, including potters in other Maya towns and those newly inhabiting the Spanish capital at Santiago.

Communities and Constellating Practices: Beyond Continuity

The ceramic data presented here corroborate Robinson's (1990, 1997) findings of settlement continuity in the Antigua highland region. However, the ceramics also indicate a broader persistence not just of site settlements as individual towns weathering colonization in isolation. They speak to the persistence of communities of practice and crafts production, and the resilience and persistence of ties *between* communities: networks of exchange, interaction, and commerce. The ceramics from Aguacatepeque and other sites discussed above illustrates the presence and persistence of what Wenger (1998) calls "constellating practices": practices that bind particular communities across space and time through similar knowledges and production, consumption, use, and discard routines related to ceramic and other material goods (Mills 2016; Roddick and Stahl 2016).

At one level, the observed persistence of similar technological and stylistic choices and practices of ceramic production by communities of potters active prior to and after colonization highlights the resilience of both particular ceramic materialities and the social practices and learning that are drawn and performed in their production. Drawing on the work of Lave and Wenger (1991), such "bundles" of similar situated knowledge, social practice, and materiality constitute communities of practice within, between, and across towns and generations that remain active despite the supposed rupture of colonization. (See Mills 2016.) It is not just the ceramics that persist but rather the whole assemblage constitutive of ceramic production and its social/cultural contexts: from choices in ceramic finishing techniques and clay sources to firing methods and embodied movements and stylistic citations used to shape and decorate ceramic vessels. The ceramic producers in Mixco, Chinautla, and Chimaltenango clearly persisted as potters, using techniques similar to those of past generations of potters, producing pots indistinguishable from precolonial contexts (such as Chinautla polychrome vessels) as well as innovating and introducing new types of pots, albeit ones made with materials, technological knowledge, and embodied techniques—constellating practices—that persisted and tied them to precolonial communities of practice, despite the upheavals of colonization, as well as to modern, non-Native communities of potters and consumers to whom they became constellated.

As a result, this observed material persistence tells a tale of manifold persistence—but not continuity—of practice, both in the various elements bundled together in the production of ceramic vessels and in their distribution, acquisition, and use. The products of the same ceramic potting communities continued to find their way into the hands of the residents of Aguacatepeque, through the markets and itinerant merchants that continued to serve as important access points to goods for communities both prior to and after colonization. Perhaps most importantly is the persistence of what Mills (2016) calls communities of consumption, which illustrate similarities in choices made in the acquisition and use of things, such as ceramic vessels, that continued to bind the same producers and consumers across regions and through time. At Aguacatepeque, ceramic goods from the same ceramic potting communities in Mixco, Chimaltenango, and Chinautla continued to be consumed, providing evidence of constellating choices related to the continued demand and desire for products of these communities, and by extension the uses they were put to (such as making tortillas with *comales* from Mixco or eating from Chinautla bowls). Together, these constellating practices of both production and consumption/use, along with practices such as language, would relationally "mark" the expression of a distinct and legible Native identity through its difference from non-Native practices and lifeways, at the same time those non-Native practices and materialities—including Spanish-introduced ceramic vessels—became integral parts of Native practice and colonial persistence tactics. (See Pezzarossi 2014.) Such "distributed" persistence is crucial to undermining notions of rupture or complete disruption in the colonial period by illustrating multi-sited persistence across the landscape, as well as the continued presence and relevance of ties that bound Maya populations into similar, as well as different, communities of practice—both material and cultural—prior to and after colonization. (See Mills 2016.)

However, it is critical that the identification of persistence, particularly of ceramic/potting communities of practice, not be conflated with a finding of unchanged continuity either in ceramic production or in associated cultural and material practices of Maya producers, consumers, and users of these wares. The contexts of production at these highland Maya potting centers, likely under pressure to generate revenue for the payment of newly imposed tribute and tax demands, or to produce new, in-demand ceramic types for new industries (such as sugar production), introduced change in apparent continuity. As an example, Native potters were drawn into the Convent of Santo Domingo in Santiago Guatemala to produce Chinautla polychrome ceramics, albeit for the benefit of the clergy who distributed these wares (Paredes and Romero 2008:86). At Aguacatepeque, the apparent continuities in ceramic consumption practices hide changes in community practice caused by colonial impositions/opportunities, such as increasing market dependence for ceramic artifacts as local ceramic production ceased and the community focused on cash crop cultivation (Pezzarossi 2014).

Both of these cases highlight the pitfalls of assuming that material continuities are indicative of unchanging practice, given that such a perspective ignores how materials move into and out of new and different contexts of use and exchange, and regimes of meaning and value, despite their apparent "static" continuity. Moreover, it is key not to equate change with loss, as material discontinuities may in fact occult continuities in practice, use, and meaning, as new materials are folded into existing practices and worldviews rather than radically transforming them with their presence. Moving away from continuity as an interpretive frame opens up a conceptual space for change as critical to persistence, thus shedding light on how communities navigated new opportunities to continue existing as entities, albeit in new contexts that preclude or restrict past ways of being. Attention to context beyond the apparent material (dis)continuities provides a window into these complex dynamics of continuity in change and change in continuity as messy entangled processes contributing to Native community persistence in manifold ways.

As mentioned above, persistence, rather than static continuity (Panich 2013), helps reframe this discussion to better account for how transformations in practice and materiality arising from cultural/material innovations, arising from new opportunities, and/or catalyzed by violent new colonial arrangements did not unravel Maya communities but rather were part of the always unfinished, context-contingent, and culturally mediated process of (re)negotiating what it meant to be Maya/Native in a continually changing and often hostile world. Such a process was not unique to the colonial period in highland Guatemala, meaning that precolonial Maya communities were not static and did not practice a singular way of being Maya through time, only to change at "contact" with Spanish colonists. Rather, these processes of negotiating identity and community had been ongoing in the deeper past and continued to be so during the sixteenth, seventeenth, eighteenth centuries and beyond.

In recent work, Law Pezzarossi and Sheptak (2018) have provided an important consideration of how studies of long-term indigenous entanglement can highlight the dynamics of community and identity persistence beyond static continuity. They argue that more attention needs to be placed on recognizing how Native community identities and practices change, transform, and are redefined in ways not necessarily referential of continuity with past precolonial practice and lifeways, albeit always from a particular standpoint informed by past(s) and present(s). The valence of such a perspective on persistence and entanglement lies in its expansion of the influences—of various origins—and cultural/material contexts and practices of longer and shorter histories that are considered "authentic" or simply an unproblematic aspect of dynamic Native lifeways and their historically situated practices.

Mitigating Violence: Discourses of Persistence through Long Durée Maya Archaeologies

The Guatemalan highlands, as a base of modern descendant Maya populations, provides a unique opportunity to draw archaeological knowledge into the project of deconstructing narratives of colonial rupture and mitigating their violent discursive effects. My argument is simple: archaeologists working in Guatemala's highland Maya (and indeed all) regions must treat the colonial period as part of the archaeology and history of the Maya rather than as an endpoint of both. This means more archaeological projects focused explicitly on the highland Maya colonial experience, as well as more intensive, integrative analysis of colonial components of archaeological sites encountered during fieldwork (for example, treating colonial components as part of the archaeology of the site). While colonial Maya life has been well studied by ethnohistorians through ethnohistoric documents and official archival sources, historical archaeologists have long argued for archaeology as more than just a "handmaiden" to history in contexts with writing and documentary sources. Instead, archaeology offers a way to investigate beyond the gaps, biases, and constraints of the archive(s), "through the examination of the quotidian, the overlooked, and 'taken for granted' that the traces of subaltern voices and experience can be constituted" (Buchli and Lucas 2001:14; see also Beaudry 1988; Deetz 1996). Mayanists need little reminding of this point, as Classic-period texts have long complemented, but not replaced, archaeological research on the lowland Maya.

Working to bridge these disciplinary and discursive ruptures by emphasizing

Maya history as continuous across precolonial and colonial divides is of manifold importance. It allows archaeology to tell more complete histories of descendant Maya populations that mitigate the violence done by discourses of rupture, and rupture by archaeological omission (that is, ignoring colonial Maya archaeology). Providing insight into the dynamics of Maya persistence and change over nearly five hundred years, as attempted in this chapter, is an important avenue for undermining dominant narratives of rupture, collapse, acculturation, and extinction that continue to hold sway in academic, popular, and national discourse in Guatemala. It bears explicit mention that arguing for such persistence does not entail a minimization of the impacts of colonization, much of it outright violent, on Maya communities. Fully acknowledging the scope and scale of colonial violence is crucial, as it reveals the hostile conditions within which Maya communities creatively made do to remain connected to their pasts, albeit as knowledgeable, engaged inhabitants of a differently cosmopolitan present, while providing context for the necessity and opportunities to change that may have made persistence possible for many communities.

Finally, such a reframing of the colonial period as an important period of Maya persistence, survival, and even fluorescence intersects productively with the goals of Maya revitalization and community activism. An emphasis on colonial Maya archaeology offers additional heritage sites, histories, landscapes, and artifacts for Maya communities to claim as part of their cultural revitalization and refashioning projects, which do not all have to be rooted in the baggage-laden Classic-period heritage. Frühsorge (2007:49) has called the spiritual, economic, and political overtones of Maya rituals at archaeological sites in the region a manifestation of the "claim on the places" that produces "strong images of unbroken tradition . . . from prehispanic times to the present," using "period" materials, practices, and knowledge identified by archaeological research. Maya colonial heritage provides the means for similar Maya claims to "unbroken" tradition or connection, albeit through colonial "period" sites and materials. In turn, archaeology can begin to address the discursive violence done to Maya histories and descendant communities by highlighting material bridges between modern, colonial, and precolonial Maya communities, both for and with the Maya and the Guatemalan and global public.

FOUR

Spanish Colonialism and Spatial Violence

KATHRYN E. SAMPECK

Contributions to this volume discuss violence in terms of acts, experience, places, and times *of* violence. This work, in contrast, posits space itself *as* violence. Examples from colonial Latin America illustrate spatial violence that had the same shock as a slap in the face, the same humiliation, and devastating consequences because it was common, daily, insidious, and difficult to evade. Because spatial violence occurred in multiple, simultaneous, and recursive ways, violence was insidious, infecting public, private, urban, and rural places, knitting together locales that otherwise might seem disconnected. The permanence and pervasiveness of spatial violence in colonial Spanish America was generated by a process of translation of (indigenous) place into an ideal space (imperfectly executed even in Europe) for civilizing and creating moral order by and through design. This ideal model positioned physical, geographical relationships as implementations and exemplars of elements of law and empire-building doctrines, arrangements that were ineluctably formed from and generative of violence. The violence of Spanish colonial application of spatial regimes and policies occurred through means that included Foucauldian spatial disciplines, subtle but pervasive structural violence, and symbolic violence. Comparing each of these modes of spatial violence highlights how each—the overseen, unseen, and unknown, respectively—together generated space as potent violence. The on-the-ground results of applying these ideals, the deployment of space to place, varied wildly in many ways from one locale to another but were consistent in one crucial way: the conversion made places perpetrators of violence in ways that had not existed before, gaining new or increased power.

These forms of real, humiliating harm were a persistent experience in colonial Spanish America. In fact, spatial violence is a main point of concordance between two regions where I have conducted substantial archaeological fieldwork and that seem worlds apart. One is in western El Salvador, in the territory of people who called themselves Pipil and spoke Nahuat, a language in the same family of Nahuatl spoken by the Aztecs. The other is in the us Southeast, in the ancestral homelands of Ani-yunwiya (Cherokee) peoples (Figure 4.1). Archaeological and documentary evidence from the sixteenth century from just these two locales in Spanish America offers a few among many examples of different modes of spatial violence. These examples focus particularly on how illicit and legal implementation of Spanish spatial policies of *congregación* (forced resettlement) resulted in the unmaking of places and how recrafted places exerted harm. Colonial relocation and reorganization of place were overtly violent—tearing down and rebuilding—but even more vicious than containing residents in new ways through forced resettlement was to unsee their very presence, which simultaneously divorced being from place. Spanish imperial policies thus relied upon multiple, simultaneous dislocation. From this perspective, the implementation of spatial policies in specific places was not just a violent means but was an enduring and pervasive violent end whose effects still persist today.

The imposition of violence through applying spatial regimes was imperfect, however, because cultural landscapes are a palimpsest rather than a tabula rasa; those traces, some more subtle than others, in concert with the unconceived or incompletely implemented elements of spatial regimes, provided opportunities to thwart pervasive spatial violence. Even though Spanish colonial places exerted violence in multiple ways, they also harbored contexts of refuge. People worked within and around violences of places to maintain practices and populations that the violence sought to extinguish.

In the following sections, I highlight how archaeological and ethnohistoric research in the Izalcos region and the interior of La Florida shows that this violence occurred in different regions of Spanish America, and shows that through physical, structural, and symbolic modes, colonial space regimes were forms of violence. The implications for this work include heightened awareness that the violence is not a relic of the past but rather that these processes continue today. Archaeology can play a role in understanding the genesis and scope of violence and thereby help confront enduring processes of spatial violence.

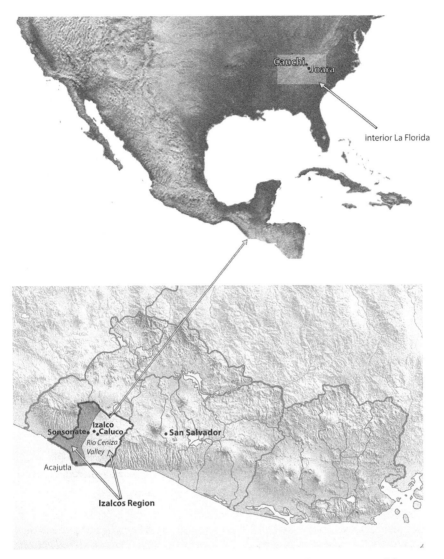

FIGURE 4.1 Map showing the locations of study regions: the Izalcos region, part of the *audiencia* of Guatemala, and ancestral Ani-yunwiya (Cherokee) settlements in the interior of La Florida. Map by Kathryn Sampeck. Base map for inset courtesy NASA/JPL-Caltech.

Space, Place, and Violence

Henri Lefebvre (1991:14) was careful to distinguish "conceptual" space—an ideal paradigm (a Cartesian "empty container," such as a house or room) that involves distance—from historically contingent, particular locales of social practice, what I refer to here as *place*, noting that "each of these two kinds of space involves, underpins, and presupposes the other" (Feld and Basso 1996; Tilley 2010; Tuan 1977:6). As many landscape archaeologists have emphasized, socially produced space "serves as a tool of thought and of action; that in addition to being a means of production it is also a means of control, and hence, of domination, of power; yet that, as such, it escapes in part from those who would make use of it. The social and political forces that engendered space seek, but fail, to master it completely" (Lefebvre 1991:26). Scholars have devoted significant attention to the colonial reordering of space and its social, economic, and political consequences (Edmonds and Banivanua Mar 2010; Feld and Basso 1996; Harvey 2009; Jamieson 2002; Lovell 2005; Mignolo 2003; Rice 2013). This previous work shows how places such as factories, great houses, or gardens can be expressions that reify power inequalities and result from oppression (Camp 2016; Foucault 1975, 1977; Mrozowski, Ziesing, and Beaudry 1996; Orser 2005; Sampeck 2014b). For example, Beaudry (1989) and Mrozowski, Ziesing, and Beaudry (1996) explain how US factories were simultaneously conscious statements of the goals of industrial capitalists; useful tools to serve the needs of industry for efficient, cheap production; and, surprisingly, and a way to project an image of America as an agrarian republic (Van Bueren 2006). Mark Leone and colleagues argue that spatial arrangements in Maryland gardens and architecture were a means to display and enact ideologies of a rightful place of elites at the apex of a natural hierarchy among humans (Casella 2001b; Leone 2010; Leone, Harmon, and Neuwirth 2005; Miller and Tilley 1984; Shackel 2001). Public buildings, private great houses, and gardens, such as the Maryland Statehouse dome of the 1780s, the Wye Hall Plantation of the early 1790s, and the William Paca Garden, were panopticons, acting as devices of surveillance as much as generative spaces of ideologies of power (Brown and Samford 1990; Epperson 1999). Examples of prisons and confinement as places of violence are women's prisons in Tasmania. Established in the late eighteenth and early nineteenth century, institutional designs were architectural expressions, a kind of spatial orchestration, to deploy criminal reform philosophies (Casella 2001b, 2007a, 2007b). I build upon this previous work by suggesting that we can learn from evaluating the potential for space itself to be violent not just in overt forms such as prisons and internment camps but, just as importantly, in everyday spaces of domestic, laboring, and spiritual life.

Lefebvre (1991:416–17) observed that socially produced space is a "confrontation of diverse values, ideas, and preferred arrangements," resulting in a "trial by space." As is the case in other kinds of colonial encounters, this confrontation of space is an ongoing process; it is in this way that the trial by space continues to exert harm. The worst harm is the undoing of people and place: "Groups, classes, or fractions of classes cannot constitute themselves or recognize one another as 'subjects' unless they generate a space" (Lefebvre 1991:416). I would amend the phrasing slightly to "a trial by space to generate a place." The lack of constitution of a group means that it is placeless.

This trial by space harbors the potential for violence. More precisely, this effort to dominate by creating and maintaining structures of power through spatial practices is necessarily violent. It is not so hard to understand how a jail cell is violent, as the form, physical properties, and intent of the construction and use of the structure are to execute discipline in accordance with laws. These specialized structures, however, dealt with publicly acknowledged laws and perpetrators. The relation of law to violence is that they are ineluctably intertwined; law does not necessarily decrease the amount or intensity of violence but instead governs its deployment (Giddens 1985). Walter Benjamin (1986 [1921]:277) explored the relationship of violence, law, and justice, characterizing violence as a means to a just or unjust end, criteria that determine whether violence is sanctioned and legitimate or not. His argument is that legitimate violence is the origin of law. The state has the right to use force to attain certain ends, rights upheld and elaborated by laws.

That legal dividing line does not necessarily differentiate the forms, frequency, duration, or other characteristics of violence; the crucial difference between illicit and sanctioned violence is its legal foundation. Benjamin (1986 [1921]:281) argued that "violence, when not in the hands of the law, threatens it not by the ends that it may pursue but by its mere existence outside the law." Law is so intertwined with violence, Benjamin (1986 [1921]:288) claimed, that "when the consciousness of the latent presence of violence in a legal institution disappears, the institution falls into decay." That latent presence of violence also is a constituent of the material existence of the institution; institutions must have physical instantiations, whether buildings, bodily actions, or other material forms, to create and enforce law. Consequently, those observable existences must be as constituted by and executing of violence as the laws themselves.

Law-related violence (which is a redundant phrase) exists in a wider context of harm. The discussion so far has emphasized that violence creates; violence, of course, destroys, but even more importantly, violence is self-destructive: "[A]ll law-preserving violence, in its duration, indirectly weakens the lawmaking violence represented by it, through the suppression of hostile counterviolence" (Benjamin 1986 [1921]:300). The universe of violence—lawmaking, law preserving, and illegal—is fragile and volatile, making and unmaking by its very existence. Manifest violence then stands to be powerful, contradictory, and widespread, yet observable.

What, then, is not violent? Benjamin (1986 [1921]:289) in fact turns to the material world, arguing that small-scale, personal relationships can be nonviolent but that they "never apply directly to the resolution of conflict between man and man, but only to matters concerning objects. The sphere of nonviolent means opens up in the realm of human conflicts relating to goods." Although reciprocal exchanges are supposed to build social bonds, Mauss (2000) long ago convincingly demonstrated the simmering hostility in exchanges. This dilemma of latent violence in seemingly nonviolent means of exchange and the world of objects is similar to the appearance of peace created by law that is in its genesis violent.

Furthermore, what if violence is an end and not just a means? From this perspective, violence is literally structural. Colonial dislocation was a violent end, treating land as one thing and its residents as something separate, objectified, commodified, and thus removable. Anthropologist Audra Simpson (2014:21) describes this distinction and dislocation as a stepwise process that "moves Indigenous peoples and their polities in the settler imaginary from nations, to people, to populations—categories that have shifted through time and in relation to land and its dispossession." Jodi Byrd (2012) phrases this rupture as "colonial agnosia": colonialism is simultaneously everywhere and nowhere; it permeates places yet seems dissociated from space. A review of specific Spanish policies shows relationships among violence, space, and place.

SPANISH SPATIAL VIOLENCE:
CONGREGACIÓN, REDUCCIÓN, AND POLICÍA

The Spanish colonial policy of congregación was (usually) forced resettlement into nucleated communities. Was forced removal a brute demonstration of power? Of course, but the framework of Spanish reordering of space had ideological and ethical intent: to make orderly, *reducción*, and to foster *policía*, moral order. It was not enough to force people to move but to do so as a means to implement particular spatial regimes and enable violent practices, though such acts and places were publicly touted as a way to civilize.

REDUCCIÓN

Many scholars tend to interpret the Spanish prime directive of reducción as synonymous with congregación, forced resettlement. The anthropologist William Hanks has shown that colonial sources defined the term as "persuade" rather than the modern dictionary definition "reduce" (Hanks 2010). For example, Sebastián de Covarrubias (1995 [1611]:854), chaplain for King Philip II, glossed *reducido* as "convencido y vuelto a mejor orden" (convinced and turned into a better order). This sense of reducción addresses the dispositions and conduct of people, not just that they are gathered together but that they are gathered together in a particular way. From this perspective, social space, the human body, and everyday social conduct were all equally subject to reducción (Hanks 2010:3). This definition of reducción also underscores that it was a process that was performed and experienced as much as arranged, and that people manipulated material culture to fully embody it (Hanks 2010:211). While Hanks (2010:2) concentrated on the impact of the dynamic of reducción on spoken and written indigenous language, he argued that the drive was for indigenous subjects to embrace reducción in their daily lives, "to habituate them to a new way of being in the everyday social world. The appearance and neatness of collective life, the 'small details,' would help transform the Indios' disposition. . . . Much as in Elias's (1969) civilizing process, or Bourdieu's (1977) concept of habitus, the idea of policía was to instill ways of perceiving, experiencing, and behaving, rooted in the little details of the body in its social life and in the disposition to reproduce them." The *how* of reducción, to reform the everyday life of the individual for the *why* of moral and social improvement, was intimately linked with *where* this transformation took place.

POLICÍA

Place and moral order were intimately entwined in Spanish ideology and practice. Hanks observed, "To be reducido was above all to live in a stable place, in which things were done in their proper settings and people behaved in ways appropriate to those settings. The concept here derives from policía, moral order, itself derived linguistically from *polis* 'town.' Consequently, the order imposed by reducción revolved around the pueblo 'town'" (Hanks 2010:25). Policía was the moral law for every colonist—Spanish, indigenous, or African. Dislocation and relocation were thus the important first step and ongoing project to enforce the day-to-day conformity with moral laws. The removal of residents to new places was a coercive act in itself, moving people physically away from, or at least in a new relationship to, ancestral lands—a material tearing out by the roots, so to speak.

Spatial violence was concrete but also a spatial practice with symbolic weight. Scholars such as Michel Foucault, Pierre Bourdieu, and Paul Farmer provide obvious theoretical foundations, but their attention to space differs from that of an archaeologist. Because the center of archaeological work lies in physical objects and experiences, it has the potential to evaluate forms of violence and nonviolence by using methodologies particularly suited to systematic and holistic assessment of material remains, approaches less consistently employed by scholars in other disciplines.

Material Violence: Spatial Discipline and Punishment

One of the most widely known discussions of violence in relation to spatial organization and use is the work of Michel Foucault. He picked apart both the social dynamics within and the formal organization of space as a deployment of power. One of his more dramatic examples was equating the horror of an ineptly done drawing and quartering with the rules and schedule for a young prisoner's day. He presented these examples as parallel in level of violence, although the temporal and corporeal regimes of the prisoner were less overtly gory. Prison violence was potent because it was instead bloodless brutality hidden in plain sight under the trappings of peaceable order. Foucault (1977:3–8) identified the shift from the public act to the institution as "punishment of a less immediately physical kind, a certain discretion in the art of inflicting pain, a combination of more subtle, more subdued sufferings, deprived of their visible display." It is the difference between the overt (public, gory violence) and the implied but not entirely covert: official oversight, self-policing, and enduring daily encumbrance, but violence nonetheless. That these disciplinary measures were quotidian made them pernicious; archaeological assessments of contexts as diverse as formal gardens (Brown and Samford 1990) and Virginia plantations (Epperson 1999) reveal these daily, persistent elements of policing.

This discipline of a body's rhythms, movements, and comfort was enacted at large and small scales. Foucault (1977:188) described how the quarantine of plague victims implemented what he called "a compact model of the disciplinary mechanism" of "segmented, immobile, frozen space. Each individual is fixed in his place. And, if he moves, he does so at the risk of his life, contagion or punishment." Power was visibly mobilized to combat the extreme situation of plague infection to create order, control the mixing of bodies, and maintain respect for laws rather than let fear overwhelm legal and social prohibitions. These same concerns—creating order, controlling mixing, and fortifying moral conduct in the face of turmoil—and their disciplinary consequences occur in contexts as early as the sixteenth century in Spanish America and are observable archaeologically as spatial practices and arrangements.

As much as any of Foucault's institutions of schools or prisons, quotidian Spanish policies created physical, observable consequences that were violent by preventing access to resources and segregating people into more controllable, containable spaces for achieving imperial schemes (Hanks 2010). Not only was this reformulation a trauma that each individual settlement perpetrated, but shocks also resonated through the reordering of the network of settlements and activity spaces. This transformation in late pre-Columbian to early colonial networks is manifest in the number and distribution of settlements in the Río Ceniza Valley, the heartland of the Izalcos region. Archaeological survey recovered a late pre-Columbian pattern of evenly dispersed, remarkably unnucleated settlement just before Spanish invasion. In fact, it was difficult to establish a "site" as a bounded space in the traditional sense. In contrast, it is clear that by the mid-sixteenth century, Spanish colonists had relocated the majority of the population into nucleated centers that erected physical barriers to interchange that had not existed before (Sampeck 2010:261–82).

In the interior of Spanish colonial La Florida, colonists created policies that reconfigured spatial relationships, even if the space itself did not change in its footprint. One 1576 meeting between southeastern indigenous and Spanish leaders at the Cherokee settlement of Cauchi was meant to determine where some of them were to pay tribute. Juan Pardo, in charge of the effort to colonize the region, ordered food to be taken to the garrison of soldiers at Cauchi but deerskins to "another Guancamu" at Joara (Hudson 2005:100). Spanish colonists endeavored to reconstruct the system of settlements and resources to act as a disciplinary form. Archaeological evidence of settlements in the region where Cauchi was likely located, the Nolichucky Valley of today's eastern Tennessee, does not indicate the broad Spanish-directed reconfiguration of settlement systems through congregación that occurred in the Izalcos region (Sampeck, Thayn, and Earnest

2015). Instead, the documentary record hints at both violent and nonviolent re-
fusal to dislocate, and the archaeological evidence of especially large settlements
with rich and diverse resources strongly affirms rootedness in place. The spatial
violence of applying an ideal plan of space, for the location and connections
among settlements, to these two places, the Izalcos and the Ani-yunwiya territories, was profound and overt in the first and subtle in the second.

PHYSICAL AND MORAL ORDER OF THE POLIS

Congregación brought Native peoples not only into fewer spaces but also into
spaces that were decidedly Spanish in form. Places recast in Spanish models for
scale, materials, organization, orientation, and design were modes of Spanish
moral laws that physically shaped one's constitution. The goal was to instill moral
order by living at best willingly, at worst unwillingly, in an ordained spatial regime.
No less than the pope issued a directive about proper town plans, and this mandate became a principle to invoke in settlements in the Americas. Philip II man-
dated an ordinance that restricted Indians from participating in the construction
of Spanish towns because "when the Indians see it, it will cause admiration, and
they will understand that the Spaniard residents are populating there and they
will fear and respect and want their goodwill and not to offend them"[1] (Escalante
Arce 1992:1:39). The experience of a Spanish town was meant to inspire fear and
respect for those who built it and lived there. This overt desire for fear and respect
conforms to Foucault's notion of place as law-abiding discipline and power.

An exemplary feature of manifest reducción was the grid street system of the
traza, a central plaza bounded by municipal buildings with, ideally, a church
slightly set apart and above it all, with everything aligned along a grid plan system
of streets as the ideal form (Figure 4.2). One coercive effect of the traza plan was
to segregate people and space into more crisply defined elements. The mosaic of
these elements displayed a divine plan, policía. Lefebvre (1991:151) argued for the
pivotal importance of the grid-plan town, calling it "an instrument of production:
a superstructure . . . [serving] a political means of introducing a social and economic structure in such a way that it may gain a foothold and indeed establish
its 'base' in a particular locality." In this case, the social and economic structure
of reducción accomplished by the grid plan was also the legal moral structure of
policía (Kagan 2000, 2016).

All the congregaciones in the Izalcos had a gridded traza plan. The perfection
in regularity of the grid was an ideal, and its execution conformed to topographic
irregularities as well as, in some cases, to previous spatial arrangements (Figure 4.3;

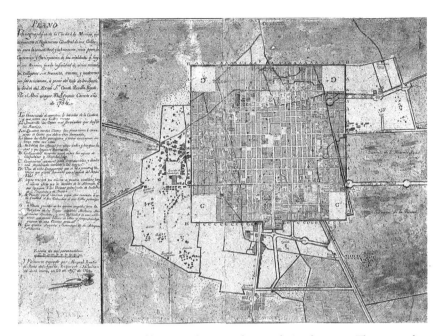

FIGURE 4.2 Map prepared by Manuel Ygnacio de Jesus de Aguila in 1794. The image of the grid-plan city and the map title show efforts to enforce *policía*. The title is "Iconographic Plan of Mexico City Showing the General Layout of its Pleasant and Beautiful Streets: As well as the repair and elimination of the negative features of the various neighborhoods, with their myriad hidden places, deserted alleyways, ruins and the negligent residents who cause them, in spite of all the efforts of the officers of public law and order under the command of His Excellency Count Revilla Gigedo, in the administration of Metropolitan Mayor Don Ignacio Castera." Courtesy Library of Congress, Geography and Map Division. Permalink https://lccn.loc.gov/00560609.

Wernke 2013). In the case of Caluco, the lack of any substantial archaeological evidence prior to the construction of the Spanish urban center indicates that it colonized a place that generations of prior inhabitants had rejected (Fowler 1995; Sampeck 2007; Verhagen 1997). A rocky hilltop that still today has problems with reliable access to water, the Spanish *pueblo de indios* (Indian town) of Caluco was a dramatic reorganization of indigenous settlement. Foucault's "frozen, segmented, and immobile" aptly describes boundaries of urban house lots that strongly inhibited mobility and were statically defined to maintain control and possession.

For the quarantine victims Foucault (1977:197) described, spatial segregation proscribed "the ultimate determination of the individual, of what characterizes

FIGURE 4.3 The *traza* plans of the Izalcos region towns of Caluco (left) and Nahulingo (right). Drawings by Kathryn Sampeck.

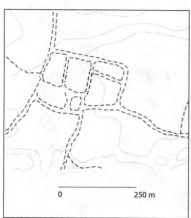

him, of what belongs to him, of what happens to him," a point equally true of residents in Spanish colonial towns. Much of what characterized a person was what religious, ethnic, or *casta* group they were considered to be a member of. A papal bull of August 8, 1442, Eugene IV's *Dundum ad nostram audientiam*, ordered the complete separation of Jews to their own residential area, a "ghetto," away from Christians, and subsequent spatial doctrines in the Americas continued to implement segregation on the basis of social, ethnic, and other factors that later (by the eighteenth century) included ideologies of race. While the regional network endeavored to control the extent and kinds of connections from location to location, within the city, the urban plan was to control the mixing of bodies.

The grid of the town segregated space into crisply separated units, and those ideally conformed to distinct social segments that then together formed a mosaic of *policía* that proscribed the "ultimate determination of the individual." A common feature across Mesoamerica for Spanish towns was a designated barrio (neighborhood) of Tlaxcallans (Fowler 2011; Matthew 2012; Murillo 2009). People of Tlaxcala were Native allies for Spanish conquest and colonization efforts, beginning with Hernando Cortés and reaching as far south as Peru. Towns in Spain already had segregated neighborhoods before Columbus's first voyage. The parishes of San Bernardo, San Roque, and several other Sevillian barrios were known for their numerous African, Moorish (North African Muslim), and Morisco (Spanish Muslim) residents, with Triana, the quarter of the seafaring population of Seville, the home of many Moors and Moriscos (Pike 1967). This spatially segregated difference in what the resident was supposed to be like, the kind of work, and social engagements ("what happens") has material evidence in belongings, with different areas of the town of Caluco in the Izalcos, for example, having different patterns of architecture and ceramics, some of which rely on forms that hark back to pre-Columbian practices (Hodges 2015; Kizior 2013). Similarly, at the settlement of Joara in the interior of La Florida, the area of the Spanish fort was separated from that of Native settlement and had distinctive architectural and artifact patterning (Beck, Rodning, and Moore 2016; Beck et al. 2017).

Furthermore, the function of the fort was to keep watch over the indigenous community. Foucault (1977:209) argued that the eighteenth-century utilization of surveillance in the form of the panopticon was an everyday, generalizable, sustained discipline mechanism, "a way of defining power relations in terms of the everyday life of men . . . a design of subtle coercion for a society to come." The archaeological remains of Fort San Juan attest numerous sturdy and specially provisioned structures, with imported trade goods, weights, and measures, all protected by a palisade wall. Fort San Juan was not unusual in the Southeast; Spaniards had infrastructure in Cauchi even before they built Fort San Pedro. At Spanish request, Native residents built a house to receive the Spanish and built a storehouse to keep grain for Spanish consumption. It is the last town this far west that prepared a house for the Spanish (Hudson 2005:97). In 1567 eleven men stayed at Cauchi to man the fort (DePratter, Hudson, and Smith 1983; Hudson 2005:96). The forts and towns in the interior of La Florida were physical installations of buildings and people to directly oversee the reorientation of commerce and political obligation as well as to establish and uphold colonial prohibitions.

In the ideal plan of the Spanish polis, the church was to have the privileged perspective of a panopticon, a constant moral gaze. Figure 4.4 shows one example of the sixteenth-century Church of San Pedro y San Pablo at the town of Caluco in the Izalcos region. The remains of the church loom on the horizon and are visible for miles around; the majority of sixteenth-century domestic settlement in the area, not just the town but smaller rural settlements as well, was within its viewshed. The Church of San Pedro y San Pablo of Caluco was a panopticon par excellence.

Another example of a Spanish colonial panopticon is documentary. The

FIGURE 4.5 Map of La Florida showing trans-Appalachian settlements of Xuala (Joara) and Guaxuli (Guasili). From Abraham Ortelius, *Theatre de l'univers, contenant les cartes de tout le monde* (Antwerp: Plantin Press, 1598). Courtesy John Carter Brown Library, Brown University.

chronicle of Juan de Bandera of the colonizing effort by Juan Pardo in 1567 in the interior of La Florida, what is today the Appalachian Summit area, offers a grand view and orientation provided in one statement of distances and directions (Table 4.1). While in some ways the chronicler Bandera is objectively reporting locations, the center point for these observations is the Spanish installation at Joara, an indigenous settlement within which Juan Pardo founded the Spanish

TABLE 4.1

Distances to Spanish Towns and Forts from Joara, La Florida

SIXTEENTH-CENTURY NATIVE AMERICAN SETTLEMENT/SPANISH TOWN/FORT	DIRECTION	DISTANCE (LEAGUES)
Chiaha/San Pedro	W	50
Cauchi/San Pablo	NW	28
Guatari/Santiago/Salamanca	NE	40
Canos/Santo Tomás	SE	45
Canos/Santa Elena	S	55

town of Cuenca and Fort San Juan (Figure 4.5). The table of distances Bandera provides was based upon surveillance of the entire region.

The complement to official panopticons was the public gaze upon events of upholding laws and order. The public square at the center of the traza was the locale for residents to observe the consequences of transgressing policía (Kagan 2009, 2016). Regular, public corporeal punishment was a strategy to prevent fear and the threat of death from overwhelming the observance of prohibitions. Public space was then a theater of violence. For example, an indigenous resident of Izalco spoke in favor of the *alcalde mayor*, Torres, saying that Torres "carried out prosecution against many Indians from the village of naolingo [Nahulingo] and yzalco [Izalco] for being drunks and adulterers and other crimes for which he punished them" (Escalante Arce 1992:1:197).[2] Public discipline was also a way to mark social difference, as the same infraction had different consequences depending on who you were. In the sixteenth century in the Izalcos region, Spaniards who sold goods on credit were fined thirty pesos, while Indian, mulatto, mestizo, and black infractors were publicly beaten (Escalante Arce 1992:1:239). Public castigation was an effort to make the possibility of violating prohibitions even worse than the specter of less overt and official threats.

Foucault opposed the overt against the subtle, the drama of a moment against the everyday to emphasize the evolutionary growth of institutions as coercive spaces. Taking a starting point in Latin America and about a century earlier, it is clear that what Foucault presented as evolutionary dynamics of discipline were actually all already in play, all at the same time, in sixteenth-century Spanish America. Rather than Foucault's evolution of overt, public violence to insidious, institutional forms of violence, cases in just two places in Spanish America show that these were simultaneous processes in the sixteenth century, medieval spectacles of horror as well as the working out of formal and informal institutional and quotidian disciplinary procedures.

It would seem that Spanish colonial material spatial violence was insurmountable. These colonial policies and practices, however, operated within constraints. Spaniards relied upon indigenous systems of labor mobilization and social hierarchy to extract and manage wealth and keep social order. Reducción was thus situated within competing political, economic, and social agendas, so the trial by space had strong contenders in both the Southeast and Central America (Bricker 2009; Cardós de Méndez 1959; Chapman 1957; Jones 1982). The Spanish economy often centered upon local products and production strategies, a siphoning off rather than a complete remaking of the local economy (Hill 1990, 1996; Hill and Monaghan 1987; Lockhart 1992:45; Sampeck 2014a). The Spanish used Native inter- and intrapolity boundaries to establish jurisdictions, departments, municipalities, and *encomiendas*, rewards of labor and tribute for service to the crown. The persistence of these pre-Columbian spatial patterns shows up archaeologically in the positioning of settlement-free areas and the relationship of settlements to stable landmarks (Sampeck 2014a). Archaeological evidence of access to imported goods and creative improvisations in daily material practices in and about these spaces indicates resilience in the face of threats and injury.

Inverting Foucault: Structural Violence

Foucault's scheme of overt, public violence evolving to insidious, institutional forms of violence goes a step further with what Paul Farmer and others call "structural violence" (Farmer 2004b; Farmer et al. 2006). In this case, "[t]he arrangements are structural because they are embedded in the political and economic organization of our social world; they are violent because they cause injury to people . . . neither culture nor pure individual will is at fault; rather, historically given (and often economically driven) processes and forces conspire to constrain individual agency" (Farmer 1999:79). The violence is corporeal in that it damages well-being in the short and long term through lack of access to health care or food, for example: "Structural violence is structured and *stricturing*. It constricts the agency of its victims. It tightens a physical noose around their necks, and this garroting determines the way in which resources—food, medicine, even affection—are allocated and experienced" (Farmer 2004b:315; emphasis in the original). At the same time, structural violence is subtle, often invisible, especially compared to the spatial ordering of the panopticon, which makes pinpointing a specific person to be held responsible difficult or impossible. In contrast to Foucauldian overt behavioral violence and less public, insidious institutions of surveillance, structural violence is a "non-opticon."

FEEDING VIOLENCE

The *entrada* of Hernando de Soto across La Florida in 1539–1540 was an exercise in draining places of people and food. As mentioned earlier, the colonization effort of Juan Pardo about thirty years later redirected flows of resources. Even though Juan Pardo gave the directive for food to be taken to Cauchi but deerskins to Joara, the effect and intent was to establish colonial policies and procedures. In this sense, the new scheme was not personal at all. The structural violence parallels that of examples from the Izalcos relating to food security and access. The clear effect, even within only a few months of Spanish incursion, was of food stress (Hudson 2005). Suddenly adding to the population with demanding new residents meant that large shifts in need had to be satisfied with resources that indigenous people produced based on a different set of relationships of people and places. The acute distress was spatial in its dimensions in that those locales of Spanish reconfiguration suffered inordinately, establishing spatial discontinuities in places that had archaeological evidence of previous prosperity and access to abundant resources (Sampeck, Thayn, and Earnest 2015).

Residents in the Izalcos suffered spatial structural violence related to food security, quality, and access as well. Here, the structural violence was spatial in that access to resources, in this case the most fundamental of all, food, was not at hand; food precarity was a looming specter. Imports provided staple foods such as corn and beef, indicating that a great proportion of the Izalcos economy for much of the colonial period was devoted to nonfood production. *Jueces de milpas* (agricultural judges) were an attempt by the crown to force Indian villages to produce more staples to remedy the short supply felt in the 1620s (MacLeod 1973:205–6). The access to means to produce food, however, had become much more limited. Because rural areas had a much lower population in the 1600s than a few decades earlier, land grants to *vecinos*, Spanish residents, faced few obstacles. During the seventeenth century, Spaniards took to the countryside in great numbers; indigenous populations returned, but as hired laborers rather than owners (MacLeod

1973:206). This increase in rural settlement is observable archaeologically by an increase in the number of smaller hinterland sites compared to late sixteenth- to early seventeenth-century settlement (Figure 4.6).

Colonial towns were in some cases centers for food monopolies. The mid-sixteenth-century *encomendero* of Izalco, Diego de Guzmán, had the monopoly on all beef sold in Izalco and supplied much of the beef for Sonsonate (Escalante Arce 1992:1:238). As part of Guzmán's careful control of meat sales, indigenous *alguaciles* (sheriffs) did not allow Afrodescendants of other pueblos to go to the Izalco market to sell cooked meat (Escalante Arce 1992:1:248). Furthermore, Guzmán's product sold at a relatively high price, for two hundred cacao beans (one real) per pound rather than the twenty to thirty beans of other vendors. This control over food distribution, source, and quality was spatially governed: access to the space of the market in Izalco was only with permission.

Food quality was another means of structural violence enacted through spatial relations. In a 1580 complaint, Gómez Díaz de La Reguera denounced the encomendero Guzmán for having an exclusive public meat market using *vacas magrantas* (migrant cattle). Guzmán was also accused of ordering that any chickens that died be made into tamales and sold without regard to whether they had been healthy or sick when they died (Escalante Arce 1992:1:248). Guzmán's control over the town's market space ensured that marketgoers did not have many alternatives to the tainted food because it was difficult or impossible to go to another market.

Other laws sought to limit sales as insurance against food scarcity. Jorge de Alvarado, acting as *tieniente de gobernador* (lieutenant governor) for Santiago de los Caballeros, the first capital of Guatemala, ordered that no one could sell maize they had stored for their own sustenance (Libro Viejo 1934:23). While policies in the capital city of Santiago de los Caballeros evinced a certain nervousness about basic food supply in the early years of the city, Sonsonate and other Izalcos region towns had a greater concern for social order and control over space and practices therein. The restrictions on what could be sold and who could buy it in Sonsonate replicated and enforced social hierarchies, and trade in certain commodities, such as wine, superseded such hierarchies.

The production of meat by encomenderos was doubly damning, as cattle negatively affected the agricultural space of Native populations. Cattle being fattened roamed freely, often in areas of cacao agriculture. They had no mercy for the sensitive trees or the infrastructure that supported their growth. Cattle trampled seedlings, destroying orchards (Escalante Arce 1992:1:159). One acequia (irrigation

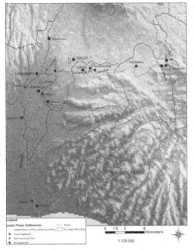
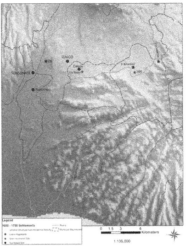
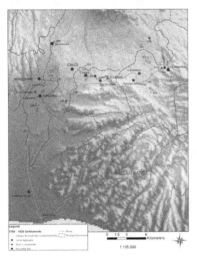

FIGURE 4.6 Archaeologically recovered settlements of the Río Ceniza
Valley in the heartland of the Izalcos
region. Marroquín phase (1580–1615)
settlements (top left) have many
congregaciones, while 1615–1720 settlement is sparse, with a few new rural
and hacienda settlements (top right);
1750–1820 settlement shows a prolif-
eration of individual households and
small rural settlements. Maps by Sean
Stretton and Kathryn Sampeck.

canal), named Atatucpan and located in Caluco, was ruined and contaminated
by cattle in the late sixteenth century: "[S]aid cattle love the irrigation canals of
said orchards, they have made them broken and blind and they wander below the
cacao orchards, in which they damage much, knocking off the fruit and breaking
them and in this way in all of the cultivation areas confined with said cabins they
are lost and without any profit" (Escalante Arce 1992:1:243).[3]

The rampant, damaging free range of cattle violated places defined for Native production. The practice of free grazing had severe spatial impact of structural violence, making less land available for agricultural production for subsistence or commodities, coercing people to purchase low-quality, high-cost staples.

An official concern for wealth and health fostered policies that proponents argued were in the best interests of Native residents, an effort to control what they did, its outcome, and where they carried out activities of daily existence. In 1570 Gonzalo de Alvarado, brother of the conquistador of Guatemala, Pedro de Alvarado, recommended that because Izalco was growing, tribute should increase from one thousand to fourteen hundred *xiquipiles* of cacao, plus poultry and fanegas of corn. Not just wealth in cacao but also basic foodstuffs needed to be part of the burden. The rationale was that Izalco was "one of the idle towns on the whole coast and the people of said village have so much extra cacao that they spend it unwisely" (Escalante Arce 1992:1:235).[4]

What is evidence of the spending habits of Izalqueños? Archaeological ceramic assemblages of households of the period in indigenous contexts include about 5 percent Ming Dynasty porcelains, mostly illicit goods from the Manila galleon trade (Sampeck 2015). This may seem a small amount, but it matches the relative proportion of porcelains in wealthy Spanish households and exceeds frequencies in other regions of Mexico and Central America. These wares were material evidence of wealth. The official concern was that if Native residents spent their wealth poorly, they needed to be relieved of it through higher tribute requirements; it was a program of benevolent structural violence. Being idle was unacceptable; Izalco was a place of lazy, spendthrift people; and the solution was to work harder, produce more, and give in tribute rather than spend wealth garnered from their agricultural land so that they did not acquire unneeded belongings in their homes and in their lives. Here, the trial by space was in each home, and structural violence concerned the very dishes for serving the food that was in short supply.

LIMITS OF STRUCTURAL VIOLENCE

Despite these persistent and pervasive forms of spatial structural violence, examples of overcoming challenges exist for both La Florida and the Izalcos. During the expedition of Hernando de Soto in 1540 through the trans-Appalachian area of La Florida, Spanish tastes in food were a way for Native residents to rid themselves of something they considered inedible: dogs. The Soto accounts describe small, delicious, barkless dogs ("perillos, que es buen manjar," "perros pequeños que no ladran") (Oviedo y Valdés 1851:562). The account by the Gentlemen of

Elvas related how the people at Guasili, a settlement likely in the Nolichucky Valley, possibly the archaeological site of Jackson Farm/Plum Grove Site (40WG17) (Sampeck, Thayn, and Earnest 2015), served them three hundred dogs (*cāes*) because they saw that "the Christians enjoyed them even though they [the Indians] did not eat them" (Delvas 1557). This was a taste the Spaniards developed in Mesoamerica and evidently brought with them to the Southeast. Those dogs must have been really delicious because the place became synonymous with good luck; soldiers used the phrase "casa de guasuli" to say good luck or a good turn when playing dice (Oviedo y Valdés 1851:563).[5] Indigenous bounty defined the place in colonial eyes yet was a creative solution for minimizing impact on highly desired foods.

An example from the Izalcos relates to implements for preparing and serving food, ceramics. Like other practices within the context of reducción, ceramic forms and decoration conformed to expectations in some ways yet did not in others. Tin-enameled earthenwares (maiolica) were a Spanish ceramic import of forms and techniques in pottery making. The pervasiveness of maiolica and its attributes even in locally made pottery suggests a genesis of a shared colonial identity, a seeming conformity to colonial governance predicated on the practice in use and aesthetics of serving wares (Sampeck 2015). The many rural and urban contexts for both maiolica and locally made ceramics with attributes copied from Spanish maiolica indicate that it was less an index of "Spanishness" than a visual identifier of vessels for serving, Spanish or not. The indigenous potters did not copy the entire suite of maiolica attributes but only a select few, and onto pre-Columbian forms, not only Spanish ones. The appearance of only a select few distinctly Spanish attributes of decoration and/or rim shape on specifically indigenous serving vessels violated Spanish ceramic canons, however. Vessels with this Spanish element occurred in the majority of contexts across Izalcos society and thus were not limited to Spanish or Ladino households. Furthermore, the continued production of Native forms indicates some maintenance of traditional foodways and forms of polite interaction, but within a Hispanicized context. This perhaps had the effect of making Native foods and serving styles appealing to Hispanic consumers as well as rendering Hispanic conventions and aesthetics relevant and intelligible to indigenous consumers. Within a context of structural violence that worked to limit the quality and availability of food, the presence of creatively subversive vessel forms for serving food is a hopeful sign that in domestic spaces, people not only nourished themselves but did so in a way that suited their tastes. They had a place at the table, so to speak.

A Landscape of Symbolic Violence

Space as violence in Spanish America occurred in symbolic form as well, which invokes a distinct set of implications. While Farmer's structural violence is *unseen*, Bourdieu's symbolic violence is *unknown*, or at least misrecognized: symbolic violence "is the violence which is exercised upon a social agent with his or her complicity" (Bourdieu and Wacquant 2004:272–74). Powerful and insidious, misrecognition is "the fact of recognizing a violence which is wielded precisely inasmuch as one does not perceive it as such. . . . Of all forms of 'hidden persuasion,' the most implacable is the one exerted, quite simply, by the order of things." Charles Orser illustrated how the creation of an appearance of antiquity in an Irish demesne was an example of Bourdieu's idea of symbolic violence, wherein symbols were manipulated to appear normal and natural but to permit domination in cases where overt violence was impossible or inadvisable (Orser 2006). The Tanzyfort demesne landscape was reshaped to emphasize the recognition of a new "ruin" that lent a patina of legitimacy to the demesne's new English owners. In the case of Tanzyfort, the violence was made *temporal* by creating a false depth in history that was observable through alteration of the landscape.

UNMAKING EXISTENCE: THE MOST BRUTAL VIOLENCE

Symbolic violence of Spanish American spaces introduces the most complete, and therefore violent, violence. Part of the colonial process of reordering space through congregación and reducción involved treating land as one thing and its residents as something separate—objectified, commodified, and thus removable. This reconceptualization of human subject and landscape object involved employing new technologies of landscape representation that emerged in the early modern period of landscape painting, mapmaking, and topographic writing (Dalglish 2012; Johnson 2007; Thomas 2012; Wood 2010).

Spatial violence in the case of many Native Americans was extreme, to the point that colonial schemes involved not just containing residents in new ways, as in policies of forced resettlement, but unseeing their very presence. The ideology and processes of referring to and treating land as "wilderness" or uninhabited (*tierras baldías*) created a mandate for colonization—a divine gift of unrealized potential (Dent 2013; Gazin-Schwartz 2008:25–26; Gosden 2004). The anthropologist Michael Taussig (1986:82) brings out an even more vivid sense of urgency for colonists confronting wilderness: to tame the wild was a mandate for self-preservation. The account of the Capuchin Francisco de Vilanova, writing in the 1920s about the Amazon, described (indigenously inhabited) wilderness this way: "[T]he jungle is an irrational fact, enslaving those who go into it—a whirl-wind of savage passions conquering the civilized person possessed with too much self-confidence. . . . The rational civilized man loses self-respect and respect for his home. He throws his heritage into the mire from where who knows when it will be retrieved. One's heart becomes morbid, filling with the sentiment of savagery, insensible to the pure and great things of humanity" (Taussig 1986:82). This "empty" land was the locale of Native American settlements or subsistence, ritual, and other activities (Hall 2014). Foucauldian spatial violence acknowledges the existence of the structure, wall, or topographic feature. Spatial structural vi-olence, likewise, recognizes that food should go some places instead of others. Symbolic violence is instead willful blindness to the very existence of places and people, a fundamental illogic of notation without recognition.

In the case of a 1756 metes and bounds land survey to give legal title for com-munal lands for residents of Caluco in the Izalcos region, the symbolic violence was spatial, not temporal: the antiquity of pre-Columbian political boundaries was less contested than their location. The new survey measure of the territory to achieve social, political, and economic orderliness was the goal—to see, record, and, in the end, partition off some territories and envelop others in a fixed and permanent way. Although the 1753 survey of the municipal border of Caluco was done to assign permanent, legal title to the municipality (in *ejido*) or to a *cof-radía*, a religious sodality that held land communally, the correct proportion of land among ejido, cofradía, and the crown also involved whether the land was in disuse, vacant. The judge for the case found that the ejido had twenty-two *caballerías* "too much" land. Those twenty-two were "saco de cacao á favor de su majestad," taken from cacao lands to please His Majesty (Caluco Archive 1753:Folio 109). That cacao lands were taken as "excess" reinforced the idea that Indians deserved only so much potential for wealth. These lands were not aban-doned if they were under cacao cultivation. It was a recognition of value and po-tential, and at the same time a blindness toward the people and their investments of time and resources.

In some cases, if colonists and officials recognized past presence of indigenous peoples, the landscape was "widowed"; due to disease, the indigenous population was significantly reduced by the time systematic settlement began in some areas (Gosden 2004:117). Colonists then cared for the orphaned place and in the pro-cess ignored human survivors. In widowed landscapes, the memory of the former settlements and their missing occupants faded as subsequent colonial generations dwelled there (Dent 2013; Guernsey 2008). It was genocide in practice if the fact of invasion and colonization had not completely done the job.

Though colonists judged and recorded resources in La Florida, they demonstrate this kind of lack of recognition of people connected to the land. The Pardo party founded the city of Cuenca in early January 1567, picking the spot of the Native settlement of Joara because of the large number of Indians and caciques who were resident or came to the region (Bandera 1990 [1569]:f5; Worth 2007). Despite vivid accounts of fertile agricultural fields and large towns filled with substantial populations, this action was in fact an unseeing of Native residents, erasing them from the landscape. Pardo chronicles describe that the goal was to work so that the "place called Joara should not remain a wilderness" (Bandera 1990 [1569]:f5v). The trial by space of reducción and policía versus orientations, meanings, and constructions of indigenous southeastern peoples involved severe dislocation.

It was the myth of the pristine: by casting the place as undeveloped, even though it was a settled town and the principal source of survival for the Spanish army, the whole territory became open for improvement by empire. Along the same vein, multiple examples of southeastern Native American town names recorded in the conquest and colonization efforts of Hernando de Soto and Juan Pardo are still known today but are overwritten by current, Anglo city names. The Native American part of history in these places is affixed to the remnants of town house mounds, while the rest of the indigenous settlement is obscured by contemporary development of "Franklin" or "Bryson City" or an unnamed agricultural field (Figure 4.7). Alice Te Punga Somerville's point is well taken: "There is no pure location: all of us (Indigenous and non-Indigenous) see certain places as 'bare' and all of us struggle sometimes to tell the difference between 'comments' and 'names'—and all of us benefit from deliberately seeking and cultivating ways

FIGURE 4.7 A nineteenth-century photograph of the council house mound at Nikwasi, a historic Ani-yunwiya (Cherokee) town. The credit reads, "From photograph of 1890 furnished by Mr H. G. Trotter, owner of the mound." From James Mooney, *Myths of the Cherokee* (GPO: Washington, DC, 1902):Plate XVI.

FIGURE 4.8 "Guatimala," in Thomas Gage, *Nouvelle relation, contenant les Voyages de Thomas Gage dans la Nouvelle Espagne* (Amsterdam: Chez Paul Marret, Marchand Libraire dans le Beurs-straat, 1694). Courtesy John Carter Brown Library, Brown University.

of recognizing and reaching for names. How differently might histories—might academia—look if we all always assumed Indigenous presence?"

In the case of Cherokee settlement of the interior Southeast, the process of erasing Cherokee names from Cherokee places, making them seem vacant, continues today. This symbolic unseeing is real, brutal violence, as it unmakes one's very existence. There's nothing to survive if it is seen as never to have existed in the first place.

UNRAVELING SPATIAL SYMBOLIC VIOLENCE

The case of the 1753 survey of Caluco is also an example of how the hegemonic sway of spatial symbolic violence was incomplete. Testimony and even acrimony in the genesis of what officials recorded as "seen" (recognizing one landmark, not another) was surprisingly unhegemonic (Figure 4.8). Colonial power was the product of a messy debate and rather haphazard consensus building of many actors rather than a unilateral pronouncement (Sampeck 2014a). The effect, however, was violent, as residents had to buy their own land to receive the title and ended up giving some of the most agriculturally productive lands permanently to the crown through the symbolic violence of unseeing. Communal landholding in

FIGURE 4.9 In retribution for European greed, Native Americans oblige the invaders' craving for gold by pouring molten metal down their throats. From Girolamo Benzoni, *La historia del mondo Nuovo* (Venice: Appresso Francesco Rampazetto, 1565), 49r. The text describes the Spanish, under the leadership of the governor of Panama, Pedrarías Dávila, raiding the coast for gold. Courtesy John Carter Brown Library, Brown University.

MONDO NVOVO.   49

quefta coftiera per coftume di mangiar huomini, &
quando mangiauano de gli Spagnuoli, n'erano di
coloro che ricufauano di cibarfene, temendo anco-
ra che nel lor corpo, non gli faceffero quelle carni
qualche danno, & quegli che pigliauano uiui,fpe-
tialmente i Capitani, legategli le mani & i piedi:

Come gli Indiani colauano l'oro in bocca
a gli Spagnuoli, e dell'habito che lor por-
tano in diuerfi lochi di terra Ferma.

gettatigli in terra, colauano loro, dell'oro in bocca,

the area was undermined and impoverished in the process, and alienated properties became part of a new geography of municipal management.

Pardo's willful blindness in La Florida may have been his undoing. After establishing the network of towns and forts across the interior Southeast, he was
called away to deal with French incursions along the Carolina coast. While at
Santa Elena, he received word in 1568 that not a single fort or town remained.
Archaeological work at Joara confirms continued indigenous settlement in the
spot, but the burning and destruction of fort-related buildings. It was a Native act
of counterviolence, eliminating those who did not see them (Figure 4.9).

Giving Place to the Placeless

The challenge of historical archaeology has long been known to be giving voice
to the voiceless (Orser 1996:178). I would add to this that archaeological investigations can help give place to the placeless. To recognize the perhaps obscured

but ultimately indelible record harks back to what Ingold (1993:152; Ingold 2000) called a "dwelling perspective," wherein the "landscape is constituted as an enduring record of—and testimony to—the lives and works of past generations who have dwelt within it, and in so doing, have left there something of themselves." Spatial violence occurred in many ways: as a disciplinary mechanism, as structural violence, and as symbolic violence, often concurrently. These modes often reinforced one another, making the violence of spatial regimes a relentless attack. Archaeological evidence of the formation of and change in spatial regimes, however, shows how, in Spanish America, resilience was the antidote to such violence.

Acknowledgments

Archival and archaeological research in this chapter was supported by many sources. For the work in El Salvador, a Tinker Grant through the Roger Thayer Stone Center for Latin American Studies at Tulane University funded the feasibility study. Multiple seasons of archaeological research were made possible by several grants from the Middle American Research Institute, as well as dissertation research grants from Fulbright-Hays, the Wenner-Gren Foundation for Anthropological Research (Grant 5919), the Social Science Research Council, and the National Science Foundation (Dissertation Improvement Grant 9521749). Further research in El Salvador was supported by a CIES Senior Scholar Fulbright Fellowship. I am deeply grateful to Brad Phillippi and Chris Matthews for organizing the panel at the 2016 Society for Historical Archaeology that gathered all the contributors in this volume together for the first time, and for the cogent reflections of the reviewers.

Several seasons of archaeological research in eastern Tennessee and North Carolina were made possible by institutional support from Illinois State University, numerous grants and logistical support from the Tribal Historic Preservation Office of the Eastern Band of Cherokee Indians, and a grant from the Cherokee Preservation Foundation. Susan Danforth, as the George S. Parker Curator of Maps and Prints at the John Carter Brown Library at Brown University, graciously provided invaluable assistance for this research. I also wish to thank Russ Townsend, Beau Carroll, Johi Griffin, Miranda Panther, Bran Burgess, and Tyler Howe for their insightful comments and support.

Notes

1. "quando los indios las vean, les causa admiración, y entiendan, que los Españoles pueblan allí de assiento, y los teman y respeten, para desear su amistad, y no los offender."

2. "hizo procedió contra muchos yndios del pueblo de naolingo e yzalco por borrachos e amancebados e otros delitos por los cuales los castigó."

3. "el dicho Ganado está aquerenciado en las acequias de agua de las dichas milpas, las tiene rompidas y ciegas y se andan debajo de los cacaguatales, en las cuales hazen mucho daño derribándoles las maçorcas y quebrándoles y ansí todas las millpas que con las dichas cabañas confinan están perdidas y sin provecho alguno."

4. "uno de los pueblos descansados que hay en toda esta costa y les sobra cantidad de cacao la los vecinos del dicho pueblo que gastan malgastado."

5. "é por ser esta Buena parada, llamaban despues los soldados en los dados casa de guasuli, ó buen encuentro."

FIVE

"An Incurable Evil"

Direct and Structural Violence in the Mercury Mines of Colonial Huancavelica (AD 1564-1824)

DOUGLAS K. SMIT AND TERREN K. PROCTOR

The Indians are brought in groups of fifty and one hundred, chained up
like criminals, with branches and shackles of iron, the women and children
and relatives bidding farewell from the churches, leaving their houses closed
up, and they followed them, crying out to the sky, pulling their hair, singing
sad songs and lugubrious laments in their language, saying goodbye to them,
without hope of ever seeing them again, because there they will stay,
to die sadly in the mines and labyrinths of Huancavelica.

Fray Buenaventura de Salinas y Córdoba (1957 [1653]:297)

These quicksilver ores, when they extract them in the mines,
they give out a dust that enters itself into the Indians as they breathe
and it settles into the chest, of such evil quality, that it causes them a
dry cough and light fever and at the end death without repair,
because the doctors have it for an incurable evil.

Viceroy Luis de Velasco (Brown 2001:472)

Violence—physical and symbolic, direct and structural—is fundamental to the colonial encounter. Spanish colonialism in the Americas began with the immediate
physical violence of conquest, notably the 1521 sack of Tenochtitlan by Hernan
Cortés and the capture, ransom, and garroting of the Inka emperor Atahualpa by
Francisco Pizarro in 1532. These early moments of plunder illustrate two funda-

mental components of the Spanish colonial project: the role of gold and silver in motivating colonial expansion, and the use of violence to acquire these sources of wealth.

The cruelty of the conquistadores occupies popular narratives, but colonial viceroys who deployed systematic violence through administrative decree soon replaced the initial generation of sword-wielding colonizers. In the viceroyalty of Peru, Viceroy Francisco Toledo's arrival in the 1570s marks this transformation from conquest to colonialism, as the Hapsburg monarchy of Philip II in Spain sought to move beyond the chaos of inter-conquistador civil wars of the 1540s and 1550s to institutionalize a more mature colonial state (Hemming 1970). More bureaucrat than soldier, Viceroy Toledo enacted several reforms that shifted the search for gold away from plunder to mining, notably a campaign that coerced indigenous peoples into forced labor to extract mercury and silver (Lohmann Villena 1949).[1] This chapter examines the most infamous labor regime, the mining *mita*, a draft-labor system that required indigenous communities to annually send one-seventh of their population to mine mercury in Huancavelica (Brown 2001). With miners working in brutal underground conditions, Huancavelica soon became known as *la mina de la muerte*, or "the mine of death" (Robins 2011).

As the name "the mine of death" suggests, colonial Huancavelica and the mita labor system were among the inspirations for the Black Legend, a problematic historiographical shorthand for the pervasive atrocities committed by Spanish colonial regimes (Juderías 1960 [1914]). While the core assumptions of the Black Legend are undeniably true—the colonial project in Spanish America did inflict massive violence upon indigenous and African bodies—an uncritical deployment of Black Legend tropes can simplify the complexity of the colonial encounter. Moreover, portrayals of the Spanish colonial project as *uniquely* violent are incorrect; they merely repeat British and Dutch accusations of the Atlantic world that were more about inter-European colonial competition than a concern for indigenous and African peoples of the Americas. So the Black Legend narrative presents a challenge: how to examine the violent aspects of the Spanish colonialism without reverting into the tropes that flatten the contours of the colonial encounter, resulting in ahistorical binaries of the Spanish villains and passive indigenous victims.

This chapter contends that a critical analysis of the form, function, and materiality of violence within the colonial project is one answer to the challenge of the Black Legend. We expand on earlier critiques of the Black Legend by analyzing the case study of indigenous miners in colonial Huancavelica, arguing that Black

Legend narratives focus excessively on examples of direct violence at the expense of more pervasive and consequential structural violence. An exclusive emphasis on the direct violence of specific historical individuals breaks past from present, minimizing the structural consequences of colonialism that continue into the twenty-first century. In short, Black Legend discourses remove the legacy of colonial violence from ongoing exploitation and dispossession, thus relegating Spanish brutality to the dustbin of history. However, by unpacking the nature of structural violence imposed during the colonial period, we can not only achieve a more complete understanding of daily life during the colonial encounter but also provide a new avenue of engagement between the past we study and the descendant communities in which we work.

La Leyenda Negra (The Black Legend)

Examining the role of violence in Spanish colonialism in the Americas requires a historiographical discussion of La Leyenda Negra, or the Black Legend. A Spanish diplomatic officer named Julian Juderías used the term *Black Legend* in a series of essays in 1912 and later in a book to take umbrage at what he perceived as an unfair characterization of Spanish actions abroad (Greer, Mignolo, and Quilligan 2008). Juderías defined the Black Legend: "In a word, we understand by the leyenda negra the legend of an inquisitorial Spain, ignorant, fanatical, incapable of existing among cultivated peoples today as in the past, always prepared for violent repressions, the enemy of progress and innovation" (Juderías 1960 [1914]:28). Since this initial formulation by Juderías, subsequent Spanish and English language scholarship further defined the Black Legend by emphasizing the historical specificity of Spanish colonial practices. As Powell notes: "The basic premise of the Black Legend is that Spaniards have shown themselves, historically, to be uniquely cruel, bigoted, tyrannical, obscurantist, lazy, fanatical, greedy, and treacherous; that is, that they differ so much from other peoples in these traits that Spaniards and Spanish history must be viewed and understood in terms not ordinarily used in describing and interpreting other peoples" (Powell 2008 [1971]:11). The Black Legend, therefore, is not merely a reference to Spanish colonial atrocities. Instead, it posits that the Spanish are *uniquely* prone to extreme moments of violence in service of colonial or imperial ambitions. While many origins have been proposed, most scholars point to the 1583 publication, translation, and spread of "A Very Brief Account of the Destruction of the Indies" by Bartolomé de las Casas, which solidified an inexorable link between the Black Legend and Spain's colonial ambitions (Arnoldsson 1960; Edelmayer 2011; Greer, Mignolo, and Quilligan 2008).[2]

The initial academic response to the Black Legend was to simply deny its historical accuracy, a debate that dominated Spanish colonial historiography during the twentieth century. To many, refuting the Black Legend required the construction of a new White Legend, which emphasized Spanish colonial paternalism and its supposed "beneficiaries." A strong historical tradition rejecting the Black Legend on factual grounds developed out of Juderías's work, with implications that Spanish colonial atrocities were the legacy of exaggerated Protestant propaganda (Edelmayer 2011; Keen 1969). In Spain, the White Legend became dominant after the civil war of the 1930s, as nostalgia for empire became codified by nationalist rhetoric under the dictatorship of Francisco Franco (Keen 1969).

While Juderías and his contemporaries supplied much of the initial intellectual stimulus for debates over the Black Legend, academic debates over the degree and impact of Spanish violence in Latin America became even more widespread in the Anglophone world, particularly as the United States began to develop its own imperial project in Latin America (Greer, Mignolo, and Quilligan 2008).[3] This scholarship became more entrenched as American imperialism in the Western Hemisphere became linked with anticommunism after the Second World War (Powell 2008 [1971]). In the 1960s, Latin American history textbooks began portraying the Black Legend as historical fallacy (Keen 1969). A popular mid-twentieth-century introductory textbook from the United States captures this sentiment: "Spain did not destroy great Indian populations: there never were great populations. . . . Spain did not destroy ancient systems of noble moral standards: the Indians were masters of gluttony, drunkenness, sexual excesses, and refined torture" (Herring and Herring 1968:152–53, in Keen 1969:708).[4]

While the first phase of debates over the Black Legend focused on historical accuracy, more recent discussions have examined the Black Legend as a form of historical discourse (Mignolo 2007). For example, a recent edited volume examined the comparative aspects of the Black Legend in relation to identity construction between competing ideas of empire during the Renaissance period of European, Ottoman, and Chinese expansion (Greer, Mignolo, and Quilligan 2008). The English in particular used the Black Legend to differentiate themselves from the Spanish at a time of imperial confrontation, which "inaugurated a racialized discourse within, that is, internal to, capitalist empires of the West" (Mignolo 2007.322). In this formulation, the Black Legend was one of many discourses mobilized by European powers during the early colonial moments of the sixteenth century that contributed to the broader construction of the classificatory system for human beings that we now know as "race" (Mignolo 2007; Quijano 2007).

Finally, the uncritical deployment of Black Legend tropes can sanitize our understanding of relations between "colonizer" and "colonized," creating binary colonial power relations of perpetrators and victims. While the figures of the barbaric Spaniard and the indigenous victim can create a coherent narrative, they also remove agency from the colonial equation. Here we emphasize that indigenous peoples had a wide range of options, including accommodation, negotiation, passive resistance, and military responses to colonial projects (Liebmann and Murphy 2011). This is not to minimize the severity of colonial violence; nor should it be taken as an argument that the violence was somehow less consequential for indigenous populations. However, it does require a nuanced perspective to understand indigenous strategies used to contend with the violent acts of colonial agents. Likewise, casting Spaniards as *uniquely* villainous removes colonial violence from broader historical narratives and instead considers Spanish violence to be related to a more general defect of character.[5] Rather, Spanish acts of violence were products of a specific context: the growing expansion of global commodity markets and search for metallic wealth in the Atlantic and Pacific worlds during the sixteenth, seventeenth, and eighteenth centuries.

While these aforementioned discussions of the Black Legend are ostensibly about violence, these commentaries often gloss over the specifics of the actual moments of violence and how colonial agents enact violence at the local level. As a result, the default understanding of the Black Legend emphasizes the direct violence of Spanish colonialism: the brutal, physical violence of murder, sexual violence, and plunder associated with specific actions of Spanish individuals. Direct violence should not be overlooked; however, it is easily sensationalized and can obscure more institutionalized forms of violence that had significant consequences for the health and well-being of indigenous populations in the Americas both during and for generations after the colonial encounter. So we characterize colonial violence on a spectrum, ranging from direct violence between individuals to structural violence embedded within larger political and economic relations of power.

Structural Violence

Originally defined by Norwegian researcher Johan Galtung in the late 1960s, the concept of structural violence expanded the commonly held meaning of the word *violence* (Galtung 1969, 1987). He argued that the general formula behind structural violence lies in inequality, specifically in the distribution of power and authority, which serves to uphold unjust social structures and stratification. As these inequalities become part of the society, they are maintained by those who participate in its structure. In the years following the introduction of the theory of structural violence, the concept has been refined and elaborated by numerous social scientists as a fundamental and insidious component of the modern state and its effects on mental and physical well-being (Bernbeck 2008; Farmer 2003, 2004a; Köhler and Alcock 1976; Žižek 2008). The introduction of structural violence theories into archaeology has served to incorporate empires and colonial states into the collection of structures we might deem violent by extending the reach of the concept into the distant past. Recently, the notion of using a theoretical framework based around structural violence was introduced to bioarchaeology (e.g., Klaus 2012; Nystrom 2014; Stone 2016). If the body is perceived as both a biological and a social object, shaped by social context, it holds that social context will create physical changes in the body.

Haagen Klaus's research (Klaus 2012; Klaus and Tam 2009) contains the clearest explication of a model of structural violence for archaeology, and his work serves as the framework for the following discussion of colonial Huancavelica. The majority of Klaus's evidence for structural violence comes from the bioarchaeology of burials from a coastal Peruvian cemetery that dates to the colonial period. The site's indigenous inhabitants were forced into economic servitude and poverty, and experienced political powerlessness under the rule of the colonists (Klaus and Tam 2009). His work expands the domain of subjects of bioarchaeologists, creating space for investigations of violence centered on health rather than trauma.

In more commonly understood violence (such as physical abuse, domestic violence, and warfare), the proximate cause is generally easily identified. Structural violence cannot be blamed upon a single individual or group of individuals but instead results from oppressive social and political structures that are both long-standing and multigenerational (Klaus 2012). In developing his theoretical model, Klaus emphasizes that "culturally induced stressors appear to be the primary locus of structural violence, as these elements can physically constrain a subordinate social entity's access to nutritional resources, adequate living conditions, and uncontaminated drinking water" (Klaus 2012:33). In the case of colonial Huancavelica, indigenous miners endured heavy labor; were deprived of adequate food and water; and were exposed to toxic substances, such as mercury and cadmium, that led to respiratory illness, neurological damage, and, ultimately, death (Robins 2011). Although structural violence is often embodied and therefore visible in archaeological skeletal populations, we must be careful not to limit our application of the concept of structural violence to bioarchaeological investigations; we must also expand our lines of evidence to consider other avenues whereby structural relationships may have inflicted violence in the recent past.

Huancavelica and Santa Bárbara

In 1563 a local indigenous leader, or *kuraka*, named Gonzalo Navincopa showed the Spanish *encomendero* Amador de Cabrera a source of mercury in the Central Andes, approximately one hundred kilometers east of Lima (Lohmann 1949). Cabrera registered the mercury mine the following year, and a small mining boom soon developed as claims expanded across the hillside above the Ichu River valley. Silver miners across the Spanish Empire had desired mercury since the 1550s, when the Spanish prospector Bartholomew Medina developed a more efficient method for refining pure silver. Known as the patio process, this method required mercury as the critical ingredient (Bakewell 1984). However, silver refiners were slow to adopt the patio process in the colonial Andes, which limited demand for mercury (Bakewell 1984; Lohmann 1949).[6]

Francisco Álvarez de Toledo began serving his eleven-year term as viceroy when he arrived in Lima on November 30, 1569. Although he never visited Huancavelica, Toledo administered a series of decrees that reshaped the political economy of Huancavelica and the organization of indigenous labor for mercury mining. Toledo immediately seized control of mercury, which he then leased back to a royal guild, or *gremio*, which organized production. Controlling the flow of mercury to the silver mines of Potosí provided colonial administrators the ability to calculate how much silver should be produced, and therefore taxed. This public-private mining guild was frequently at odds with royal authorities of taxation and mining rights; however, the colonial administration retained two points of control over the mining sector. First, the crown set the price of mercury and could therefore indirectly control silver production by withholding the critical element for refining (Lohmann 1949). The second lever of control was labor. The colonial state would provide indigenous labor to the mine owners to be paid at a fixed cost, employing a draft system known as the mita to serve the mines of Potosi and Huancavelica (Bakewell 1984; Brown 2001; Lohmann 1949).[7]

Mita is an appropriation of the Quechua word for "turn," given because male members of indigenous communities rotated through the mines (Lohmann 1949). These indigenous miners became known as mitayos, and thousands of mitayos came to the mercury mines every year until the end of the eighteenth century. The colonial administration paid mitayos near-subsistence wages, and often in goods in kind rather than coinage (Bradby 1982). In Huancavelica, workers rotated in and out of the mine every two months, but many of them stayed to work off debts accumulated during their terms of service (Lohmann 1949; Stern 1993). At the mines, Spanish and mestizo overseers assigned mitayos a variety of tasks. Mitayos known as barreteros hacked at ore containing cinnabar, the host mineral for mercury. Carguiches carried the ore to the surface, where they handed the material off to mitayos with mules or llamas (chacneas). They took the material to the mercury refineries. Horneros smelted the ore to produce liquid mercury, storing the final product in leather bags that often leaked. Finally, large llama or mule trains carried the liquid mercury to the Peruvian coast, where it was taken by ship to Arica and then to Potosi (Bauer et al. 2017).

By 1581, two mining operations, silver at Potosi and mercury at Huancavelica, structured the extraction of metallic wealth like "two poles of the kingdom" (Hanke and Rodríguez 1978:150). Each of these mines required massive amounts of indigenous labor, provided through the taxation system of the mita. For communities, the exacting labor obligation was made even more overwhelming in the wake of dramatic population declines throughout the sixteenth, seventeenth, and eighteenth centuries (Lohmann 1949; Robins 2011). In the case of Huancavelica, given the trauma of mining mercury, it is no surprise that the number of mitayos who arrived every year decreased throughout the colonial period and that, slowly, this gap was overcome through the hiring of wage laborers (Brown 2001). However, despite many attempts to reform the system by successive viceroys, the basic labor regime remained in place until the end of the Spanish colonial period.

By the 1640s, much of the mercury refining occurred in the urban zone of Huancavelica, and material evidence of the daily life of mitayos who refined mercury has been subsequently destroyed by several centuries of urban development. However, the ruins of two colonial mining camps, three kilometers north of the city of Huancavelica and adjacent to the main mercury source, survived into the twentieth century. The first, Chaclatacana, dates to the 1570s; it was buried by capital-intensive mining operation in the 1970s. The second, Santa Bárbara, is located one hundred meters from the main subterranean entrance to the mine that mitayos built from 1604 to 1643. In the late sixteenth century, a group of mitayos first constructed and began living in Santa Bárbara, which now consists of the ruins of 180 stone and adobe structures surrounding a plaza and church. Since 2013, Proyecto de Investigación Histórico Arqueológico-Santa Bárbara (PI-HA-SB) has worked with the contemporary descendant community, Comunidad Campesina de Santa Bárbara (CCSB), to understand the lives of indigenous mercury miners, including the types of violence they faced from colonial state administrators, merchants, and overseers.

Direct Violence in Colonial Huancavelica

Spanish and mestizo overseers employed violence to coerce labor from indigenous peoples who came to Huancavelica to pay their tribute in the mines, beginning when left their homes to travel to Huancavelica. As one of the epigraphs to this chapter describes, mitayos were sometimes chained to one another and marched to Huancavelica or Potosi to complete their service. Accounts of the mita from Potosi suggest that indigenous miners were beaten or whipped if a Spaniard judged their labor output to be poor. In an infamous account from Potosi in 1580, the Spanish mine owner Luis Capoche described an indigenous carguiche, or ore carrier, who fell into a deep pit while trying to avoid being beaten. The ore carrier was "dashed into a hundred thousand pieces" (Bakewell 1984:143).

However, while the mitayos were subjected to violent acts, directly comparing their lived experiences to those of other forced laborers, such as enslaved Africans, is a poor analogy. For one, mitayos were not enslaved but rather ostensibly free subjects of the Spanish crown carrying out their labor tax. Additionally, while the archival information above demonstrates that mitayos did face beatings and whippings as a violent mechanism for compelling their labor, they did not face the same daily application of direct violence characteristic of the plantation, nor the same curtailing of day-to-day freedom of movement. The archaeological data showed no evidence of direct violence, such as tools for corporal punishment, weapons, or mechanisms of confinement. Finally, Santa Bárbara was not a planned institutional space akin to a prison but was rather an organic settlement, constructed by the mitayos themselves, containing approximately 150 stone and

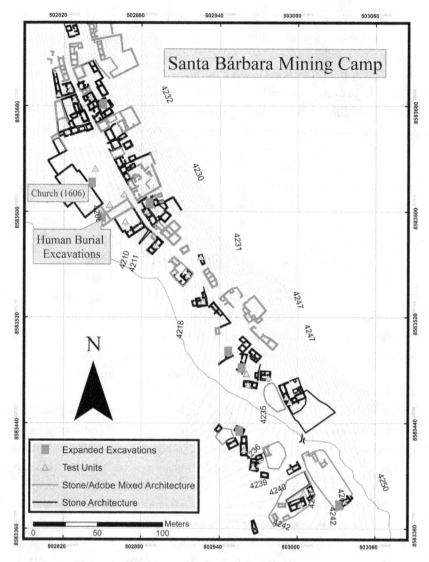

FIGURE 5.1 Planview of excavations at Santa Bárbara, Peru.
Courtesy Karin Flores Rodríguez.

adobe buildings along a ridge outside the main entrance to the mine. There is no evidence that Santa Bárbara was a *reducción* or another planned settlement laid out on grid lines, as was common in Peru during this period. (See Sampeck, this volume.)

Skeletal remains near the churchyard, however, retain evidence of direct violence. The burials are located to the west of the church, outside the official cemetery, and appear to have been made informally. There is no evidence of nails or other coffin implements, indicating simple burials; their exclusion from the formal cemetery and the inside of the church may suggest that these individuals were not baptized (Ortiz et al. 2017). The remains were oriented north or south, not east per traditional Catholic rites. Notably, however, they were buried in an extended position rather than the flexed position common in the pre-Hispanic Andes. This orientation, in conjunction with the extended burial style, has been documented at other colonial sites in the Andes and suggests the emergence of a hybrid burial practice through the sustained interaction between indigenous and Catholic belief systems (Klaus 2008; Klaus and Alvarez-Calderón 2017). Copper buttons and other diagnostic artifacts date their internment to sometime during the eighteenth century. In sum, the evidence implies that the burials contained the remains of those not accorded full burial rites in the official cemetery, namely indigenous men and women. The sample analyzed here includes the remains of three adults, two adolescents, and three third-trimester perinates (Table 5.1).

Investigating the mistreatment of the miners necessitated identifying trauma related to both violence and accidents. Only one adult cranium (Individual 5) has signs of trauma: a circular, depressed wound on the frontal bone just above the nasal cavity and a broken left nasal bone. The proximity of the wounds and their similar stage of healing suggest that the individual sustained these injuries in the same encounter, well before they died. Frontal bone injuries are incurred more often from instances of interpersonal violence than from accidents (Judd 2002; Tung 2012; Walker 2001). A second individual (Individual 2) also shows evidence of a violent encounter. Specifically, the older male sustained massive injuries to his shoulder blade (scapula) and collarbone (clavicle) that, similar to the other individual, show signs of healing. The linear fracture and angle of the break suggest that the scapula and clavicle were likely hit simultaneously from behind, over the shoulder, with extreme force (Elmadag et al. 2012; Kimmerle and Baraybar 2008).

In both cases of direct violence noted in the aforementioned sample, the injuries were sublethal and so were likely intended to inflict trauma upon, rather

TABLE 5.1

Demography of Burial Population, Santa Bárbara, Peru

INDIVIDUAL	ESTIMATED AGE AT DEATH	SEX	TRAUMA	OSTEOARTHRITIS	MUSCULOSKELETAL MARKERS (ACTIVITIES)
1	15-18 years	male	none		shoulder rotation; kayaker's clavicle; squatting
2	44-49 years	male		hips and back	shoulder rotation
3	27-33 years	female		shoulder and elbow	
4	35-39 years	male		upper back	shoulder rotation; high mechanical loading of forearms
5	18-22 years	female			kayaker's clavicle
6	7-9 months	unknown			
7	7-9 months	unknown			
8	7-9 months	unknown			

than kill, the victims. The shoulder injury particularly is consistent with being struck with a rod or a staff from behind; an accidental injury, like being crushed by falling rock, would create a different pattern. Although the sample size is limited, both of these injuries are consistent with interpersonal, direct violence to compel labor. However, examining only the direct violence of the colonial encounter precludes a thorough understanding of the lifeways of the indigenous subjects. These seemingly discrete, ephemeral events are only one facet of the experiences of Huancavelica inhabitants, whose daily existence was rife with the banal abuses of the colonial regime.

Structural Violence
in Colonial Huancavelica

Skeletal evidence of structural violence is more elusive than the obvious traumas of direct violence, but correlates have been suggested in other studies (Klaus 2012; Klaus et al. 2009; Klaus and Tam 2009; Martin, Harrod, and Fields 2010). The most utilized among these indicators of structural violence are osteoarthritis and musculoskeletal markers (changes in the bone related to muscle use) (Larsen 2015). The most important contributing factor to the incidence of osteoarthritis is mechanical stress on the joint and, by extension, the physical activities people habitually undertook in their daily lives. Osteoarthritis can manifest in the form of lipping (the formation of elevated rings of bone) and increased porosity along the joint surface. The most severe cases of osteoarthritis lead to eburnation, in which the joint takes on a shiny, smooth appearance (Larsen 2015; Weiss and Jurmain 2007). Musculoskeletal markers, in turn, may be seen on the bone in three different forms: stress lesions, enlargement of the bone at the site of muscle attachments, and ossification exostosis (the formation of bony spurs) on the bone (Hawkey and Merbs 1995). These markers are commonly used to infer activity patterns and are particularly useful when ethnographic or ethnohistoric data are available for comparison (e.g., Lieverse et al. 2013; Mariotti, Milella, and Belcastro 2009; Thomas 2014). Herein, we identify pathologies in the Santa Bárbara population that have been accepted as evidence for structural violence, as well as propose other indicators for locating structural violence in the body.

In the Santa Bárbara population, labor manifests itself on the body in several ways. Four of the individuals—an adolescent male (Individual 1), the male in his late forties with the shoulder fracture (Individual 2), a male in his late thirties (Individual 4), and a female in her early twenties (Individual 5)—all show evidence of bony changes related to labor, with a patterning of muscle exertion consistent with activities related to pickaxing. The two latter individuals show increased robusticity at attachment sites related to the rotation of the humerus and scapula around the shoulder girdle. In addition, both exhibit robusticity at the insertions for the pectoralis and deltoideus muscles, suggesting repeated flexion of the shoulder muscles. Individual 4 also shows extensive entheseal remodeling along the radius, suggesting high mechanical loading on the forearms and wrists, as well as the leg and gluteal muscles involved in repetitive bending or squatting motions. The muscle involvement in Individuals 1 and 2, the adolescent and older males, is concentrated at the pectoral and latissimus dorsi attachments of the humerus, with extensive involvement of the costoclavicular ligament, all of which are engaged during substantial shoulder activity. Individual 5, the young female, also exhibits remodeling at the attachment of the costoclavicular ligament, albeit less pronounced. This pattern is similar to that of "kayaker's clavicle" as described by Hawkey and Merbs (1995), involving the repeated rotation of the shoulder and flexion of the elbow; the movement is analogous to swinging a pickax. The bony changes in Individual 1 manifest in the form of osteolytic lesions, or the formation of holes in the bone's surface. This is likely due to the young age of the individual, as the bones are not yet fully formed and thus are weaker (White, Black, and Folkens 2011). In the older male (Individual 2), these bony changes present as increased robusticity as well as bony spur formation.

Osteoarthritis is seen in Individuals 2, 3, and 4. This is expected, given that the condition is aggravated with age and that each of these individuals was at least about thirty years old. Individual 3, a female in her late twenties to early thirties, shows porosity on both the proximal and distal ends of the humeri. Osteoarthritis in Individual 4 is confined to lipping along the thoracic vertebrae. The highest degree of osteoarthritis is seen in the oldest male. This individual shows osteo-arthritis in the hips in the form of lipping, as well as extensive spicule formation and ossification on the majority of the vertebrae. The most critical presentation is located on the right side of the joint between the first sacral segment and the fifth lumbar vertebra, due to a hemi-lumbarization of the top of the sacrum; this congenital condition is a malformation of the first sacral segment that causes it to develop as a hybrid between a sacral and a lumbar vertebra. This congenital anomaly led to the improper articulation of the joint, creating deep grooves at the joint due to improper pressure and articulation. This imbalance in the spine is likely also the cause of the severe scoliosis seen in the individual; working with this spinal deformity would have been extremely painful, yet it is clear that he was still engaged in strenuous labor.

The perinatal remains and skeletal deformities seen in Individual 4 are two additional lines of evidence interpreted here as effects from structural violence. The presence of three third-trimester fetal burials within a sample of eight in-dividuals suggests that miscarriage and stillbirths occurred with some regularity. Clinical studies show that mothers exposed to heavy metals during pregnancy experience high rates of spontaneous abortion (Adam et al. 2015; Rahman, Ku-marathasan, and Gomes 2016; Sanders et al. 2015); thus a similar pattern might be expected in this colonial sample. The fact that these individuals were all in the third trimester of development makes it much more likely that the indigenous women had stillbirths rather than intentional abortions; the fetuses also showed no signs of trauma related to intentional killing, such as cutmarks or broken bones. Finally, Individual 4 shows evidence of vitamin D deficiency resulting from malnutrition, a lack of sun exposure, or a combination of the two. Severe twisting and bowing of the lower legs (tibiae and fibulae), pronounced bowing at the wrists, and the presence of Schmorl's nodes (holes in the bodies of the vertebrae) all speak to a weakening of the bones consistent with a lack of mineral deposition. Despite this metabolic deficiency, the muscle-related changes in the bone described above suggest that he was engaged in strenuous labor.

Finally, there is the question of mercury poisoning, which became known as the "sickness of Huancavelica" (Brown 2001).[8] Mitayos could have absorbed mercury through a variety of mechanisms, including breathing in dust while underground, absorption through the skin, or inhalation of mercury vapor during the refining process. Dust containing mercury also attached itself to the clothes of the mitayos, thus entering their homes to finally settle in the meals of the miners and their families (Robins 2011). Mitayos poisoned by mercury were known as *azogados*, from the Spanish word for mercury, *azogue*.[9] Azogados first showed signs of mercury poisoning by trembling, which sometimes became so violent that "wives or mothers had to feed them as though the men were young children" (Brown 2001:481). Tremors became headaches and emotional instability, eventually leading to neurological disorders and death (Bernhoft 2012).

In Klaus's model for structural violence (2012), he cautions archaeologists against using the concept of structural violence to create an impression of passive victims unable to mitigate their circumstances. While our research suggests that mercury contamination was one avenue of structural violence endured by the indigenous miners of Huancavelica, it also highlights how different miners may have pursued different strategies to minimize their exposure to mercury. Indigenous miners certainly knew of the dangers of mercury poisoning. Colonial records suggest that they employed several strategies for dealing with mercury poisoning, including consuming alcoholic corn beer (*chicha*) to process and sweat out the toxic elements (Robins 2011) and placing a coin in the mouth, with the hope that mercury would be attracted to the coin and not enter the body (Brown 2001). It is uncertain how the young male was able to mitigate his exposure to mercury; perhaps he worked as a wood carrier to supply the refineries with fuel, or carried ore from the surface to the refineries, limiting his time underground.

Regardless, his example suggests that structural violence is not always totalizing; rather indigenous peoples retained some degree of agency to work the system to their benefit, even at a place like la mina de la muerte.

Discussion

Since it was named in 1914, scholars have debated for or against the Black Legend narrative of uniquely violent Spaniards, who committed horrific acts of violence upon indigenous and African populations in the Americas for the sake of colonial ambitions. While it is clear that violent acts were not unique to the Spanish colonial project, we contend that an exclusive focus on direct violence in the Black Legend comes at the expense of understanding the role of structural violence in the colonial encounter. Moreover, we argue that providing a tapestry of individual stories, rather than constructing a single experience of the marginalized, is one method by which we may avoid the essentializing pitfalls of victims and victimizers. By documenting individual lifeways, it is possible to represent the heterogeneity of experiences of indigenous groups rather than of an indigenous "subject."

Legends imply a different conception of time than historical narratives in that they describe events or actions removed from historical time. In the case of the Black Legend, historians and archaeologists often focus on examples of direct physical violence committed by Spanish conquistadores and administrators, yet these narratives lack the ability to connect our research to ongoing issues of marginalization and exploitation faced by contemporary Andean populations. In the case of Huancavelica, ongoing research by the Environmental Health Council, an NGO composed of historians and environmental scientists, has shown that urban Huancavelica faces ongoing structural violence. The toxic legacy of colonial mercury mining has left the adobe homes (Hagan et al. 2015) and soil contaminated at one of the highest rates in the world (Robins and Hagan 2012; Robins et al. 2012). Recent analysis of hair samples demonstrates that these toxic environments are contributing to a host of health problems among the population, disproportionately affecting young children (Hagan et al. 2015; Robins et al. 2012).[10] In short, the repercussions of the structural violence of colonial mercury mining in Huancavelica did not cease with the end of Spanish colonialism in Peru but endure into the twenty-first century.

As archaeologists continue to examine the histories of violence in the past, we must also remain engaged with the present. Colonial histories are full of violent encounters, yet moments of interpersonal violence between colonizer and colonized three hundred years ago hold less relevance for contemporary populations. In contrast, investigating the role of structural violence illuminates how colonial structures have produced contemporary inequalities, providing opportunities for dialogue with indigenous descendant communities. Structural violence has exhibited a powerful force in Latin America for more than five hundred years. Archaeologies of structural violence, drawing on historical, material, and ethnohistoric lines of evidence, can provide a powerful link between past and present to explain the historical roots of ongoing marginalization and exploitation.

Acknowledgments

We thank the people of the Comunidad Campesina de Santa Bárbara for their vital support and collaboration in our research.

Notes

1. The mining mita also forced indigenous Andeans to mine silver in Potosi, as well as at a host of other small silver mines (Brown 2012).
2. Others have implicated the art of Theodore de Bry in framing the Black Legend (Keen 1969), while recent critical examinations of de Bry's work contend that this line of argument relies on a misunderstanding of how de Bry's engravings were produced and disseminated (Brooks-Kelly 2016).
3. For example, see the debate by Keen (1969) and Hanke (1971) in *Hispanic American Historical Review*.
4. This is not to say that the Black Legend was exclusively portrayed to be false in the United States. For example, DeGuzmán notes the role of the Black Legend in nineteenth-century literature, specifically as a racialized trope that created "figures of alien whiteness or whiteness morally and physically blackened by the Black Legend against Spain" (DeGuzmán 2005:34)
5. Greer, Mignolo, and Quillagan (2008) contend that this belief in character defects of the sixteenth- and seventeenth-century Spanish can be traced to British and later American fears over the greater degree of intermarriage with indigenous populations in the Spanish colonies, further cementing the racialized aspects of the Black Legend.

6. The patio process was not adopted initially in Potosi due to political-economic reasons rather than technological ones. Most of the silver was refined by indigenous miners through pre-Columbian techniques (*guayras*). It was only when the Spanish state under the guidance of Toledo injected massive capital into refining operations that Spanish operators began employing the patio process, which both increased the yield and decreased indigenous control over the refining process (Bakewell 1984).

7. Spanish mine owners did not use enslaved African peoples for underground labor, arguing to administrative and royal officials that a combination of high altitude, climate, and diet decreased their ability to survive and to efficiently mine silver and mercury. However, this preference for indigenous mitayos over enslaved Africans was also about profit, as one African enslaved person cost hundreds of pesos, while indigenous mitayos cost nearly nothing and were required to provide all their own subsistence. Instead, the thousands of enslaved Africans who lived in the mining towns of colonial Peru worked as servants, cook, artisans, and guards (Bakewell 1984:192–93; Robins 2011:45)

8. Mitayos were also vulnerable to a wide range of other airborne disorders common to mining operations, including lung disease through silicosis, carbon monoxide poisoning (known as *umpe*), and tuberculosis acquired through weakened immune systems (Brown 2001:475).

9. The Spanish word *azogue* comes from the Arabic word *azzáwq*, a legacy of mercury mining at Almaden in Islamic Spain prior to 1492 (Tascón 1958).

10. As Robins et al. (2012:153) notes, children are especially at risk in Huancavelica considering that most of the mercury is in the soil, and children ingest larger quantities of soil every year than do adults.

SIX

The Violence of "A More Sensitive Class of Persons"

Privilege, Landscape, and Class Struggle in Northeast Pennsylvania

MICHAEL P. ROLLER

Violence and domesticity are complexly entangled in the history of the coal mining industry of Northeast Pennsylvania. In 1897 a posse of middle-class businessmen and law enforcement shot as many as nineteen immigrant coal miners in the town of Lattimer in the anthracite region of Northeast Pennsylvania. Confronted with the evidence of explicit historical episodes of violence between groups or individuals, archaeologists face great difficulties in interpreting and presenting this data. The circulation of this ambiguous evidence can be distractingly provocative. By structuring the analysis of artifact assemblages through the triumvirate classification of subjective, systemic, and symbolic violence, archaeologists can connect individual small objects to the objective forms of violence they materialize. Analyzing the event through the material differentiation of regional company town landscapes and the racializing discourse of governmental and scientific documents suggests that from the perspective of those charged with maintaining the safety and stability of society, this may have been enough to elicit their lethal response.

In a Pennsylvania anthracite coal mining town in 1897, as many as nineteen immigrant miners marching on a strike were killed by a posse of police and deputized merchants and businessmen. On the day after the event, known today as the Lattimer Massacre, a reporter visited the scene. He evocatively described the setting in the resulting article: "The shooting occurred at the bend of a dusty road leading from Hazleton and bordered by a rank growth of bush. For a background, however, the affray had a row of half a dozen frame cottages, mean enough in appearance, yet in the little yard in front of each a few bright-hued flowers grow. Today only a step from these desert blossoms lay a portion of a man's brains, and a little beyond a horrible bundle of gory rags, upon which the blood was still wet" (*Philadelphia Inquirer*, September 12, 1897). Suggestively juxtaposing the domestic materiality of the company town with the products of horrific violence, the author uncannily reveals the darkness lurking below the surface of the industrial landscape. Residents' quotidian efforts to brighten the landscapes of their living spaces (with "little yards" and "bright-hued flowers") are revealed as hopeless efforts at normalcy, merely the "background" for brains and gory rags. In fact, these objects are presented as practically growing from the soil of the very same garden.

Lattimer was one of about ten operations run by the Pardee family around the town of Hazleton (Foulke and Foulke 1979). Such family-run operations resembled feudal systems of land tenure, entailing a family managing large tracts of land dotted with isolated small mining operations coupled with worker settlements, "strewn, by the caprice of the worn and upended strata" (Berthoff 1965:262). This particular arrangement of a company town, known colloquially in the region as a patch town or colliery, reflects complete company ownership of practically everything within its boundaries: land parcels, houses, roads, infrastructure, and retail business. In these isolated environments, workers became dependent upon company paternalism, often through the binding power of debt (Aurand 2003:122–24; Mulrooney 1989).

Violence and domesticity are complexly entangled in the coal mining industry of Northeast Pennsylvania. The coal mining complexes of the region are assemblages of industrial and domestic elements. Both are subservient to the intensive functions and interests of coal extraction: to create a profit from its operations. On the one hand, they include the mine workings, such as industrial complexes of mineral processing and the infrastructure of administration and management. On the other, they include domestic settings: the homes, churches, and community buildings of their laborers, management, and ownership. The latter are not only subservient to the former; they are also productive of a social order that supports the industrial mission. In a sense, company towns are like factories without a roof; the dwellings of the miners and laborers lining the coal stripping are like the batteries of a machine. It is the capacity of the miners to survive each workday, despite the traumatic lack of investment in their welfare, and of their families to negotiate these deficient economic conditions that forms the surplus value captured by coal operation owners. Thus coal is not the primary product produced in the company town. Rather, the domestic settings are the sites of an invisibly violent production: the shaping of the subjectivities of a pluralist workforce of competitive, productive, pliant, and resilient workers and their families, who are forced to adapt their own capacities to negotiate this tragic environment. At times, these tensions erupt in moments of overt intersubjective violence, such as the Lattimer Massacre (Roller 2013, 2015, 2018; Shackel 2018; Shackel and Roller 2012).

Coal is the "mucky material bottom" of the energy, light, and movement underwriting modernity (Arnold 2014:266-67). The rise of mass manufacturing, characterized by urbanized, mechanized, segmented labor processes, can be attributed to the physical qualities of the energy source provided by coal. Capitalists and managers took advantage of the predictability and intensity of the energy produced from coal to compress production schedules and to de-skill work. Arnold asserts: "It was coal that enabled managers to strip craftsmen of their status; coal freed intellectuals and corporate managers to embrace the seemingly more certain science of abstract economic theory over the seemingly less certain alchemy of democratic politics . . . coal helped shift the nation . . . to a faster paced, more dynamic, modern society" (Arnold 2014:2). In essence, the material changes brought on by coal, beginning in the first half of the nineteenth century, produced the social conditions for class division within capitalism. The segmenting of work regimes into de-skilled processes reinforced the divisions between wage laborers, managers, and monopolistic wealth (Chandler 1972:177-78). In a sense, the mine workers ironically labored to produce the very stabilizing conditions for the formation of the privileged middle class that managed them. In turn, this more "sensitive class of persons" was often willing to defend the structures that propped up its position with coercive intersubjective violence.

When confronted with the historical evidence of explicit episodes of violence between groups or individuals, archaeologists can face great difficulty interpreting and presenting these data. If significant amounts of archaeological evidence exist, as is often the case at battlefields or massacres, they may be used to challenge or support the historical record of an event (González-Tennant 2016; Ludlow Collective 2001; Nida 2013; Reckner 2009). Often, however, instances of violence occur rapidly and leave only ephemeral evidence. The circulation of this slight and often ambiguous evidence can be distractingly provocative. In cases in which emotions or tensions are unresolved among descendant communities, these objects may, on the one hand, attain to a fetishistic significance or, alternately, provide an extraordinary opportunity for engagement and healing. Furthermore, providing physical evidence of these dark episodes of history can spark reinvigorated attention. Such applications, however, may not provide a broader understanding of the causes of violence.

Without careful contextualization, evidence of discrete episodes of subjective violence can divert us from scrutinizing the liability within epochal objective forms that serve to incite and justify violence. By "subjective," I mean the forms of explicit violence attributable to identifiable agents that populate the news: massacres and riots, abuse, murder, rape, and torture. These episodes occur between subjects and have a history tied to the circumstances of particular times and places. Like the crime reported from four perspectives in Akira Kurosawa's film *Rashomon* (1950), they often occur within an overwhelming context of divergent or conflicting interests, perspectives, and justifications, which can make it hard to tease out cause, culpability, and resolution.

Types of objective violence, divided into symbolic and systemic forms, are seemingly peaceful or stabilizing structures that serve as the "background which generates . . . outbursts" of subjective violence (González-Tennant 2018; Žižek 2008:1). Systemic forms of violence include the subjugation and control of material, social, political, or economic structures that compel or channel justice, attention, empathy, achievement, or resources away from those without power. Privilege is one such objective form; it takes forms of inequality among groups as unquestioned givens. Such systemic violence is unconsciously supported by symbolic forms of violence. Symbolic violence includes the structures of language and meaning—the interpretive grids—through which groups are subordinated to the interests of discursive forces outside their control. Symbolic violence relies on the mischaracterization or simplification of the complex histories or cultures of marginalized individuals, communities, or groups to coerce them into determinist or essentialized economic or political destinies. For example, racialization, sexism, and gender discrimination all operate through the production of a constellation of internally consistent, self-referential symbolic references that amplify or distort aspects of material life to the disadvantage of a group, subjugating them into a relative position of otherness or marginalization within society at large. On the other hand, symbolic violence operates from the semiotic groundings of a constructed normativity, an all-pervading interpretive grid through which individuals and groups understand and evaluate themselves and the behavior of others. This semiotic field is the discursive counterpart to systemic privilege: a normative background of reassuring causality, meaning, and symbolic behaviors. In capitalism, this normativity clusters around the characteristics of a predominantly white middle class that seems most naturally at home within the socioeconomic ecosystem it creates: entrepreneurial, self-sufficient, self-governing, paternalistic, and patriotic.

If we fail to account for the role systemic and symbolic structures play in inciting or justifying violence, we may mistakenly see incidents of subjective violence as simply accidental or circumstantial—as mere deviations from "the smooth functioning of our economic and political systems" (Žižek 2008:1, 2). I argue here that objective violence in systemic and symbolic forms supports the stability of hegemonic power in myriad ways—discursive, semiotic, and material. All these forms, objective and subjective, must be within the research domains of a critical archaeology of violence and privilege (González-Tennant 2018).

Arguably, historical archaeologists are most comfortable and effective examining material history at the subjective scale. Archaeological analysis, however, implies the usage of small and forgotten things to derive insight into broader truths that may otherwise be obscured in the background of society and history. Contra Žižek, I argue that by rooting analysis in those situated objects, sites, and memories of subjective experience, archaeologists can make violence at all scales visible, at least as it arises in a particular historical constellation: a discrete time, place, and set of actors. By structuring analysis of material life through the triumvirate classification of subjective, systemic, and symbolic violence, archaeologists can draw out the connections between individual episodes of subjective violence and the objective forms they materialize (González-Tennant 2018). The goal is to reveal the underlying causes of violence that often hang in delicate balance in moments of danger (Matthews 2002).

Conducting interdisciplinary research in the anthracite coal region of Northeast Pennsylvania, archaeologists from the University of Maryland investigate artifacts and landscapes that materialize subjective, symbolic, and systemic violence (Roller 2015, 2018). The tragic massacre of 1897 most clearly inflects the region's history of subjective violence. But an examination of this event in the context of the built environment of coal company towns and the transnational discourses of New Immigrant racialization reveals the culpability of objective forms.

Landscapes of Violence in the Anthracite Region and the Development of the Middle Class

The anthracite coal industry developed rapidly in the early nineteenth century to meet increasing national demand for home heating, transportation, and industry. The geographical and geological provenance of anthracite rendered tremendous danger and cost to its extraction and transport. Each advance into a coal seam, sandwiched between strata of rock of various thicknesses and declinations, involved some combination of caprice, foreknowledge, and risk. The everyday violence of these working conditions presented constant threats to the mortality and health of mine workers, ranging from explosive and poisonous gases to ceiling collapse, drowning, crushing by equipment, and kicking by mules (Dublin and Licht 2005:20–21). If a crippling injury did not force the early retirement of a miner, long-term exposure to black lung–producing coal dust often did (Dublin and Licht 2005:20–24; Wallace 1987). Coal operations required the technological means to ventilate poisonous and explosive gases, drain water, and transport coal. These took the form of a vast assortment of pumps, boilers, and fans, as well as elevators to deliver product, workers, and tools into and out of the ground. Mere survival, not comfort, was the goal of such technologies. For these reasons, coal operations required major capital investment to sustain the survival of their labor forces, bring the ore to the surface, and send it to distant markets.

Steep investment costs drove constant demand for expendable and progressively cheaper labor and production. The first miners came from northern and western Europe, bringing with them artisanal skills from Old World coalfields. Some continued traditions of organization and solidarity. In the 1880s, the industry began to mechanize its operations, as did other industries of the time (Aldrich 1997; Aurand 1985; Roberts 1901). In many such cases, de-skilling and mechanization not only added speed and efficiency to production, but it also served to destabilize established regimes of skilled labor (Paynter 1988). In the coal industry, two new labor processes integrated unskilled labor with mechanization to capture surplus production: steam shovel–aided coal stripping and washery coal. Available by the 1870s, steam shovels bypassed the delicate constraints of the craft/skill entailed in the shaft mining process. Depending on the thickness of the overburden, stripped coal could be produced by companies at half the cost of shaft mining (Roberts 1901:22). Washery operations used water and mechanization to recover coal that had been mixed with discarded by-products from the region's ubiquitous waste piles of post-processed ore.

In the last two decades of the nineteenth century, the New Immigrants, chiefly eastern and southern Europeans, including Italians, Poles, and Slovaks, entered the region. Often their introduction was facilitated by companies seeking to undercut the increasingly effective labor organization of previous generations with an army of surplus labor. These groups filled out the bottom of a racialized labor hierarchy, taking on unskilled positions as day laborers or unskilled labor.

Companies used this surplus labor opportunistically to their greatest advantage, hiring them in great numbers only when they were needed. These immigrants settled in and around isolated company towns such as Lattimer, sometimes building their own enclaves of shanties on the margins of the regular company housing occupied by longer-established groups. Materially, these organic settlements reflected the precarious political, social, and economic conditions the New Immigrants faced. At times they reinforced for middle-class observers aspects of a racialized symbolic violence. These observers responded with pity, curiosity, repulsion, and sometimes charity (Bender 2009).

Alongside the company-owned settlements, "free towns" also developed in the region, providing services to the coal industry as well as rental housing for workers. In time, these commercial centers developed relatively diversified economies, producing a middle class of professionals, managers, merchants, and public service employees tied directly or indirectly to the coal economy (Aurand 1970:9). In lower Luzerne County, the city of Hazleton developed after 1820 and was incorporated by 1840. Between 1850 and 1890, its population grew from fifteen hundred to twelve thousand people (Rose 1981:66). Many of its middle-class professionals were drawn from earlier generations of immigrant mine laborers from western Europe. Like the coal barons above them, and the laboring classes below them, this middle class came to develop its own interests defined by social and economic stability and maintenance of law and order.

Melvyn Dubofsky (1996) reports that throughout the country in the mid-nineteenth century, striking workers often benefited from the support of the middle-class citizens of their local communities. This backing sometimes even came from locally elected law enforcement, even when industrialists aggressively suppressed worker resistance with the increasing support of the state (Dubofsky 1996:47). By the late nineteenth century, however, this support reversed, as workers were increasingly isolated by local merchants and professionals. Employers succeeded in courting broad support for the suppression of strikes by instituting legal principles that defined certain behaviors and types of people as threats to civility. These frequently revolved around the definition of the liberty or negative freedom of individuals to pursue work or commerce unmolested by the collective action of either labor organization or industrialists. Judges throughout the country declared unconstitutional any actions or legislation that "regulated the hours of labor, wages, and working conditions" of any citizens entitled to such freedoms. Striking behavior was one such action said to conflict with the principles of democracy, challenging the liberty of workers and employers alike (Dubofsky 1996:57). Through these means, industrial powers courted the "ideological sympathy" of community merchants and professionals (Dubofsky 1996:59).

The Archaeology of Subjective Violence: The Lattimer Massacre

The massacre occurred in September 1897, preceded by a summer of strikes saturated with amplified racial and class tension. To offset the losses from an economic depression, coal company owners, operating in concert, introduced a variety of cost-saving measures, including limiting production and cutting wages. These actions targeted the bottom rung of the region's labor pool, predominantly eastern European and Italian laborers (Blatz 2002:43–44). New Immigrant laborers first struck in response to cost-saving measures by the superintendent of a mining operation located to the south of the town of Hazleton. The newly appointed superintendent removed some jobs from the payroll, lowered wage rates, and added a tax on coal used by employees. The company also consolidated some operations, such as the mule stables. This last change added several hours of unpaid travel time to mule drivers' workdays, essentially externalizing the costs to employees. The drivers, many of them boys from eastern Europe or Italy, struck on August 14. They were presided over by a Slovak leader and supported by an Italian assistant (Greene 1968:130).

The strikers set up a picket near the entrance to the coal workings, urging other workers to join. Confronting the picket, Superintendent Gomer Jones swung an ax handle or crowbar, breaking the arm of a young mule driver (Novak 1996:19–20). Word of the assault spread quickly, and by August 16, many of the region's laborers had gone on strike in sympathy with the drivers. By the August 23, the company had agreed to meet some demands, ending the strike. However, tension remained high in the region (Blatz 2002:55–57).

Throughout the remainder of the summer, strikes continued as new cost-saving measures were rolled out (Blatz 2002; Greene 1968; Turner 1977). A march beginning in the town of McAdoo on September 1 was described as composed of "about three hundred men, mostly Italians, who marched on the Monarch coal washery. Here they drove the employees from the place. . . . The shouts and yells of the half maddened men could be heard throughout mountain town, growing momentarily in volume" (*Hazleton Sentinel*, September 2, 1897). To conclude his article, the correspondent portended the potential necessity of violence: "The strong arm of the law cannot be subordinated to the designs of the inflammatory leader, and order must be maintained. Does it mean bloodshed? We hope not." Eight days later, the anticipated violence indeed occurred, perhaps primed by the fear-mongering tones used in local newspapers, which described the strikers as irrational and implacable.

As colliery after colliery fell to strikes, the local coal operators grew anxious. Determined to stop the loss of profit and the threat of instability to the social order they profited from, local coal company operators called upon the sheriffs of three regional counties to stop the strikes. James Martin, sheriff of Luzerne County, applied the law of *posse comitatus* to draw up a posse of eighty-seven deputized citizens. Local businessman Thomas Hall, who sold blasting powder to coal companies, was appointed as one chief deputy. A. E. Hess, an employee of the Lehigh Traction Company, and Samuel Price, a lieutenant in the Coal and Iron Police, took charge of two other divisions (Novak 1996:119, 125). At the suggestion of some deputized coal miners, Martin authorized Hall to select the men for the posse, an action the law specifically forbids a sheriff to delegate (House of Representatives 1901:137). Nearly all the men involved had middle-class or professional positions in the city or surrounding regions. All had some interest, employment, or business with the coal industry (Novak 1996:119, 125). By name, all were of western European origin, including Anderson, Babcock, Barton, Cook, Diehl, Hess, McShea, Mulhall, Nichols, Osborne, Pardee, Platt, Siewell, Turn-bach, Warriner, and Zierdt. Among them were half a dozen college graduates. By profession, many had close financial links to the coal industry, including a banker, two civil engineers, a construction foreman, a mine superintendent, a businessman involved in the sale of blasting powder, a superintendent of Bell Telephone, a lumber merchant, a bookkeeper and company store manager for a coal company, a schoolteacher, and a tea company agent. (Novak 1996:118–19, 124–26, 131, 158; Pinkowski 1950:9).

By September 9, most of the coal operations to the south of Hazleton were shut down. Italian and eastern European laborers in Lattimer, to the north of the city, sent an emissary to the newly formed union local in the south, request-ing assistance (Novak 1996:105). The next day they sent a group of men to shut down the mines at Lattimer as well. The posse was sent to guard the entrance of the town, where their force was supplemented by local men, including com-pany employees, police, and members of the Coal and Iron Police. Exactly what happened next is clouded in mystery and conflicting accounts. What is clear is that the posse, under the command of the local sheriff, fired upon a column of about four hundred unarmed striking laborers. At least nineteen were killed and as many as forty more were wounded (Novak 1996; Pinkowski 1950). Many details of the event have been obscured by the passage of time, and by many conflicting accounts.

THE ARCHAEOLOGY OF THE LATTIMER MASSACRE

In 2011 archaeologists from the University of Maryland, aided by members of the Battlefield Restoration and Archaeological Volunteer Organization (BRAVO) of Monmouth, New Jersey, led by Dan Sivilich, surveyed the site of the massacre. The goals of the survey were to produce an archaeological account of the event and to return it to the active attention of the public. Specifically, we sought to determine the location of the massacre site, identify a firing line, and locate the initial engagement. Further goals for the study included reconstructing the size of the posse, identifying the variety of munitions they employed, and tracing their movements throughout the site. Such details constitute the material traces of subjective violence.

The rough location of the massacre site was identified using archival sources and local knowledge. The roughly 6.25-acre parcel is located near the west entrance into the town of Lattimer. Ten-foot-interval transect lines were laid through the underbrush, and on each day a crew of about eight field technicians conducted a systematic and then a semi-systematic metal detector survey (Sivilich 2011). A total of forty-three artifacts were recovered. They included seven bullets of various calibers, twenty-two cartridges, six copper jackets, and a variety of non-arms-related artifacts most likely unrelated to the massacre (Scott 2011; Sivilich 2011). Battlefield archaeologist Doug Scott (2011) aided in the analysis of munitions, employing the techniques of firearm identification. Artifacts were examined for tool marks, such as those left by firing pins, extractor and ejector marks, and barrel rifling. XRF analysis was conducted on the copper jackets, revealing the presence of trace elements that suggest that they post-date the massacre. Of the seven bullets recovered, four could date to the massacre. They include two .38-caliber pistol rounds and a single .22-caliber round, which demonstrated the morphology of period armaments and were found clustered near the site of the initial engagement. An anomalous .32-caliber round was identified toward the back of the field, in the area believed to be where the posse stood. Figure 6.1 shows the locations of the bullets identified during the survey relative to the positions of the deputies, the marchers, and the raised bed of the trolley line as described in historic accounts of the event and reconstructed through existing landscape features.

At the conclusion of the survey and analysis, some of the project's goals were met while others require further study. No cartridges dating to the massacre were found. The location of the initial engagement was identified by a cluster of three bullets. This assemblage was unexpected in a number of ways. First of all, historic accounts focus on the .44-caliber Winchester repeating rifles used by the posse, whereas all recovered armaments were from small-caliber revolvers. This leads us to believe that the initial shots fired issued from law enforcement or the Coal and Iron Police, also present at the scene. The fourth bullet, a highly patinated .32-caliber revolver bullet, is an anomalous find that may suggest a number of possibilities. It may be from an unrelated event, such as hunting or target shooting. It may have been a misfire or shot into the ground by a reluctant or anxious

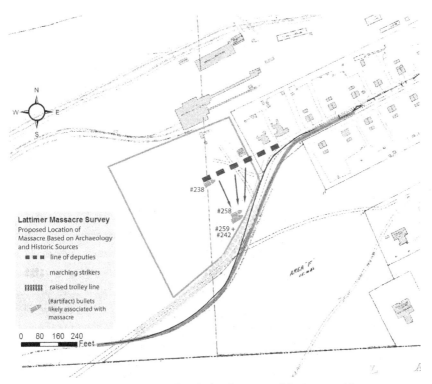

FIGURE 6.1 Map showing bullets identified in the survey of the Lattimer Massacre site in relation to the proposed location of the deputies and the raised bed of the trolley line. Map by Michael P. Roller.

member of the posse. Or it may have been, controversially, return fire from a striker with a pistol.

The day after the massacre, a newspaper editorial reflected that though the sheriff and his deputies might be questioned in coming days as to the righteousness of their actions, in fact, "It must be remembered that confronting the sheriff and his legal force was a desperate mob of *unreasonable and unreasoning men whose carelessness of life* both the sheriff and his deputies were thoroughly acquainted" (*Wilkes Barre Times*, September 11, 1897; emphasis mine). In this narrative, a kind of justificatory predestination guided the course of violence. The machinations of this predestination, however, are not to be found in the structure of the events but in the realm of everyday forms of objective violence, systemic and symbolic.

The Archaeology of Systemic Violence: The Landscapes of Lattimer Nos. 1 and 2

Known locally as patches, the company towns of the region were isolated environments in which coal companies owned practically everything within their bounds: land, houses, roads, and retail businesses. Workers were bound by paternalism and systems of credit and debt. As industrial settings, these towns were massive fixed investments, designed to aid in extracting surplus value from their occupants (Harvey 1985, 1989; Marx 1978:492). Like the time- and space-collapsing arrangements of factory assembly lines, they were machinic assemblages that rationalized production and extracted surplus value by heterogeneous means.

Capitalist engineering of space serves not only to concentrate production to minimize costs; it also serves the productive function of differentiating and reproducing a striated labor force, physically (that is, systemically) and symbolically, in a manner conducive to productivity (Harvey 1989:111). In time, the coal company towns of the anthracite region came to reflect the racialized labor-class hierarchy that prevailed throughout the late nineteenth and early twentieth century. Their differentiated spaces, physical and social, materialized divisions within their plural labor regimes, articulated in intersecting vectors of racialized ethnicity and class.

Lattimer Mines consisted of two separate patches, Nos. 1 and 2, constructed on northern- and southern-facing hillsides overlooking a stream valley coal deposit. Pardee Family and Associates developed the operations in 1865 (Foulke

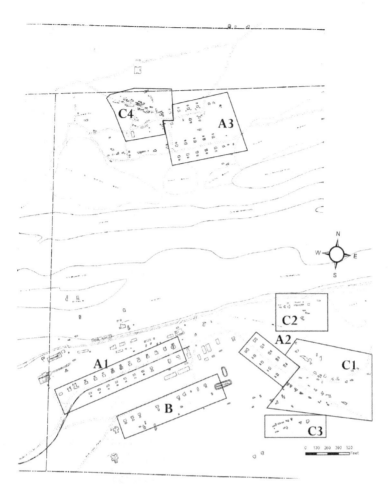

FIGURE 6.2 Company map from the 1920s adapted to show the development of areas reflecting geographical, spatial, material, and racialized social differentiation in the town. Base map from coal company records; adapted by Michael P. Roller.

and Foulke 1979:131). In their earliest configuration, the towns reflect classic company town landscapes, with a single road entering Lattimer No. 1 from the west, lined with about thirty company double houses in regimented homogeneity. Typical double houses were two-story, single-pile, wood-frame duplexes with a side-gabled roof. The homes of management secured a panoptic vantage point, set back from the dust and noise of the mining operation and the homes of the workers (Figure 6.2, Area B). The variations in lot size and house design in this area sharply contrast with the homogeneity of the workers' homes. No. 1 also had auxiliary industrial buildings, including a company store, a school, a coal breaker, and a sawmill. Across the valley to the north was the settlement of Lattimer No. 2, which included a second breaker and a smaller grouping of nine double houses.

Beginning in the late 1870s, worldwide transformations in agricultural practice, land tenure, and state governance precipitated a series of global depressions that affected the prosperity of the anthracite industry. Coal operators had recourse to a few options to maintain profitability, including the mechanization of production, the maintenance of a segmented surplus labor pool, and the regulation of prices through work stoppages or other means. The same conditions stimulating global depression also intensified migration from eastern and southern Europe. Throughout the depressions of the late nineteenth century, these migrants filled the ranks of surplus labor in the region, joining or replacing earlier generations. Capital interests benefited from, if not purposely exacerbated, the destabilizing competition that developed between ethnic groups and longer-established generations of labor in the anthracite region. Maintaining this pool of surplus labor allowed coal operators the logistical flexibility to respond to the exigencies of an unpredictable market. Through a variety of factors, racialized nationalities of each group came to occupy a place in a relatively positioned hierarchy. As in other industries, the New Immigrants were at first given relatively less-skilled laboring roles and therefore could be paid considerably less (Dubofsky 1996; Gutman 1977). In turn, the racialized differentiation of the New Immigrants was reified and exacerbated by companies through the hierarchization of labor processes, the institutionalization and reinforcement of particular spatial and material conditions, and discriminatory litigation (Berthoff 1965; Mulrooney 1989; Novak 1996). In the earliest period after their arrival, between about 1875 and 1910, New Immigrant workers occupied shanty enclaves on the margins of the ordered space of the company towns. This social marginalization was materialized in differentiated architecture and spatial patterning, consumer goods, and working and living conditions.

By the end of the 1870s, the landscape and demographics of Lattimer Nos. 1 and 2 had changed dramatically, reflecting the new split racialized labor regimes of skilled and unskilled labor coordinated with mechanized production. By the late nineteenth century, company houses along Main Street in Lattimer No. 1 were occupied chiefly by families of western European origin, including those of English, Welsh, German, and Irish descent, as well as a growing majority native born (Figure 6.2, Areas A1, A2, A3). By at least the 1890s, the majority of the company houses in Lattimer No. 2, expanded to twenty houses by this time, were occupied by eastern Europeans (Figure 6.2, Area A3).

On the edges of both towns, settlements of irregularly shaped housing enclaves of New Immigrants formed (Figure 6.2, Areas C1, C2, C3, C4). In these areas, company land was rented to families who built their own houses. The organic floor plans and the close proximity of these irregular structures reflect intimate communal spaces strikingly at odds with the linear planning of the company homes. Densely clustered small buildings lining a small road or alleyway at the southeast corner of Lattimer No. 1 (Figure 6.2, Area C3) are described on a company map from 1913 as "Italian Dwellings." The northwest corner of Lattimer No. 2, where excavations were conducted in 2013 (Roller 2015, 2018), contained the largest and densest ethnic enclave, consisting of Italians and eastern Europeans beginning in the 1880s. As many as forty-two homes were once concentrated here around a crossroads dominated by a Catholic church (Figure 6.2, Area C4). A shanty enclave on Canal Street in Lattimer No. 1 occupied a plot of land concealed from Main Street behind a large culm, or coal processing waste bank (Figure 6.2, Area C2).

Archaeology of Canal Street, Lattimer No. 1

The enclave on Canal Street was settled on about 1.8 acres of sloping land, wedged between the bank and the canal separating the town from the colliery operations. Today a single-family home stands on the wooded lot. Archaeology and historic maps from between 1878 and 1941 reveal that in this time, between nine and fifteen houses were clustered around a narrow alley. Privies, icehouses, storage shanties, and coal sheds were also present.

Archaeologists from the University of Maryland investigated the forgotten landscape and architecture of the enclave in 2011 using company maps and aerial photography. At the time of excavation, only a shallow depression from a house was evident on the ground surface. Excavations documented a total of twenty-eight features on the lot, including architectural posts or piers, foundation remnants, roof drip lines, and traces of landscaping such as animal pens and postholes. Garden features including fence postholes, shovel scrapes, planting holes, and planting supports were also identified at the base of yard soils. A total of 10,027 artifacts were recovered from a variety of stratigraphic contexts.

Architectural piers representing the northwest and northeast corners of a portion of the house were constructed of dry laid fieldstones spaced exactly eighteen feet apart. The westernmost pier, constructed of three large stones, had a flat rock that provided a platform for the frame structure to rest on. The absolute elevation of the piers differed by less than 0.125 feet, suggesting that they would have provided an even surface for the architectural framing strung between them. The piers were each placed in shallow pits excavated into subsoil. Artifacts recovered from these builder's trenches include a blob-top soda bottle with a tooled finish, Albany-slipped stoneware, and ironstone ceramics (n = 5), each of which has its peak usage in the last quarter of the nineteenth century. However, terminal usage for each extends into the first two decades of the twentieth century. A builder's trench for a slot fence extended eastward from the low wall. The slot fence may represent the border of a walkway or the enclosure of an animal pen.

Upper levels of the house fill included artifacts ranging in date from the mid-nineteenth to the late twentieth century, including undecorated whitewares (n = 2), items of Bakelite, plastic, a porcelain insulator, and embossed and undecorated glass. Soils from the top of the feature included a number of cut and wire nails, many still adhering to wood board.

A rear addition to the house, post-dating construction of the main body, was represented by a small foundation of shale collected from an abundant supply in the culm bank forty feet to the south. Measuring about five by eight feet, it consisted of three courses of stone. The center of the feature contained a concentrated layer of charcoal and charred wood overlying crushed horsehair plaster, indicating that the structure had burnt. Identifiable glass vessel forms included fragments from mason jars; wine, liquor and soda water bottles; drinking glasses; and spice or condiment bottle fragments demonstrating machine-made characteristics. One soda water bottle exhibited a red ACL label, post-dating the deposit to after 1930 (1930 to 1950-plus [SHA 2014]). The recovery of a melted fragment of a radio vacuum tube further dates the addition to the 1930s.

To the west of the addition, mottled clay and silt-rich soils lined the base of a shallow trench used to collect waste or rainwater and direct it away from the house. A posthole excavated into the edge of the slope and filled with rocks and coal ash likely served to anchor a post supporting a roof overhang. Soils in upper strata indicate a later effort to fill and level this trench, perhaps as architectural features were replaced or demolished. Sometime in the 1960s, the settlement on Canal Street was abandoned and the structures razed.

Archaeology and historic map analysis of the structure at Lot 354 on Canal

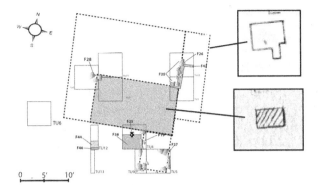

FIGURE 6.3 Super-imposition of selected archaeological features and house plans from 1885 and the 1940s. Map by Michael P. Roller.

Street reveals, on the one hand, a systemic violence at work and, on the other, residents resiliently taking control to ameliorate these conditions across more than sixty years of occupancy. Figure 6.3 superimposes the excavated features identified in the 2012 survey with the site's footprint from maps dating to 1885 and the 1920s. The housing and landscape of these places lacked the sanitation, space, and infrastructure offered by company houses, which were themselves below the standards of the time (Aurand 2003:25–29). The enclave was settled on the floodplain of an industrial canal; local informants and company maps indicate that it transported all manner of industrial and organic effluvia only feet away from the houses. Owners of these miniscule houses frequently accommodated boarders to make extra capital, such that houses were unimaginably overcrowded (Aurand 2003:31, 116).

By differentiating the racialized boundaries of the labor hierarchy, the owners of coal mining operations made the antagonistic relations of production possible. Margaret Mulrooney charts a feedback loop whereby racialized identity defined the limits to social and economic movement in the coal company towns of Southwest Pennsylvania:

> [T]he ethnic group to which a miner belonged determined the status of the job he held; this, in turn, determined his earning power. Companies then used earning power to compute the amount of rent an employee could afford.... Each company then used that figure to calculate how much it would spend on construction so that, ultimately, the amenities provided were a direct result of how much the employee earned. And to bring the cycle to a close, companies based the exclusion of provision of certain amenities on the ethnicity of their workers ... an employee might alter the status of his occupation, and hence his earning

power, but he could never change his ethnic origins and so remained somewhat limited in terms of housing. (Mulrooney 1989:135)

The feedback relationship between racialized ethnicity, laboring role, and housing set the material limits for movement within the economic sphere.

In the face of this systemic material violence, residents worked to ameliorate these conditions by resourcefully altering their homes and environment. Devices to drain sewage and effluvia were constructed by residents. Using a great variety of building methods and materials, houses were dynamically adapted to meet families' changing needs and capacities. Deficient wages were subsidized by the taking in of boarders and by the growing of copious gardens.

Even with these material efforts to ameliorate physical conditions, the broader differentiation of landscape, spatial position, and architecture remained clearly marked on the landscape, even when the once clearly distinct racialized labor hierarchy began to break down in the early twentieth century. Objective violence is composed of both systemic and symbolic forms, whose relationship is not causal but componential. Systemic violence is entangled with the symbolic aspects of racial discourse, with very real, and even deadly, implications.

The Archaeology of Symbolic Violence: "Can You Read Character from Handiwork?"

It was in the material context of a racialized landscape that the New Immigrants from around the Hazleton region went on strike for better wages and fair working conditions in the summer of 1897 (Novak 1996; Pinkowski 1950; Roller 2013, 2015, 2018; Shackel and Roller 2012). Following the massacre, a magazine reporter and artist for the *Century* magazine visited the shanty enclaves of Lattimer to report on the "foreign element" of the region to the magazine's largely urban middle-class readership (Hambidge 1898; Rood 1898). Embedding their observations in arguments for immigration restriction, the authors warn that the Slavic and Italian immigrants are "much more dangerous to the body politic than the excluded Chinese; for not only are they eager to work for wages on which an English-speaking family would starve, but they are superstitious and murderous" (Rood 1898:811). For middle-class observers, the domestic materials and landscapes of the New Immigrants are interpreted through the semiotic lens of racism, such that the contingencies of economic variability are always construed as expressing deficiencies of character rooted in inferior physiology. This is how symbolic violence operates.

The artist, Jay Hambidge, is particularly observant of aesthetic dimensions, moralizing the connections between lived materiality and perceived mentalities in what he witnesses in the New Immigrant shantytown. The domestic spaces of the shanty enclave are wide-open signifiers awaiting his structural analysis and interpretation. Like an amateur anthropologist, he opines,

> This is a place to be described by metes and bounds and degrees of instruments, and to do it would tax the ingenuity of the best of surveyors. Can you read character from handiwork? If so, this would be a place to practice your art. Each little house, with the boxes, cubby-holes, and fences about it, has been built by the man who lives in it. And he is a laborer, a struggler for mere existence, not deft in the use of tools, nor with an eye for the symmetrical, nor with an appreciation for anything beyond the most primal facts of living. (Hambidge 1898:824–25)

He describes the settlement as, "a hazy-looking mass with many poles sticking out of it," consisting of "the queerest structures, some of them not much larger than dog-kennels. . . . There is no sewage system here, and the alley is the dumping-ground for all offal. At every few steps of this winding, reeking way are little openings leading into other passageways, not much wider than will permit a man to walk through" (Hambidge 1898:824). And elsewhere:

> The roofs of the buildings slant at all angles, with no two sides of the same length or deflection. One portion will have eaves, while its companion will scorn the luxury. The same incongruity prevails everywhere. Some of the small openings used for windows are high, while others are low. One door will open in, and another out. The hinges have evidently come from the company scrap-pile, and the staples and latches and locks from the same source. Some of the roofs have shingles, others weather-boards, while others are formed of great pieces of rusty sheet-iron. (Hambidge 1898:825)

Hambidge and Henry Rood perceive a built environment attributable to only the immigrant laborers and isolated from the many material entanglements that contribute to its nature. The authors are entirely ignorant of the structural role the mine owners have taken in engineering its existence and maintaining its conditions to their advantage through regimented racial hierarchy, poverty, and debt. Moreover, the authors cannot see the dynamic character of the enclave, which has already been in a state of constant improvement and adaptation by its long-term residents for more than twenty years. Like the settlements of Native peoples encountered by Euro-American explorers centuries before, this place has no history and no future for these authors. Likewise, they imagine its residents symbolically frozen in a human past before civilization.

Transnational History of New Immigrant Racialization: The Case of Italians

Racial, racialized, or ethnic identification in the archaeological record is a major topic of research, explored in a variety of localities and contextualized within different scales of analysis. Within this body of research, academic debate surrounds the manner or degree to which the racialization or ethnic identification of groups is imposed, negotiated, or fashioned within the context of relationships to other groups or within structures of power (Orser 2011). In an examination of the material traces of these processes, archaeological scholarship has looked for patterning that reflects or contradicts the racial, racialized, or ethnic identification of groups in ways that range across processes internally constructed or externally imposed (Barton 2012; Franklin 1997; Orser 2004, 2007; Singleton and Bograd 1995; Wilkie 2001).

The material signature of ethnic or racial identity of the inhabitants of Lot 354 provides us with little to go on. A few works have examined, often with critical nuance, material traces attributable to Italian household occupation (Fitts 2002; Fitts, Klein, and Milne 2000; Matthews 2012a; Reckner 2009; Webster 2016). Perhaps unsurprisingly, many have found little in the way of patterned ethnicity in these assemblages. Rather, interpretations point to expressions of class, poverty, or the performance of Americanization. In his research on the pluralist immigrant factions of the early twentieth-century strike camp at Ludlow, Colorado, Reckner (2009) attempted to identify the ethnicity of individual tent sites using a combination of archaeological, ethnographic, and documentary evidence. The goal of his research was only to affirm or disprove the presence of any particular group in areas of the Ludlow tent camps. Reckner proposes tentative patterning from these ephemeral assemblages, assaying reflections of diet such as sardine cans or olive oil bottles, though he qualifies that these equally may reflect the presence of Greek or Spanish occupants of the strike camp. More concretely, however, Reckner identifies discrete small finds, such as medallions from religious or ethnic societies and linguistic evidence on food or medicinal packaging. At Lot 354, only one such item was found—a ten centesimi coin dated to 1867. On the front of the coin is the profile of Vitturio Emanuele II Re D'Italia, the first king of a united Italy since the sixth century. To achieve this status, he waged a sustained war upon the southern Italians to occupy their lands. Though the coin must have imbued these southern Italian immigrants with diasporic longing, the face of this particular king may not have been quite so well regarded.

The imagery memorialized on the coin evokes a history significant to the experience of southern Italians who occupied the shantytowns of the Lattimer mines. Much of what happened before, during, and after the massacre can be connected to the xenophobic fears directed at southern and eastern Europeans that dominated American political and social life in the late nineteenth and early twentieth century. The racialized treatment of these migrants functioned as part of an ideology institutionalized in scientific racialization, supported and exploited by capital interests, and popularly accepted and elaborated upon. In this period the relationship between racial whiteness and the nation-state was in the process of a kind of codification as racial definitions for citizenship were being drawn (McKeown 2008; Ngai 1999, 2004a, 2004b). The migrants from eastern and southern Europe making up the New Immigration existed for a time in American society as "in between peoples," occupying an epistemological gray area between whiteness and ethnic or racial Other. Scholars of race and ethnicity debate the trajectory of this passage for individual groups, contesting the pace, sequence, and causality of this trajectory (Barrett and Roediger 1997; Guglielmo 2003; Roediger 2005). The only common agreement among scholarship is that the passage was messy and contingent upon a variety of historic and political factors.

The specific racialized generalizations regarding New Immigrants by Hambidge, Rood, and other Americans of the period have their origins in nineteenth-century European intellectual ideas about criminology, scientific racism, and the populations of southern Italy. The influence of this thinking was propagated not only in works of popular fiction and journalism but also by government agencies such as the federal fact-finding mission known as the Dillingham Commission (Zeidel 2004). Anthropologist Daniel Folkmar, author of the commission's *Dictionary of Races or Peoples* (1911), was greatly influenced by the work of Italian criminologist Cesare Lombroso and his contemporaries.

The racialization of Italy's southern populations developed in the context of its fragile post-unification in the mid-nineteenth century. However, these ideas were selectively and opportunistically absorbed by American scholars, capitalists, and lawmakers dedicated to informing rationalized immigration reform and to applying scientific racism for the management of the diverse new Americans arriving en masse to factory shop floors, farm fields, and mining towns all over the country. These ideas affected the particular management choices made by social and economic engineers of the anthracite region. In turn, they would direct the actors responsible for the Lattimer Massacre.

Lombroso and his followers were patriots invested in northern Italian nationalist movements seeking to differentiate and dominate the racial groups of the Mezzogiorno, or southern Italy (Dickie 1999). Lombroso and his colleagues founded a positivist school of criminal anthropology devoted to the recording and classifying of physical traits believed to be scientifically connected to criminal or degenerate behavior. Working as a doctor for the northern expeditionary forces, Lombroso collected the heads of brigand resistance fighters so that he could measure them, documenting what he interpreted as the physical characteristics of racial inferiority. In the prisons and lunatic asylums of Rome, Lombroso invented a new subspecies of human, *Homo delinquens*, to classify the racial differences between bourgeoisie northern Italians and the criminally inclined rural populations of the Mezzogiorno. Regarding their propensity for crime, Lombroso explained to an American audience in 1895, "Like savages, criminals display great insensibility to pain, which explains their longevity, their ability to bear wounds, their frequent suicide. As with savages also, their passions are swift but violent," and "vengeance is considered a duty" (Lombroso 1896:37). Guerrilla resistance, brigandry, and criminal institutions from the Italian South, such as the Mafia or the Black Hand, were all considered manifestations of the barbarism or moral failure of these people. His colleague Alfredo Niceforo describes the Mafia, for instance, as an atavism, a survival of "the feudal spirit, the Arab spirit of independence and boldness [and] the medieval spirit of chivalry" (D'Agostino 2002:326).

Ultimately, Lombroso's rigid racial systematization did not find support in Italian politics, though forms of discrimination against the south of the country continue even today. However, in American thought, his ideas found fertile ground. They were used in systematic and symbolic ways to support administrative, industrial, and legal policies regarding race and immigration. Most pointedly, the ideas of Lombroso and his colleagues were used as scientific backing to inform Congress's passing of the Johnson Act of 1921 and the Immigration Act of 1924, restricting numbers of immigrants from southern and eastern Europe (D'Agostino 2002; Zeidel 2004). The racialized science advanced by government volumes such as the Dillingham Commission's reports on immigrants in industrial work both reflected and were constitutive of racialized administration of plural labor forces. In a government report on the bituminous coal region from 1911, racialized aptitude and nationality of the pluralist workforce are compared for "Relative Efficiency," "Industriousness and Efficiency," "Adaptability and Supervision," and "Sobriety." The section concludes with a chart neatly matching the hierarchically arranged *chaîne opératoire* of the extraction process with the preferred racial groups for each task (Dillingham Commission 1911a:549–50). With the equating of race, nation, and aptitude, the solidity of these boundaries and their consequent divisions in quality of life, salary, work, and living conditions were justified with a basis in naturalized structure.

The predilection of the southern Italian peasantry for violence, pain, and danger cited by Lombroso is echoed in a volume on migrant workers in the anthracite industry (Dillingham Commission 1911b). Here these racial characteristics are used to justify the neglectful and dangerous working conditions imposed by mine ownership upon New Immigrant workers. The Dillingham Commission's report on the demographics of the industry suggests that immigrant insensibility to pain explains their abundant presence in the industry rather than the insistent demands of an economy structured to limit their options: "A feature of the occupation [of mining] which enhances the reward is the element of danger, which, however, does not act deterrently upon the immigrants, as their limited imagination shields them from the fears which would harass *a more sensitive class of persons* in such hazardous employment" (Dillingham Commission 1911b:656, emphasis added).As a racially defining characteristic of New Immigrant laborers, a deficiency in self-preservation signified for management a suspension of its responsibility to protect these workers, who had taken it upon themselves to put themselves in danger. Thus they were differentiated from "a more sensitive class of persons." In the minds of the posse ordered to protect the homes and industrial operations of Lattimer, this same predilection for danger was a vengeance that could be stopped only with violence.

Symbolic violence often has no principal material component. Rather it serves as the interpretive grid through which subjective violence is justified. Symbolic violence provides the justifications for unfair treatment by conceptually producing populations as "deserving" or "undeserving" of criminal reform, entitlement, or poverty (Chicone 2011; Orser 2011; Spencer-Wood and Matthews 2011). Thus it operates within an unconscious realm of cognitive infrastructure, causal relationships, ideas, and definitions that do violence unto themselves by excluding or occluding the possibility of alternatives.

Conclusion: Violence And Privilege

A shaft of light shot upward from the steel, and I felt as if a long,
thin blade transfixed my forehead. At the same moment all the sweat that had
accumulated in my eyebrows splashed down on my eyelids, covering them
with a warm film of moisture. . . . Every nerve in my body was a steel spring,
and my grip closed on the revolver. The trigger gave, and the
smooth underbelly of the butt jogged my palm. And so, with that
crisp, whipcrack sound, it all began.

Albert Camus (1942:38)

To isolate a moment of subjective violence from its historic and social context
is to risk a fatal misapprehension. There is a moment in *The Stranger* (Camus
1942:38) when the protagonist justifies the shooting of an Arab man because the
sun and sweat blinded him into action. Such accounts leave open the possibility
that such acts of violence are merely accidents or aberrations. It is through just
such a narrow judicial context that, for example, racially biased police brutality is systematically acquitted on a case-by-case basis. Like the murder in *The
Stranger*, in each case there is an object that is mistaken for a gun, a posture
that appears threatening, a misunderstood direction, or an attitude that demands
the escalation of a confrontation. Yet when the broad statistics of racially biased
police brutality (Eppler-Epstein 2016; Prison Policy Initiative 2015) or the racial
demographics of imprisoned populations are examined objectively and across a
broad scale, the aggregate racist truth behind these events cannot be written off
as an aberration.

As linked components of objective violence, systemic and symbolic forms
play off each other, reinforcing and amplifying their effects to create a series of
integrated hegemonic systems. One such system rarely implicated in subjective
violence is racial privilege. Privilege is the invisible infrastructure of racist systems,
a passively aggressive assemblage of exemptions, favoritisms, assumptions, benefits, and materialities. In opposition to the explicit forms of violence outlined
above, privilege seems innocuous, evidencing no hostile intent on the part of its
benefactors. In fact, as "the invisible background" upon which coercive violence
plays out, privilege too benefits directly from coercive violence. As a result, it is directly integrated with, or even responsible for, systems of subjective and objective
violence. Often taken for granted as a matter of course, privilege depends upon

the stability of a social status quo to operate. But the sudden withdrawal or threat to social stability can quickly draw coercive forces to action. At such moments, we must recognize that the threat of coercive violence is always present whenever the stability of a social structure is threatened. Quickly, violence can erupt, justified by those very systems of symbolic and systemic violence.

Even the power or right to draw upon society's forces of coercion is a form of privilege reserved for the few. In the case of the archaeological survey of the Lattimer Massacre, a single, highly patinated .32-caliber revolver bullet was recovered in a location suggesting that it may have been fired by a striker. In all written accounts of the events, the possibility that the strikers fired back at the posse is controversial. Yet it is well documented that the posse fired hundreds of rounds, emptying the magazines of their Winchester repeating rifles into the backs of retreating strikers. For researchers, the contradiction and complexity arising out of the discovery of the anomalous bullet offered an opportunity to consider exactly when, on behalf of whom, or by whom the use of violence is ever acceptable.

Systems of objective violence such as privilege have material components visible to archaeological analysis, though often it may take the gestalt of explicit violence to bring these unconscious materialities into the foreground. They may include differentiated domestic spaces and differential access to infrastructure, capital, environmental health, sanitation, privacy, and convenience. Domestic spaces, which serve as the most common scale of archaeological research, can be examined within the broader context of such affordances and relative to an expanded social sphere. In the case of the archaeological study of the shanty enclaves of Northeast Pennsylvania, it is important to understand not only the context of the adjacent neighborhoods of company-built and maintained houses but also that of the "free town" settlements of nearby Hazleton.

As an instance of explicit subjective violence, the Lattimer Massacre transpired over a period of only about three minutes. Its import is in the way it illuminates how everyday life is punctuated by forms of everyday violence. In the lead-up to the Lattimer Massacre, the middle-class businessmen of the anthracite region benefitted from the profits issuing out of industrial-scale coal extraction. The privileges of their bourgeois lifestyles, affording them a comfortable and stable domestic life, isolated from the precarity and danger of the nearby coal industry, depended upon steadily increasing profits. Threatened by increasingly organized generations of craft labor and fickle economic markets, the industry turned to a combination of mechanized production and unskilled New Immigrant labor, at first far more pliant and less demanding of wages, work stability, and expensive safety measures. Systems of objective violence differentiated these populations through domestic landscapes and racialized character, justifying a split labor force. When the New Immigrants sought equal rights to those of earlier generations of workers, this same interpretive frame structures their judgment. During the Lattimer Massacre, the power over life and death hung delicately in the balance in the hands of an armed posse of middle-class businessmen. From the perspective of that "more sensitive class of persons" charged with maintaining the safety and stability of society, this was a sufficient excuse to elicit their lethal response.

Acknowledgments

I would like to thank my mentor, Paul Shackel, and the many colleagues and friends who made this research possible through their hard work, insight, and energy throughout this and other pursuits of the Anthracite Heritage Project. Most of all, I would like to thank the residents of Pardeesville, Lattimer, and Hazleton, Pennsylvania, who generously shared their community's history with our project. Special thanks go to Joe Michel for sharing his wonderful archive.

SEVEN

Sifting through Multiple Layers of Violence

The Archaeology of Gardens at a WWII Japanese American Incarceration Camp

KOJI LAU-OZAWA

Ken Hayashi and his father were imprisoned at the Gila River Incarceration Camp for more than a year due to what a congressional commission would later find was a combination of "race prejudice, war hysteria and a failure of political leadership" (CWRIC 1983:18). Returning to the camp in 1995, Hayashi's father, one of the oldest survivors of the incarceration on that trip, gave an interview. He began to cry as he looked out across the landscape and noticed the numerous irrigation ditches that still crisscrossed the remains of the site. He noticed the ditches when he arrived at the camp in 1942, when there was much uncertainty around the fate of Japanese Americans, with rumors swirling through the community. Convinced that he and his family would be shot, he thought the ditches were for mass burials (Hayashi 2015). His visit to the camp resurrected those memories and the palpable fear he felt so many years before.

The story of Ken Hayashi and his father reminds us of the trauma of events that lie silently inscribed upon landscapes. Only through a deliberate search for these vestiges of violence can they be found; if we do not seek them out, they will remain hidden and untold. Alfredo Gonzalez-Ruibal (2008) notes the power of archaeology to challenge narratives of power. We risk missing opportunities to discover these hidden pasts by discounting archaeological remains and oral histories. Without Hayashi's testimonial, the drainage ditches lining the camps revert to nothing more than utilitarian features in a banal landscape. But, within the context of incarceration, even the banal and quotidian are filled with meanings—meanings that resonate across time with those who were once forced within the walls of confinement. The sound of firing squads never echoed through this or any of the internment camps, yet Japanese Americans remain scarred by the trauma of their mass incarceration more than seventy years prior (Inouye 2016). Many of those who were incarcerated carry this with them to the present day, and for the subsequent generations, the incarceration experience has become a powerful postmemory. (For more on postmemory, see Hirsch 2012.)

This chapter considers the various forms of violence imposed upon and experienced by Japanese American internees at the Gila River Incarceration Camp, where my own family was incarcerated. The forms of violence to which I speak are both subtle and overt, relatively hidden and dramatically conspicuous, but equally insidious and traumatic. In its most obvious form, violence against Japanese Americans materialized in their forced mass removal, physical exclusion, and bodily incarceration. Violence need not be so flagrant, however. Take, for instance, the placement and construction of the Gila River Incarceration Camp on Akimel O'odham and Pee Posh land. The location and material fabric of the prison, designed to hold thirteen thousand incarcerated individuals, are themselves acts of violence. The very narratives that have been used to remember the camps must be interrogated to understand a different kind of violence: erasure. Finally, the gardens constructed by the incarcerees call to mind the most prolific profession of Japanese Americans in the Los Angeles area: gardening. The number of Japanese Americans who partook in the gardening industry speaks of exclusionary policies and structural racism. In turn, these forces amalgamated to produce gardens within the camp. Thus the archaeological remains of gardens stand as materialities of the violence surrounding the incarceration.

Japanese Incarceration during WWII and the Gila River Incarceration Camp

While the events of World War II undoubtedly acted as a catalyst for this mass confinement, racial discrimination and anti-Japanese sentiment had long been festering, especially in the western states, contributing to the political pressure to incarcerate Japanese Americans (Robinson 2009). Ultimately, President Franklin Roosevelt's decision to sign Executive Order 9066 created an exclusion zone along the western coast of the United States and paved the way for the mass removal and imprisonment of all people of Japanese ancestry. Those of Italian or German descent, whose countries of origin the United States was similarly at war with, were not subjected to similar displacement.

Approximately 110,000 people of Japanese descent were incarcerated in ten camps across the country: two in California (Manzanar and Tule Lake), two in Arizona (Poston and Gila River), two in Arkansas (Jerome and Rohwer), and one each in Colorado (Amache), Idaho (Minidoka), Utah (Topaz), and Wyoming (Heart Mountain). Another ten thousand people were born in these camps, resulting in a total of 120,000 incarcerees across seven states. Two-thirds of those imprisoned were *nisei* or *sansei*, second- and third-generation American citizens, respectively. The remaining third were *issei*, first-generation Japanese-born immigrants who were barred from naturalization by a series of racially motivated laws and judicial rulings (Chuman 1976). A civilian organization, the War Relocation Authority (WRA), oversaw the administration of the camps.

Euphemistic language obfuscated the severity of the situation. The WRA labeled mass removal as *evacuation*, the camps as *relocation centers*, and the incarcerees as *colonists*. Later the camps would be called *internment camps*, though this is incorrect again, as *internment* refers to a specific legal status of enemy aliens. Roger Daniels (2005) treats this subject in depth, explicating the power of the language employed and the importance of using accurate terminology. I use *incarceration camp* to describe the ten general population camps. *Concentration camp* is perhaps more accurate and was used at times by members of the government and by President Roosevelt himself to describe these camps (Ishizuka 2006:166). However, the association of *concentration camp* with the Nazi death camps of the same period has made this usage distracting and problematic. Though the technology of the concentration camp was applied to Japanese Americans, the US structures should not be treated as the same as those utilized in Europe during World War II.

The Gila River Incarceration Camp, or the Rivers Relocation Center as it was known during its operation, opened in July 1942. It was composed of two smaller camps separated by three miles and located on the land of the Gila River Indian Community (GRIC) in southern Arizona. Camp I was named Canal Camp and was the first to be opened, with 520 incarcerees arriving from the Turlock Assembly Center on July 20, 1942 (Brown 1945:10). Although it was constructed to house forty-eight hundred people, by August of that year, approximately fifty-four hundred people were living at Canal Camp, with many of the barracks overcrowded (Brown 1945:11). Most of the people who arrived at Canal Camp came from rural

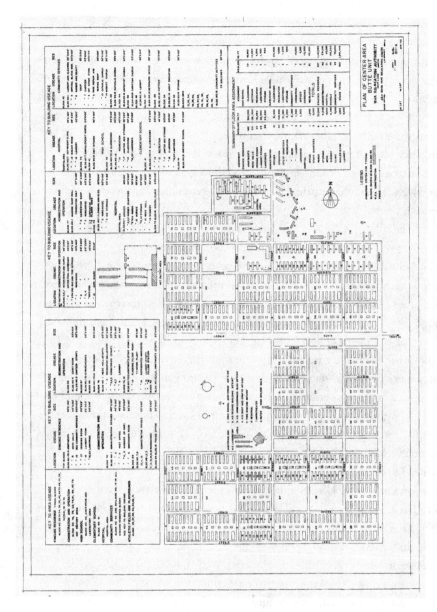

FIGURE 7.1 "Plan of Center Area: Butte Unit," NARA College Park Cartographic Section, Record Group 210, Gila River Relocation Center. Plan photographed by Lynne Horiuchi.

parts of California and had passed through the Turlock Assembly Center. These people had lived in less integrated areas and reportedly had a strong sense of communal identity (Tamir et al. 1993:29).

Camp II was named Butte Camp, sitting under the shadow of the Sacaton Butte. This was the larger of the two camps, housing 8,301 people by 1943 and absorbing some of the overflow from Canal Camp (Brown 1945:10). At its peak, the entirety of Gila River housed approximately 13,348 people, though ultimately more than sixteen thousand Japanese Americans passed through the camp during the war (Burton et al. 1999:61). The residents of Butte Camp came primarily from the Los Angeles area of California, though some came from other parts of the state, and a few came from Hawaii (Tamir et al. 1993:29). Most had lived in relatively urban areas and had passed through the Santa Anita and Tulare Assembly Centers. Consequently, while the Japanese Americans at Canal Camp were primarily farmers, people with a more diverse array of occupations settled in Butte Camp.

The divisions between Canal Camp and Butte Camp caused some tension between the two populations, with each harboring some small resentment toward the other. Members of Butte Camp reportedly looked down at those from Canal as being ignorant and uncivilized. Conversely, those from Canal Camp contained a certain amount of scorn for people coming out of the "white zone" (Tamir et al. 1993:29). Despite these tensions, many people collaborated and pursued group activities between the two camps. In an oral history, Tok Yoshihashi, a Butte Camp resident, remembered traveling and hanging out with young boys from Canal Camp (Yoshihashi 2015).

As with all the incarceration camps, both Butte and Canal were divided into residential blocks, consisting of standardized rectangular units. These provided an orderly arrangement of individuals for the administration. Canal Camp contained twenty-seven units—eighteen residential blocks, six recreational fields, and three administrative offices. Butte Camp contained forty-nine units—thirty-six residential blocks, seven recreational fields, five administrative and warehousing facilities, and one hospital. Each residential block contained fourteen evenly spaced barracks arranged in two rows, with a mess hall at the end of one row and a recreational hall at the end of the other. Every barrack was further subdivided into two apartments (one twenty-four by twenty feet; the other twenty-eight by twenty-four feet) (Brown 1945:25). Every residential block also contained a laundry room, an ironing room, and a men's and women's lavatory.

FIGURE 7.2 "Block 60, 7/18/43." Historic photograph of Block 60, Butte Camp, Gila River, taken from a nearby butte. Courtesy Ozawa Family Collection; photographer unknown.

Archaeology and Incarceration

Archaeologists have examined sites of incarceration and confinement with increased scrutiny over the past decade (Beisaw and Gibb 2009; Casella 2007a; Myers and Moshenska 2011; Mytum and Carr 2013). Their studies largely focus on the relationships between institutions and individuals, and the unequal distribution of power between the two. Casella (2007a) stresses in her work the importance of recognizing historically specific types of institutions and the diversities of their populations. Others (Farrell and Burton 2011) note the importance of sites of confinement as places of memory and remembrance, continuously engaged in dialogue with the present.

The National Park Service (NPS) leads much of the work on Japanese American incarceration sites, especially at the well-studied Manzanar War Relocation Center. Archaeologist Jeff Burton extensively surveyed Manzanar, identifying dozens of archaeological sites, including hundreds of features related to the operation of the incarceration camp (Beckwith 2013; Burton 1996, 1998, 2015; Burton and Farrell 2013, 2014; Burton, Haines, and Farrell 2001; National Park Service 2006). In addition to the NPS work, several insightful master's theses and a doctoral dissertation focus on Manzanar (Branton 2000, 2004; Ng 2014). The NPS also surveyed each of the ten incarceration camps and other sites of confinement, documenting in detail Minidoka, Tule Lake, Poston, and Honouliuli (Burton and Farrell 2001, 2005, 2006, 2007, 2008; Burton et al. 1999).

The Granada, or Amache, Camp in Colorado is probably the second most archaeologically researched camp. Bonnie Clark from the University of Denver directs a multiyear project at the incarceration camp, investigating a variety of subjects, including children, femininity, gardening, and sake production (Kamp-Whittaker 2010; Shew 2010; Slaughter 2006). The work at Amache focuses on the integration of oral histories with various methodologies, including surface survey, excavation, ground-penetrating radar, and botanical analysis.

Archaeological investigations at other sites of incarceration range widely. A cultural resource management firm surveyed and documented the remains of the Topaz Center in Utah (Ellis 2002). The Wyoming Recreation Commission surveyed the Heart Mountain Center and nominated it for the National Register of Historic Places (Gorman 1985). The Jerome and Rohwer Camps in Arkansas have not to date had any extensive archaeological investigations published. Stacey Camp's (2016) work at the Kooskia Internment Camp in Idaho shows that it was a fundamentally different type of camp. It held only non–US national men, subjecting it to rules and restrictions set forth by the Geneva Convention. Such protections were not available to those imprisoned at the general population camps (Camp 2013; Ng and Camp 2015; Fitz-Gerald 2015).

Archaeology at the Gila River Incarceration Camp

Archaeological work at the Gila River Camp has been fairly limited in scope. A total of five archaeological survey reports detail the camp and its surrounding area (Effland and Green 1983; Sawyer-Lang 1989; Sullivan et al. 1987; Tamir et al. 1993; Wright 2010). This work was primarily produced in compliance with historic preservation regulations. Due to the nature of these projects, none of them have undertaken in-depth analyses or documented in detail the residential portions of the central camp areas. I collaborated with the Gila River Indian Community Cultural Resource Management Program (GRIC-CRMP), surveying approximately

TABLE 7.1

Summary of Survey Results from Blocks 55-61
at Gila River Incarceration Camp

BLOCK	POND	TYPE	COMPLETENESS	SIZE	SHAPE
55	22	barracks garden	whole	small	two ovals
	23	open space garden	whole	large	square
	24	barracks garden	whole	large	square
56	34	barracks garden	whole	medium	long thin
	35	barracks garden	fragmented	medium	oval
	36	barracks garden	fragmented	small	two circles
57	28	open space garden	whole	small	bathtub
	29	barracks garden	fragmented	small	rectangle
	30	barracks garden	whole	medium	rectangle
	31	open space garden	fragmented	small	semicircle
	32	barracks garden	whole	medium	irregular
	33	open space garden	fragmented	medium	long thin
58	38	open space garden	whole	large	irregular
	39	barracks garden	whole	medium	long thin
	40	barracks garden	whole	medium	irregular
	41	barracks garden	whole	medium	bell shaped
	43	open space garden	whole	small	bathtub
59	8	barracks garden	whole	medium	square
	9	barracks garden	whole	medium	keyhole
	10	open space garden	whole	small	heart
	42	barracks garden	whole	medium	l shape
60	6	barracks garden	whole	medium	keyhole
	7	barracks garden	whole	large	long thin
61	1	barracks garden	whole	medium	circle
	2	barracks garden	whole	small	three circles
	3	barracks garden	whole	large	long wide
	4	barracks garden	whole	medium	long thin
	5	barracks garden	whole	large	two triangles
	53	barracks garden	fragmented	small	two circles
	54	barracks garden	fragmented	small	pinched oval

one-third of Butte Camp, the larger of two camp areas at Gila, documenting garden pond features (Ozawa 2016). GRIC-CRMP archaeologist Wesley Miles and I documented sixty-four such features spread throughout fourteen residential blocks. Of these, forty-two garden ponds were found to be located adjacent to specific barracks, closely abutting their footings and suggesting a direct relationship to their residents. Tables 7.1 and 7.2 summarize the results of the survey. We divided gardens into three types: barracks gardens for those found adjacent to a barrack's footings, mess hall gardens for those found next to a block's mess hall, and open-space gardens for those found farther away from buildings. We judged the completeness of each pond as either mostly whole or fragmented. Ponds were further divided into three size categories based on their maximum dimension: small (0.1–2.9 meters), medium (3.0–5.0 meters), and large (longer than 5.1 meters). Finally, we attempted to roughly describe each pond's shape.

Many of these ponds suggested Japanese-influenced aesthetics, incorporating asymmetry and rock garden elements, while many did not appear to, utilizing more symmetrical designs or minimal ornamentation. Some appeared to be the products of highly skilled craftsmen, and others less so. What is apparent is a high degree of variability in garden construction at Gila.

Concrete was used in all the ponds found at Gila River. However, the durability and composition of concretes utilized varied widely. Some ponds had dense and durable concretes while others had brittle and crumbling concretes. In its most basic form, concrete is composed of a paste, cement, which binds to an aggregate when mixed with water and hardens into a solid durable form. Commonly, both coarse aggregates, such as crushed rock, and fine aggregates, such as sand, are used. The quality of concrete is largely dependent on the ratio between these elements: cement, coarse and fine aggregates, and water (Portland Cement Association 2017). The variability observed suggests variations in these ingredients. The notes of Robert Spencer suggest that incarcerees would often "beg, borrow or steal" bags of cement to use in construction (Spencer 1942c:22). Oral histories and newspaper articles corroborate these claims (Madden 1969; Sato 1944).

The Realities of Incarceration

The veil of violence hangs its shadow over all aspects of the incarceration event. In its most obvious and apparent form, it manifests itself with the mass removal and imprisonment of a people based upon their ethnic heritage. The examination

TABLE 7.2

Summary of Survey Results from Blocks 63–74 at Gila River Incarceration Camp

BLOCK	POND	TYPE	COMPLETENESS	SIZE	SHAPE
63	11	open space garden	fragmented	large	irregular
	12	barracks garden	fragmented	medium	two ponds
	13	open space garden	whole	medium	J shape
	14	open space garden	fragmented	small	asymmetrical
	44	open space garden	fragmented	large	irregular
	45	barracks garden	fragmented	small	D shape
	46	barracks garden	whole	small	oval
	47	barracks garden	whole	medium	long thin
	48	barracks garden	fragmented	large	rectangle
	49	barracks garden	whole	large	square
	50	barracks garden	fragmented	small	circle
	51	open space garden	fragmented	medium	C shape
	52	open space garden	whole	small	oval
64	15	barracks garden	whole	medium	irregular
65	16	open space garden	fragmented	large	irregular
	17	open space garden	whole	small	circle
66	18	barracks garden	fragmented	small	asymmetrical
	19	open space garden	whole	small	bathtub
	20	open space garden	whole	small	two circles
	21	barracks garden	fragmented	medium	irregular
	25	barracks garden	fragmented	medium	long thin
	26	barracks garden	fragmented	small	oval
	27	open space garden	fragmented	small	oval
	37	barracks garden	fragmented	medium	irregular
72	55	barracks garden	fragmented	small	L shape
	56	mess hall	whole	large	large
	57	open space garden	whole	medium	irregular
	58	barracks garden	whole	medium	L shape
	59	open space garden	whole	medium	long thin
	60	barracks garden	fragmented	small	oval
73	61	barracks garden	whole	medium	long thin
74	62	open space garden	fragmented	small	oval
	63	mess hall	whole	large	rectangle
	64	barracks garden	whole	large	two circles

of gardens at Gila River reveals the many ways in which people reacted to this violence of displacement and imprisonment.

The removal and imprisonment of all people of Japanese descent from the western United States was an act of state power and violence par excellence. In financial terms, it cost the Japanese American community millions of dollars. Many lost their homes, their work, and the majority of their material possessions. At facilities such as Gila River, the harsh camp conditions resulted in heat exhaustion and other physical ailments. Although rare, at least one shooting of a Japanese American by camp guards occurred (CWIRC 1983:176). The psychological effects of incarceration drove many to depression and some even to suicide. Yosh Nakamura, in an oral history, spoke about the effects of the camp on his father: "He was a very proud guy and so, when he was put in the camp and he wasn't able to provide for the family, it did a number on him, morale wise . . . being placed in the camp made him just, lose a lot of the dignity he had of himself" (Nakamura 2015). The humiliation and losses suffered from unjust imprisonment left scars on the Japanese American community for decades afterward.

The environmental conditions at Gila River proved to be particularly punishing for the largely Californian population. Daytime temperatures ranged from 50°F in the winter to well over 100°F in the summer. When Japanese Americans first arrived, temperatures were so unbearable that many chose to sleep outside to escape the heat (Marubayashi 1944:54). A historic drought hit the Gila River area in 1942, lasting until 1960 and leaving the ground particularly arid (Lillquist 2007:467). Dust storms were frequent occurrences; incarcerees often recalled their harsh nature (Ekinaka 1944:27; Matsumoto 1943:63).

Jane Dusselier (2008) argues that the creation of gardens was a way of making home, reterritorializing a foreign landscape, and creating a psychological and spiritual refuge. Laura Ng (2014) in her analysis of gardens at Manzanar contends that creating gardens acted in part as a way to build community within the confines of imprisonment. My research at Gila River supports these interpretations of gardens. They can be read as innovative reactions to violence and as forms of resistance toward the rigid impersonal structures of the camps.

As many adults who were incarcerated during World War II chose not to talk of their experiences, oral histories often provide the perspective of children at the incarceration camps. For younger incarcerees, gardens provided places to play and socialize. Ken Hayashi recalled, "We used to use the castor bean seeds for a blow gun. In the camp, they used to have the water coolers, and they used a lot of plastic tubing. We used to cut up the tubing and use them as blow guns; use them for shooting" (Hayashi 2015). Frances Kuramoto remembered gardens as places of play: "I don't know about the other blocks, we had a bunch of trees, several dozen trees around it. So, it happened that one of the years that we were in, the two years that we were in camp, was the year of the cicadas. And those trees were just covered with millions of cicadas making noises, and several kids you know were picking them off the trees and playing with them [laughs]" (Kuramoto 2014).

Anthropologist Robert Spencer, working at Gila River for the Japanese American Evacuation and Resettlement Study (JERS), wrote that those who built the gardens spent large quantities of time on their maintenance, taking great pride in tending their constructions and often incorporating ironwood and cactus plants from the surrounding desert (Spencer 1942a:17). Camp newspaper announcements further suggest that as time progressed, seeds were purchased through mail-order catalogs. Australian rye, Bermuda grass, canna lilies, poplars, and Chinese elms, among others, are listed as being imported into camp (Gila News-Courier 1942b:4; 1943:3). Some incarcerees fished in the irrigation canals surrounding the camp, bringing back carp to place in the ponds (Spencer 1942c:23). Spencer speculated than many of the gardens had religious connotations, noting that one man's gardens contained "charms of paper in his yard attached to the stone lanterns which he has made. These are called *ofuta* and impart qualities of good luck" (Spencer 1942b:40). It is unclear how closely aligned gardening and religious practices were at Gila River. What is certain, however, is that incarcerees invested large amounts of energy into the design, construction, and maintenance of gardens.

On September 25, 1942, two months after the first Japanese Americans arrived at Gila River, the camp's newspaper announced, "Contests will be held in both the Canal and Butte sections of the city to determine the most artistic gardens and the blocks surpassing all others in beauty and cleanliness . . . cash awards and banners will be presented respectively to winning gardens and blocks" (Gila News-Courier 1942a:2). Gardens helped create senses of home and community, offering ways to counteract the alienation felt by Japanese Americans in their incarceration.

Furthermore, garden construction alleviated the environmental and psychological stresses of incarceration at Gila River. Forty-two of the ponds recorded at Butte Camp sat next to or incorporated a barrack's footings into their designs. Several of these ponds undercut the barracks, with footings placed on small islands. The placement of these ponds so close to the barracks may have lowered

FIGURE 7.3 "60-3-A, 1944." Historic photograph of Patty Ozawa sitting on the steps of Barracks 60-3-A, Butte Camp, Gila River. Around the sides of the barracks, large castor bean plants grow, providing shade. Ozawa Family Collection; photographer unknown.

temperatures in the buildings, with water acting as a thermoregulatory device. Historic photographs have shown tall plants such as castor beans incorporated into garden designs. Kuramoto (2014) recalled that they offered shade to the barracks, further helping to cool them. The construction of these gardens also reduced the frequency of dust storms, greatly improving incarcerees' quality of life (Imagire 2008). Thus, despite the harshness of the desert conditions, the act of gardening made homes out of alienated environments.

The creation of gardens at Gila River was in part a response to the violence of the state. Dislocation, imprisonment, and the harsh environment of the desert all adversely affected the Japanese Americans incarcerated there. By examining gardens, we can begin to understand the ways they ameliorated some of these conditions for a better life within the camps. Yet while pursuing this project, I found that a whole spectrum of violence can be seen within an examination of gardens. While the exercise of state power is perhaps one of the most obvious forms of violence, others must be deliberately sought out in the archaeological record lest they remain hidden or forgotten.

Violations of Sovereignty

As we recorded the numerous ponds in the 2015 survey, we noted the high volume of materials and foundations still present across the camp. Stepping back and reflecting on this, it became apparent that the presence of the camp and so much material on GRIC land was itself an act of violence. The placement of the Gila River Incarceration Camp followed a decision process the ignored the sovereignty of the Gila River people in an attempt to limit costs to the government. This was another violent act, violating government-to-government agreements and territorial boundaries.

The GRIC reservation, created in 1859, was the first Native American reservation established in Arizona and one of the few to be placed on the ancestral land of its people, the Akimel O'odham and Pee Posh peoples (DeJong 2016:21; Lillquist 2007:476). Since its formation, the GRIC government has had a contentious relationship with the US government, primarily over the diversion of the Gila and Salt Rivers, resulting in reduced water for irrigation and subsequently famine and poverty (DeJong 2011, 2016).

The placement of all the incarceration camps was the result of three primary factors: accessibility by train for transportation, distance from potential military and civilian targets, and ability to cultivate the land (National Park Service 2006:96). While the federal government considered other locations for camps in Arizona, they were ruled out due to proximity to military bases and the expense of construction (Lillquist 2007:478). John Collier, the director of the Bureau of Indian Affairs (BIA), advocated for the camps to be placed on Native American reservations. He argued that this would create infrastructure for the local populations to use after the camps were decommissioned and that the BIA, with its experience in "handling a minority group," could successfully administer the camps (Bernstein 1991:83). The two camps in Arizona, Gila River and Poston, would be the only ones placed on reservations, though the BIA did not ultimately administer either for the entirety of the war.

The placement of the Gila River Camp was decided and finalized by four separate federal agencies—the War Relocation Authority, the Bureau of Indian Affairs, the War Department, and the Interior Department—before the tribal council at Gila River was asked or notified (Bernstein 1991:84). The tribal council voted against approving any construction or leasing permits twice. Despite this opposition, construction began anyway (Lillquist 2007:477). Ultimately the GRIC government approved the project with a third vote after most of the camp was already built. A marginal majority voted in favor only after BIA superintendent A. E. Robinson made it clear that GRIC would lose money if they didn't and after the WRA agreed to the development of several improvements upon the land (Tamir et al. 1993:108).

During the closure of the camp in 1945, the federal government initially planned to remove structural and foundational elements of buildings. It found that this was too costly and reneged on its commitment, leaving them in place and providing only marginal compensation. Furthermore, many of the improvements promised by the WRA were never realized. Recompenses for these actions were achieved by the GRIC only after several years of legal action (Bernstein 1991:85; Tamir et al. 1993:111). The conduct of the US government toward the GRIC constitutes an act of violence. It violated territorial borders with the construction of the camp, ignored the rights and wishes of the GRIC government, and attempted to leave without honoring its commitments, ultimately an act of attempted theft. Today the foundations of the camp lay strewn across the desert floor, a reminder of these violations of sovereignty and broken promises. Our ability to survey the remains of the camp is itself the result of this violence. This is very often overlooked. The incarceration of Japanese Americans had a wide impact on diverse communities. With an inspection of the material remains of these camps and their placement in the landscape, archaeology can highlight these impacts.

The Erasure of Diversity

An examination of the material constructions and styles of gardens at Gila River helps to uncover even more subtle forms of violence surrounding the incarceration. Though many of the garden ponds were extremely complex, others were simple in form. Some were well built, retaining a high level of integrity to the present day. Others did not stand the test of time, crumbling slowly and fading into the desert sands. A few of the ponds contained multiple chambers, elaborate rock ornamentations, rivers, and islands. Several were no more than concrete circles with a few minimalist stone embellishments. The diversity of garden varieties speaks to larger diversity within the incarcerated community, a quality often ignored in narratives of the incarceration.

As noted above, the ponds found at Butte Camp varied widely in both design and the quality of material. These variations suggest either a difference in knowledge of cement composition or unequal access to resources and networks.

FIGURE 7.4 Photo of Pond 5 in Block 61, looking southeast in 2015. It was one of the largest ponds found in the survey of Gila River and was composed of four large concrete chambers with blocks of embedded sandstone and quartz. Photograph by Koji Lau-Ozawa.

While some Japanese Americans could count on the acquisition of cement of the necessary quantity and quality, as well as the knowledge of desirable proportionality, others its seems were not so fortunate. Whether they were uneducated in the art of concrete production or unable to purchase or borrow cement, the end result was the same: brittle concrete ponds. The materiality of the ponds highlights this heterogeneity of knowledge and access to resources. The differences in styles and qualities of gardens at Gila River serve to remind us of a subtle form of violence—historical erasure.

Portrayals of Japanese Americans within the camps often show quiet, passive victims or heroic soldiers who fought in the 442nd and 100th battalions. The Japanese American population is portrayed as a large homogenous block with limited reactions to incarceration (Murray 2008). The emphasis of this history was an important aspect in the struggle for redress and in gaining recognition of the civil rights violations incurred by the incarceration. However, the myth of homogeneity persists, often as a political tool directed by community elites. It obfuscates the unjust treatment and marginalization of outcast segments of the population. The Japanese American Citizen League initially privileged this narrative, and those who spoke out against it were shunned or ostracized (Lyon 2012). Archaeological work can serve as a powerful counternarrative to this history, helping these marginalized communities tell their stories (Farrell and Burton 2011).

Recent historical scholarship suggests that remnants of pre-Meiji-era caste systems followed issei migrants to the New World (Geiger 2011). The *buraku jumin*—the lowest group in the Tokugawa-era caste system—were systematically discriminated against in Japan, excluded from opportunities and social mobility. Some migrated to the United States to escape social and economic disenfranchisement. Upon arrival, these people found themselves similarly excluded from the larger Japanese American population (Geiger 2011:193). In his field notes, Robert Spencer wrote that many people were unhappy with sharing facilities with members of the lower castes and that consequently community relations were at times tense (Spencer 1942d). Divides also occurred generationally and between groups with opposing political views. The most dramatic example culminated with the severe beating of a man perceived to be too in line with the WRA administration at Gila (Hansen 1985). The narrative of a homogeneous community and of the quiet, passive victim glosses over the multiplicity of identities within the Japanese American community.

Diversity at Gila River took many forms, from divergent castes and classes to divergent generations and political leanings. Failing to recognize this diversity is an act of violence by erasure. Though a subtler form of violence than those previously traced through the recordation of ponds, erasures still silence the complexity and nuance of the community. The wide range of garden aesthetics, modes of construction, and the apparent skill of the constructors hints at a wide range of garden builders. It reminds us that we are looking at complex communities and that we must seek out the narratives that have been silenced. Close inspection of the material forms of the archaeological record can bring attention to the messiness of the historical one.

Histories of Racial Discrimination

The subject of study, gardens at Gila River, calls to mind another form of violence. Interpretations of the high density of gardens at Manzanar have attributed it to the high volume of gardeners and landscapers incarcerated as well as the high number of farmers (Burton 2015). The same could be said of Gila River, where 761 people had gardening or a garden-related profession listed as their primary occupation and 2,904 had farming. When examining the immigration history of Japanese migrants to the United States, it is apparent that structural racism tightly constrained the opportunities of issei, forcing many into the gardening and farming professions.

Discriminatory immigration policies prohibited Japanese migrants from pursuing citizenship while European American–dominated unions often excluded them from pursuing traditional labor professions (Ichioka 1988:145; Ngai 2004b). During the first two decades of the twentieth century, gardening was the fourth most common occupation among Japanese American men, accounting for about 10 percent of the working population, with farming being the most common profession. Agriculture offered a large amount of stability to issei, allowing them to raise families and pursue a sedentary lifestyle (Ichioka 1988:152). Within a short amount of time, Japanese migrants in western states dominated the cultivation of niche crops such as potatoes and strawberries (Azuma 2005:64). These types of produce required intensive labor for lower yields compared to staples such as wheat and corn.

In reaction to these successes, state legislatures enacted racially charged and exclusionary alien land laws, forcing many issei out of the agriculture industry. These laws prevented "aliens ineligible for citizenship" from owning or leasing land. Many issei found ways around this type of legislation, joining in corporations and cooperatives to purchase and lease land, and signing deeds in their American-born children's names (Azuma 2005:66). However, states continued to pass increasingly harsh and targeted legislation, making it difficult or in some cases highly impractical to continue farming.

Because of these pressures, many issei transitioned into gardening. Gardening presented itself in southern California as a viable alternative to farming for young issei due to its relatively low start-up costs and the fact that fluency in English was not required (Tsuchida 1984:441). By 1934 fully one-third of Japanese American men in the Los Angeles area were employed as gardeners, by far the leading occupation of the area. The majority of these people worked as maintenance gardeners, mowing lawns, cutting trees, watering plants, and removing trash (Tsukashima 2000:67). European Americans in Los Angeles were eager to hire Japanese gardeners, filled with orientalist expectations of exotic paradises and in need of year-round care of their grounds (Esaki 2013; Tsuchida 1984). Issei exploited this need, playing off these racialized assumptions for their own benefit. Such strategies were not uncommon within Japanese American communities as people attempted to navigate around racial discrimination (Azuma 2009).

Issei provided for themselves and their families within the niche of gardening.

FIGURE 7.5 Photo of Pond 8 in Block 59, looking east in December 2014. The pond is composed of two varieties of concrete with mosaicked quartz stones embedded. A small island in the center holds a barracks footing, suggesting that the structure overlapped the pond feature. Photograph by Koji Lau-Ozawa.

It was for some the only viable chance to pursue financial security and upward economic mobility (Tsukashima 1991). Prohibitions from citizenship, racialized exclusion from unions, legislative barriers to farming, and stereotypic expectations constrained the field of choices available. The high volume of gardeners in camps such as Manzanar and Gila River, both of which were populated by many southern Californians, stands as a testament to these constraints.

During the recording of gardens constructed by incarcerees, it became apparent that the skill sets and knowledge for garden construction might have been related to the high number of people employed in both gardening and agricultural industries. Japanese Americans in both fields gained the experience necessary for the construction and maintenance of gardens and garden ponds. While these professions did not determine the creative output of the incarcerees' energies, they helped provide the requisite knowledge for its production. The gardens at Gila River and at other sites of incarcerations, with their sophistication and intricacies, speak to the skills gained and refined by Japanese Americans.

The medium of expression traced through the archaeological record thus serves as a record of the structural violence Japanese Americans were subjected to. By tracing the history of discrimination through the prewar years, this facet of gardens is revealed. Archaeologists must consider these diachronic linkages in the production of features such as garden ponds. They are not only the consequences of singular events but also the product of longer historical forces. For the Japanese Americans incarcerated, gardens were assemblages of the knowledge and skills accumulated over sixty years of navigating the racial barriers of the United States.

Multiple Layers of History

Gardens built within the camps reflect a strong sense of determination and perseverance. They are one expression of resistance toward a violent act of forced removal and imprisonment. And, if we dig deeper, they also speak to a wider spectrum of violence. It is important that the stronger and more apparent forms of violence do not eclipse the less obvious ones. If archaeology is to truly challenge narratives of power, it must seek out these various forms of violence. The study of the Gila River Incarceration Camp highlights a period of unjust imprisonment and persecution. The creation of garden ponds helps to reveal the strategies that incarcerees deployed to alleviate their circumstances. The location and preservation of archaeological features speak to infringements of the sovereignty of the Gila River Indian Community. Varieties in form and construction quality challenge narratives of a singular homogenous community and the suppression of diversity. And the very medium of gardens as ways of making home and expression speaks to the structural racism that pushed many Japanese Americans toward the professions of gardening and agriculture.

The study of the Gila River Incarceration Camp reminds us that the violence of the World War II incarceration rippled through space and time, impacting communities and individuals in ways not always immediately obvious. By sifting through the multiple layers of violence surrounding the camp, it is possible to better understand the complex and intersubjective experiences of incarcerees and the structures that resulted in their confinement. Each component contributed to this totality of violence: years of discrimination and racist hostility, the marginalization of Native American communities, caste and class divisions. These forces are not exclusive to the singularity of Japanese American incarceration. They have operated through countless historical moments up to the present day.

That the particularities of violence at Gila River must be sought out with such intense scrutiny is a function of the camp's designs. Hidden away and far removed from most American cities, it can easily be forgotten by those who were not directly impacted. The privilege accorded to many is to rest in benign ignorance, often unaware of the entire history of the incarceration, let alone its less salient details. This is a privilege kept from Japanese American communities that have internalized the violence of incarceration. It is kept from the Gila River Indian Community, whose land bears the scars of incarceral infrastructure. The enterprise of archaeology is to challenge this privilege and acknowledge those who were subjected to the violences of the past. In this way, reiterations of such iniquities might be prevented from occurring again.

Acknowledgments

This research was undertaken in conjunction with the Gila River Indian Community Cultural Resource Management Program and the Pima-Maricopa Irrigation Project, with funding from the Department of the Interior, US Bureau of Reclamation, under the Tribal Self-Governance Act of 1994 (P.L. 103–413), for the design and development of a water delivery system utilizing Central Arizona Project water. Further funding was provided by the Kiana Dressendorfer Scholarship at San Francisco State University. I would like to thank Christopher Matthews and Bradley Phillippi for inviting me to participate in this volume; Stacey Camp, Laura Ng, and Jeff Burton for many productive conversations around the archaeology of Japanese American incarceration; and the reviewers for their insightful comments. I give a great thanks to my grandmother Shigeko Elizabeth Ozawa and to my whole family for their support, contributions, and sacrifices on behalf of this work.

EIGHT

Race and the Water

Swimming, Sewers, and Structural Violence in African America

PAUL R. MULLINS, KYLE HUSKINS, AND SUSAN B. HYATT

In January 2016, Visit Indy, the tourism agency of Indianapolis, proposed building a seasonal beach along the White River, the waterway that meanders through the heart of Indiana's capital city (Schoettle 2016). The idea was modeled on temporary summer beaches in Paris, where sand is placed on roadways along the Right Bank. The artificial Parisian beachfront hosts a variety of popular leisure activities, though there is no beachside swimming in the Seine itself. The proposal to reproduce Paris's seasonal beaches along the White River in Indianapolis was greeted with local skepticism and outright ridicule. At the heart of such doubt was the river's reputation for being an unsightly and unpleasant artery that has been polluted and poorly integrated into the cityscape over more than a century. This revulsion concerning the city's waterways and the notion of an urban beachfront is rooted in a complex range of material, social, and historical ideas that paint Indianapolis waterways as polluted, unsightly, and mostly forgettable spaces.

Our interest is in how the condition of those waterways, along with the lack of access to other public spaces, such as swimming pools, illuminates the profound sway of anti-black racism in the past and present alike. Many stretches of the White River, its tributary Fall Creek, and the Central Canal that are today disparaged as polluted and unappealing ran through modest working-class neighborhoods that became overwhelmingly African American around the turn of the twentieth century. Those African American neighborhoods were disproportionately subjected to sewer discharges, concentrations of industrial waste, and poorly maintained or nonexistent water and sewer services. Over the course of the twentieth century, white residents generally settled in segregated urban and suburban communities that secured utility services, escaped industrial and utility pollution, and had access to well-maintained recreational amenities. The present-day White River and its local tributaries are often stereotyped or ignored precisely because they evoke anxieties about class and color privilege.

On the one hand, many of the city's exclusively white waterways were not universally spoiled: Some northern Indianapolis stretches of the White River, such as a segment that runs through a Northside neighborhood known as Ravenswood, began to host seasonal riverside cottages in the late nineteenth century; another Northside neighborhood, Broad Ripple, and the banks along the city's Riverside Park were popular boating and recreational spots with scenic riverfront access; there were even scattered stretches of exclusive elite housing along both the White River and Fall Creek. On the other hand, there is a genuine historical reason to characterize some of Indianapolis's waterways as tainted by a century and a half of pollution. The White River, its Indianapolis tributaries (such as Fall Creek), and waterways such as the Central Canal have long been fouled by sewage, industrial discharges, and upriver pollutants, and those impacts were clearly disproportionately inflicted on African American neighborhoods. By the early twentieth century, the southern reaches of the White River's course through downtown Indianapolis had become especially contaminated by unsightly, foul-smelling, and unhealthy industrial discharges and raw household sewage. That pollution lingers in many Indianapolis residents' imaginations today because it is not simply a historical artifact. Well into the late twentieth century, the city resisted extending modern sewer services to many African American communities, which were subject to constant raw sewage overflows. Simply considering the African American experience of the city's waters uncomfortably compels contemporary communities to acknowledge more than a century of environmental and social injustices against African Americans.

Many cities like Indianapolis denied equitable utility service and recreational spaces to black residents and failed to uniformly enforce their own sanitary and housing codes. Indianapolis administrators ignored waterway pollution and inequity in sewer and recreational services through willful racism and ignorance of everyday African American material life. Nevertheless, such injustices are not necessarily easily blamed on circles of consciously racist city leaders. Instead, that racism was invested in deep historical and systemic processes that privileged particular communities and that were naturalized as if they were beyond public contemplation.

Similar everyday acts of environmental racism and social injustice were inflicted on African American communities throughout the country. Such acts were

FIGURE 8.1 In 1921 the beach along the White River at Broad Ripple Park was strictly segregated. Courtesy Bass Photo Company Collection, Indiana Historical Society.

not simply reducible to the will of individuals or even discrete entities; rather,
these were examples of what Johan Galtung (1969:171) calls "structural violence,"
in which the "violence is built into the structure and shows up as unequal power
and consequently as unequal life chances" (cf. Farmer 2004b:308). Certainly
many individuals were consciously complicit in anti-black racism, and fathom-
ing their defense of color and class privilege is one element of interpreting how
persistent injustice was imposed on black residents and condoned by so many
white residents. Nevertheless, an analysis of race and water requires systematically examining the ways in which a landscape of inequality was created and
reproduced and was virtually unremarked upon in white public discourses. Our
interest here is in examining specifically how environmental and social injustices
associated with water in particular were disproportionally directed toward African
Americans and their neighborhoods.

   This analysis of the materiality of race and water expands the conventional
archaeological focus on excavated objects and aspires to situate those objects
within systems of structural violence, which is utterly material in its effects. Paul

Farmer's (2004b:308) research on structural violence and health injustice advocates illuminating what he calls the "materiality of the social." Farmer indicates that this term "underlines my conviction that social life in general and structural violence in particular will not be understood without a deeply materialist approach to whatever surfaces in the participant-observer's field of vision—the ethnographically visible." Few dimensions of materiality could be more affecting than the sensory landscape of Indianapolis's waterways, but the city's broadly defined waterscapes—from riverways to sewers to pools—have rarely been viewed as archaeological expressions of structural violence. Our interest is in examining these waterscapes as material products of structural inequality that profoundly shaped everyday African American life despite their invisibility in white imagination. Concessions of environmental racism in Indianapolis have been quite rare, and there has not been an especially sustained focus on the concrete ways in which access to the waterscape and spaces of privilege have been controlled by the city. The story of race and class injustice projected onto Indianapolis's waters is clearly told in how the city's landscape was materially transformed by the city and how that landscape was distinctively experienced by African Americans.

Waterways as "Pariah and Outcast": Color Line Experiences of Urban Waterways

In the late nineteenth century, Indianapolis became spatially segregated along the color line, so many white residents had no sustained experience of the river's most deplorable reaches. In 1896, for example, the *Indianapolis News* (1896b:7) observed that during a local event along the river, "tens of thousands of residents who rarely see White river, but often are reminded by sadly-tainted breezes from the southwest as to its locality and its special propinquity to the pork houses, made a closer acquaintance with the stream. . . . They saw a stream of great natural beauty and sweetness, which has been treated as a pariah and an outcast: a stream which has, year after year, been made to receive the refuse of a great city, until the breath of the river has become an offense to decency and a menace to health." The newspaper singled out the "pork houses," including the massive Kingan and Company packing plant, as largely responsible for spoiling the water, but by the late nineteenth century it sat alongside railway yards, a paper mill, and a massive cannery, all of which contributed to polluting the river.

Pockets of African American residents were scattered throughout Indianapolis

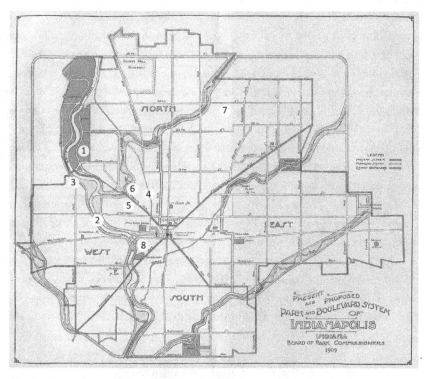

FIGURE 8.2 This 1909 plan of Indianapolis parks features many of the sites of the city's segregated waterscape, including (1) Riverside Park; (2) the White River; (3) Emrichsville Beach; (4) the Central Canal; (5) Indiana Avenue, the heart of the city's African American community; (6) Fall Creek; (7) Douglass Park, which opened in 1921; and (8) the Kingan and Company plant. Broad Ripple Park Beach and Ravenswood were both just north of the area show in the map. Courtesy Indy.gov.

by the second quarter of the nineteenth century. From the 1860s onward, some of the largest concentrations were in the city's Near Westside from the 1860s onward, which lay along the White River and Fall Creek. By the 1870s most of the Near Westside was settled, but strict spatial segregation did not really exist until the very end of the nineteenth century. Color line segregation came very rapidly around 1900, at the very moment that many African Americans began to arrive in the half-century African American exodus from the South known as the Great Migration. Between 1900 and 1920 Indianapolis's African American population doubled, with most African Americans settling in the neighborhoods along Indiana Avenue (Figure 8.2). Cities like Indianapolis offered employment and an established network of African American institutions, neighborhoods, and a business district.

The long and steady decline of the Near Westside's waterfront reflected city leaders' unwillingness to challenge industrialists. The potential profits of industrial growth apparently justified inequitable services in the predominately African American neighborhoods near the riverside factories. For instance, while sewer service reached some Indianapolis homes in the late nineteenth century, much of the Near Westside was served by wells and privy vault outhouses, and sewer service was not extended to many Near Westside residences until relatively recently. The city enacted its first ordinances regulating privy vault outhouses in 1873 to control "unwholesome, noxious, or offensive smells" (City of Indianapolis 1904:667–68), but these codes were hardly ever enforced. The unhealthiness of such sanitary conditions and polluted water sources was well-known to the city's physicians. For example, in May 1880 homeopath Moses T. Runnels reported that White River waters feeding the city's waterworks were "little better than sewage" (*Indianapolis News* 1880a:2). A month later he followed with an extensive chemical analysis of citywide water testing and stated, "I found the alleys, by-ways, back yards and stables all through the city in a very filthy condition" (*Indianapolis News* 1880b:3; cf. Runnels 1883). In 1881 Runnels indicated that during an ongoing typhoid outbreak, "nearly every case of typhoid fever can be traced to impure water, defective drainage, or filthiness of the home of the patient" (*Indianapolis News* 1881:3).

Indianapolis's public health crusaders like Runnels focused on household sanitation, a move that gravitated toward the vivid sensory dimensions of sanitation and mortality in impoverished African American communities. However, that observation fixed on the visible material culture of impoverishment and evaded acknowledging structural inequality in city services. While they lamented the public health implications of housing conditions, city administrators never seriously regulated or enforced housing codes until well after World War II, when such enforcement fueled "slum clearance" displacement. Almost no city leaders were willing to challenge industries along the White River, so the blame was often laid at the feet of the city's poorest residents. For example, an ambitious 1917 study of the city was critical of Indianapolis's sanitary shortcomings, but it suggested that "as Indianapolis develops it is likely to attract a class of transient laborers to whom any shanty is acceptable for temporary quarters. ... The increase of the colored population coming from the South and bringing with them the lowest standard of housing and sanitary conveniences, is also likely to create a danger against which the city should be armed by giving the health department adequate powers of condemnation" (Bureau of Municipal Research 1917:342).

The community adjoining Indianapolis's waterfront industry was subject to some of its most unpleasant airborne discharges and waterfront pollution. In 1916, for instance, the *Indianapolis News* (1916:1) delivered an alarming report that the White River just south of the African American Near Westside "is devoid of natural fish life and birds." The state board of health's John C. Diggs pronounced that from the Kingan and Company packing plant south, the river was "a malodorous, septic stream, bearing on its surface floating matter of sewage origin." Diggs concluded that the river "was of the same character as ordinary household sewage"; south of the Van Camp's cannery, "pieces of tomato are on the surface of the water." Slightly farther south, "floating slime is on the water; the odor is foul. Banks are covered with slime. Bubbles of gas rise to the surface" (cf. Diggs 1914).

The Aesthetics of Indianapolis Waterways

The river's stereotype as an unpleasant space has been significantly shaped by the contemporary aesthetics of the downtown stretches of the White River and the Central Canal. Urban planners often aspire to produce aesthetically attractive and functional cities centered on waterways, and some Indianapolis planners imagined the city's streams as its most important feature. For instance, in 1894 landscape architect Joseph Earnshaw proposed creating continuous waterfront parks that would reach through most of the Near Westside (*Indianapolis Journal* 1894:6). Earnshaw's plan was solicited by the Commercial Club (the precursor to the city's chamber of commerce), but the city council was cool to the seemingly expensive plan (*Indianapolis News* 1894:1).

Two years later John Charles Olmsted, Frederick Law Olmsted Jr., and Charles Eliot provided a parks plan to Indianapolis's freshly created parks commission. It echoed the tenor of Earnshaw's plan to focus a park system along the city's waterways. The Olmsted firm proposed a variety of parks linked by "a handsome parkway along Fall creek. . . . We believe it would be worth all it would cost to extend this parkway down Fall creek from Michigan road to White river and along White river to a point as near Washington-street bridge as might be found practicable, from which point it should be made to connect with one or more of the broad streets north of Military Park" (*Indianapolis News* 1896a:5). The Olmsted proposal emphasized that the city's waterways were its most important landscape planning feature: "In conclusion, we may say that the best, and indeed almost the only, park sites worth considering are those including some portion of the rivers or runs which pass through or close to the city, and that it is high time that desirable and conveniently situated lands for parks and playgrounds should be secured." Yet some city councilors concluded that the overwhelmingly African American "lands south of Indiana avenue are least likely to advance rapidly in value, and that consequently it will be best to abandon for the present the southern end of the system" (*Indianapolis News* 1897:4).

George Kessler's 1909 Indianapolis plan borrowed the Earnshaw and Olmsted plans for parkways along the city's waterways, and Kessler's designs shaped much of the city's waterways. The *Indianapolis Star* (1909:3) indicated that "Mr. Kessler urged the importance of securing to the city the use and control of both banks of all natural waterways and the preservation of their natural beauty." The banks of all the city's waterways were not universally purchased by the city, but Kessler's boulevard system remains one of the contemporary city's most prominent landmarks. The parkways were intended to deliver residents to green spaces throughout the city. Kessler's 1909 plan proposed the construction of a boulevard through the Near Westside along the east banks of the White River, but that road was never constructed.

In 1912 *Indianapolis Star* columnist Walter Sidney Greenough (1912:1) championed an Indianapolis park system "having as its backbone beautiful waterways" that would be "not only for beauty's sake, but for sanitation's sake." Yet Greenough lamented the condition of the city's waterscape, which he characterized as the "garbage-strewn White River, the sewage-polluted canal, tin-can-lined Pogue's Run and fishless Fall Creek." Greenough feared his proposal would be greeted with skepticism, ironically for reasons much like those Visit Indy would withstand over its White River beach proposal a century later. Greenough admitted that "the idea may be laughed at by those who have seen ocean fronts," and he recognized that it was likely that "Big Business will rail at the beautification plan and seek the parks for factory lands even more assiduously than now."

Indeed, while Indianapolis did construct some creative park spaces and linked greenways that had been planned for more than a decade, the city largely ignored downtown waterways and accommodated industries along the White River's stretches through the African American Near Westside. After a devastating 1913 flood, much of the White River in the city's Near Westside was widened, got new levees, and was lined with massive concrete flood walls that remain the contemporary waterway's most striking feature. When the downtown canal was remodeled seventy years later, it too was dramatically made into a concrete artery. In the 1980s, after most of the Near Westside's residents had been uprooted by urban renewal, the city developed a project to transform the depopulated canal into a tourist destination. The long-ignored canal was lined with concrete and pedestrian walkways, got fountains and decorative footbridges, and was emptied of nearly all its historic structures to make way for a host of new apartments and businesses.

Swimming and Segregation in Indianapolis Waters

The deep-seated picture of Indianapolis's waterways as polluted arteries is complicated by residents' long-standing recreation in those waterways, and it risks ignoring their connections to segregated pools scattered throughout the Indianapolis area. In the early twentieth century, waterfront beaches were found along northern reaches of the White River in Ravenswood, Arden, and Broad Ripple, and swimming holes could be found along Fall Creek and Pleasant Run. A 1917 study concluded that certain stretches of the White River were still relatively unpolluted (Indiana State Board of Health 1917). At Broad Ripple, "the river is free from floating matter or objectionable odor"; at Crow's Nest just south of Broad Ripple, "water is clear, free from floating matter"; and at Riverside Park, the "water is clean but has a slightly weedy odor" (Indiana State Board of Health 1917:140).

At least initially Indianapolis's recreational waters were not racially segregated. In about 1877, for instance, Otto Schissel opened a recreational swimming hole and adjoining bath house on the canal at West and Wabash Streets (Dunn 1912:450–51; *Indianapolis News* 1890:5). In 1890 the *Indianapolis News* indicated that the canal swimming holes and bath houses were places where "whites and blacks mingle in the foam." However, most twentieth-century swimming spots were segregated from the very outset, a pattern that was typical of American leisure space segregation at the turn of the century (Wiltse 2009; Wolcott 2012). Indianapolis's YMCA dedicated a building with a swimming pool in 1887, stating that "bath room privileges are alone, now that Fall Creek and fresh water are so far away, worth 'more than double the price of admission' to him who holds cleanliness next to godliness" (*Indianapolis News* 1887:1). However, the YMCA rejected all membership applications from African Americans. A segregated black YMCA

FIGURE 8.3 In 1930 industrial smokestacks dotted the horizon of downtown Indianapolis along the White River. Courtesy Bass Photo Company Collection, Indiana Historical Society.

was formed in Indianapolis in 1900, and the city's "colored" YMCA was admitted to the state YMCA in 1902 (Pierce 2012). After an extensive fund-raising campaign, Indianapolis's segregated Senate Avenue YMCA opened in 1913, with a swimming pool among its featured attractions. Legions of African Americans learned to swim in the Senate Avenue pool between 1913 and the building's closing in 1959.

Indianapolis had thirteen park swimming pools in 1914, most barring everyday access to African Americans. In July 1914 a segregated black pool was opened by the parks board on Almont Street, and in 1919 black children were allowed access to one city pool one day a week (*Indianapolis Star* 1914a:12, 1914b:13, 1919:12). The city embarked on an ambitious effort to construct swimming pools in the public parks after World War I, a move that was driven in part by the deplorable condition of the city's waterways. In 1919 parks director R. Walter Jarvis advocated building nineteen new swimming pools, acknowledging that the city's health board had concluded that city waterways were not safe for bathing or recreational swimming (*Indianapolis News* 1919a:18). The parks "board decided that it would have signs put up at swimming holes in Fall creek and White river warning the public that the water is insanitary. 'The only solution of the swimming problem in Indianapolis is the swimming pool,' Mr. Lowry told the board. 'The system of combination overflow and storm water sewers in Fall creek and the sewage in White river, make it impracticable to consider the establishment of swimming places in these streams.'"

However, a week after Jarvis's proposal, Indianapolis's parks board decided that sewage overflows into the African American Near Westside were not consequential after all. The board decided not to construct pools in the Near Westside, arguing instead that residents of those neighborhoods should continue to swim in the White River and Fall Creek (*Indianapolis News* 1919b:13). Parks superintendent James H. Lowry argued, "This does not mean that the department will give up its plans of placing swimming pools in neighborhoods not accessible to streams. . . . But if Fall creek and White river near Riverside are safe from a health standpoint to use there is no reason why we should go to the expense of putting in swimming pools in neighborhoods accessible to the streams." Jarvis's initial 1919 plan for nineteen pools continued the segregation of the parks and pools, specifying that two would be reserved for African Americans (and another for Italians and a fourth for Hungarians). Eventually the city built only one black pool, opening the Douglass Park pool in 1921. It remained the city's only public black pool into the late 1950s, but its location in the city's Eastside required most residents of the Near Westside to reach it by bus or car.

The city parks were not legally segregated, but residents and the parks board itself clearly understood parks and pools to be racially exclusive. In July 1926 staff from the city's African American newspaper, the *Indianapolis Recorder*, tried to reserve a picnic space at Brookside Park, but they were denied a permit (*Indianapolis Recorder* 1926b:1). The superintendent of parks stressed that Douglass Park was the official "Jim Crow Park," and he insisted that Douglass Park was an inviting leisure space for the city's "colored citizens" (Jarvis 1923). The African American newspaper's staff was told by the superintendent that they should go to Douglass Park to limit animosity.

Rebuffed by the parks board, African Americans aspired to establish private black beaches or pools, but most of these efforts failed or were short-lived ventures. In 1927, for instance, a group of African American entrepreneurs, led by Henry Fleming, announced a plan to purchase the former Casino Gardens, a club

FIGURE 8.4 Sometime around 1950 this group of African Americans gathered at Douglass Park for the *Indianapolis Recorder*'s annual picnic. Courtesy Indianapolis Recorder Collection, Indiana Historical Society.

along White River that lay just south of a municipal golf course (*Indianapolis Recorder* 1927a:1). The Casino Gardens owner had been unable to sell the property to the city's parks board, but Fleming assembled sufficient funds to purchase the club and convert it into a venue that would be known as the Spring Hill Country Club. The city council first responded by introducing a bill barring the sale of the property to African Americans, but the bill failed to pass (*Indianapolis Recorder* 1927a:1). Undeterred by the city's resistance, Fleming held an event at the club on February 20, 1927, but the "announcement created quite a stir among the poor whites who live in vicinity of the place" (*Indianapolis Recorder* 1927b:1). Fleming touted the venue's riverfront location and plans to develop a beachfront along the White River, but his potential neighbors "besieged the City Council to buy the property" (*Indianapolis Recorder* 1927b:1). The neighboring Haughville and Riverside civic organizations pleaded to the parks board to condemn the property rather than allow it to be sold to African Americans (*Indianapolis Recorder* 1927c:1). That proposal echoed parks board member John E. Milnor's warning that "if the group of colored men bought the property it would be condemned" (*Indianapolis Recorder* 1927b:1). Despite the parks board's initial reluctance to purchase the property, it bowed to white neighbors' resistance and purchased the former Casino Gardens, merging it with the neighboring golf course.

The most successful African American resorts were outside the city limits. Idlewild, Michigan, was the most prominent African American resort in the Midwest, and in March 1916 the *Indianapolis Recorder* (1916:1) celebrated that "beautiful Idlewild is to be an exclusive, high-class colored summer resort." Idlewild was indeed class exclusive, though, so few Indianapolis residents were sufficiently wealthy to purchase property at the Michigan resort (Stephens 1913). The Fox Lake resort began to sell lots near Angola, Indiana, in 1926, and it was long an African American getaway, but it was likewise too costly for most African Americans in Indianapolis (Polley 1993). A resort calling itself Idlewild of Indiana (with no connection to the Michigan resort) began selling open lots in Johnson County in 1926 (*Indianapolis Recorder* 1926a:5). This was not an especially realistic option for many families, because after purchasing property they would then need to build a structure, and the Idlewild of Indiana venture collapsed within a year. A few efforts were made to establish African American beaches in Indianapolis itself. In June 1933, for instance, the newly opened Eaglewood Beach promised to be a "sojourn in heaven," offering swimming and recreation "in company with Refined folks" (*Indianapolis Recorder* 1933:8). However, the far Westside swimming and picnic grounds along Eagle Creek seems to have closed at the end of the 1933 season.

In the absence of unpolluted swimming spaces or accessible pools, many African Americans instead continued to swim in the White River and its tributaries. In August 1936 an African American beach was cleared on the west side of the White River adjoining Belmont Park (*Indianapolis Recorder* 1936:8). Located near the Emrichsville Dam, the beach was within easy walking distance of the Near Westside. Yet by 1941 the *Indianapolis Recorder* was complaining that the beach was poorly maintained (*Indianapolis Recorder* 1941a:1). The newspaper found "weeds and dead fish in the water not more than six or seven feet from where young children were 'paddling in the water'" and complained that there was "no guard for a sixty-foot hole several yards from the beach, a hole which claimed the life of a young boy several seasons ago" (*Indianapolis Recorder* 1941a:8).

As the *Recorder* acknowledged, the White River, its tributaries, and the canal were treacherous swimming spaces that claimed numerous drowning victims. In June 1934 the *Indianapolis Recorder*'s Lee A. Johnson lamented that "drowning season is on" (Johnson 1934:2). Indeed, a month earlier seventeen-year-old John Edward Bennett drowned in Fall Creek near Indianapolis City Hospital

(*Indianapolis Recorder* 1934:1). Drownings in the White River, the canal, and Fall Creek were unpleasant staples of summertime news coverage well into the 1960s, inevitable realities of a structurally segregated waterscape that was largely invisible to white residents.

Waterway conditions grew progressively worse and persist in many city streams today. Into the 1950s, Indianapolis constructed a combined sewer system that, when precipitation is particularly heavy, causes raw sewage to overflow, ejecting it into much of the White River and Fall Creek. In 1941 African American resident Curtis Terry filed a suit against the city because "refuse dumped into the creek will cause the stream to overflow its channel and flood his property. . . . Noxious odors in the neighborhood are often caused by a sanitary sewer . . . located near City Hospital" (*Indianapolis Recorder* 1941b:2). A decade later Terry's home was targeted for demolition by the city's redevelopment commission; his family moved in about 1952, when their home was part of 178 acres razed during an urban renewal project.

The Terry home was near a combined sewer overflow, but new sewers were still being built and connected to combined sewers into the 1960s (West 2006). These new connections actually increased sewer overflows into tributaries (such as Fall Creek) in predominately African American neighborhoods. In 1999 a federal civil rights complaint was filed against the city for its unwillingness to address sewer overflows, and Mayor Stephen Goldsmith responded by suing the state and claiming that the city could not financially meet the state's environmental requirements to make the water "swimmable." In 2006 the city agreed to construct thirty-one combined sewer overflow mechanisms to reduce the 7.8 billion gallons of yearly sewer overflows, which were roughly one hundred times too high to satisfy the safe swimming standard (Department of Justice 2010). In 2010 the Department of Justice and the Environmental Protection Agency agreed with the state's plan to enact a second set of changes to reduce yearly sewage discharges to 414 million gallons (Department of Justice 2010). That project is expected to be completed in about 2025. Nevertheless, a 2016 report cautioned that seventy-one communities in forty-eight Indiana counties could have significantly underfunded combined sewer overflow systems (Palmer and Schmidt 2016:3). The cost of those projects is amplified by even more costly drinking water infrastructure projects as well as wastewater conveyance and septic system projects.

Imagining Racist Waterways

The transformation of the White River into a seasonal beachfront could perhaps rehabilitate the public's somewhat limited imagination regarding the city's waterways. However, that imagination seems to either fancy the river mostly as an aesthetic feature or cast water as a narrowly defined and race-neutral spatial dimension of the landscape. City officials and many residents have long deplored pollution of the city's waterways, but that pollution has rarely been acknowledged to be a product of anti-black racism, and its deep historical roots extending from utility service to leisure space have never been admitted. Recognition of pollution's material reality tends to project it into an industrialized past, and acknowledgment of segregated services such as park and pool access tends to situate segregation in an alien historical moment, largely disconnected from the contemporary world. Admissions of persistent pollution have never acknowledged its connection to a broad range of structural policies that have consistently denied African Americans utility services, public leisure and recreation, health care, and educational equity.

A White River beach perhaps hazards reducing the river to an aesthetic feature and leisure space. Like the remodeled canal, the transformed White River is likely to serve white suburbanites and a newly resettled community of affluent urban dwellers. An ambitious picture of the city's waterways could underscore their implication in racist and classist sentiments that have long been at the heart of everyday practice in places like Indianapolis. An unwillingness or inability to imagine the dense systemic connections between inequalities in pollution management, health care, and public rights risks leaving underlying structural violence unexamined and unchallenged. The White River could perhaps be one modest springboard for a rich narrative examining American cities' relationships with both bodies of water and African American communities.

Acknowledgments

This research was conducted with the generous support of the 2016–2017 Charles Bantz Community Fellowship project "Invisible Indianapolis: Race, Heritage and Memory in the Circle City."

NINE

Binocular Vision

Making the Carceral Metropolis in Northern New Jersey

CHRISTOPHER N. MATTHEWS

> Whiteness is blindness. It is the wish not to see what it will not know.
> *Michael Eric Dyson, 2016*

In an op-ed for the *New York Times* titled "Death in Black and White," Michael Eric Dyson (2016), a prominent scholar and critic of race in America, expressed and contextualized the rage of the black community that came in response to recent police violence. The violent acts he spoke of included police shootings of unarmed African American men and the retaliation by black shooters in both Dallas and Baton Rouge.[1] Dyson took that moment to reflect on what he thought was not addressed in the effort to make "real racial progress" in America. For him, the key issue is the unacknowledged material results of white privilege. Speaking directly to whites, Dyson wrote: "At birth, you are given a pair of binoculars that see black life from a distance, never with the texture of intimacy. Those are privilege; they are status, regardless of your class. In fact, the greatest privilege that exists is for white folk to get stopped by a cop and not end up dead when the encounter is over" (Dyson 2016).

Dyson's metaphorical reference to binoculars captures the spatial reality of America's racial groups; residing in different places, they see one another only across gulfs of spatial, social, and cultural difference. Of course, those holding the binoculars in his story are white. As a group, whites isolate themselves in advantageous positions to surveil and contain nonwhite communities. To make his point clear, Dyson references white concerns over "black-on-black" crime, noting, "It is not best understood as black-on-black crime; rather, it is neighbor-to-neighbor carnage. If their neighbors were white, they'd get no exemption from the crime that plagues human beings who happen to be black. If you want interracial killing, you have to have interracial communities" (Dyson 2016). Interracial communities would eliminate the need for binoculars, since whites, African Americans, Latinos, Asians, and others would see each other face to face, as neighbors, and thus as people equally invested in the well-being of their shared community. This paper examines how segregated metropolitan communities developed in late twentieth-century America. My argument furthermore is that segregation has entailed not only racial separation but also the cultivation of distinct and unequal experiences that mirror the structure of the prison.

Echoing Lyndon Johnson's observation from fifty years earlier, Ta-Nehisi Coates (2016) argues that that black poverty is still not the same as white poverty. He shows that black families live in concentrated areas of poverty (that is, where 40 percent of the households live below the poverty line) at rates four times greater than their white counterparts (Jargowsky 2015). In addition, "the majority of black people in this country (66%) live in high-poverty neighborhoods [while] the vast majority of whites (94%) do not." Layered over differences in black and white poverty are disproportionate experiences of violence, police surveillance, and incarceration. In Chicago, "the incarceration rate in the most afflicted black neighborhood is *40 times worse* than the incarceration rate in the most afflicted white neighborhood. . . . There is no gradation, nor overlap between the two. It is almost as if, from the perspective of mass incarceration, black and white people—regardless of neighborhood—inhabit two 'fundamentally distinct' worlds" (Coates 2016; emphasis in original). Coates's articulation of racial separation, concentrated poverty, and extreme differences in incarceration provides a powerful vantage point for reflecting on the racial isolation inherent to the urban African American experience.

This chapter considers how such fundamentally distinct worlds emerge and affect the people who inhabit them. The focus is a historical and material portrait of communities in Essex County, New Jersey, which cohered as a starkly segregated metropolitan region after the 1950s (Figure 9.1). Newark is the urban center of Essex County, but I show that the center has expanded to include neighboring towns and cities to create a majority nonwhite urban core that effectively contains the poor. A series of autonomous suburban towns surrounds the core. Supported by the institution of home rule, these majority-white suburban enclaves reserve the privilege of looking through the binoculars rather than being the subject of their gaze. The result is a highly segregated settlement pattern with

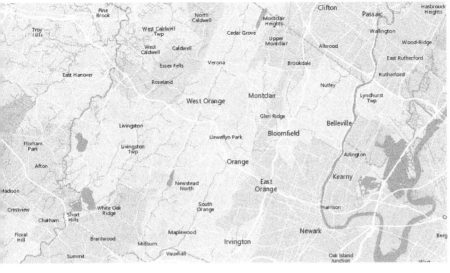

FIGURE 9.1 Map of Essex County, New Jersey, showing townships and the route of I-280 (in white) running between Newark and East Hanover.

municipalities immediately adjacent to one another whose actual connections—quite real though largely unacknowledged—are "more tragic than what separates them" (Baldwin 1972:87).

The question is, when and how did white suburbia obtain binocular vision? As an archaeologist, I focus on the material objects and forms that constitute this fractured metropolitan landscape. Specifically, this chapter is organized to describe the making of a landscape that both privileges suburban towns and experiences while imposing a carceral structure over the nonwhite urban core. A key feature of the carceral landscape in Essex County is Interstate 280, which passes through the cities of the county's urban core as it provides motorists rapid access to America's highway network and the key nodes connected to it. Reflecting on the historical and material context of I-280 provides a broader understanding of how distinct black and white worlds emerged in the region. Additionally, analyzing the materiality of its construction exposes those who find solidarity in the racial-spatial distinction (Coates 2016) and how they came to occupy a physical and mental terrain separate from their impoverished and besieged neighbors.

Reimagining the Metropolis
as a Carceral System

In "A Report from Occupied Territory," James Baldwin (1966) provides key insights into the condition of African American life in urban America and for understanding how fundamentally distinct racial worlds are symptomatic of deeper relations between white privilege and urban incarceration. His essay also provides a relevant historical perspective since Baldwin's focus is the 1960s, especially the aftermath of the Harlem Riot of 1964, which set the stage for many other urban uprisings, including the Newark Rebellion in 1967, whose effects are vital to understanding the carceral landscape that formed in Essex County. For Baldwin, the key to understanding urban black neighborhoods is the relationship of residents with the police and outsiders, especially those who engaged in the discourse about the supposed "Negro problem," which circulated widely in the public consciousness of the time. Harkening to W. E. B. Du Bois, Baldwin explains that the "Negro problem" can be easily explained as one of unemployment, inferior education, substandard and overcrowded housing, and aggressive policing—all creating and mixing with widespread frustration and hopelessness. Yet the imposition of privilege and de facto segregation allowed the rich and powerful to remain ignorant of the structural violence empowering them. Thus those with the capacity to alter the material conditions saw race as the root problem. Baldwin pins the issue on how police are used to enforce this racist standpoint:

> Now, what I have said about Harlem is true of Chicago, Detroit, Washington, Boston, Philadelphia, Los Angeles and San Francisco—is true of every Northern city with a large Negro population. And the police are simply the hired enemies of this population. *They are present to keep the Negro in his place and to protect white business interests, and they have no other function.* They are, moreover—even in a country which makes the very grave error of equating ignorance with simplicity—quite stunningly ignorant; and, since they know that they are hated, they are always afraid. One cannot possibly arrive at a more surefire formula for cruelty. (Baldwin 1966; emphasis added)

Baldwin argues that urban black communities are "occupied territories" where the police serve as a self-regulated armed force stationed to keep residents in line and have the sole legitimate right to use force when tensions overflow. But the occupied population in this case is not a vanquished foe. Rather they are fellow citizens, though they are deprived of access to necessities like decent jobs and sufficient education and housing, as well as basic rights to organize, protest, and protect their own. Moreover, they are marked as different because of race. Rather, as Baldwin notes, in the occupied territory, the police have the backing of "no-knock" and "stop-and Frisk" laws, "which permit a policeman to enter one's home without knocking and to stop anyone on the streets, at will, at any hour, and search him. Harlem believes, and I certainly agree, that these laws are directed against Negroes. They are certainly not directed against anybody else."

Baldwin makes a strong case for understanding both the economic and cultural contexts that led to violence and rioting in American cities in the 1960s. To drive this home, he lets seventeen-year-old Daniel Hamm, who was arrested, beaten, and falsely accused of murder in April 1964, explain: "They don't want us here. They don't want us—period! All they want us to do is work on these penny-ante jobs for them—and that's *it*. And beat our heads in whenever they feel like it" (Baldwin 1966; emphasis in original). Baldwin reflects: "There is a very bitter prescience in what this boy . . . is saying, and he was not born knowing it. We taught it to him in seventeen years." Baldwin concludes his essays thusly: "It is the bitterest possible comment on our situation now that the suspicion is alive in so many breasts that America has at last found a way of dealing with the Negro problem. *'They don't want us—period!'*" (Baldwin 1966; emphasis in original).

The conflict accordingly is between a powerless "ghetto" community under siege and an empowered suburban community that lives in safety. The concern is that urban and especially suburban residents have lost sight of their coexistence, that suburban safety and advantage are the result of urban decline and despair. This is why Baldwin characterized his essay as "a plea for the recognition of our common humanity [because] without this recognition, our common humanity will be proved in unutterable ways," by which he means the violence endemic in the lives of those in the occupied territories and the imminent threat of retaliation that simmers below the surface of the city.[2]

From Baldwin we gain clear evidence to propose that modern American metropolises have the qualities necessary to be considered carceral landscapes. Carceral landscapes are usually envisioned as the spaces contained in formal sites of incarceration, such as jails, prisons, asylums, workhouses, almshouses, and concentration camps (e.g., Barnes 2016; Beisaw and Gibb 2009; Camp 2016; Casella 2001a, 2007a; Garman 2005; Leone 1995; Ozawa 2016; Skiles and Clark 2010; Spencer-Wood 2009; Starzmann 2015). Key attributes of the carceral landscape include architectural forms and spatial arrangements that support the necessary distinctions between inmates, guards, administrators, visitors, and other outsiders. In broad strokes, the carceral landscape is an enclosed space meant to provide total control over inmates' lives. Prisoners are marked by distinct uniforms and housed in contained and locked cells and buildings, whose entrances and connecting paths are tightly controlled by armed patrols. Guards and administrators also have surveillance positions that afford them a controlling view of the inmate population from a distance. Towers overlooking prison borders and yards, elevated viewing platforms inside prisoner-occupied areas, and the classic form of Bentham's panopticon are architectural designs meant to physically and symbolically monopolize power and control. Outsiders enter and exit the carceral landscape in ways that closely mirror the entry of inmates. Families and loved ones, delivery persons, and contractors follow specific pathways under the direct surveillance if not accompaniment of guards. As with inmates, an outsider's time in the carceral space is also directly monitored and limited. Finally, the prison walls and internal landscape work dialectically: inasmuch as they contain the inmates, they also define the alternate landscape of freedom that inherently supports the formation of a sense of solidarity for those not incarcerated (Leone 1995). In sum, the carceral landscape is designed as a heavily controlled and bounded spatial form that is supported by supervised and restricted access and movement, and is backed up by a threat of violence that simultaneously defines both imprisonment and freedom.

We learn from Foucault (1977) and others how to see evidence of the carceral form in other private and state institutions, such as plantations (Epperson 1999), farms (Phillippi 2016), factories (Nassaney and Abel 2000), and schools (Dewan 2016), where the control and surveillance of laborers and students follow the same sorts of schematics as those used to detail the control of prison inmates. Researchers have not placed the same sort of attention on the elaboration of carceral landscapes in other settings, especially those outside institutions. Yet I argue that the model of the carceral landscape fits the late twentieth-century metropolitan urban core quite well.

This claim is similar to one made by the prominent social scientist Loïc Wacquant (2004:321), who argues that the ghetto is an "ethnoracial prison [that] encages a dishonored category and severely curtails the life chances of its members in support of the 'monopolization of ideal and material goods or opportunities' by the dominant status group (Weber 1978:935) dwelling on its outskirts." I support this assessment, but I contribute more empirical data and interpretive structure than is found in Wacquant's sweeping study of the long-term domination of African Americans. In short, the parallels between the prison and the urban core are that the majority nonwhite resident population of the occupied urban territories are the inmates, the urban police are the guards, government officials serve as the prison administrators, and those living in the suburbs, who are a majority white, are the privileged people who live in an "utterly distinct" world of freedom. The borders between the zones of incarceration and freedom are marked by stark divisions in the landscape well-known to residents and outsiders alike, and they are patrolled by both police and the overriding political and economic forces that define each place. Residents in the carceral space live under siege as they are surveilled, beaten, and killed by an armed police force that has the backing of the state. They are typically marked by color, which is used to differentiate their existence from the majority white outsiders and to serve as a badge of their supposed location of residence and potential criminality. That key aspects of this landscape can be traced to turn of the twentieth century (Abu-Lughod 2007; Du Bois 1920; Muhammad 2010) only embeds the perceived reality of the urban core by those holding the binoculars as a normal if not appropriate part of metropolitan space.

Making the Carceral Landscape in Essex County

Several processes and events coalesced in Essex County, New Jersey, to form a carceral landscape that powerfully segregates urban and suburban communities. This section reviews varied data to show the 1960s emergence of Essex County's carceral landscape and the primary mechanisms to create a marked population who live in dangerous neighborhoods controlled and surveilled by police. The majority white and "free" outsiders use one of these mechanisms—I-280—to safely travel through the carceral landscape. The city of Orange provides an important element to this story. Drawn into the urban core in the 1970s and 1980s, Orange transformed from an independent "suburban city" into one section of Essex County's incarcerated urban core.

The most dramatic event leading to regional change and segregation was a race riot in Newark in mid-July 1967. The riot, which raged for six days and was sparked by the police assault and violent arrest of African American cab driver John Smith, is remembered today as the Newark Rebellion. The violence and lootings peaked after police shot Rebecca Brown to death through a second-story window in her home (Mumford 2007; Porambo 1971:19). On the third day, New Jersey governor Richard Hughes ordered the state's almost all white National

Guard to quell the violence, which intensified the community uprising into a police riot as law enforcement upped its attacks. As witness Eric Mann recalled:

> One [riot] was started by black people and one by the State Police. The first riot was over in two days. It took a very few lives but a hell of a lot of property. The second riot was pure retribution on the part of the National Guard and State Police. For instance, in the first three days not a black store was touched . . . [in the next three days] police went to each black store and smashed in its windows. . . . The policy of the National Guard was to use the snipers . . . as an excuse to put down what they understood to be a very popular rebellion and as a result they felt that anybody in the neighborhood was fair game. (Porambo 1971:22)

In the end, twenty-six people died (twenty-four black citizens, one white police officer, and one white firefighter), more than eleven hundred people were injured, and fourteen hundred were arrested. There were 350 arsons, and law enforcement expended more than thirteen thousand rounds of ammunition (Mumford 2007:125). The riot altered the landscape of Newark substantially, in the way property and human life were destroyed but also in the way the city's population and capital base changed after whites subsequently left the city. Many think the Newark Rebellion was a violent reaction to years of state violence that put black residents at odds with the police and by extension the white community at large.

A second event in the late 1960s, though less dramatic, was just as catastrophic and transformative in the long run. This was the construction of I-280 through the urban core of Essex County (Figure 9.1). Building the concrete pathway involved the demolition of hundreds of homes, businesses, churches, and community centers; displaced thousands of people; and ultimately destroyed significant historic working-class and minority urban communities in the cities of Newark, East Orange, and Orange. The federal government and state of New Jersey proposed the new thoroughfare in the 1950s, and their efforts to relocate families and households began in the early 1960s as the state purchased properties individually and used eminent domain to take others. The state began demolishing properties in 1963 in anticipation of highway construction, which included the excavation of a deep trench through the center of both Orange and East Orange. The highway opened in 1973. Aerial photos (Figure 9.2) from 1954 and 1970 show the highway's path and the number of structures in Orange demolished by the highway.

The Newark Rebellion and I-280 made an unprecedented impact on the landscape in terms of the destruction of buildings and the uprooting and loss of lives in the urban core of Essex County. However, they should be understood

FIGURE 9.2A-B Aerial photographs of Orange from 1954 (before I-280)
and 1970 (showing I-280 under construction). Images purchased from
Nationwide Environmental Title Research, LLC.

alongside other processes of change that that also spurred the carceral landscape to emerge. To illustrate, I have compiled statistics about population and crime in Essex County between 1950 and 2010 that provide a longer view of key social trends before and after that pivotal era. I also narrate the story of a 1979 police shooting of a young African American man in Orange, extending the carceral metaphor by showing the emergence of a strained resident–police relationship in Orange that closely mirrors those of inmates and guards. I then show how I-280 provided the final pieces of the carceral landscape by supporting a sense of Orange as a ruined and dangerous place. Ultimately, the carceral landscape promotes an experience of present absence that reinforces an image of urban destitution and decline while enabling the image of suburban safety and privilege.

CREATING THE "IRON RING OF SUBURBIA" IN ESSEX COUNTY

The shifting distribution of racial groups living within distinct municipalities provides a way to document the emergence of a racially marked urban core in Essex County. As illustrated in Figure 9.3, the percentage of the population that was nonwhite in the county's urban core (Newark, East Orange, and Orange) shifted from a small minority in 1950 to a slight majority in 1970 to an overwhelming majority after 1980. Notably, 86 percent of all nonwhites in Essex County lived in the urban core in 1980 while the suburban population at the time was 79 percent white, figures revealing each section to be a racial mirror of the other. In comparison to the urban core, Montclair, a suburb neighboring Orange, had the highest percentage of nonwhite residents of any town in Essex County in 1950. The percentage of nonwhites in Montclair in subsequent decades, however, increased at a much slower rate, with a lower total (the highest percentage being 40 percent in 2000) than in the county's urban core, where the nonwhite population in all cities exceeded 80 percent by 1990. In fact, the percentage of nonwhites in Montclair declined after 2000, the reverse of the continuing upward trends in the urban core.

In 2010 the regional population changed in an interesting way as the cities of the urban core accounted for only 65 percent of all nonwhites in the county. This decrease in the percentage of nonwhites living in the urban core is the result of a substantial increase in nonwhites moving to close-by suburbs such as Irvington, whose population grew from 47 to 97 percent nonwhite between 1980 and 2010, as well as South Orange, Maplewood, Bloomfield, and Belleville, which each saw the nonwhite population grow to account for more than 40 percent of its people. It is notable that despite the increase in nonwhites living in these

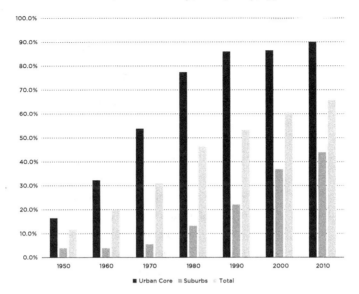

Nonwhites as a percentage of population in the urban core
and suburbs, Essex County, New Jersey, 1950–2010

■ Urban Core   ▓ Suburbs   ░ Total

FIGURE 9.3 The urban core in Essex County consists of Newark, East Orange, and Orange. Suburbs include West Orange, Montclair, Belleville, Bloomfield, Caldwell, Cedar Grove, Essex Fells, Fairfield, Glen Ridge, Livingston, Maplewood, Millburn, North Caldwell, Nutley, Roseland, South Orange, Verona, and West Caldwell. With the exception of Belleville, Bloomfield, and Nutley, these towns did not have the twenty-five thousand residents required to be included in county and city data books. To determine the number of nonwhites living in these towns in 1950, 1960, and 1970, the total number of nonwhites recorded for larger towns and cities was subtracted from the total number of whites recorded as living in all of Essex County. Data indicating the number of nonwhites living in each Essex County municipality were reproduced in the New Jersey data book for the 1980 census and later. Sources: US Bureau of the Census (1952, 1962, 1967, 1972, 1977); Center for Government Services (2016).

suburban towns, the suburbs in Essex County overall remained majority white (56 percent of all residents) and even more notable that the percentage of whites in the county overall who lived in the suburbs in fact increased from 79 percent in 1980 to 86 percent in 2010. These figures also show that the majority of whites in Essex County in 2010 lived in the farther, large-white-majority western suburbs located across First Mountain, which has long served as a natural barrier to urban expansion.

Another way to statistically document the emergence of the carceral landscape is to track crime statistics in the region through time. The FBI's uniform crime reporting statistics (US Department of Justice 2016) provide counts of various offences recorded by police. To represent changes in Essex County, I collected crime data in ten-year intervals between 1950 and 2010 for the small city of Orange, suburban Montclair, and the urban center Newark. Montclair is roughly the same size as Orange, though it has always been considered a suburb, while Orange has always been a small "suburban" city. Newark, a large city, has always been significantly larger than both Orange and Montclair. One factor important in this analysis is that there are historically lower crime rates in suburbs and small cities compared to larger cities.

Data in Table 9.1 show that Orange shifted from having crime statistics closer to those of suburban Montclair in 1950 and 1960 to having statistics that are virtually the same as Newark after 1990. This change is especially evident in violent crimes and the percentage of the population who were victims of violent crime. In 1950, for example, only 2.7 percent of crimes in Montclair were violent, and they affected just 0.02 percent of the town's residents. In Orange, 9.4 percent of crimes were violent; they affected only 0.07 percent of the population. In Newark in 1950, 14.0 percent of all crimes were violent, and they affected 0.21 percent of the population. These figures match what is expected, with the suburb (Montclair) being safer than the small city (Orange) and the small city being safer than the large city (Newark). In 1970 the number of violent crimes and the percentage of those affected in each community grew, but the same and expected differences between the types of towns were maintained. In 1990 there was a noticeable change in crime patterns as the percentage of violent crime declined in Montclair and remained stable in Newark, while violent crime increased in Orange. This trend continued such that by 2010 the percentage of crimes that were violent remained almost unchanged in Montclair and Newark but had risen to 23 percent in Orange. The intensification of violent crime in Orange is also evident in the figures reflecting the percentage of the population affected by violent crime in each community. In 1950 and 1970, residents of Orange were about 3.5 times as likely as residents of Montclair to be victims of violent crime. By 1990 this ratio had grown slightly, such that residents of Orange were four times as likely to be victims of violent crime. By 2010 the ratio had grown further: Orange residents were 5.5 times as likely as those living in Montclair to be victims of violent crime. In fact, as of 2000, residents of Orange were more likely to be victims of violent crime than residents of Newark.

These figures objectively show a rapid transformation of Orange within the

TABLE 9.1

Crime Data for Select Cities and Towns in Essex County, New Jersey, 1950–2010

	POPULATION	TOTAL CRIMES	VIOLENT CRIME	PERCENT	PROPERTY CRIME	PERCENT	CRIME/POP	VIOLENT CRIME/POP	PRPERTY CRIME/POP
1950									
Montclair	39,807	295	8	2.70%	287	97.30%	0.70%	0.02%	0.70%
Orange	38,037	286	27	9.40%	259	90.60%	0.80%	0.07%	0.70%
Newark	438,776	6643	935	14.10%	5708	85.90%	1.50%	0.21%	1.30%
1960									
Montclair	43,129	525	11	2.10%	514	97.90%	1.20%	0.03%	1.20%
Orange	35,789	597	43	7.20%	554	92.80%	1.70%	0.12%	1.50%
Newark	405,220	23217	3241	14.00%	19976	86.00%	5.70%	0.80%	4.90%
1970									
Montclair	44,043	1356	172	12.70%	1184	87.30%	3.10%	0.39%	2.70%
Orange	32,566	2305	413	17.90%	1892	82.10%	7.10%	1.27%	5.80%
Newark	382,417	40063	9630	24.00%	30433	76.00%	10.50%	2.52%	8.00%
1980									
Montclair	38,301	2347	84	3.60%	2263	96.40%	6.10%	0.22%	5.90%
Orange	31,106	4125	733	17.80%	3392	82.20%	13.30%	2.36%	10.90%
Newark	329,298	45107	11484	25.50%	33623	74.50%	13.70%	3.49%	10.20%
1990									
Montclair	37,729	2272	209	9.20%	2063	90.80%	6.00%	0.55%	5.50%
Orange	29,925	3422	651	19.00%	2771	81.00%	11.40%	2.18%	9.30%
Newark	275,221	44739	10684	23.90%	34055	76.10%	16.30%	3.88%	12.40%
2000									
Montclair	38,977	1310	101	7.70%	1209	92.30%	3.40%	0.26%	3.10%
Orange	32,868	2749	550	20.00%	2199	80.00%	8.40%	1.67%	6.70%
Newark	273,546	19663	4092	20.80%	15571	79.20%	7.20%	1.50%	5.70%
2010									
Montclair	37,669	705	75	10.60%	630	89.40%	1.90%	0.20%	1.70%
Orange	30,134	1430	335	23.40%	1095	76.60%	4.70%	1.11%	3.60%
Newark	277,140	12094	2885	23.90%	9209	76.10%	4.40%	1.04%	3.30%

Source: US Department of Justice, Federal Bureau of Investigation, Uniform Crime Reporting Statistics.

larger region. A small city of about 35,000 people concentrated within 2.2 square miles, Orange is significantly denser (about 15,000 people per square mile) and more urban than neighboring Montclair (6,450 people per square mile). Population density in Orange is comparable to Newark, which has maintained a density of about 14,500 people per square mile since 1950. The similar crime rate in Orange and Montclair before the Newark Rebellion and the opening of I-280 is thus quite remarkable given the much higher population density of Orange. That the crime rates in Orange quickly matched and then exceeded the crime rates in Newark after 1970 is one testament to the decline of the city, especially in the era after I-280 opened in 1973 and the subsequent expansion of the urban core.

To broaden this analysis, I also compiled crime statistics for East Orange, situated between Newark and Orange, and West Orange, which is on the other side of Orange. Both of these communities were also impacted and divided by the construction of I-280, though West Orange was relatively less developed at the time of the construction so the impact of the interstate was not as pronounced. In addition, the Orange–West Orange boundary is marked by the steep elevation climb up First Mountain, which has long served as a natural border between the eastern low-lying and western upland settlements (Pope 2001).

Crime data from East Orange show that the figures for total crime and violent crime were better than those in what was then a more densely settled Orange in 1950 and 1960. However, there was a significant jump in the crime rate in East Orange, which matched and surpassed the figures for Orange in violent crimes and in the likelihood that an East Orange resident would be the victim of a violent crime. East Orange and Orange remained comparable after 1970, by 2010 having barely distinguishable violent crime rates that more than doubled the figures for nearby suburban Montclair. In contrast, the crime figures for suburban West Orange trended closer to those for Montclair. In both Montclair and West Orange there were very low figures for violent crime in the 1950s and 1960s, followed by a slight increase to a new plateau after 1970, when violent crimes rose to about 7 to 8 percent of all crimes, affecting 0.2 to 0.3 percent of residents each year. Both of these figures are significantly lower than those for Newark, East Orange, and Orange.

The upshot of this analysis of population and crime statistics is an overview of the historical creation after 1970 of an expanded urban core region in Essex County along the I-280 corridor, accompanied by an increasingly sharp urban–suburban distinctions in terms of the racial makeup of the communities and their experience of violent crime. The urban core of Newark, East Orange, and

Orange can be defined today as having high-density settlement, an overwhelming majority nonwhite population, and a higher frequency of violent crime. Suburban towns surrounding the core exhibit the opposite trend, with low-density settlement, a majority white population, and a lower frequency of violent crime. As noted above, this urban–suburban distinction was not nearly as pronounced in the region before the Newark Rebellion and the construction of I-280 in the late 1960s. Rather, Orange and East Orange shifted from having crime figures that lay between those of Newark and the suburban towns from 1950 to 1970 to figures essentially indistinguishable from Newark's after 1990. Recognizing this process allows a view on how the carceral landscape formed through time by eliminating the middle sorts of communities between the city and suburbs in favor of a stark dualistic settlement system consisting of an urban core surrounded by an "iron ring of suburbia" (Paul Ylvisaker in Mumford 2007:100).

BLACK, WHITE, AND ORANGE

In addition to population changes and crime statistics that demonstrate the creation of a starkly segregated landscape in Essex County over the last fifty years, another key component of the carceral landscape is the establishment of a police force used to control the urban population. One measure of police activity can be found in incarceration rates for Essex County, which show a sharp disparity by race (Vera Institute of Justice 2017). Countywide, the difference in incarnation rates for African Americans after 1990 ranged from six to eighteen times greater than those for whites. These figures are based on a racial disparity in incarceration in which the approximately even population of both groups (about 40 percent of the total) is unevenly matched by the representation of each racial group in the incarcerated population, which is an average of 77 percent African American versus only 7.5 percent white. Unfortunately, data for segments smaller than the county level are not available. So I consider other source information to understand the dynamic of policing in communities within Essex County, specifically concerning tensions between police and the black community in Orange.

   I have already discussed James Baldwin's highly negative characterization of police-community relations in Harlem and their role in the riot there in 1964. Similar assessments of police overreach and violence against nonwhites have also been noted in multiple studies of the 1967 Newark Rebellion (e.g., Mumford 2007; Porambo 1971) as well as uprisings in many other American cities in the late 1960s (National Advisory Commission on Civil Disorders 1968). To further this analysis, I discuss another example of police violence that almost led to a riot in Orange in 1979. The purpose here is not just to tell another tragic story but to show the effects of how the "suburban city" of Orange was folded into the urban core of Essex County during the decade after the Newark Rebellion and the opening of I-280. Based on observations of city residents, it is apparent that the police were mistrusted by the black community. It is also clear that the tensions that resulted are connected to other factors that were leaving Orange in ruins at the time.

The shooting by two Orange police officers on October 31, 1979, resulted in the death of seventeen-year-old Darrell Walker. Walker was shot in his car after a four-mile chase that started when he ran a red light and ended when he lost control of the car and crashed into a tree. When the two Orange police officers approached the disabled car, Walker supposedly "reached for something shiny," at which point the officers fired their weapons and shot the youth five times. They then handcuffed his lifeless body to an ambulance gurney for transport to East Orange General Hospital, where he was pronounced dead (Bolger 1979a). Parallels with the police shooting deaths of other youths in Newark can be made, but the similarities are greater than the race, ages, and circumstances of death of these young men. Shared aspects are also found in the community's response.

In the week after Walker died, the black community in Orange protested to "express support for the Walker family, and outrage at the attitudes of police and public officials" (Bolger 1979b). The protests peaked on November 5, after Walker's funeral service, with a "stormy meeting" of eight hundred to one thousand people at city hall, who came to hear speakers James Cosby and Morris Thomas of the NAACP, the Reverend Buster Soaries of the New Jersey Leadership Institute, and the Reverend George Ryder of People United to Save Humanity. Among the demands, Cosby called for the resignation of the white mayor, the entire city council, and the police director in Orange "for allowing the city to deteriorate" (Bolger 1979b). The Reverend Russell White delivered one of the most powerful statements: "We are just insignificant people, but we'll boycott every business along Main Street. And when we just stop spending our insignificant dollars in the City of Orange, the City of Orange will become insignificant overnight" (Bolger 1979b). Following the rally, protesters stormed the mayor's office to begin a three-day sit-in to express their outrage. Those inside were supported by protestors holding vigil on the sidewalk out front.

The occupation of the mayor's office ended on November 9 when an Essex County grand jury failed to indict the police officers who shot Walker. After this decision, which was greeted by "jeers, tears, and disbelief" (Bolger 1979c), the community resumed protests outside city hall and later at a rally at Saint Paul's

AME Church and again the next evening at Mount Olive Baptist Church in East Orange. Soaries spoke at both rallies and led a call for state and federal attorneys to review the case again. Eventually the state took the case, but its grand jury also failed to indict the officers. Soaries noted that he worked extremely hard to calm the emotions of "factions pressing for a violent reaction to the grand jury's decision" (Bolger 1979c). Clearly, the ingredients were in place for a riot in Orange.

The frustrating struggles with police that helped provoke the rebellion in Newark in the 1960s stoked similar feelings in the black community in Orange. Farid Saunders (1979) described his take in a letter to the *Orange Transcript*: "Nationwide statistical evidence indicates that over 70 per cent of all people killed by cops are black! Suppose Walker had been a white youth in [suburban] Milburn or Short Hills and 'fleeing the police' . . . not even the tires of his car would have been shot at!" In another letter, Elsie Jones (1979) wrote:

> Yes, let's face it—white cops can go around killing black Americans without anything being done. But if a black cop killed a white boy, don't you know that he would have been fired from the force? . . . Some policemen do not need to become cops, because they are sick individuals. . . . Some people are just too naïve to see that some policemen are sick, sick, sick and need psychiatric help. Being a policeman does not exempt one from needing help. Being a policeman does not exempt one from obeying the law. And surely, being a policeman does not mean that one can go around killing people without paying the price one day. (Jones 1979)

Jones's call for psychiatric testing and evaluation was in fact part of the demands that protestors put to the mayor earlier in the week. As the Reverend Harry Batts stated, they need to "stop allowing men to carry guns through the community with the intent of discharging them at the slightest provocation" (Bolger 1979b).

Critique of police actions was paired with palpable fears of the police in the black community. Morris Thomas said that the failure of the state's grand jury made it "open season on blacks, especially in Orange" (*Orange Transcript* 1980). African American city councilman Ben Jones noted that "death came to Darrell Walker as a hunted animal" (Bolger 1979b). In a speech at the YWCA, Soaries (Bolger 1980) stated that "right now in Orange the average black person is afraid of being stopped by the local police, afraid of what could happen to them. When taxpayers of a city have to live in fear because of the Police Department, that is a sick city." With eloquence, Soaries declared that "laws facilitate, but they cannot reconciliate. You can change laws, but you cannot change what exists in a man's heart." A particularly potent sense of these feelings was noted in an anonymous letter to the *Orange Transcript*. It stated, "We as black people are in a life and death struggle for survival. We are locked in a mortal combat with our oppressors." The writer concluded, "My frustration was summed up by an old man [after the Walker shooting protests]. He said 'I'll see you at the next one.' Ominous words." (*Orange Transcript* 1979a).

Amid the news coverage of Darrell Walker's death and subsequent protests, other stories in the *Orange Transcript* described related problems frustrating African Americans. Just after the Walker shooting, former African American city council candidate Mims Hackett was exonerated after serving three years in prison for a 1976 kidnapping he did not commit. The story was featured on *60 Minutes* in November 1979 in a report that showed how white police officers orchestrated the fabricated kidnapping to undermine Hackett's election bid and to clear a path to the election of another white officer (Bolger 1979d; Gunin 1979; UPI 1986). Also in November 1979, William Cook, one of the first African American disc jockeys in America and owner of a grocery store on Hickory Street, was arrested for purchasing stolen goods (*Orange Transcript* 1979b). The circumstances of this crime were questioned since Cook was a vocal advocate of Mims Hackett in the *60 Minutes* report. It was suggested that Cook's arrest was in retaliation for his anti-police statements.

Given these traumatic race and police relations incidents in November 1979, Orange residents were rightfully on edge into the new year. The former head of the Orange chamber of commerce, George E. Englert, captured these feelings in "Black, White, and Orange," a January 10, 1980, op-ed in the *Orange Transcript*. There he characterized these events "as a one-two punch" for the city. He also reiterated Russell White's statement that Orange was "sitting in the middle of a Hurricane . . . as members of the black community have no confidence in the police department or the system of justice in this town" (Englert 1980).

While Englert's essay was an explicit attempt to quell hard feelings, correct misinformation, and return normalcy to the city, he opened his piece by saying that "none of us needs to be reminded of the several large companies that left Orange in the recent decade [1970s], adversely effecting employment opportunities, the general economic viability of the community, and the increased taxes that must be shared by those of us who still live and work in Orange" (Englert 1980). Two of those companies were the Monroe Calculator Company (closed in 1975), which employed as many as seven hundred people, and the Rheingold Brewery (closed in 1977), which employed about six hundred workers. These factory closings are still remembered in the city today, since the urban landscape bears the ruins of these and many other abandoned factories. In fact, the factory closings are better remembered than Darrell Walker's shooting, probably because of these ruined physical reminders. Still, the near riot after Walker's shooting and the closing of the factories are two sides of the same coin in the formation of the carceral landscape that developed in Orange in the 1970s. Each provides evidence of the decimation of the city such that it lost the resources that sustain prosperity and safety, and it became instead a place of ruin and violence noticeably distinct from the towns surrounding it. The last piece in this story is the particular role of I-280 as a material agent of destructive change.

INTERSTATE 280 AS A CARCERAL ARTIFACT

During an interview session with a group of former Orange residents from the city's historic Italian American community, Anthony Battista yelled across the crowded room, with palpable vitriol, "280 ruined Orange!" As everyone in the room agreed, it became more than clear to me that the highway is seen as a powerful agent on the landscape of the city, both past and present. This meaning was typically expressed as a loss or a feeling that there was something special in Orange that the highway itself took away. Of course, the highway was designed and constructed by people and is itself not the perpetrator, but it is nevertheless treated as one because of the way it reminds former residents of how their communities were destroyed. Yet the highway's impact on the landscape in Orange is not just as a "memory-scape" of loss. It has at least two other faces, or materialities, that residents deal with every day. One is a "highway-scape" that consists of the street surfaces adjacent to and over the highway. Where there used to be homes, stores, churches, and community centers, there is now a spatial void consisting of concrete, asphalt, chain-link fencing, and high-speed traffic. Another is the "motorist-scape" that runs below the surface of the city, at the same time cutting through its very heart. This is defined in the experience of Orange for those traveling on the highway. Understanding how the city coexists and interacts with motorists on the highway brings particular clarity to processes by which Orange was folded into Essex County's carceral core.

THE MEMORY-SCAPE IN ORANGE The construction of I-280 involved the demolition of more than two hundred structures in the center of Orange, and the African American and Italian American communities were most directly impacted. In interviews with former residents from both communities, happy memories and strong feelings are mobilized to reconstruct a dynamic and successful city before the interstate was built, as well as an understanding of what specifically was lost that led to its decline.[3]

On the stretch of Oakwood Avenue that crosses over 1-280 today used to stand the "colored" YMCA and YWCA (Figure 9.4). On the north side of Parrow Street where the highway now runs is the former location of the Friendship House. The Colgate, also known as the Italian YMCA, was on the former Hurlbut Street. These institutions were community anchors, and their loss is remembered among the most important factors leading to decline and abandonment. Past residents note with certainty that these institutions held their communities together by offering a place for children and adults to go for a wide range of social and athletic activities. Italian American former residents also recalled that the Italian Y took kids to the YMCA's Camp Arrowhead, a subsidized summer camp near the Jersey shore. Gordon Roberts grew up down the street from the "colored" Ys. He recalled being so tired after playing basketball and other sports there that there was "no time to get into trouble." Walter Preston credits the "colored" YMCA with teaching him "how to be a man," because "all [the] leadership people came through that Y. All professional people, all the Doctors and Dentists were there." At the YMCA young African Americans shared the locker room with men dressed in suits and ties and could see what successful people looked like and learn from them directly. Gordon Roberts credits the relationships he built at the YMCA with his chance to attend Howard University on a scholarship provided by one of the community's leading African American families. Losing the YMCA and YWCA meant losing access to community leaders, since these adults left the community after 1-280 came through. Like Anthony Battista, Preston concludes that "280 destroyed our community. Point blank. It destroyed us as a people here."

Former residents also speak about the loss of local businesses that provided a foothold for minority groups. Mildred Harris, Gordon Roberts, and Goldie Burbage recall several African American–owned businesses lost to the highway, including Whitlock's sweet shop, Golden's general store, Titian's pool room, Reed's temple, Shorty's barbershop, and Brownie's hot dog stand, all located on Oakwood, Parrow, and Hickory Streets. Similar sorts of businesses were lost in the Italian neighborhood, though there were also Italian-owned butcher shops that served both communities. Some Italian-owned businesses, such as Trezza's junkyard and Rossi Paints, still operate in Orange, though they moved to new locations after the highway was built. These small businesses were all family owned and the families were Orange residents. Some, such as the Modugno family,

FIGURE 9.4 Detail of a Franklin Survey Company plate showing the location of the "colored" YMCA along Oakwood Avenue in Orange, 1932. The YWCA was part of a complex in the small building south of Charles Saver Inc. Downloaded from Historic Map Works, Rare Historic Maps Collection, http://www.historicmapworks.com.

which lived in an apartment above John's Market, lived in the same neighborhood as their businesses. But while John's Market, Rossi Paints, Trezza's junkyard, and even the African American–owned Cotton and Woody funeral homes are still in business, none of the business owners still live in Orange.

Shorty's barbershop, formerly on Hickory Street, was both a business and a community center. Shorty's was established by Morris Thomas Sr., who moved to Orange from North Carolina in 1930. He was a college-educated minister who served as associate pastor at Bethany Church in Newark. Like most African American ministers, Thomas worked other jobs to support his family, which is how he came to open a barbershop. Being educated and devout, Thomas set up a library in the back of the barbershop for the community to use. He also encouraged people to stop in for not just haircuts but also intellectual and political discussion. Thomas raised his children in the shop, training his son Morris Thomas Jr., who took over in 1957 in both business and politics. Thomas Jr. worked with

FIGURE 9.5 Exterior of Shorty's barbershop on Hickory Street in Orange. This picture was taken during the 1963 election campaign. Shorty's was the campaign headquarters for Ray Murphy and the Nonpartisan Organization for Liberal Action (NOLA). Courtesy Rebecca Doggett.

the NAACP and ran for public office several times in the 1950s and 1960s. The barbershop was his base of operations (Figure 9.5).

After a series of protests and actions led by African Americans, a new city charter was put in place in Orange in 1960 in an attempt to dismantle racial segregation (Thompson and Thompson 1976). The new charter established a ward system that helped the first African American be elected to the city council in 1962. Shorty's became the headquarters for the candidacy of Ray Murphy, supported by the Nonpartisan Organization for Liberal Action (NOLA). According to Thomas Jr. and Rebecca Doggett, NOLA was an interracial group of "young radicals" who had met each other in church, NAACP meetings, and as customers at the barbershop. They had good reasons for backing Murphy, but this put them at odds with older, more established African Americans who had led the fight for the charter change. In the end Murphy lost to Ben Jones, the candidate backed by the older group. Still, Shorty's offered opportunities for learning and engaging in local politics—opportunities lost when the barbershop was torn down to make way for I-280.

The diverse communities where young people interacted with older people of different class backgrounds were wiped away after I-280 as the community's professionals and skilled workers left the city. Dr. Walter Alexander II, a dentist, moved to South Orange in the mid-1960s. He was the son of Dr. Royal Alexander, also a dentist and the great-nephew of Dr. Walter Alexander Sr., a physician and in 1921 the first African American elected to the New Jersey State Legislature (Rutgers Oral History Archives 2009). The Alexander brothers were the dentist and physician for many African Americans interviewed in this study. Frank McClain, a camera operator at a Newark television station, moved to Orange in 1951 and moved again to Union as the city declined. Many middle-class Italian families also left. Paul Ianiro, who took over his father's excavation business, moved to West Orange in the mid-1960s. Paul Modugno, who took over John's Market from his father, moved to Caldwell in 1969. Debbie Freda Gallo moved to West Orange in 1976 to start her adult life after living in Orange for her first twenty-three years. Even Anthony Benevento, who was a police officer in Orange for twenty-five years and police director from 1998 to 2008, moved to West Orange around the time I-280 opened.

The loss of these middle-class families drained the two neighborhoods of the men and women who would have otherwise served as role models for the next generation. Moreover, as many of these men and women were born in Orange and were the children of successful business owners, they took with them both the financial capital and intangible social and cultural qualities that second-generation "native" elites bring to local communities as they come of age. Many of these people either left Orange behind or became absentee business owners, increasingly disconnected from and disinterested in their old neighborhoods. As Fran McClain, Frank McClain's daughter, noted, her childhood neighborhood and the memories associated with it were "erased" and replaced with a "sterile" neighborhood after I-280 opened and the leading families left.

It is worth noting that the loss of these communities in Orange also fed into the intensifying racial segregation in the region. Every member of the Italian community interviewed left Orange and moved west, essentially following the path of I-280 into West Orange, Caldwell, and Livingston. Being white, Italian families were welcomed in the suburban developments built over the mountain. In fact, Paul Ianiro's company was successful in large part because it excavated the basements for many of these new homes. That said, Ianiro also expressed great regret about leaving Orange. He was convinced by friends and family to move to a new home in West Orange, but he missed knowing his neighbors and especially the camaraderie of his home community. In contrast, many African Americans moved east to East Orange or Newark, or like Walter Preston and Gordon Roberts they stayed in Orange, leaving only after they retired. Thus, even though there were middle-class families in both the African American and Italian communities, the post-280 choices regarding where to move were quite distinct, if not restricted, as people of color remained in the urban core while whites left for the suburbs.

As an agent of memory, I-280 provides few positive stories for past and present residents of Orange. It marks an end of an era remembered for its happiness, prosperity, and successful communities, none of which are thought to still exist in Orange. To some extent this is objectively true, as the city is poorer and more fragmented than it was. However, the negativity of the narrative has its own materiality in the way it seems hard for people see Orange as a city with promise. Rather, Orange is seen as a ruin, a place whose time has passed. Of course, one source of this narrative is comparison with the suburban communities to the west where many of the Italian Americans eventually settled. While many miss the neighborhood in Orange, they did leave and never returned except to visit. One reason was what became of their neighborhoods after I-280 opened.

THE HIGHWAY-SCAPE   In the place of diverse, well-rounded, and historic minority communities, the landscape of I-280 in Orange today is a monolithic void. This highway-scape is defined by the sunken highway route, Freeway Drives East and West (service roads that run parallel to the highway), and a series of overpasses for north–south streets that preexisted the highway (Figure 9.6). The highway-scape is a physically and socially empty space made of asphalt, concrete, chain-link fencing, and a few small grass patches where short sections (and reminders) of former streets such as South and Parrow Streets can still be found. The buildings along the two Freeway Drives face the side streets rather than fronting the highway. These materials and arrangements make the highway-scape seem like a scar or an unhealed wound, since in the heart of Orange there is now a space that people have turned their backs on. Like the ruined factories found nearby, no one wants to be in the highway-scape because there is nothing for them there. At best people hurry across the bridges to reach the other side. In fact, the desolation inherent to the highway-scape has divided the city, as people living on either side of the highway grow distant as they face away from each other.

A prime example of the way the highway-scape is now a distinct material space is the tragic death of African American police officer Joyce Carnegie in 1999.

FIGURE 9.6 The Hickory Street bridge over I-280 in Orange, New Jersey. Photo by Christopher N. Matthews.

Carnegie, a native of Orange, was shot while she attempted to question a criminal suspect. She died from the gunshot wounds next to her cruiser on Freeway Drive West near the corner of South Day Street. As the *New York Times* described the incident, "She approached a man who fit the description of the suspect at the intersection of South Day Street and Freeway Drive West, near an overpass of Interstate 280, a strip of decrepit vacant storefronts and a go-go bar called Rah-Rah's" (Newman 1999). Carnegie was the first police officer in Orange to be killed on duty in thirty-five years. A memorial (Figure 9.7) erected at the site of her death includes her service photograph, which, as she keeps a virtual watch, makes her the only person actually in and looking over the otherwise empty highway-scape in the center of Orange. Notably, the area around the memorial remains much the same as it was described in 1999.

THE MOTORIST-SCAPE A third landscape feature of I-280 is the experience of Orange from the highway itself, or the motorist-scape. Passing through Orange, motorists have no reason to notice that they are in the city at all. The highway is

FIGURE 9.7 Memorial for Officer Joyce Carnegie, Freeway Drive West, Orange, New Jersey. Photo by Christopher N. Matthews.

three dozen feet below the street surface in the city, and there are just two exits into Orange, one heading east and one heading west. The city lies above the highway and is mostly out of sight except for the seven bridges that cross over (Figure 9.5). These, of course, are enclosed by chain-link fencing that contributes to the desolate highway-scape in the city itself. Yet the highway does not pass through a marginal part of the city; it goes right through its heart, two blocks south of Main Street and the NJ Transit railroad tracks. The present absence of motorists in the city is thus highly pronounced given that they are really in the center of the city as they pass through.

Yet there is more to the motorist-scape's experiential materiality. An important factor is the role of highways like I-280 in America more generally. Paul Hoffman of the Studebaker Corporation wrote in 1940, "In highways . . . lies a new frontier for the pessimist who thinks frontiers have disappeared. It challenges the imagination and spirit of enterprise which always have been the distinctive marks of American life" (Rose and Mohl 2012:1). Hoffman captures here a core part of the American identity, its basis in expansion and the claiming of new "frontier" lands that found a renewed expression in the suburbs after World War II (Jackson 1985). Those passing through Orange embody this identity as they use the highway to navigate the space between a suburban home and an urban workplace.

Arguably this is the most significant result of I-280, if not its true purpose. I-280 was the first and only major route to pass over First Mountain. All previous transportation routes had been stymied. This includes the commuter train line, which, heading out of the city, turns sharply south at the base of the mountain. The lack of any path over the mountain is also evident in the very small populations of the towns west of Orange in Essex County until after I-280 opened. However, a mountain is no match for an interstate, especially if that path opens to a suburban frontier. In this case, the path for I-280 was created by blasting away a passage over the mountain, producing so much rubble that a temporary train line was built along the highway path to haul it away.

I-280 was built to provide a rapid route between Newark and points west. However, as these western places were new suburbs, I-280 also effectively drained the white populations of Newark and later East Orange and Orange. Yet despite the open passage via the interstate, racial covenants, loan restrictions, and other racist attitudes and actions kept nonwhites from flowing out of the cities as well (Jackson 1985; Massey and Denton 1993). Instead, the mountain remains an effective barrier only to nonwhites. Moreover, lacking a way to engage the modern suburban frontier, nonwhite Americans were denied the essence of Hoffman's sense of being American. Rather, they have been held captive in the urban core, at best witnesses to what free people in America are able to do beyond limits of their urban incarceration.

I-280 has thus replaced the African American and Italian American neighborhoods with a vacant, dangerous, and uncaring landscape. Like prisoners, the residents are provided only a minimally functional space to survive. There is housing and corridors for human and vehicle traffic, but the space itself is not conducive to dwelling. Rather, people want to or are expected to be on the move and in some cases at very high speeds. Unlike the welcoming homes, stores, and community centers that occupied the same spaces previously, the current landscapes of I-280 are designed so that people do not want to be there.

Discussion

This chapter has compiled and reviewed several sources of data to show the transformation of communities in Essex County, New Jersey, since the 1950s. The result has been the creation of a settlement system consisting of a densely packed urban core with an overwhelming majority nonwhite population suffering with high crime and poverty rates and a scarred landscape of ruins and loss surrounded by suburban, majority-white municipalities with low crime and poverty rates untouched by urban renewal and highway construction. This two-faced system did not exist in the 1950s and appeared only after the construction of I-280 and white flight from the urban core, which was itself largely a negative reaction to African American resistance and militancy in the urban center after years of racist oppression. I have argued that the result was not only separation but also a form of incarceration in which the urban core took on key aspects of imprisonment, including especially a threatening police force, the use of race to mark inmates, and the disinvestment and destruction of the resources supporting community well-being. Here I consider the sense of powerlessness felt by current and former residents that came from being excluded from the opportunities whites gained in their suburban adventure.

Powerlessness was a repeated theme in interviews with former residents. Both Italian Americans and African Americans felt that I-280 happened *to* them. It was a symbol of state power and the way highway, housing, and other major urban initiatives were imposed on communities from the top down. While early planners argued that urban highways were a "'positive social good' . . . 'eating out slums' and 'reclaiming blighted areas'" (Mohl 2000:233), in Essex County, this reclamation never happened. Rather, I-280 created a "no-man's land" or "DMZ," according to Newark residents interviewed in 1986 (Jett 1986). Former Orange residents speak in the same terms about the highway in their city as they do about the factory closings after the highway opened, especially because the hulking ruins of these workplaces still stand empty in the city, and their closings also led to a sharp increase in unemployment and vacant housing. The result of the highway and its part in creating the carceral urban core is arguably how it promotes a sense of present absence, illustrated and sustained by empty buildings and homes and the dangerous voids in the urban scene that define the highway-scape.

Powerlessness is also expressed in the fear and distrust of the police that was voiced in the aftermath of Darrell Walker's shooting. The police force in this case was defined as isolated from and opposed to the local community it was supposed to serve. Rather, it was seen as yet another outside, top-down arm of the state used to control and oppress a marginal population and to cultivate a feeling of powerlessness. James Baldwin (1966) described the attitude toward police in Harlem this way: "This is why those pious calls to 'respect the law,' always to be heard from prominent citizens each time the ghetto explodes, are so obscene. The law is meant to be my servant and not my master, still less my torturer and my murderer. To respect the law, in the context in which the American Negro finds himself, is simply to surrender his self-respect" (Baldwin 1966).

Like the highway and abandoned factories, the police are another form of present absence. As people with power, and because they are a majority-white force, they do not mirror their host communities but illustrate and embody key reasons why these communities suffer.

The police play a similar role to the motorists on I-280. As noted, the motorists tearing through Orange at high speeds on the depressed section of I-280 are more than likely unaware that they are actually in the city as they pass through. There is virtually nothing to tell them they are; nor are most drivers actually even looking to know where they are as they speed to their destinations. Rather they are following a path that moves them through the urban core of Essex County without them actually ever having to be in it. This is the fiction of the highway, for drivers are always somewhere, yet they are empowered neither to need nor to care to know anything about where they are. This experience plays out as another form of present absence: while motorists on I-280 are present in Orange, this is more so another form of absence as they do not know they are even there, though the fumes and noise from their vehicles make a direct impact on the city as they pass through.

From motorists, we can expand this interpretation to the broader suburban communities surrounding the urban core, which serve in this model as the free people living outside the prison walls. A key point to remember is that there are no actual walls. Rather, the boundaries are built with other materials, notably the building blocks of municipal lines, white supremacy, and Dyson's binoculars. In New Jersey, the basis of segregation by race, class, and income, in schools and other services, is a deeply entrenched practice of home rule. Starting at the end of the nineteenth century with the Village Act of 1891 and codified in the 1917 Home Rule Act, New Jersey's 566 municipalities had firmed up their borders by the time the urban crisis was exposed in the 1960s. Home rule practices created a uniform municipal structure such that each municipality could act autonomously from others regarding local governance. In this way neighboring towns can take on quite distinct characters as they make their own rules regarding taxation, school funding, development, and other key "public" issues that often create costs of living high enough to keep the struggling and the poor out. The result is a sorted-out metropolitan landscape (Fullilove 2013; Hanchett 1998) that has divided communities into increasingly homogenous municipalities across the state. Situated within their own towns, people are less and less socially connected to neighbors living just a few miles, if not a few blocks or even few houses away. Nevertheless, municipalities remain tied together by county- and state-level governance and by virtue of being neighbors.

The step that moves this process from being about just municipal separations to being about white supremacy is when town lines are combined with historically racist practices such as redlining and racial profiling, as well as differential distributions of wealth and crime across space. The resulting segregation forms the population into "fundamentally distinct worlds" of whiteness and nonwhiteness paired with wealth and poverty and safety and crime. For those living in separate places, only binoculars provide a view of the other, but, as Dyson notes, only whites use what they see through binoculars to make sense of the difference between themselves and their struggling neighbors. Nonwhites do not need binoculars to see the differences. Rather, racialized and impoverished, they witness and struggle with the effects of racial difference every day. Dyson's binoculars serve, in other words, to symbolize the present absence of suburban whites in the urban core. With binoculars, suburban residents can see they are connected, but through home rule and white privilege they successfully preserve their distance. That is, urban residents know the present absence of whiteness in the same way that inmates know about the free people beyond the prison wall.

Epilogue: Reverse Archaeology

This chapter examines the formation and meaning of the carceral metropolis in metropolitan America, especially as it was built in Essex County, New Jersey. I owe much to my collaborators in the city of Orange whom I worked with to create "A Reverse Archaeology of Interstate 280."[4] However, this project is not only about documenting the negative impact of the interstate. Rather it is an urban intervention using history, anthropology, community engagement, and the dramatic and visual arts to recover what was lost and to project a future that tells an alternate story of the city. By "reverse archaeology," we mean to put back in Orange what the excavation done for the interstate removed, and in the process we have learned that we need to reject the many forms of powerlessness and present absence that infect the city. I describe some of these in the discussion section above. However, my collaborators have defined others, many of which I predict will lead to more productive efforts than working to redress the regional racism of home rule and municipal separation. Rather, they are documenting what is actually present in Orange, such as vibrant "new" immigrant communities, dedicated educators, survival stories, and an emergent arts community but also violent crime, abandoned buildings and homes, transit-oriented development, high taxes, and constant fiscal shortcomings and municipal conflicts. Using critical views on the past and the present, our project seeks to shed light on the chasm that separates Orange from other places but also to recognize that this chasm can be bridged. It is, in one way, as simple as asking neighbors to put down their binoculars and get to know each other face to face.

Acknowledgments

I owe a deep gratitude to my colleagues in Orange, especially those from the University of Orange who have inspired and pushed me to produce good work. This includes especially Mindy Fullilove, Aubrey Murdock, and Molly Kaufman. I have also benefited from the insights and support of other reverse archaeology colleagues, including Kate McCaffrey, Mike Malbrough, Khemani Gibson, and Rachel Bland. This research was in part funded by a grant from ArtPlace America. While this chapter in particular has been improved by editorial suggestions from Zoë Burkholder, Paul Mullins, and Brad Phillippi, all errors and omissions are my own responsibility.

Notes

1. Alton B. Sterling was shot by a police officer in Baton Rouge, Louisiana, on July 5, 2016, and Philando Castile was shot by an officer in Saint Paul, Minnesota, on July 6, 2016. On July 7, 2016, Micah Xavier Johnson shot five police officers in Dallas, and on July 17, 2016, Gavin Eugene Long shot six police officers in Baton Rouge.
2. It is notable that Baldwin's use of the term *occupied territory* repeats language used in the mayor's commission report produced after a riot in Harlem in 1935. It "singled out endemic tension with the police, who were 'overzealous in arresting black youth.' In return, young blacks tended to view police as 'the boldest examples of northern racism. . . . Critics of the police compared large concentrations of patrolmen in black ghettos to 'an army of occupation' and complained of constant brutality" (Abu-Lughod 2007:180).
3. The research reported in this section draws from oral interviews collected between

2013 and 2016 with former residents of Orange from the African American and Italian American communities who were directly and indirectly displaced by the construction of 1-280. All quotes are attributed to their sources in the body of the text. Digital audio recordings and summaries of interviews are on file in the Department of Anthropology, Montclair State University. Most of those interviewed are older than sixty and lived in Orange during childhood and early adulthood. Many left around the time 1-280 was built, though some stayed in Orange longer and a few still live there. In my interviews with more than forty individuals in one-on-one and small group settings, I did not meet anyone who felt the construction of 1-280 was good idea or that it has served Orange in any positive way. Instead, their memories detail aspects of two working-class communities devastated by the construction of the highway. This part of the research was funded by a grant from ArtPlace America.

4. These include Mindy Thompson Fullilove, Molly Kaufman, Aubrey Murdock, Mike Malbrough, Katherine McCaffrey, Khemani Gibson, Rachel Bland, Candace Lee, Pat Morrissey, Katilin Stillwell, and Bryan Murdock.

TEN

Commentary

The Violence of Violence?

LOUANN WURST

The primary focus of this volume is to address structural or objective violence. The noble goals evident in all these papers entail developing ways to talk about violence that move beyond obvious contexts of subjective or interpersonal violence. Of the eight papers making up this collection, three articles deal with colonialism and colonial contexts, three address questions of race and structural racism, one relates to class and labor history, and one emphasizes theory and the role of archaeology more generally. The goal in compiling these papers was obviously not to be comprehensive, but the topics under purview do conform to the standard bailiwick of historical archaeology, even in the frequency distribution of their representation. The ever-present danger of a collection of articles such as this lies in the distribution; are we to presume that these are the most important contexts in which to address violence? Or does this simply reflect the individual interests of the participants? Either way, expectations are set about what counts as appropriate venues to reflect on structural violence. One strength of this collection is that these topics move beyond the obvious connection of violence with battlefields, conflict, war, dictators, and political repression that is found in so much other archaeological work on violence (González-Ruibal and Moshenska 2015; Starzmann, Pollock, and Bernbeck 2008).

The three articles about colonial violence all deal with Spanish New World contexts. Pezzarossi's case study uses archaeological data on settlement patterns and ceramic technologies from the Guatemala highlands to challenge violent discourses of collapse and rupture that position the "authentic" Maya as existing only in the past. His detailed analysis demonstrates clear continuities in the ceramics and settlement across the colonial "rupture," and he uses these patterns to emphasize the persistence of Maya communities. Pezzarossi argues that deconstructing narratives of Maya collapse can "mitigate the violence done by discourses of rupture" and tell "more complete histories."

Sampeck uses the examples of the Izalcos region of colonial Guatemala and the trans-Appalachian region of La Florida to explore how Spanish colonial regimes reordered space itself to be violent. She argues that this spatial violence created inequities by physically barring people from necessary resources and segregated people into controllable spaces, as well as "unseeing their very presence" by treating land as unpeopled wilderness that could then be easily appropriated through the colonial mandate. Sampeck considers these processes of unmaking indigenous peoples' very existence the most brutal or violent violence.

Smit and Proctor use bioarchaeology to address structural violence in the Huancavelica mercury mines in the Central Andes. Their goal is to challenge the exclusive focus on Black Legend narratives that see the Spanish colonial project as uniquely violent. These narratives also emphasize direct violence and thereby obscure the structural violence and long-term consequences of colonialism. Their bioarchaeological examination of five individuals documents evidence for direct violence interpreted as forms of labor coercion, and well as data showing how the *mita* labor system left evidence of structural violence literally "recorded on the body" through patterns of muscle exertion, repetitive motion, and mercury contamination.

Three of the articles focus on racial violence. Mullins, Huskins, and Hyatt address racial aspects of water privileges in Indianapolis by focusing on how the color line influenced access to rivers, swimming pools, and beaches. The fact that contemporary attempts to develop a seasonal beach along the White River in downtown Indianapolis were met with ridicule provides an opening to discuss the community's views of this water body as tainted in the context of the city's long history of structural racism as evidenced by water pollution, inequitable utility provision, and segregated recreational space. This is a powerful example because of the implicit ironies of the name *White* River and the focus on water that underscores how racial violence is fluid. Racial violence seeps and percolates into all aspects of social life rather than being a concrete and immutable thing.

Lua-Ozawa uses the gardens constructed by Japanese Americans at the Gila River Incarceration Camp to interrogate multiple layers of violence: mass incarceration as a form of state violence; state appropriation of land from the Gila River Indian Community that ignored their sovereignty and territorial boundaries; the fact that many of the Japanese Americans incarcerated at Gila River were employed in the gardening industry, which provides evidence of the structural racism that excluded them from other forms of employment; and common narratives that erase the diversity within the camp and cast the incarcerees as a homogeneous community of passive victims. The gardens that the incarcerees built become a powerful material emblem of the resistance and innovative reaction to the violence of the camp. Lua-Ozawa argues that the inmates used the gardens to create a sense of community and to counteract the alienation of incarceration.

Chris Matthews's article represents a significant intervention that challenges the way we think about race in urban contexts, moving away from the more neutral idea of racial segregation as simply separation to the idea of calling cities carceral landscapes. He presents a historical and material portrait of Essex County, New Jersey, that "describes the making of a landscape that both privileges suburban towns and experiences while imposing a carceral structure over the nonwhite urban core." He uses Interstate 280 as emblematic of a settlement system that consists of a majority nonwhite population in the dense urban core suffering from high crime and poverty rates while living in a scarred landscape of ruins and loss surrounded by suburban, majority-white communities with low crime and poverty rates and untouched by urban renewal and highway construction.

Only one article in this volume specifically addresses class violence. Mike Roller uses an archaeological case from Pennsylvania's coal county to argue that discrete episodes of violence such as the Lattimer Massacre can distract us from interrogating objective or structural violence. He warns us that by focusing on identifying discrete moments of subjective violence, archaeology risks the danger of interpreting these events as historical accidents or aberrations. Instead, he uses archaeological data from the "Italian Dwellings" at Lattimer to provide an example of how archaeologists can connect the small objects that we find in the ground to the systemic or structural forms of violence that they materialize.

Reinhard Bernbeck's article is the only contribution to this volume that provides substantive theoretical and methodological discussion about violence and how we study (perpetuate?) it. Bernbeck's theoretical discussion revolves around notions of power, ideology, interpellation, and subjectivation. His provocative framing is worth quoting: "I wish to pursue a line of thinking that considers relations between individuals as nonviolent when they are based on a mutual recognition as subjects, even when such relations include stark power differences.... It is the lack of recognition in intersubjective encounters that amounts to violence." To understand this lack of recognition, Bernbeck builds on Honneth's idea of reification as contrasted with recognition. Recognition emphasizes intersubjective relations of care, respect, empathy, and mutuality—an attitude of one's counterparts as subjects of equal value. In contrast, reification entails nether care nor respect but rather the complete dismissal of all personal traits of others, a forgetting of the Other as subject and the nature of intersubjective relations. Between these extremes, Honneth posits objectivation as a third "process that stays aware of an Other's subjectivity even when the relationship itself has the trappings of reification." Bernbeck suggests that what distinguishes violence is this lack of recognition of the subjectivity of the Other. He discusses how in the controversies over the display of Nazi war photographs, the forgetting of the victim's rights to not be displayed at all is itself an act of violence perpetrated by those on both sides of the debate. It is worth reflecting seriously on this point. Bernbeck cautions us that any historical archaeology that investigates sites of violence runs the risk of reification even when our work is meant to address past injustice. His argument is bolstered by reflecting on how virtually all anthropological writing entails reification and therefore symbolic violence. Our archaeological de rigueur emphasis on multivocality, public archaeology, and including multiple stakeholders is not exempt, since the Other "cannot undo a narrative order created by archaeology that is tantamount to structural violence." Bernbeck's warning, which I am sure many readers will not internalize, is that the very structures of our academic discipline, from field practices to publications, contain inbuilt reificatory tendencies indicating that archaeology itself is a violent process.

Common Themes

Even though the subjects of these articles range widely, several common themes are easily discerned. Several of the articles emphasize the importance of deconstructing or challenging common narratives about the past. This goal is obvious in the way Smit and Proctor challenge Black Legend tropes that position Spanish colonists as uniquely violent, Lau-Ozawa's critique of the homogenizing impact of narratives about Japanese incarceration camps, and Pezzarossi's emphasis on challenging the narratives of rupture that structure our views of Maya history. The larger warning that they all recognize is that confronting some forms of violence often leads to other silences and erasures. A clear example is Roller's caution that narratives about subjective violence (in the case of the Lattimer Massacre) can result in ignoring subtler forms of structural violence.

In their varied case studies and contexts, many of these papers intentionally connect the past and present. Mullins, Huskins, and Hyatt use the contemporary Visit Indy tourism agency's attempt to construct a beach along the White River as an entry point to examine race and water. Pezzarossi argues that archaeology can productively intervene to mitigate the effects of violence on contemporary Maya people. As one last example, Smit and Proctor speak to the legacy of mercury mining at Huancavelica that has resulted in a toxic environment and health problems that continue to plague people living in the area today.

Another commonality that runs through these articles is the resilience of the subjects in the face of structural violence. Lau-Ozawa discusses the gardens at the Gila River Incarceration Camp as reflecting a strong sense of determination and the perseverance of the inmates in the face of the alienation of their incarceration. In this, the gardens serve as expressions of resistance to the violent act of forced removal and imprisonment. Roller suggests that archaeology conducted in domestic places such as the "Italian Dwellings" at once reveals "a systemic violence at work" and "residents resiliently taking control to ameliorate these conditions." Sampeck describes how people used the continued production of Native ceramic forms and traditional foodways to nourish themselves to their own taste in the face of Spanish structural violence that worked to limit the quality and availability of food. Smit and Proctor conclude that structural violence was not always totalizing and that people "retained some degree of agency to work the system to their benefit." The idea of resilience is also central to Pezzarossi's goal of shifting typical narratives of the Maya away from collapse and rupture to instead emphasize continuity and persistence.

The concept of seeing, vision, and making clear is another theme that runs through these papers, providing an important counterpoint to ideas about structural violence as largely invisible and that the nature of direct or subjective violence often distracts us from examining structural forms. Žižek (2008:2) notes that "objective violence is invisible since it sustains the very zero-level standard against which we perceive something as subjectively violent." Matthews uses the metaphor of binoculars to capture the spatial differentiation of America's racial groups, which see one another only across a gulf of spatial, social, and cultural difference. He suggests that only binoculars can make sense of these differences for whites; nonwhites do not need binoculars to see since they live these differences every day. This aspect of seeing also figures in Bernbeck's discussion of war photographs when he states that it is "obvious that these photographers were absolutely incapable of seeing in the captured victims subjects like themselves." Sampeck argues that the spatial violence of colonial schemes resulted in erasing people from space: "unseeing is real, brutal violence, as it unmakes one's very existence."

All these papers focus on the importance of seeing structural violence, yet I wonder how the authors would respond to Alain Badiou's comment that "it is better to do nothing than to contribute to the invention of *formal ways of rendering visible* that which Empire already recognizes as existent" (Žižek 2008:216; emphasis added).

These ideas of seeing connect directly to another commonality: explicit statements about the powerful ability of archaeological studies to *reveal* and challenge violence. Roller suggests that "archaeologists can connect individual small objects to the objective forms of violence they materialize," revealing "the underlying causes of violence that often hang in delicate balance in moments of danger." Lau-Ozawa argues that "archaeological work can serve as a powerful counternarrative to this history, helping these marginalized communities tell their stories." Pezzarossi also makes some pretty strong statements about the power of archaeology to "mitigate the violence done by discourses of rupture" and "undermine (in some form) the violence done by dominant narratives." Mullins, Huskins, and Hyatt are more cautious, suggesting that simply acknowledging the African American experience "compels contemporary communities to acknowledge more than a century of environmental and social injustices." In their view, it is not that archaeology itself challenges violence but that our work can play a role in the struggles of the larger communities in which we work.

Individually, all these papers present important ways to recognize and think about structural violence. They also all make important contributions to the subject areas and contexts they deal with, representing a positive addition to the burgeoning field of historical archaeology. Even so, I find myself a bit more unsettled reflecting on the volume as a whole. While I am sympathetic to the authors' goals, especially to their arguments about the role and importance of archaeology, these strong statements seem to ring hollow since their interventions are as enmeshed in the "violence of archaeology" that Bernbeck discusses as the positions they critique.

Classification and the Violence
of Academic Privilege

Žižek notes (2008:6) that "a cold analysis of violence somehow reproduces and participates in its horror." Many of the papers in this volume are involved in the standard academic process of classification, naming, and definition. Various articles talk about direct violence, interpersonal violence, subjective violence, structural violence, and symbolic violence, as well as adding new terms, such as *spatial violence* and *discursive violence*. It almost seems as if defining terms and creating a classification was the goal of the exercise. Here lies the cold analysis that Žižek mentions, the violence of naming and containing social reality, the violence of abstraction. This reification of concepts fractures our social understanding and is not just an academic exercise but has real implications for people's lives.

Part of this classification process entails defining not just what violence is but how it differs from similar concepts. Moshenska and González-Ruibal (2015:5) note that structural violence is a problematic term that is synonymous with other concepts, including oppression and structural inequality. Even given this ambiguity, they argue that the "value of structural violence is that it illuminates and forces us to confront the aspects of our society, culture and everyday lives that impact negatively on others" (González-Ruibal and Moshenska 2015:5). Reading these articles, I was really struck by the lack of engagement with previous archaeological research that tackled the very same issues under different names and using different framing concepts. In particular, I was missing any real attention to the concept of ideology or inequality that framed a great deal of similar work in the 1980s and 1990s or research from the 1990s and 2000s that tackled questions of power.

Bernbeck firmly situates power in his discussion and distinguishes violence as those structures based on forgetting the subjectivity of the Other. But other papers gloss the differences between structural violence and forms of social inequality that are typically conceived as class. It seems as if a focus on violence precludes engagement with previous scholarship—almost as if exploring a new concept can be untethered from the past, itself a reificatory process. Landon refers to this as "intellectual deforestation": the tendency to dismiss "all past work in favor of the theory or approach of the moment" (2005:24). The ironic unforeseen consequence of this is that it conveys violence as an intellectual fad, a polemic or rhetorical posturing that is itself part of the violence of archaeology that Bernbeck discusses. We should think seriously about how to reconcile the opportunities and excitement that new concepts or approaches bring to our studies with the insights provided by researchers using other related concepts and perspectives. This would help us avoid the "old wine in new skins" and "reinventing the wheel" phenomena that have so plagued the history of archaeological thought.

Other reificatory tendencies are easily spotted in these papers, through the naming and framing that are an essential part of archaeological research. One example is the way Smit and Proctor refer to the crania they examine by *individual number*—a concept implicated in the ideology and alienation of capitalism that Chris Matthews so clearly articulated in his book *The Archaeology of American Capitalism* (2012b). I do not mean to criticize Smit and Proctor unfairly. Indeed, referring to skeletal remains as individuals may well be better than using specimen numbers. However, calling them individuals is not necessarily based on a greater recognition of their subjectivity, as Bernbeck discusses. And frankly, I do not know a better way, leading exactly to Bernbeck's point that "there is no exit from this paradoxic situation." One solution that may help ameliorate this paradox is to more clearly focus on the everyday lives of these individuals. Smit and Proctor argue that "documenting individual lifeways" avoids the essentializing pitfalls of a facile dualism of victims and victimizers, but by ignoring the larger community and social relations, they may themselves fall prey to other reificatory tendencies. In particular, I wondered about the larger implications of the patterns of "labor recorded on the body" within the larger mita context, where workers cycle into and out of the mines for two-month rotations. The reificatory tendency here is to assume that all these indigenous individuals were miners, a role just as defined by the colonial encounter and itself a dehumanizing and violent act. And doesn't Pezzarossi's vehement claim for Maya continuity also deny them as subjects of colonization? Thus many of these papers are as embroiled in processes of "othering" as the contexts they critique. This is not a specific criticism of these articles but is rather part of the violence of archaeology itself that we all fall prey to. Like Bernbeck, I find myself pessimistic "about the prospects for a significant reduction of the violent structures of our discipline. Excavation practices, academic narratives, and their pictorial illustrations all contain strong inbuilt reificatory tendencies."

I guess what unsettles me most is that the real difference between previous research using other concepts and the papers in this volume may be in terms of political engagement. As noted above, the goal of these papers seems pretty anemic (revealing, challenging narratives) and academic. In other words, they are safe. But violence is anything but safe. What I was missing in these papers is the passion and rage that a concept like violence engenders. Sampeck does call violence a "slap in the face," Roller uses a contemporary newspaper article about the Lattimer Massacre to reveal the "horrific violence" and "darkness lurking below the surface of the industrial landscape," and Pezzarossi's paper is full of righteous zeal to correct discursive wrongs. I think the political impotence in these articles stems from the almost total lack of engagement with the violence of capitalism and the "archaeology of perpetrators" in the sense that Bernbeck and Pollock (2007) have discussed.

The Violence of Capitalism
and an Archaeology of Perpetrators

Bernbeck and Pollock (2007) present a powerful critique of identity-based archaeology and instead advocate for an archaeology that exposes the perpetrators of injustices: "It is a noble goal to give the oppressed a place in history, but that still leaves those responsible for their plight in a neutral, sanitized space, conveniently separated from the structures of repressive power" (Bernbeck and Pollock 2007:220). The idea of perpetrators makes sense to us when thinking about violence enacted by political regimes with dictators who can easily be vilified, and Bernbeck and Pollock (2007:220) argue that an archaeology of perpetrators exposes the actions of people such as dictators, warmongers, and promulgators of racist policies and their followers. The perpetrators are easy to see in this volume when the authors discuss subjective forms of violence: the state as perpetrator in the Gila River Incarceration Camp, Spanish colonists as perpetrators at Huancavelica, Izalco, and La Florida, or the coal company operatives along with local law officials as perpetrators at Lattimer.

The authors are correct when they state that the perpetrators of structural violence are not so easy to identify. Mullins, Huskins, and Hyatt suggest that racial injustices are not easily blamed on consciously racist city leaders but are instead invested in deep historical and systemic processes. Smit and Proctor follow Klaus (2012) to argue that structural violence cannot be blamed on individuals or groups but instead results from long-standing multigenerational oppressive social and political structures. Sampeck argues that structural violence is subtle and often invisible, "which makes pinpointing a specific person to be held responsible difficult or impossible." While these statements are true in the sense that structural violence is different than direct, interpersonal, or subjective violence, where an individual or group can be identified as perpetrator, these ideas are also terribly unsettling since they imply that structural violence is faceless and anonymous, leaving academic study as the only action we have to battle, see, and reveal it. This positioning has the unforeseen consequence of naturalizing structural inequality. Instead I would argue that we need to ask serious questions about the social relations of who benefits from structural violence. Who are the perpetrators, and whom do we blame for structural violence?

It is in this context that I would build on the contributions in this volume that discuss colonial violence and structural racism to confront the violence of capitalism. Capital, according to Marx, "comes dripping from head to toe, from every pore, with blood and dirt" and assumes the form of "an animated monster" (1967:926, 302). In this, the very logic of capitalism—its inner workings—is monstrous, fraught with violence, and it jeopardizes our ability to realize our own humanity. This is exactly what Žižek (2008) calls systemic or objective violence: "the often catastrophic consequences of the smooth functioning of our economic and political systems," the violence inherent in the normal state of things. This violence results from the very logic of capitalism based on abstract labor and its laws of motion (Harman 2009; Holloway 2010; McNally 2011; Ollman 2003, 2014). As Bernbeck notes, it is the capitalist logic of abstract exchange that is the major force behind our capacity to reify almost anyone. I would argue that interrogating this is as much an archaeology of perpetrators as of naming dictators, and failing to do so creates other silences and leaves structural violence unscathed. The perpetrators here are not individuals whom we can name and vilify but the structures of capitalism itself.

As an example, Matthews's powerful discussion of urban cores as a carceral landscape leaves us no way to understand this except through "white privilege," which is both true and false at the same time. This inadvertently frames the discussion as white perpetrators versus nonwhite victims, leaving unscathed the actual structures: the capital flight that created the urban core as a place of ruin and violence occupied by people who are a reserve army of unnecessary labor within the contemporary economic system. Matthews cites Baldwin as saying, "They don't want us—period," but this "they" is not simply white people. It just as clearly refers to capitalist structures that no longer need black urban labor. Saying this is not an excuse for whites' "blind eye" or the condoning of color-blind racism, but it does recognize that not all whites benefit equally. Recently, Roediger (2017:384) suggested that "we may be due for discussion on whether 'white privilege' now serves us well in naming patterns of white advantage inside a system in which most people are miserable." Framed another way, blaming "whiteness" is as dangerous and violent as blaming "blackness" since it leaves structures of repressive power uninterrogated.

Roller provides another example in his discussion of symbolic violence, which includes structures of language and meaning that subjugate groups "to the interests of discursive forces outside their control." Our perpetrator here is discursive forces! Roller comes closest to naming the perpetrators of the Lattimer Massacre as "a posse of middle-class businessmen and law enforcement" and states the "middle-class businessmen" benefited from steadily increasing profits. Even so, I don't typically think about coal mine owners as middle-class businessmen, and this vagueness serves to elide the structural violence inherent in the very nature of the capitalist system. The violence of the capitalist system is one that commoditizes and reifies everything and alienates us all from our own production and thus humanity. In the context of these larger structures, we can see that the motorists on Interstate 280 or the guards at Gila River are subject to violence as well, although obviously not with the same consequences to their material conditions and life chances as for nonwhites incarcerated in urban cores or the Japanese Americans imprisoned in concentration camps.

Without this engagement with the larger structures of capitalism—the structural perpetrators of violence—does our work serve simply to perpetuate it? As Žižek (2008:216) suggests, is it "better to do nothing than to engage in localized acts the ultimate function of which is to make the system run more smoothly"? Like Bernbeck, I remain pessimistic about the possibilities of a significant reduction in the violence of archaeology or even the violence of capitalism. Because of this, I worry about the violence of violence.

ELEVEN

Forum

Thoughts and Future Directions

Reinhard Bernbeck

My comment centers on two facets of violence that stand at opposite ends of the theme. One is the question of "actionable" consequences of the realization that we live and are entangled in a world full of violent relations; the other concerns the scholarly response to structural violence and privilege.

The volume argues that violence, and especially structural violence, generates privileged groups. This happens through multifarious processes, not all of which are intentional. The bombing of civilians in Yemen and the blocking of ports that are instrumental for the provisioning of a starving population are both actively pursued by the military of Saudi Arabia and are also actively supported by US political circles. However, the production of arms, bombs included, that are sold at low prices to Saudi Arabia is based in part on taxes paid by average US citizens who do not necessarily know about or agree with such use of their money. The same citizens enable other kinds of structural violence by paying for the maintenance of electric infrastructure. Amazon, Uber, and other internet giants exploit labor worldwide through vicious mechanisms such as crowdsourcing or in-game labor (Scholz 2017). Structures themselves do not act, whether they are military organizations, tax systems, maintenance services, or international relations. They need to be constantly reenacted to persist. But at the same time, structures frame and orient such reproduction. This "structuration," as Anthony Giddens (1984) called it, works on many scales.

Can structures be violent then? Taking a "structurationist" perspective, the answer is no. They enable but do not commit violence. Only structuration cycles can be violent. Following the argument presented in my contribution, I think that conditions can be rated as violent when actors reify Others in order to reach specific goals within a structuration logic. Dialectical relations of structure and agency can be violent, whether in research environments, official or business administrations, or elsewhere. This occurs when the basic acknowledgment of Others as subjects drops out of sight. Such reificatory processes have a strong tendency to exclude and ostracize. Large groups of people, even entire populations may turn into what Judith Butler (2009) has called "ungrievable." Notorious and obvious cases are the refugee camps of Jordan, Bangladesh, and Greece. Less obvious is that the acquisition of flowers for a friend on Valentine's Day boosts ecological and economic disaster through the desiccation of soils and the use of toxic chemicals in the huge flower factories in Kenya, Uganda, and elsewhere. No specific person is behind such multiscalar effects; the perpetrators consist of well-meaning, naive consumers in neoliberal globalized capitalism. No matter what we do, we cannot extricate ourselves from this system. We generally profit from it, even when we recognize its deadly grip.

Scholars are chained to a violent structuration cycle in two ways: in daily life, in which one cannot eschew consumption based on an all-pervasive system of (reifying) commoditization; and as researchers who shape their "objects" of interest by classifying them into abstract categories in order to make them manipulable. Is the recognition of this situation a reason for utter despair?

I think not. In academia, as hinted at, I perceive a need to reorient archaeology in the direction of the "new forensis": on the one hand, to consider the past (and present) as a long continuous process of misconduct that consists of setting up cycles of violent structuration, whether by large collectives, small groups, or individuals; on the other hand, to single out past single events of atrocities and infringements on others' most basic right: to exist as a human being (Forensic Architecture 2014). A necessary accompaniment for a turn toward such a forensic understanding in archaeology is a sustained discussion about the universality of basic ethical standards and the right or possibility to speak for others, as I mentioned in my contribution to this book. Yannis Hamilakis (2018) has shown a concrete way forward with his recent edited volume on forced and undocumented migration.

Second, a feeling of being implicated in structural violence and horrendous injustice lays the ideological grounds for political inaction. We need to be careful about the message we produce when insisting on the all-pervasiveness of structural violence. It leads ultimately to an indulgent self-pity that involves lamenting a privileged position and partaking in the production of knowledge as power. However, a qualitatively new development that archaeologists and other scholars have lately had to become used to is the emergence of a different discursive form of violence: hate speech. It is violent not just because it is devoid of recognition but because it actively and explicitly promotes brutality in a murderous rhetoric of scorn and contempt. Once ideological facets of xenophobia, racism, homophobia, and sexism have made their way into public discourse, they become part of a reproducible frame and turn into vicious structuration dynamics. Our precarious present is characterized by (mostly elected) officials with dictatorial tendencies, the so-called populists who willfully use demeaning speech to promote a Darwinian social world that legitimizes their power in a perverse ethics of the powerful.

This is decidedly not the same as the structural violence of scholarly knowledge production. This type of active endorsement and stirring of violence should lead us in a very different direction, formulated with exceptional clarity by the writer, politician, and concentration camp survivor Stéphane Hessel (2011:17): "The worst possible outlook is indifference that says 'I can't do anything about it; I will just get by.' Behaving like that deprives you of one of the essentials of being human: the capacity and freedom to feel outraged." Outrage as the condition for the possibility to rein in violence may on the surface seem to be a strange proposition. It means "paying back in kind." Ultimately, this is as close a call to arms as one can get. That is exactly the point Hessel wants to make: to reflect on the threshold where violence requires a response that does not remain peaceful. The Nazi "rupture in civilization," as Dan Diner (1988) called it, bears a terrifying threat of reoccurrence.

Guido Pezzarossi

Violence, and the privilege it affords, emerges as something new in archaeological inquiry by becoming the primary focus and shared analytical thread in comparative archaeological studies. Framing particular types of violence beforehand—class, race, gender, and so on—has been exceedingly successful within archaeology. However, it does place limits on the potential for cross-context comparative analyses or forces us to impose a framing concept on a context where it may or may not be applicable or useful. Yanagisako and Collier (1987) provided an important critique of the centering of biological sex as a stable axis of difference across human spacetime. Despite the political potential of exploring the "universal" violence of "female subordination" (see Ortner 1972), new violences are enacted by deforming local contexts to the contours of these imposed frames.

Shifting our analytical lens onto violence itself it allows for a refocusing on the actual violence-generating practices/processes and their emergent effects that both produce and are produced by manifold inequalities. This shift enables a certain analytical flexibility that can account for diversity and variation in how violence is enacted, and to what effect on those subjected to it. Coronil's (2007) approach to comparative imperialism via what he terms "imperial effects" intersects with such a focus on violence. Focusing on how violence manifests avoids defining ahead of time the structures and social relations through which violence takes place and instead pushes us "to recognize systems of domination by their significance for subjected populations rather than solely by their institutional forms or self-definitions" (Coronil 2007:243). Voss (2012) has adapted this approach to the investigation of sexuality/sexual effects, allowing the particular formations of sexual practices, identities, gender, and regulation to emerge in the analysis. In my own work (Pezzarossi 2015, 2019), I draw on Coronil to explore capitalist effects as a way to sidestep the fuzziness in definitions of capitalism and to reorient analyses on the particulars of how unequal power and violence afford/generate the diverse practices and relations generative of the dispossessions attributed to abstract capitalist structures to the benefit of some and detriment of others.

Perhaps the most effective aspect of the analysis of violence is in its direct identification of the mechanisms by which violence is done in varied contexts rather than the searching out of abstract logics and structures as the targets of our interventions. Braidotti (2015) reminds us that there is no "Winter Palace" of capitalism to storm but only situated doings where violence manifests and affects those subjected. It is in these contexts that interventions need to happen, be they in the "slow" violences of industrial environmental toxicity affecting urban subaltern laborers (Mrozowski 2006; Nixon 2011), the structural violence of colonial legacies of exploitation and indebtedness in the former colonies (Farmer 2004b), or the "privilege" of purchasing low-cost consumer goods (such as sugar; Mintz 1985) thanks to the use of variously coerced "cheap labor." In the case study I discuss for Guatemala, identifying who benefits from and/or perpetuates the discursive violence of historical erasures and imposed conceptions of "authentic" indigeneity directly implicates the biases of archaeological research and its practitioners. Archaeology is not positioned to solve all the issues affecting descendant Maya communities. However, in this case it does have the potential to intervene in correcting a broadly shared (mis)conception of Maya history that the discipline has helped construct.

Abu-Lughod (2002) reminds us of the dangers of a cultural relativism that supports disengagement despite the power inequities, violence, and suffering that have emerged in part due to the West's imperial meddling around the globe.

Instead, we should be "asking how we, living in this privileged and powerful part of the world, might examine our own responsibilities for the situations in which others in distant places have found themselves" (Abu-Lughod 2002:789). Within archaeology, reflexivity around the violence and colonialist legacies of archaeological practice in and out of the United States can cut close to such relativism when the solution is to simply do nothing and stop archaeological work for fear of reifying these legacies and the unequal relations that sustain them.

In contexts with histories of colonialist archaeological relations, such as Guatemala (Chinchilla 2012), simply disengaging after decades of narrative-making archaeological practice does not seem like much of a solution. Indeed, I argue that disengagement can amount to an elision of responsibility for the misrepresentation and use of Maya heritage in Guatemalan national historiography and the public imagination. Moreover, more recent imperial legacies of the United States in Guatemala have created an ongoing dependency on Western funding agencies for archaeological research at the same time that archaeological and historical heritage has become an important source of global cultural capital for indigenous communities and the nation. The infrastructures and legacies of archaeological heritage practice have become an avenue for employment as well as a backbone of the country's cultural heritage tourism.

These are not ideal circumstances or perhaps even desirable ones. However, simply stopping archaeological work does not seem satisfactory given the enduring and well-established importance of archaeological knowledge and heritage in Guatemala. Now that these entanglements exist, there is a responsibility to collaborate, address erasures, and decolonize, rather than leaving the discursive and structural violences of archaeology to linger in dominant narratives of history and contribute to the erasure of colonial and modern articulations of indigeneity. In some cases, archaeological knowledge and practice may be appropriated into community/cultural revitalization, as the Movimiento Maya has done, as well as other Maya communities that draw on decipherment of Classic Maya glyphic writing as part of language revitalization and a reconnecting with heritage purposefully ruptured from descendant Maya communities. Given these examples, and drawing inspiration from colonial material culture studies (e.g., Thomas 1991), I am perhaps more optimistic about the potential of archaeology to decolonize, address legacies of colonial violence past, and mitigate archaeological violence present. The long-term entanglements of archaeology in Guatemala should push us to conceptualize how archaeology itself can and has come to be appropriated and redeployed as a "braided" (Atalay 2012) Maya/Western knowledge-producing practice, in the service of Maya goals and interests. Archaeologists may have the privilege to pull back from these contexts of violence and work where they do not have to face their troubling disciplinary legacies. Perhaps it is easiest on us to simply "do nothing." However, would this not generate new violence for the communities we leave to clean up the messes of our colonial endeavors? The mutually constituting dialectical relation between violence and privilege places additional pressure on us to be allies and to deploy that privilege to undercut legacies of violence that have benefited archaeologists to the detriment of our community partners.

Kathryn E. Sampeck

The archaeology of violence and privilege offers a fresh view of sometimes familiar territory. It is territory, however, worth revisiting because much of it is a foundation for historical archaeology. Numerous archaeological studies of violent events (strikes, massacres, battles) and contexts (prisons, plantations, factories) foreground issues such as class, race, gender, and subjecthood, with violence sometimes looming, sometimes lurking, but ever present. It is a literature so deep and rich that a laundry list cannot do it justice. Justice is in fact the point.

Previous work provided not just the inspiration but also the crucial information for the shift in perspective to violence itself. This shift in attention is overdue, as other disciplines and institutions have devoted increasing attention to one of the greatest challenges that people face today. This reorientation in historical archaeology reveals how privilege and its consequent violence were potently consistent factors and experiences across time and in different locales. Other crucial elements, such as, say, the formulation of race, distinguish different contexts. For example, Patrick Wolfe (2006:388) points out how "Indigenous people obstructed settlers' access to land, so their increase was counterproductive . . . the restrictive racial classification of Indians straightforwardly furthered the logic of elimination. . . . Indigenous North Americans were not killed, driven away, romanticized, assimilated, fenced in, bred White, and otherwise eliminated as the original owners of the land but as Indians." Native American contexts of racialization have a different character than, for example, those experienced by enslaved African Americans on nineteenth-century plantations in the United

States. The violence used to establish and enforce such racialization, however, is a common element between the two circumstances. Focusing on violence and privilege encourages researchers to compare contexts that would be less likely under the aegis of other themes.

The dialectical approach that contributors to this volume take to violence and privilege prompts us to assess more deeply who benefits from violence. Some are obvious—*encomenderos*, officials, entrepreneurs—but the more subtle cases become less so with attention to violence. The seemingly innocent nineteenth-century farmstead can exist only because of settler colonialism and violent removal of Native peoples. People built upon stolen land the spectacular wealth of the sixteenth through eighteenth centuries through the horror of captive, coerced labor. The lack of recognition of the very presence, much less the contributions, of people of African descent in the establishment and independence of Latin American nation-states is a further assault within a dynamic of physical and historical erasure. The price of the finery of privilege is human suffering. While these brutal relations exist within a network of capitalism, violence extends beyond and starts before fully capitalist systems. This volume thus contributes to an effort to show how violence is a primary medium through which people form and maintain social relations.

Alain Badiou's critique of analytical distance endeavors to dissuade scholars from reifying agendas and systems of inequality. The problem is that it negates inquiry into processes of invisibilization. The violence of invisibility is an important theme in critical indigenous studies and Afro–Latin American studies, for example (Moreton-Robinson 2016; Picq 2018; Reiter and Eison Simmons 2012). These and many other studies, especially efforts in relation to activist struggles, show that "formal ways of rendering visible" willful, harmful blindness are not such bad thing.

The cold and calculating approach, Žižek's violence of dispassionately naming and containing social reality, is perhaps not what it seems. In some cases, it can be the calm in the storm. Screams and tears, visceral and dramatic, recognize violence. For some, giving that acknowledgment of the moment of harm feels demeaning, like giving perpetrators exactly what they want. Novelist Toni Morrison observed that "Martin Luther King didn't have any guns, he didn't blow up anything, he didn't lynch anybody. He trained boys and girls to just sit there and accept insults. That is a thing that is bigger than hope. It is survival and it is resistance and it is triumph" (Collette 2013). People can feel dignity in calmness in the midst of pain, violation, and cruelty to show that they are not broken by clearly and confidently pointing a finger.

Koji Lau-Ozawa

In this book, the themes of violence and privilege are foregrounded. This is not new in itself; archaeologists and anthropologists have long been interested in such themes. However, the pairing of the two concepts in dialectical opposition is a productive move in the study of violence. The invitation to participate in the conference session that inspired this collection, and the writing of my own contribution to the volume, forced me to seriously consider what the implications of such an orientation might be. In terms of Japanese American incarceration, this refocusing makes us consider the multiple layers of violence expressed in the material remains of mass incarceration.

While many types of violence are well represented in archaeological litera-tures (structural, symbolic, discursive, and so on), less frequently are we asked to consider violence and privilege side by side. In doing so, the tensions and com-plexities of racial, class, gendered, and national violences are highlighted. Those who are embedded in the mechanisms of repression or exploitation, whether consciously or not, are frequently subjected to their own forms of oppression. As Wurst points out in her remarks, the guards in the watchtowers of the incar-ceration camps were themselves subjects of cycles of violence. She asks if we do enough to engage with these larger structures embedded in capitalist systems.

Though I concede that my own work here has not perhaps addressed this ques-tion satisfactorily, I would not go as far as Žižek's suggestion that this may serve only to perpetuate forms of violence. Studies of Japanese American incarceration can be productive and can counter forces of violence through a variety of means.

The process of archaeological study does itself help to create spaces of in-clusion and to bring together communities affected by traumatic pasts. It is true that bearing witness is not enough (see Hauser et al. 2018), but community-based archaeological projects do have value when these pasts are considered during their design and execution (Atalay 2012).

With regard to the violences of Japanese American incarceration, archaeolog-ical surveys and excavations often integrate descendants and former incarcerees into their designs (Burton 2017; Clark 2017). These do not just mine communities for information about sites but legitimately aid in helping to mediate the mem-ories and postmemories of the incarceration. In one instance at the Manzanar National Historic Site, recording an oral history of a former incarceree led to the excavation of a family pond built by the incarceree's father. The excavation of the pond helped her connect with her childhood memories of the incarceration and the thrill of seeing her father's work brought to life in the present day (Burton and Farrell 2014:65).

The violence of these events is still felt by descendants, and if the process of archaeology can help them process these traumas, then it can indeed be worth doing. As Farmer (2004b) implores, anthropological attention must be turned toward the histories and complexities of structural violence to understand the suffering of people.

The pairing of violence with privilege provides another insight into these structures and processes. It pushes us to recognize the multiple layers of violence inflicted upon people. The dialectical approach suggested by this volume asks us to reckon with this pair of concepts. What privileges did the recipients of violence have? What violences were the privileged subjected to? At Gila River, while it is true that guards were themselves subjected to different modes of violence, it should also be remembered that members of the incarcerated population were the recipients of different types of privilege. The incarceration was felt differentially across lines of ethnic, class, and gendered distinctions. The discursive violence of post-camp narratives is symptomatic of these expressions of privilege, amplifying the voices of those members of the community empowered to speak and suppressing others.

Primo Levi (1998) saw the camp as not erasing modes of difference and privilege for its occupants but preserving them within the morally ambiguous gray zone. Understanding these tensions of violence and privilege helps to reveal the complexities of life within landscapes of trauma. To not do so would allow for the discursive brutality of homogenization to gain epistemological authority.

Today, the apologist accounts of Japanese American incarceration by academics and pop historians are plentiful (Lotchin 2018; Malkin 2004; Smith 1995). Simultaneously, specters of the camp creep back into US public discourse, with politicians (Lachman 2017) and pundits (Bromwich 2016) invoking this history to justify contemporary policies of detention. Tent cities are erected in Texas to house migrant children (Delgado 2018), while those seeking asylum in Australia are left in indefinite limbo on islands (Held 2018; Mathiesen 2015). In these circumstances it is crucial for archaeologists and anthropologists to turn toward histories of violence and privilege, to better understand their dynamics, to reveal their complexities, and to help mediate their traumas.

I take seriously the cautions and critiques put forth by Wurst in this volume. While the work here represents a good point of departure, we must push further to understand the mechanisms at play within systems of oppression. However, I also understand the limitations of my own position. How far can the descendants of incarcerees push on these matters before they are accused of being too close to the history? How much passion and rage can be written before a paper is dismissed as another diatribe by an embittered descendant?

Michael P. Roller

Walter Benjamin (1968:256) famously stated, "There is no document of civilization which is not at the same time a document of barbarism." If we agree with Benjamin's proposal, we might then seek out the ways violence lurks within the materiality of everyday life. For if this is true, it must be somewhere present in all the arenas of twentieth-century progress, not only in the dank places we might most expect it but also in suburbs, highways, shopping malls, and everyday kitchen appliances. It too must be present in class systems of privilege, respectability, and governance.

Considering violence in the context of privilege can reveal who benefits from, and is thereby culpable for, systematized coercive violence. For example, it can reveal the hidden role of violence in the formation and policing of class structures in capitalist society. Though the posse was formed through the finances and support of aristocratic coal mine owners, middle-class businessmen and law enforcement perpetrated the violence of the Lattimer Massacre I present in my case study. Documenting such a blatant execution of subjective violence by the middle class defending their interests reveals often hidden relationships of power in society. Namely, this example connects these middle-class citizens to the coercive violence capitalists may use to control an immigrant labor force.

Class structures in capitalism are fundamentally relational. Based upon the movement of surplus capital between classes, their relative positioning structures and stabilizes the working and living conditions of each class. To fail to account for one element, therefore, may limit our understanding of the whole (Urry 1973). Perhaps owing to the mutative development of the middle classes throughout his lifetime, Karl Marx provided neither clear nor consistent analysis of their development and function in capitalist society (Friedman 1974; Urry 1973). Moreover, in Marxist writing, the middle classes sometimes appear to be almost a bystander, formed in surplus of capital production among the broader historical trajectories of the class antagonism between capital and labor.

The ambiguity and inconsistency of Marx's accounting for the role of the middle class in capitalism are largely a result of his dialectic propensities to at times formulate materialist history as abstraction and other times to report specific historical contexts in great journalistic detail. In his early works, Marx defined the middle class as those who do not own property but rather bolster the accumulation of capital as administrators, clerks, bookkeepers, agents, managers, secretaries, and technical and skilled laborers. Two major analyses structure Marx's earliest and most direct work on the formation and function of the middle class in capitalist society. The first proposes that the sole purpose of the middle class is to directly consume the excess commodities produced by the working class while not adding to the surplus production (Urry 1973:177). Such overproduction he foresaw as the inevitable outgrowth (and eventual barrier if not consumed) to the continued expansion of industrial modes of production. The second analysis concerns the need for a class of skilled workers and administrative assistants in overseeing the increasingly complex operations of industrial capitalism (Marx 2018; Urry 1973:177–78). In later writings, Marx is less clear about the importance, direction, and structuring role of the middle classes in capitalist development, at times predicting they would eventually be absorbed into the exploited proletariat (Friedman 1974:330–33). Nonetheless, he could observe their burgeoning numbers and the consequent growth of their political will in his historical documentation.

If the trajectory and function of the middle class in regard to the totality of capitalist operations remains ambiguous today, that cannot be said to result from its underdevelopment. Rather there is a contemporary preponderance and over-determination of middle-class values as the vanguard class structure of neoliberal or late capitalism. The dawning of the twentieth century seemed to turn much of the class dynamics of pre- and early industrial class struggle inside out, foregrounding consumption as the antidote to the surplus production yielded by mechanization, infrastructure development, advertising, and assembly line efficiency (Roller 2019a). Throughout the twentieth century, capitalism has stabilized its growth on grounds far more multivalent and complex than the traditional arena of accruing surplus value from labor productivity. Today, profit is siphoned from so many other aspects of social, political, and economic life, including consumerism, waste, catastrophe, financial regulation, and speculation (Roller 2019b).

The perpetrators of violence in the Lattimer Massacre were middle class. That the middle class holds an ambiguous relationship to explicit capital accumulation does not make an account of their violence in its defense an "eli[sion of] the structural violence inherent in the very nature of the capitalist system," as our commenter suggests. Middle-class privilege is part of a capitalist machine responsible for structuring, capitalizing, stabilizing, and coercing into submission an objectively violent mode of production. In the time since Marx's earliest writing describing the nascent development of a middle class, the battlefield of class antagonism has become far more complex than a chess match between capital and labor.

David Graeber, in an essay entitled "Dead Zones of the Imagination" (2012), argues that coercive violence underlies the functioning of all bureaucracies. While the smooth functioning of, for example, a school library can seem distant from the coercive apparatuses of society, Graeber suggests that if anyone tried to enter a library without an ID, instantly "armed men would indeed be summoned to physically remove them, using whatever force might be required." He concludes that "it's almost as if the more we allow aspects of our everyday existence to fall under the purview of bureaucratic regulations, the more everyone concerned colludes to downplay the fact (perfectly obvious to those actually running the system) that all of it ultimately depends on the threat of physical harm" (Graeber 2012:8).

The essays in this volume demonstrate that an archaeology of violence and privilege can contribute to a rich understanding of the hidden violence stabilizing hegemonic social and political structures and policing the divisions of society into classes. The "capitalist system" is structured, capitalized, and stabilized by so many everyday practices and materialities beyond the exploitation of labor by the forces of capital.

Douglas K. Smit and Terren K. Proctor

> The exchange rate between the plantation record and the produce it represented was reckoned in suffering: "On some estates settlements are made every evening, and the whipping follows [the weighing] immediately." For slaves, violence was the metric of production.
>
> *Walter Johnson (2013:248)*

In the 1980s, power, inequality, and oppression emerged as essential themes in historical archaeology's drive to redefine itself as "the archaeology of the modern world." Much of this research explored histories of violence, such as the brutality of colonialism in the Caribbean and La Florida, antebellum lives of enslaved peoples, and everyday inequalities amid class relations in early capitalism. While these studies examined the violent spaces across the early modern world, the research rarely addressed how violence itself was a constitutive force of modernity. In some ways this volume is an attempt to ask an old question: What can the archaeology of colonialism and capitalism tell us about the emergence of modernity? However, by focusing on violence rather than taking it for granted, we can unpack what has largely remained a black box to better understand how different forms of violence operated and created the modern world.

We deeply appreciate LouAnn Wurst's essay, particularly her commentary that future archaeologies of violence should engage more directly with capitalism. This important point epitomizes the promise and pitfalls of the archaeology of violence and privilege. While violence is essential to capitalism, it is critical to avoid universalizing violence as a category that is merely a consequence of capitalism. By orienting our focus on the contingency of violence, it is imperative that we ask, "What does violence do in a given place and time?" Matthews and Phillippi emphasize the dialectical nature of violence and privilege, noting that "for the privilege to exist there must also be forms of violence that sustain and defend it." We agree, yet we reaffirm that these categories of violence and privilege must be historicized to understand how different types of brutality produce distinct forms of privilege.

Consider the opening epigraph, taken from the Walter Johnson's history of the Mississippi cotton economy prior to the Civil War. Drawing on a long tradition of scholarship that links capitalism and slavery under the term *racial capitalism*, Johnson describes how cotton planters and overseers deployed violence to measure and increase the efficiency of enslaved labor. Violence was a critical input, a tool to extract labor and resources across the early global economy from Mississippi to Manchester. While the enslaved peoples of Mississippi and the oppressed workers of Manchester were indispensable to capitalism and modernity, they also existed in distinct political, economic, and social formations. Likewise, it is critical to understand how violence operates, the types of privileges it sustains, and the forms of resistance it engenders.

Our chapter compared two types of violence, direct and structural, between the Spanish colonial administration and indigenous labor at the Andean mercury mines of Huancavelica. We argue that overemphasizing narratives of direct violence can obscure structurally violent legacies of colonialism. Popular and historical narratives of Spanish conquest often focus on the sensational scenes of conquistadores enacting direct violence on indigenous populations. While this is undeniably true, a focus on direct violence overlooks the more subtle and enduring patterns of structural violence enacted by forced labor regimes, land dispossession, and attacks on indigenous culture under the guise of evangelization. Moreover, while we can read colonial documents for stories of direct violence, or use bioarchaeology to see traces of past brutalities on the human body, memories of direct physical force fade over generations. Yet structural violence persists well beyond the actions of a single conquistador or colonial administrator. Economic research, for example, has shown that the boundaries of the region where the Spanish forced people to work in the mines can predict contemporary Peruvian poverty and inequality (Dell 2010). Likewise, the locations of smelters from the seventeenth and eighteenth centuries in Huancavelica correspond with high mercury content in the soil, leading to a suite of health problems for contemporary residents. While archaeological analyses of atrocities and physical force are important, we argue that a structural violence perspective provides an avenue to greater public engagement, as well as an understanding of how the past produced the present.

We also share some of Bernbeck and Wurst's pessimism on the relevance of archaeology to violent legacies of prior injustices. Matthews and Phillippi conclude their introduction by noting the power and privilege of archaeology to bear witness to acts of violence, the subject of a recent Vital Topics Forum in *American Anthropologist* that brought together scholars, including several contributors from this volume, to "interrogate what it means to bear witness" (Hauser et al. 2018:535). However, what type of witness should archaeologists be? Wurst notes a lack of "passion and rage" in this volume, a critical yet potentially dangerous point for scholarship on topics prone to sensation such as violence. While emotive writing is important, it is equally important to ask, "Whose emotion matters?"

For example, while our chapter was based on fieldwork and analysis conducted in 2014–2015, our more recent and ongoing fieldwork has attempted to recenter community narratives. Historians and archaeologists might regard the mercury mining landscapes of Santa Bárbara as spaces of violence and brutality, but for the people of the Comunidad Campesina de Santa Bárbara, it is home. After a series of discussions with community leaders, in 2018 we began a heritage project that employed collaborative methodologies such as Photovoice, which allows people to document and interrogate their archaeological and community landscapes. While this research is still preliminary, it is revealing that legacies of violence are rarely depicted in isolation but rather intersect with narratives of community emergence from animated landscapes. In short, their history contains violence, but violence is not their only past.

As Barbara Voss notes in their contribution to the *American Anthropologist* forum on bearing witness, "emotional responses are not independent of political, economic, and discursive structures" (Voss 2018:540). Voss describes how their initial attempts to understand nineteenth-century racial violence against San Jose's Chinatown overemphasized tragedy, but later collaborative work embedded the archaeological evidence into descendant community narratives of survival, bearing a form of witness that balanced past violence and twenty-first-century resilience. Wurst's concern over "the violence of violence" is a critical warning to future scholarship on the archaeology of violence, yet we believe that collaborative work with descendant communities offers a way forward.

Paul R. Mullins, Kyle Huskins, and Susan B. Hyatt

Placing violence at the heart of historical archaeology may seem like a rather prosaic shift in how we rhetorically describe inequality, but it potentially addresses a persistent tension in the early twenty-first-century discipline. On the one hand, nearly all historical archaeology now seems to be an archaeology of inequality, injustice, and oppression that examines various forms of structural and direct violence alike. Nothing could be more material than violence, and given the systemic injustices that historical archaeology documents, it might seem that violence is already the discipline's central narrative thread. On the other hand, archaeological scholarship of the past five hundred years routinely celebrates human agency in the face of all those systems of inequality. Archaeologists have indeed framed a rather dark history in which captivity, impoverishment, and injustice are persistent dimensions of human life, but structural violence risks looming simply as a backdrop against which archaeologists illuminate the everyday victories people have secured in the face of inequality.

A historical archaeology of violence is on some level a rhetorical shift in how we imagine the materiality of power and injustice, but it does not simply rename inequality, dark history, resistance, or everyday agency. Structural violence refers to systemic processes that make sustained oppression and suffering the fundamental feature of social life in the last five hundred years (Bernbeck 2008; Farmer

2004b; Galtung 1969). Rather than look at these features as aberrations in a theoretically equitable society, the "normal" practices of modern life inevitably and intentionally produce injustice. Violence is not merely the "backdrop" for human agency; it is the very structural condition that produces imagination, retreat, rejection, silence, and myriad other forms of resistance that negotiate injustice. Structural violence creates concrete conditions that leave these forms of everyday negotiation as the only capacities for action left available to many people.

A focus on structural violence compels us to examine the suffering that inhabits the ethnographically and archaeologically visible world. This description of oppression and inequality comes from Paul Farmer (2004b:305), who refers to the "ethnographically visible" as the disparate local faces of structural conditions that we encounter as "what is there in front of us." Farmer presses scholars to examine the utterly material visibility of violence as the surface of historical, social, and cultural linkages between suffering and power. This is an ambitious methodological approach to what is appropriately archaeological, and in many ways the aspiration to dissect the structural conditions of everyday life is familiar to historical archaeologists. For instance, contemporary segregated neighborhoods, memories of housing racism, environmental injustice, and persistent pockets of extreme poverty are rooted in more than a century of structural violence that made the racially segregated city "normal." Archaeologists certainly encounter myriad material dimensions of such structural racism in the form of house lots, the histories of particular families and neighbors, and of course the detritus of everyday life. Linking all these artifacts, from ceramic sherds to racist housing policies, is consistent with a broadly defined anthropological archaeology, so this methodology is not at all alien to most twenty-first-century scholars.

Nevertheless, historical archaeologists have often celebrated the human spirit in ways that hazard ignoring the deterministic dimensions of structural inequality. Historical archaeologists routinely invoke the material sway of capitalism, but scholarship has tended to valorize the ways anonymous masses carve everyday lives out in defiance of or obliviousness to capital. An archaeology that focuses on structural violence instead presses the discipline to acknowledge that oppression is a normal product of modern life embedded in fundamental structural processes. This also compels the discipline to more resolutely confront the suffering that is itself central to modern life; there are many effectual ways in which people recede from oppression and secure consequential lives in opposition to the interests of structural violence, but a sober archaeological picture of life in the last half millennium should more resolutely acknowledge the profound, persistent, and enormously undemocratic suffering wrought on many of the anonymous masses upon whom archaeological scholarship has often focused.

Christopher N. Matthews

I want to thank LouAnn Wurst for her insightful comments on this collection. I could not agree more that these chapters present only a partial view of how violence can be approached and interpreted in archaeology. Certainly, no collection can cover all aspects of violence or even the slightly more limited sorts of cruelty evident in structural violence. That said, I think she effectively points out how this collection does succeed in bringing to light myriad ways that structural violence can be documented and understood in archaeology. As she points out, contributors highlight such processes as the violence of reification and abstraction, the violence of controlling narratives, and presumed discontinuities between past and present, as well as the way people and communities are made visible or concealed through violent discursive and material means. I also sympathize with her assessment that the chapters enact some of the shortcomings of academic analysis and thus lack the passion and outrage that the topics we consider can and should elicit. On the latter, I defend the voice and standpoint of the volume by hoping that the work we produce and present objectively will be useful for not only stirring the emotions of readers but also providing solid foundations for action. I think Wurst would agree that we would prefer to see this research lead to action in the world guided by informed understanding more than a visceral disgust at how horrible people have been to each other.

It is this point in particular that I'd like to discuss further. Wurst cautions that the book dwells perhaps too much on defining violence and thus falls prey to reproducing the violence of reification and abstraction that we otherwise write against. In part she feels that we work through definitions to establish the currency of violence as a topic worth the attention of archaeologists. She argues that in so doing, we have not engaged with "previous archaeological research that tackled the very same issues under different names and using different framing concepts." She cites archaeological research on ideology, inequality, and power that seems to her to cover the same terrain. I do not think this is an accurate assessment.

As she points out, "violence is anything but safe." Such a simple statement is deceptively powerful since it captures much of what I think the chapters have done so well. Rather than rendering old wine in new skins, these studies individually and collectively center structural violence itself in ways not typical in archaeology. What this collection shows and leads us to think more about is not the asymmetrical cruelty of class, race, gender, or capital, but violence as itself a structuring social force in modernizing and modern society. That we present evidence of structural violence across a range of contexts further clarifies how it needs the sort of attention it has not yet received, having been to date an aspect of other relations and processes. The point here is to revise this tradition.

For example, while my chapter on binocular vision is certainly about the making of a racist landscape through political power and residential segregation, the focus is on how these were signs or results of an increasingly violent landscape and the installation of a carceral order to define and contain those deemed dangerous in modern urban space. Certainly, this was a racially informed assessment and, as Wurst rightly calls out, one perpetrated by specific persons who authored and enforced specific actions and policies (and thus was not the result of a nebulous white privilege). Indeed, I may have elected to tell the story of the city and the interstate as part of a process of racialization, which would have highlighted how anti-black and anti-Italian racism informed the decision-making of city, county, and state leaders as well as the thousands of whites who left Orange after being welcomed in new, racially restricted suburbs built along the Interstate 280 corridor. This version would have necessarily included the same evidence of corporeal and structural violence related to police actions, urban unrest, and capital flight, but the evidence would be presented as effects of larger ideological and racial justifications for the expansion of capital. This standpoint is not mistaken, but it is organized in a way that decenters and downplays the violence that makes up the core of this story.

Instead I put the focus on the making of the carceral landscape and how it was constructed and empowered to direct the way violence would be defined and used to determine the everyday experience of all county residents. The question of who is permitted to act violently and whose actions are interpreted as violent is a distinct discourse that, while informed by race, class, and capital flow, is not subordinate to them. If the relations of violence were subordinate to other social discourses, then drivers on I-280 could be considered just the same as those living in the towns they drive through. In such a scenario, the violent effects of the suburban commuter would become visible—and the everyday experience of violence by Orange and other urban core residents would be understood—only as the result of racism and uneven capitalist development in Essex County (as many analysts, such as Jackson [1985], suggest). Instead, I argue that the carceral landscape built in Essex County was created first and foremost to define who and what is violent as residents navigate the social and spatial worlds the landscape constructed. In this landscape the suburban commuter embodies the spirit of the frontiersman, whose daring escape from the city paved the way for the American suburban dream. No violence to see there, right? Residents of the urban core, on the other hand, are constructed to represent the sorts of people incapable of achieving this dream and are therefore excluded from it (again, no violence here). Yet the difference between these groups is not just the result of uneven development through which some communities were valued more than others but rather an uneven distribution of corporeal violence meant to contain and control some segments of the population for the benefit of others. In the carceral landscape, there are no bystanders. There are only communities constructed as deserving of violence and others that perpetrate it. The carceral landscape of Essex County includes everyone.

In the end, the way violence is brought into view in this collection is expressed simultaneously in discourse and narrative as well as corporeal suffering. It is through such manifold expressions that structural violence is normalized, since it is hard to see and know the world outside of the way violence constructs it. Re-sensitizing readers to how violence was endemic to these past societies, we hope opens up new perspectives on how social relations are formed and reproduced as well as deepens our understanding of the ways that cruelty can be hidden in the frameworks people objectively use to relate to the world.

REFERENCES CITED

Abu-Lughod, Janet L.

2002   Do Muslim Women Really Need Saving? Anthropological Reflections on
        Cultural Relativism and Its Others. *American Anthropologist* 104(3):783–90.

Abu-Lughod, Lila

2007   *Race, Space, and Riot in Chicago, New York, and Los Angeles*. Oxford University Press, New York.

Adam, Khalid Mohamed, Sahar Abdalla Abdaltam, Aisha Mustafa Noreldeen,
and Wafaa Alfadil Alseed

2015   Relationship between Maternal Blood Lead, Cadmium, and Zinc Levels
        and Spontaneous Abortion in Sudanese Women. *Public Health Research*
        5(6):171–76.

Agamben, Giorgio

1999   *Remnants of Auschwitz: The Witness and the Archive*. Translated by Daniel
        Heller-Roazen. Zone Books, New York.

2004   The Witness. In *Violence in War and Peace: An Anthology*, edited by Nancy
        Scheper-Hughes and Philippe Bourgois, pp. 437–42. Blackwell, Malden,
        MA.

Ahmann, Chloe

2018   "It's Exhausting to Create an Event Out of Nothing": Slow Violence and the
        Manipulation of Time. *Cultural Anthropology* 33(1):142–71.

Aldred, Sarah, and Rosemary H. Waring

2007   Mercury. In *Molecules of Death*, edited by Rosemary H. Waring, Glyn B.
        Steventon, and Steve C. Mitchell, pp. 167–86. Imperial College Press, London.

Aldrich, Mark

1997   The Perils of Mining Anthracite: Regulation, Technology and Safety, 1870–
        1945. *Pennsylvania History* 64(3):361–83.

Alexander, Michelle

2010   *The New Jim Crow: Mass Incarceration in the Age of Color Blindness.*
        New Press, New York.

Althusser, Louis

1971   *Lenin and Philosophy and Other Essays.* Translated by Ben Brewster.
        Monthly Review Press, New York.

Aparicio, Rodrigo.

1997   La Arquitectura Industrial y Utilitaria de Santiago, Capital Del Reino de
        Guatemala y Sus Alrededores. In *Approaches to the Historical Archaeol-
        ogy of Mexico, Central and South America,* edited by Janine Gasco, Greg
        Charles Smith, and Patricia Fournier-Garcia, pp. 71–82. Institute of Archae-
        ology, University of California, Los Angeles.

Appadurai, Arjun

1996   *Modernity at Large: Cultural Dimensions of Globalization.* University of
        Minnesota Press, Minneapolis.

Ardren, Traci

2006   Is "Apocalypto" Pornography? *Archaeology,* December 5, https://archive
        .archaeology.org/online/reviews/apocalypto.html, accessed June 22, 2019.

Arendt, Hannah

1969   *On Violence.* Harcourt, Brace, and World, New York.

Armstrong Fumero, Fernando

2011   Words and Things in Yucatán: Poststructuralism and the Everyday Life
        of Mayan Multiculturalism. *Journal of the Royal Anthropological Institute*
        17(1):63–81.

Arnold, Andrew

2014   *Fueling the Gilded Age.* New York University Press, New York.

Arnoldsson, Sverker

1960   La leyenda negra: Estudios sobre sus orígenes. Göteborgs universitets
        årsskrift 66. Almqvist & Wiksell, Stockholm.

Atalay, Sonya

2012   *Community-Based Archaeology: Research with, by and for Indigenous and
        Local Communities.* University of California Press, Berkeley.

Aurand, Harold

1970   Diversifying the Economy of the Anthracite Regions, 1880–1900. *Pennsylva-
        nia Magazine of History and Biography* 94(1):54–61.

1985   Mine Safety and Social Control in the Anthracite Industry. *Pennsylvania
        History* 52(4):227–41.

2002   The Lattimer Massacre: Who Owns History? An Introduction. *Pennsylvania History* 69(1):5–10.

2003   *Coalcracker Culture: Work and Values in Pennsylvania Anthracite, 1835–1935.* Susquehanna University Press, Selinsgrove, PA.

Azuma, Eiichiro

2005   *Between Two Empires: Race, History, and Transnationalism in Japanese America.* Oxford University Press, New York.

2009   Race, Citizenship, and the "Science of Chick Sexing": The Politics of Racial Identity among Japanese Americans. *Pacific Historical Review* 78(2):242–75.

Bahrani, Zainab

1998   Conjuring Mesopotamia: Imaginative Geography and a World Past. In *Archaeology under Fire: Nationalism, Politics and Heritage in the Eastern Mediterranean and Middle East,* edited by Lynn Meskell, 159–74. Routledge, London.

2008   *Rituals of War: The Body and Violence in Mesopotamia.* Zone Books, New York.

Baird, Jennifer A.

2011   Photographing Dura-Europos, 1928–1937: An Archaeology of the Archive. *American Journal of Archaeology* 115(3):427–46.

Bakewell, Peter John

1984   *Miners of the Red Mountain: Indian Labor in Potosí, 1545–1650.* University of New Mexico Press, Albuquerque.

Baldwin, James

1966   A Report from Occupied Territory. *Nation*, July 11, https://www.thenation.com/article/report-occupied-territory/, accessed June 14, 2019.

1972   *No Name in the Street.* Dial Press, New York.

Bandera, Juan de la, II

1990 [1569] Proceedings for the Account Which Captain Juan Pardo Gave of the Entrance Which He Made into the Land of the Floridas. Translated by Paul Hoffman. In *The Juan Pardo Expeditions: Explorations of the Carolinas and Tennessee, 1566–1568,* edited by Charles Hudson, pp. 205–96. Smithsonian Institution Press, Washington, DC.

Barnes, Jodi

2016   From Caffé Latte to Catholic Mass: The Archeology of a World War II Italian Prisoner of War Camp. In *Research, Preservation, Communication: Honoring Thomas J. Green on His Retirement from the Arkansas Archeological*

Survey, edited by M. B. Trubitt, pp. 245–68. Research Series 67. Arkansas Archeological Survey, Fayetteville.

Barrett, James R., and David Roediger

1997   Inbetween Peoples: Race, Nationality and the "New Immigrant" Working Class. *Journal of American Ethnic History* 16(3):3–44.

Barton, Chris

2012   Tacking between Black and White: Race Relations in Gilded Age Philadelphia. *International Journal of Historical Archaeology* 16(4):634–50.

Batz, Giovanni

2014   Maya Cultural Resistance in Los Angeles: The Recovery of Identity and Culture among Maya Youth. *Latin American Perspectives* 41(3):194–207.

Bauer, Brian S., Douglas K. Smit, Jesus Galiano Blanco,
and Antonio Coello Rodriquez

2017   El Camino del Mercurio de Huancavelica a Potosí. In *Nuevas tendencias en el estudio del camino inka*, edited by Sofia Chacaltana, Elizabeth Arkush, and Giancarlo Marcone, pp. 380–99. Ministerio de Cultura, Proyecto Qhapaq Ñan–Sede Nacional, Lima.

Baumann, Zygmunt

1989   *Modernity and the Holocaust*. Polity Press, Cambridge.

BBC News

2014   Michael Brown Shooting: Ferguson Residents React. BBC News, August 18, https://www.bbc.com/news/world-us-canada-28841350, accessed January 3, 2019.

Beaudry, Mary C.

1988   *Documentary Archaeology in the New World*. Cambridge University Press, New York.

1989   The Lowell Boott Mills Complex and Its Housing: Material Expressions of Corporate Ideology. *Historical Archaeology* 23(1):19–32.

Beck, Robin A., Christopher Bernard Rodning, and David G. Moore

2016   *Fort San Juan and the Limits of Empire: Colonialism and Household Practice at the Berry Site*. University Press of Florida, Gainesville.

Beck, Robin A., Lee Ann Newsom, Christopher B. Rodning, and David G. Moore

2017   Spaces of Entanglement: Labor and Construction Practice at Fort San Juan de Joara. *Historical Archaeology* 51(2):167–93.

Beckwith, Ronald J.

2013   Japanese-Style Ornamental Community Gardens at Manzanar Relocation Center. In *Prisoners of War: Archaeology, Memory, and Heritage of 19th-*

and 20th-Century Mass Internment, edited by Harold Mytum and Gillian Carr, pp. 271–84. Springer, New York.

Beisaw, April M., and James G. Gibb (editors)

2009   *The Archaeology of Institutional Life*. University of Alabama Press, Tuscaloosa.

Bender, Daniel E.

2009   *American Abyss: Savagery and Civilization in the Age of Industry*. Cornell University Press, Ithaca.

Benjamin, Walter

1968   *Illuminations: Walter Benjamin, Essays and Reflections*. Edited by Hannah Arendt. Translated by Harry Zohn. Schocken, New York.

1986 [1921]   Critique of Violence. Translated by Edmund Jephcott. In *Reflections: Essays, Aphorisms, Autobiographical Writings*, edited by Peter Demetz, pp. 277–300. Schocken, New York.

1999   *The Arcades Project*. Translated by Howard Eiland and Kevin McLaughlin. Belknap Press, Cambridge, MA.

Bernbeck, Reinhard

2005   The Past as Fact and Fiction: From Historical Novels to Novel Histories. In *Archaeologies of the Middle East: Critical Perspectives*, edited by Susan Pollock and Reinhard Bernbeck, pp. 97–122. Blackwell, Oxford.

2008   Structural Violence in Archaeology. *Archaeologies* 4(3):390–413.

2013   Heritage Void and the Void as Heritage. *Archaeologies* 9(3):526–45.

2015   From Imaginations of a Peopled Past to a Recognition of Past People. In *Subjects and Narratives in Archaeology*, edited by Ruth Van Dyke and Reinhard Bernbeck, pp. 257–76. University Press of Colorado, Boulder.

2017   *Materielle Spuren des nationalsozialistischen Terrors: Zu einer Archäologie der Zeitgeschichte*. Transcript Verlag, Bielefeld, Germany.

Bernbeck, Reinhard, and Susan Pollock

2007   "Grabe, Wo Du Stehst!" An Archaeology of Perpetrators. In *Archaeology and Capitalism*, edited by Yannis Hammilakis and Phillip Duke, pp. 217–33. Left Coast Press, Walnut Creek, CA.

2018   Quotidian and Transgressive Practices in Nazi Forced Labor Camps: The Role of Objects. *International Journal of Historical Archaeology* 22:454–71.

Bernhoft, Robin A.

2012   Mercury Toxicity and Treatment: A Review of the Literature. *Journal of Environmental and Public Health* 2012:460–508.

Bernstein, Alison R.

1991   *American Indians and World War II: Toward a New Era in Indian Affairs.*
University of Oklahoma Press, Norman.

Bersani, Leo, and Ulysse Dutoit

1985   *The Forms of Violence: Narrative in Assyrian Art and Modern Culture.*
Schocken, New York.

Berthoff, Rowland

1965   The Social Order of the Anthracite Region, 1825–1902. *Pennsylvania Maga-zine of History and Biography* 89(3):261–91.

Bhabha, Homi K.

1985   Signs Taken for Wonders: Questions of Ambivalence and Authority under a
Tree outside Delhi, May 1817. *Critical Inquiry* 12(1):144–65.

Black Lives Matter

2019   Herstory. Black Lives Matter, https://blacklivesmatter.com/about/herstory,
accessed January 3, 2019.

Blaisdell-Sloan, Kira

2006   An Archaeology of Place and Self: The Pueblo de Indios of Ticamaya, Hon-duras (1300–1800 AD). PhD dissertation, University of California, Berkeley.

Blakey, Michael

1998   The New York African Burial Ground Project: An Examination of En-slaved Lives, a Construction of Ancestral Ties. *Transforming Anthropology*
7(1):53–58.

Blatz, Perry K.

2002   Reflections on Lattimer: A Complex and Significant Event. *Pennsylvania
History* 69(1):42–51.

Bleibtreu, Erika

1980   *Die Flora der neuassyrischen Reliefs: eine Untersuchung zu den Orthostaten-reliefs des 9.–7. Jahrhunderts v. Chr.* Verlag des Institutes für Orientalistik
der Universität Wien, Vienna.

Bohrer, Frederick N.

2011   *Photography and Archaeology.* Reaktion Books, London.

Bolger, Frank

1979a   Cops Kill Youth after Chase. *Orange Transcript* 81(45):1.

1979b   Hundreds March after Youth Shot. *Orange Transcript* 81(45):1.

1979c   City Wards Communicate. *Orange Transcript* 81(46):1.

1979d   Hackett Blasts Council and Mayor for "Silence." *Orange Transcript* 81(49):1.

1980   Soaries Raps State Jury Vote. *Orange Transcript* 82(5):1.

Borgstede, Greg, and Eugenia Robinson

2012   The Archaeology of the Late Postclassic Maya Highlands. In *The Oxford Handbook of Mesoamerican Archaeology*, edited by Deborah L Nichols, pp. 405–18. Oxford University Press, New York.

Borgstede, Greg, and Jason Yaeger

2008   Notions of Cultural Continuity and Disjunction in Maya Social Movements and Maya Archaeology. In *Archaeology and the Postcolonial Critique*, edited by Matthew Liebmann and Uzma Z. Rizvi, pp. 91–108. Alta Mira Press, Lanham, MD.

Boura, Frédérique

2017   My Encounter with the Writer Alain-Fournier, Who Died in World War I. In *Clashes of Time: The Contemporary Past as a Challenge for Archaeology*, edited by Jean-Marie Blaising, Jan Driessen, Jean-Pierre Legendre, and Laurent Olivier, pp. 23–28. Presses Universitaires de Louvain, Louvain-la-Nueve, Belgium.

Bourdieu, Pierre

1977   *Outline of a Theory of Practice*. Cambridge University Press, Cambridge.

Bourdieu, Pierre, and Jean-Claude Passeron

1990   *Reproduction in Education, Society and Culture*. Translated by Richard Nice. Sage, London.

Bourdieu, Pierre, and Loïc Wacquant

2004   Symbolic Violence. In *Violence in War and Peace: An Anthology*, edited by Nancy Scheper-Hughes and Philippe Bourgois, pp. 272–74. Blackwell, Malden, MA.

Bradby, Barbara M.

1982   Plan, Market and Money: A Study of Circulation in Peru. PhD dissertation, Department of Sociology, University of Sussex, Falmer, UK.

Braidotti, Rosi

2015   The Posthuman. Paper presented at the Central New York Humanities Corridor Seminar, Syracuse, February 13.

Branton, Nicole L.

2000   Rice Bowls and Resistance: Cultural Persistence at the Manzanar War Relocation Center, California. Master's thesis, Department of Anthropology, University of Arizona, Tucson.

2004   Drawing the Line: Places of Power in the Japanese-American Internment Eventscape. PhD dissertation, Department of Anthropology, University of Arizona, Tucson.

Braswell, Geoffrey E.

2003   K'iche Origins and Ethnogenesis in the PC Mesoamerican World. In *The Postclassic Mesoamerican World*, edited by Michael E. Smith and Frances F. Berdan, pp. 297–303. University of Utah Press, Salt Lake City.

Breglia, Lisa

2006   *Monumental Ambivalence: The Politics of Heritage*. University of Texas Press, Austin.

Brereton, Gareth

2018   *I Am Assurbanipal: King of the World, King of Assyria*. Thames & Hudson, London.

Bricker, Victoria R.

2009   *The Indian Christ, the Indian King: The Historical Substrate of Maya Myth and Ritual*. University of Texas Press, Austin.

Bromwich, Jonah Engel

2016   Trump Camp's Talk of Registry and Japanese Internment Raises Muslims' Fears. *New York Times*, November 17, https://www.nytimes.com/2016/11/18/us/politics/japanese-internment-muslim-registry.html, accessed June 12, 2019.

Brooks-Kelly, Amanda

2016   The Black Truth: Understanding Theodore de Bry's Role in the "Black Legend." *Bowdoin Journal of Art* 1(1):1–31.

Brown, Gordon G.

1945   Final Report: War Relocation Authority, Gila River Project, Rivers, Arizona. Community Analysis Section. *Applied Anthropology* 4(4):1–49.

Brown, Kendall W.

2001   Workers' Health and Colonial Mercury Mining at Huancavelica, Peru. *Americas* 57(4):467–96.

2012   *A History of Mining in Latin America: From the Colonial Era to the Present*. University of New Mexico Press, Albuquerque.

Brown, Marley R., and Patricia M. Samford

1990   Recent Evidence of Eighteenth-Century Gardening in Williamsburg, Virginia. In *Earth Patterns: Essays in Landscape Archaeology*, edited by William Kelso and Rachel Most, pp. 103–22. University of Virginia Press, Charlottesville.

Browning, Christopher R.

1992   *Ordinary Men: Reserve Police Battalion 101 and the Final Solution in Poland*. Harper Collins, New York.

Brunke, Hagan, Evelyne Bukowiecki, Eva Cancik-Kirschbaum, Ricardo Eichmann, Margarete van Ess, Anton Gass, Martin Gussone, Sebastian Hageneuer, Svend Hansen, Werner Kogge, Jens May, Hermann Parzinger, Olof Pedersén, Dorothée Sack, Franz Schopper, and Ulrike Wulf-Rheidt

2016   Thinking Big: Research in Monumental Constructions in Antiquity. *eTopoi: Journal for Ancient Studies* 6:250–305.

Buchli, Victor, and Gavin Lucas, eds.

2001   *Archaeologies of the Contemporary Past*. Routledge, New York.

Bureau of Municipal Research

1917   Report on a Survey of the City Government of the City of Indianapolis W. H. Burford, Indianapolis.

Burton, Jeff F.

1996   *Three Farewells to Manzanar: The Archaeology of Manzanar National Historic Site, California*. Publications in Anthropology 67. Western Archaeological and Conservation Center, National Park Service, US Department of the Interior, Tucson.

1998   *The Archaeology of Somewhere: Archaeological Testing along US Highway 395, Manzanar National Historic Site, California*. Publications in Anthropology 72. Western Archaeological and Conservation Center, National Park Service, US Department of the Interior, Tucson.

2015   *Garden Management Plan: Gardens and Gardeners*. National Park Service, US Department of the Interior, Manzanar National Historic Site, Independence, CA.

2017   Excavating Legacy: Community Archaeology at a Japanese American World War II Incarceration Site. *Journal of Community Archaeology and Heritage* 4(3):160–72.

Burton, Jeff F., and Mary M. Farrell

2001   *This Is Minidoka: An Archeological Survey of Minidoka Internment National Monument, Idaho*. Publications in Anthropology 80. Western Archaeological and Conservation Center, National Park Service, US Department of the Interior, Tucson.

2005   *Tule Lake Segregation Center*. Western Archaeological and Conservation Center, National Park Service, US Department of the Interior, Tucson.

2006   *Poston Relocation Center*. Western Archaeological and Conservation Center, National Park Service, US Department of the Interior, Tucson.

2007   *World War II Japanese American Internment Sites in Hawai'i*. Trans-Sierran Archaeological Research, Tucson.

2008   *Jigoku-Dani: An Archaeological Reconnaissance of the Honouliuli Internment Camp, O'ahu, Hawai'i.* Trans-Sierran Archaeological Research,
Tucson.

2013   "Life in Manzanar Where There Is a Spring Breeze": Graffiti at a World
War II Japanese American Internment Camp. In *Prisoners of War: Archaeology, Memory, and Heritage of 19th- and 20th-Century Mass Internment,*
edited by Harold Mytum and Gillian Carr, pp. 239–69. Springer, New York.

2014   *A Place of Beauty and Serenity: Excavation and Restoration of the Arai
Family Fish Pond.* National Park Service, US Department of the Interior,
Manzanar National Historic Site, Independence, CA.

Burton, Jeff F., Mary M. Farrell, Florence B. Lord, and Richard W. Lord

1999   *Confinement and Ethnicity: An Overview of World War II Japanese American
Relocation Sites.* Publications in Anthropology 74. Western Archaeological
and Conservation Center, National Park Service, US Department of the
Interior, Tucson.

Burton, Jeff F., J. D. Haines, and Mary M. Farrell

2001   *I Rei To: Archaeological Investigations at the Manzanar Relocation Cemetery, Manzanar National Historic Site, California.* Publications in Anthropology 79. Western Archaeological and Conservation Center, National Park
Service, US Department of the Interior, Tucson.

Butler, Judith

1997   *The Psychic Life of Power: Theories in Subjection.* Stanford University Press,
Stanford, CA.

2009   *Frames of War: When Is Life Grieveable?* Verso, London.

Byrd, Jodi A.

2012   Fracturing Futurity: Colonial Agnosia and the Untimely Indigenous Present.
Lecture presented at the University of New Mexico, Albuquerque, October 25.

Caluco Archive

1753   Decree of March 21. Survey conducted by Juan Antonio Bósquez y Artiaga,
Juez Subdelegado, to Enact the Policy of Composición Moderado. Caluco
Archive, Caluco, El Salvador.

Camp, Stacey

2013   *The Archaeology of Citizenship.* University Press of Florida, Gainesville.

2016   Landscapes of Japanese American Internment. *Historical Archaeology*
50(1):169–86.

Camus, Albert

1942   *The Stranger.* Vintage, New York.

Cardós de Méndez, Amalia

1959   El comercio de los mayas antiguos. *Acta Antropológica, Época* 2 2(1).
        Escuela Nacional de Antropología e Historia, Mexico City.

Carmack, Robert M.

1973   *Quichean Civilization: The Ethnohistoric, Ethnographic, and Archaeological
        Sources.* University of California Press, Berkeley.

Carrasco, David

1995   Cosmic Jaws: We Eat the Gods and the Gods Eat Us. *Journal of the Ameri-
        can Academy of Religion* 63(3):429–63.

Casella, Eleanor Conlin

2001a   Landscapes of Punishment and Resistance: A Female Convict Settlement in
        Tasmania, Australia. In *Contested Landscapes of Movement and Exile,* edited
        by Barbara Bender and Margot Winer, pp. 103–30. Berg Publishers, Oxford.

2001b   To Watch or Restrain: Female Convict Prisons in 19th-Century Tasmania.
        International Journal of Historical Archaeology 5(1):45–72.

2007a   *The Archaeology of Institutional Confinement.* University Press of Florida,
        Gainesville.

2007b   Detention Castles of Stone and Steel: Landscape, Labor, and the Urban
        Penitentiary. *Historical Archaeology* 41(2):185–86.

Castañeda, Quetzil E.

1996   *In the Museum of Maya Culture: Touring Chichén Itzá.* University of Minne-
        sota Press, Minneapolis.

Center for Government Services

2016   New Jersey Data Book. Center for Government Services, Rutgers Univer-
        sity, http://njdatabook.rutgers.edu/center-government-services-new-jersey
        -data-book, accessed June 14, 2019.

Chakrabarty, Dipesh

2000   *Provincializing Europe.* Princeton University Press, Princeton, NJ.

Chambers, Samuel A.

2013   *The Lessons of Rancière.* Oxford University Press, New York.

Chandler, Alfred D., Jr.

1972   Anthracite Coal and the Beginnings of the Industrial Revolution in the
        United States. *Business History Review* 46(2):141–81.

Chapman, Anne M.

1957   Port of Trade Enclaves in Aztec and Maya Civilization. In *Trade and Market
        in the Early Empires,* edited by Karl Polanyi, Conrad M. Arensberg, and
        Harry W. Pearson, pp. 144–53. Free Press, Glencoe, IL.

Charim, Isolde

2009　*Der Althusser-Effekt. Entwurf Einer Ideologietheorie.* Passagen Verlag, Vienna.

Chicone, Sarah J.

2011　Respectable Rags: Working-Class Poverty and the 1913–14 Southern Colorado Coal Strike. *International Journal of Historical Archaeology* 15(4):51–81.

Chinchilla, Oswaldo

2012　Archaeology in Guatemala: Nationalist, Colonialist, Imperialist. In *The Oxford Handbook of Mesoamerican Archaeology*, edited by Deborah L. Nichols and Christopher A. Pool, pp. 54–68. Oxford University Press, New York.

Chuman, Frank F.

1976　*The Bamboo People: The Law and Japanese-Americans.* Publisher's Inc., Del Mar, CA.

City of Indianapolis

1904　*The General Ordinances of the City of Indianapolis: Containing, Also Acts of the Indiana General Assembly, So Far as They Control Said City, to Which is Prefixed a Chronological Roster of Officers from 1832 to 1904, and Rules Governing the Common Council.* Burford Printing, Indianapolis.

Clark, Bonnie J.

2017　Digging Yesterday: The Archaeology of Living Memory at Amache. In *Historical Archaeology through a Western Lens*, edited by Mark S. Warner and Margaret Sermons Purser, pp. 210–32. University of Nebraska Press, Lincoln.

Coates, Ta-Nehisi

2016　The Enduring Solidarity of Whiteness. *Atlantic*, February 8, http://www.theatlantic.com/politics/archive/2016/02/why-we-write/459909/, accessed June 14, 2019.

Coe, Michael D.

1993　*The Maya.* Thames and Hudson, New York.

Cojtí Cuxil, Demetrio

1996　The Politics of Maya Revindication. In *Maya Cultural Activism in Guatemala*, edited by Edward F. Fischer and R. McKenna Brown, pp. 19–50. University of Texas, Austin.

Collette, Matt

2013　Toni Morrison: "Goodness" More Powerful Than Violence, Hate. *News@Northeastern*, January 22, https://news.northeastern.edu/2013/01/22/toni-morrison/, accessed June 6, 2019.

Collins, Paul

2008　*Assyrian Palace Sculptures.* British Museum, London.

Collins, Randall

2008   *Violence. A Micro-Sociological Theory.* Princeton University Press, Princeton, NJ.

Colop, Enrique Sam

1996   The Discourse of Concealment and 1992. In *Maya Cultural Activism in Guatemala*, edited by Edward F. Fischer and R. McKenna Brown, pp. 107-13. University of Texas Press, Austin.

Colwell, Chip, and Charlotte Joy

2015   Communities and Ethics in the Heritage Debate. In *Global Heritage: A Reader*, edited by Lynn Meskell, pp. 112-30. Wiley, Malden, MA.

Commission on Wartime Relocation and Internment of Civilians (CWRIC)

1983   Personal Justice Denied: Report of the Commission on Wartime Relocation and Internment of Civilians. CWRIC, http://hdl.handle.net/2027/mdp .39015019141285, accessed June 12, 2019.

Cooke, Colin A., Holger Hintelmann, Jay J. Ague, Richard Burger, Harald Biester, Julian P. Sachs, and Daniel R. Engstrom

2013   Use and Legacy of Mercury in the Andes. *Environmental Science & Technology* 47(9):4181-88.

Coronil, Fernando

2007   After Empire: Reflections on Imperialism from the Americas. In *Imperial Formations*, edited by Ann Stoler, Laura McGranahan, and Peter C. Perdue, pp. 241-74. SAR Press, Santa Fe, NM.

Covarrubias Orozco, Sebastián de

1995 [1611] *Tesoro de la lengua castellana o española.* Edited by Felipe C. R. Maldonado. Editorial Castalia, Madrid.

Crane, Susan A.

2008   Choosing Not to Look: Representation, Repatriation, and Holocaust Atrocity Photography. *History and Theory* 47(3):309-30.

Crawford, Vaughn E., Prudence O. Harper, and Holly Pittman

1980   *Assyrian Reliefs and Ivories in the Metropolitan Museum of Art: Palace Reliefs of Assurnasirpal II and Ivory Carvings from Nimrud.* Metropolitan Museum of Art, New York.

D'Agostino, Peter

2002   Craniums, Criminals, and the "Cursed Race": Italian Anthropology in American Racial Thought, 1861-1924. *Comparative Studies in Society and History* 44(2):319-43.

Dalglish, Chris

2012   Archaeology and Landscape Ethics. *World Archaeology* 44(3):327-41.

Dalglish, Chris (editor)

2013   *Archaeology, the Public and the Recent Past.* Boydell Press, Woodbridge, UK.

Daniels, Roger

2005   Words Do Matter: A Note on Inappropriate Terminology and the Incarceration of the Japanese Americans. In *Nikkei in the Pacific Northwest: Japanese Americans and Japanese Canadians in the Twentieth Century*, edited by Louis Fiset and Gail Nomura, pp. 183–207. University of Washington Press, Seattle.

Daston, Lorraine, and Peter Galison

1992   The Image of Objectivity. *Representations* 40:81–128.

Davis, Whitney

1996   *Replications: Archaeology, Art History, Psychoanalysis.* Pennsylvania State University Press, University Park.

De Backer, Fabrice

2009   Cruelty and Military Refinements. *Res Antiquae* 6:13–50.

Deagan, Kathleen

1983   *Spanish St. Augustine: The Archaeology of a Colonial Creole Community.* Academic Press, New York.

Deetz, James

1996   *In Small Things Forgotten: The Archaeology of Early American Life.* Doubleday, New York.

DeGuzmán, María

2005   *Spain's Long Shadow: The Black Legend, Off-Whiteness, and Anglo-American Empire.* University of Minnesota Press, Minneapolis.

DeJong, David H.

2011   *Forced to Abandon Our Fields: The 1914 Clay Southworth Gila River Pima Interviews.* University of Utah Press, Salt Lake City.

2016   *Stealing the Gila: The Pima Agricultural Economy and Water Deprivation, 1848–1921.* University of Arizona Press, Tucson.

Delgado, Edwin

2018   "A Dangerous Precedent": Texans Outraged at Prospect of Tent Cities for Migrants. *Guardian*, November 18, https://www.theguardian.com/us-news/2018/nov/18/texas-fort-bliss-migrant-cities-of-tents-locals-outraged, accessed June 12, 2019.

Dell, Melissa

2010   The Persistent Effects of Peru's Mining *Mita*. *Econometrica* 78(6):1863–1903.

Delvas, Fidalgo

1557   Relaçam verdadeira dos trabalhos q[ue] ho gouernador do[m] Ferna[n]do
       d[e] Souto [e] certos fidalgos portugueses passarom no d[e]scobrime[n]to
       da prouincia da Frolida. Andree de Burgos, Evora, Portugal.

Dent, Joshua

2013   False Frontiers: Archaeology and the Myth of the Canadian Wilderness.
       University of Western Ontario Anthropology Journal 21(1):59–71.

Department of Justice

2010   Clean Water Act Settlement with Indianapolis Will Reduce Pollution at
       Lower Costs. Department of Justice, https://www.justice.gov/opa/pr
       /clean-water-act-settlement-indianapolis-will-reduce-pollution-lower-costs,
       accessed November 18, 2016.

DePratter, Chester, Charles Hudson, and Marvin Smith

1983   Juan Pardo's Explorations in the Interior Southeast, 1566–1568. *Florida His-
       torical Quarterly* 62:125–58.

Dewan, Eve H.

2016   Identities in the Arena: The Archaeology of Sports and Gender at Indian
       Boarding Schools. Master's thesis, Department of Anthropology, Brown
       University, Providence, RI.

Diamond, Jared

2005   *Collapse: How Societies Choose to Fail or Succeed.* Rev. ed. Penguin,
       New York.

Dickie, John

1999   *Darkest Italy: The Nation and Stereotypes of the Mezzogiorno, 1860–1900.*
       St. Martin's Press, New York.

Diggs, John C.

1914   A Sanitary Survey of White River. *Journal of Industrial and Engineering
       Chemistry* 6(8):639–40.

Dillingham Commission (United States Immigration Commission)

1911a *Reports of the Immigration Commission.* Vol. 6, *Immigrants in Industries:
       Bituminous Coal Mining.* Government Printing Office, Washington, DC.

1911b *Reports of the Immigration Commission.* Vol. 16, *Immigrants in Industries:
       Anthracite Coal Mining.* Government Printing Office, Washington, DC.

Diner, Dan (editor)

1988   *Zivilisationsbruch: Denken nach Auschwitz.* Fischer Taschenbuch, Frankfurt.

Distelhorst, Lars

2007   *Umkämpfte Differenz: Hegemonietheoretische Perspektiven der Geschlech-
       terpolitik mit Butler und Laclau.* Parodos, Berlin.

Dobyns, Henry

1991   New Native World: Links between Demographic and Cultural Changes. In *Columbian Consequences: The Spanish Borderlands in Pan-American Perspective*, Vol. 3, edited by David Hurst Thomas, pp. 541–59. Smithsonian Institution Press, Washington, DC.

Dublin, Thomas, and Walter Licht

2005   *The Face of Decline: The Pennsylvania Anthracite Region in the Twentieth Century*. Cornell University Press, Ithaca.

Dubofsky, Melvyn

1996   *Industrialism and the American Worker, 1865–1920*. Harlan Davidson, Wheeling, IL.

Du Bois, W. E. B.

1920   *Darkwater: Voices from within the Veil*. Harcourt, Brace, and Howe, New York.

Duncan, William N., and Kevin R. Schwarz

2015   A Postclassic Maya Mass Grave from Zacpetén, Guatemala. *Journal of Field Archaeology* 40(2):143–65.

Dunn, Jacob Piatt

1912   *Memorial and Genealogical Record of Representative Citizens of Indiana*. B. F. Bowen and Company, Indianapolis.

Dunnell, Robert C.

1991   Methodological Impacts of Catastrophic Depopulation on American Archaeology and Ethnology. In *Columbian Consequences: The Spanish Borderlands in Pan-American Perspective*, Vol. 3, edited by David Hurst Thomas, pp. 561–80. Smithsonian Institution Press, Washington, DC.

Dusselier, Jane E.

2008   *Artifacts of Loss: Crafting Survival in Japanese American Concentration Camps*. Rutgers University Press, New Brunswick, NJ.

Dyson, Michael Eric

2016   Death in Black and White. *New York Times*, July 7, http://www.nytimes.com/2016/07/10/opinion/sunday/what-white-america-fails-to-see.html, accessed June 14, 2019.

Eco, Umberto

2008   *Experiences in Translation*. Translated by Alastair McEwen. University of Toronto Press, North York.

Edelmayer, Friedrich

2011   The "Leyenda Negra" and the Circulation of Anti-Catholic and Anti-Spanish Prejudices. European History Online, http://www.ieg-ego.eu/edelmayerf-2010-en, accessed October 8, 2018.

Edmonds, Penelope, and Tracey Banivanua Mar

2010   *Making Settler Colonial Space: Perspectives on Race, Place and Identity.* Palgrave Macmillan, London.

Edwards, Elizabeth

2012   Objects of Affect: Photography beyond the Image. *Annual Review of Anthropology* 41:221–34.

Effland, Richard W., and Margerie Green

1983   *Cultural Resource Assessment for the Gila River Farms Indian Community, GRIC.* Archaeological Consulting Services, Tempe.

Ekinaka, Yuriko

1944   #36. Ekinaka, Yuriko. Online Archive of California, http://www.oac.cdlib .org/ark:/28722/bk0013c585x/?brand=oac4, accessed June 12, 2019.

Elias, Norbert

1969   *Über den Prozeß der Zivilisation.* Suhrkamp, Frankfurt.

Ellis, Sheri Murray

2002   *Site Documentation and Management Plan for the Topaz Relocation Center, Millard County, Utah.* SWCA Environmental Consultants, Delta, UT.

Elmadag, Mehmet, Hasan Huseyin Ceylan, Kerem Bilsel, and Mehmet Erdil

2012   Floating Shoulder: Ipsilateral Clavicle, Scapular Body and Glenoid Fracture: A Case Report. *Malaysian Orthopaedic Journal* 6(4):35–37.

Englert, George E.

1980   Black, White, and Orange: A Negative Image. *Orange Transcript* 82(2):4.

Epperson, Terrance W.

1999   Constructing Difference: The Social and Spatial Order of the Chesapeake Plantation. In *"I, Too, Am America": Archaeological Studies of African-American Life,* edited by Theresa A. Singleton, pp. 159–72. University of North Carolina Press, Charlottesville.

Eppler-Epstein, Sarah

2016   What We Do and Don't Know about Race and Policing. *Urban Wire: Crime and Justice,* July 20, http://www.urban.org/urban-wire/what-we-do-and-dont -know-about-race-and-policing, accessed June 20, 2019.

Esaki, Brett

2013   Multidimensional Silence, Spirituality, and the Japanese American Art of Gardening. *Journal of Asian American Studies* 16(3):235–65.

Escalante, Emilio del Valle

2009   *Maya Nationalisms and Postcolonial Challenges in Guatemala: Coloniality, Modernity, and Identity Politics.* SAR Press, Santa Fe, NM.

Escalante Arce, Pedro Antonio

1992   *Códice Sonsonate: Crónicas hispánicas.* 2 vols. Consejo Nacional para la Cultura y el Arte, San Salvador.

Fabian, Johannes

1983   *Time and the Other: How Anthropology Makes Its Object.* Columbia University Press, New York.

Fahidi, Éva

2011   *Die Seele Der Dinge.* Translated by Doris Fischer. Lukas-Verlag, Berlin.

Fanon, Frantz

1963   *The Wretched of the Earth.* Translated by Constance Farrington. Grove Press, New York.

Farmer, Paul

1999   *Infections and Inequalities: The Modern Plagues.* University of California Press, Berkeley.

2003   *Pathologies of Power: Health, Human Rights, and the New War on the Poor.* University of California Press, Berkeley.

2004a   On Suffering and Structural Violence: The View from Below. In *Violence in War and Peace: An Anthology*, edited by Nancy Scheper-Hughes and Philippe Bourgois, pp. 281–89. Blackwell Publishers, Malden, MA.

2004b   An Anthropology of Structural Violence. *Current Anthropology* 45(3): 305–25.

Farmer, Paul E., Bruce Nizeye, Sara Stulac, and Salmaan Keshavjee

2006   Structural Violence and Clinical Medicine. *PLoS Med* 3(10):e449.

Farrell, Mary, and Jeff Burton

2011   Gordon Hirabayashi, the Tucsonians, and the US Constitution: Negotiating Reconciliation in a Landscape of Exile. In *Archaeologies of Internment*, edited by Adrian Myers and Gabriel Moshenska, pp. 89–110. Springer, New York.

Feld, Steven, and Keith H. Basso (editors)

1996   *Senses of Place.* School of American Research Press, Santa Fe, NM.

Fischer, Edward F.

1999   Cultural Logic and Maya Identity: Rethinking Constructivism and Essentialism. *Current Anthropology* 40(4):473–99.

Fischer, Edward F., and R. McKenna Brown

1996   Introduction: Maya Cultural Activism in Guatemala. In *Maya Cultural Activism in Guatemala*, edited by Edward F. Fischer and R. McKenna Brown, pp. 1–18. University of Texas Press, Austin.

Fischer, Edward F., and Carol Hendrickson

2003   *Tecpan Guatemala: A Modern Maya Town in Global and Local Context.* Westview Press, Cambridge, MA.

Fitts, Robert K.

2002   Becoming American: The Archaeology of an Italian Immigrant. *Historical Archaeology* 36(2):1–17.

Fitts, Robert K., J. Klein, and C. Milne

2000   Immigrant Life in Turn-of-the-Century Jamaica, Queens. Stage II and III Archaeological Investigations at the Proposed Queens Family Court and Families Court Agencies Facility, Blocks 10092 and 10093 (Former Black 10097), Jamaica, Queens, New York. John Milner Associates, West Chester, PA.

Fitz-Gerald, Kyla

2015   Cold Cream, Masculinity, and Imprisonment: The Archaeology of Japanese American Internees at Idaho's Kooskia Internment Camp, 1943–1945. Master's thesis, Department of Anthropology, University of Idaho, Moscow.

Folkmar, Daniel

1911   *Reports of the Immigration Commission, Dictionary of Races and Peoples,* Vol. 5. Government Printing Office, Washington, DC.

Forensic Architecture (editor)

2014   *Forensis: The Architecture of Public Truth.* Sternberg Press, Berlin.

Foucault, Michel

1975   *Surveiller et punir.* Gallimard, Paris.

1977   *Discipline and Punish: The Birth of the Prison.* Translated by Alan Sheridan. Vintage, New York.

2000   *Power,* Vol. 3. Edited by James D. Faubion. Translated by Robert Hurley. New Press, New York.

Foulke, Calvin Pardee, and William G. Foulke

1979   *Calvin Pardee, 1941–1923: His Family and His Enterprises.* Pardee Company, Philadelphia.

Fowler, William R.

1995   *Caluco, Historia y Arqueología de un Pueblo Pipil en el Siglo XVI.* Proyecto "Venga Y Busque Con Nosotros," Patronato Pro-Patrimonio Cultural: Fundación Interamericana, San Salvador.

2011   *Ciudad Vieja: Excavaciones, Arquitectura y Paisaje Cultural de la Primera Villa de San Salvador.* Editorial Universitaria Universidad De El Salvador, San Salvador.

Fox, John W.

1980   Lowland to Highland Mexicanization Processes in Southern Mesoamerica. *American Antiquity* 45(1):43–54.

Franklin, Maria

1997   "Power to the People": Sociopolitics and the Archaeology of Black Americans. *Historical Archaeology* 31(3):36–50.

2001   A Black Feminist-Inspired Archaeology. *Journal of Social Archaeology* 1(1):108–25.

French, Brigittine M.

2010   *Maya Ethnolinguistic Identity: Violence, Cultural Rights, and Modernity in Highland Guatemala.* University of Arizona Press, Tucson.

Friedman, Daniel

1974   Marx's Perspective on the Objective Class Structure. *Polity* 6(3):318–44.

Frühsorge, Lars

2007   Archaeological Heritage in Guatemala: Indigenous Perspectives on the Ruins of Iximche. *Archaeologies* 3(1):39–58.

Fullilove, Mindy Thompson

2013   *Urban Alchemy: Restoring Joy in America's Sorted-Out Cities.* New Village Press, New York.

Gall, Marion, and Ralph Izard

1986   The Journalist In Life-Saving Situations: Detached Observer or Good Samaritan? *Journal of Mass Media Ethics* 1(2):61–67.

Galtung, Johan

1969   Violence, Peace, and Peace Research. *Journal of Peace Research* 6(3): 167–91.

1985   Twenty-Five Years of Peace Research: Ten Challenges and Some Responses. *Journal of Peace Research* 22(2):141–58.

1987   Review Essay: Only One Quarrel with Kenneth Boulding. *Journal of Peace Research* 24(2):199–203.

Garman, James C.

2005   *Detention Castles of Stone and Steel: Landscape, Labor and the Urban Penitentiary.* University of Tennessee Press, Knoxville.

Gat, Azar

2008   *War in Human Civilization.* Oxford University Press, New York.

Gazin-Schwartz, Amy

2008   Abandoned, Avoided, Expelled: The Creation of "Empty" Landscapes. In *Landscapes of Clearance: Archaeological and Anthropological Perspectives,*

edited by Angèle Smith and Amy Gazin-Schwartz, pp. 25–45. Left Coast
Press, Walnut Creek, CA.

Geiger, Andrea A. E.

2011   *Subverting Exclusion: Transpacific Encounters with Race, Caste, and Borders, 1885–1928.* Yale University Press, New Haven, CT.

Gibb, James G.

2015   Constructive Imagination and the Elusive Past: Playwriting as Method. In
Subjects and Narratives in Archaeology, edited by Ruth Van Dyke and Reinhard Bernbeck, pp. 145–67. University Press of Colorado, Boulder.

Giddens, Anthony

1984   *The Constitution of Society: Outline of the Theory of Structuration.* University of California Press, Berkeley.

1985   *The Nation-State and Violence: Contemporary Critique of Historical Materialism,* Vol. 2. University of California Press, Berkeley.

Gila News-Courier

1942a   Contests Open. *Gila News-Courier* 1(5), https://ddr.densho.org/media/ddr
-densho-141/ddr-densho-141-5-master-f72da47131-a.jpg, accessed June 12, 2019.

1942b   Flowers, Shrubs, Lawns Beautify School Area. *Gila News-Courier* 1(3),
https://ddr.densho.org/media/ddr-densho-141/ddr-densho-141-30-master
-3c87f06df5-a.jpg, accessed June 12, 2019.

1943   Trees for Shade, Beauty Sprout in Canal Community. *Gila News-Courier*
2(11), https://ddr.densho.org/media/ddr-densho-141/ddr-densho-141-45
-master-8dc6239591-a.jpg, accessed June 12, 2019.

Gold'n, Liliana R.

2011   *Global Maya: Work and Ideology in Rural Guatemala.* University of Arizona
Press, Tucson.

Goldhagen, Daniel J.

1996   *Hitler's Willing Executioners: Ordinary Germans and the Holocaust.* Alfred
A. Knopf, New York.

Golitko, Mark, and Lawrence H. Keeley

2007   Beating Ploughshares Back into Swords: Warfare in the Linearbandkeramik.
Antiquity 81:332–42.

González-Ruibal, Alfredo

2008   Time to Destroy: An Archaeology of Supermodernity. *Current Anthropology*
49(2):247–79.

González-Ruibal, A., and Gabriel Moshenska (editors)

2015   *Ethics and the Archaeology of Violence.* Springer, New York.

González-Tennant, Edward

2016   Hate Sits in Places: Folk Knowledge and the Power of Place in Rosewood, Florida. In *Excavating Memory: Material Culture Approaches to Sites of Remembering and Forgetting,* edited by Maria T. Starzmann and John R. Roby, pp. 218–41. University Press of Florida, Gainesville.

2018   *The Rosewood Massacre: An Archaeology and History of Intersectional Violence.* University Press of Florida, Gainesville.

Gorman, Michael

1985   *Heart Mountain Relocation Center National Register of Historic Places, Nomination Forum.* Wyoming Recreation Commission, Cheyenne.

Gosden, Chris

2004   *Archaeology and Colonialism: Cultural Contact from 5000 BC to the Present.* Cambridge University Press, New York.

Gosner, Kevin

1992   *Soldiers of the Virgin: The Moral Economy of a Colonial Maya Rebellion.* University of Arizona Press, Tucson.

Gould, Rae

2014   Cultural Practice and Authenticity: The Search for Real Indians in New England in the "Historical" Period." In *The Death of Prehistory,* edited by Peter Schmidt and Stephen A. Mrozowski, pp. 241–66. Oxford University Press, New York.

Graeber, David

2012   Dead Zones of the Imagination: On Violence, Bureaucracy, and Interpretive Labor. *HAU: Journal of Ethnographic Theory* 2(2):105–28.

Greenberg, Raphael

2009   Towards an Inclusive Archaeology in Jerusalem: The Case of Silwan/The City of David. *Public Archaeology* 8(1):35–50.

Greene, Linda Sheryl

2015   Before and after Michael Brown: Toward an End to Structural and Actual Violence. *Washington University Journal of Law and Policy* 49:1–63.

Greene, Victor R.

1968   *The Slavic Community on Strike: Immigrant Labor in Pennsylvania Anthracite.* University of Notre Dame Press, Notre Dame, IN.

Greenough, Walter Sidney

1912   Making Indianapolis Beautiful by Using Its Several "Water Fronts" in Connection with a String of Parks. *Indianapolis Star,* March 3, pp. 1–2.

Greer, Margaret R., Walter D. Mignolo, and Maureen Quilligan (editors)

2008   *Rereading the Black Legend: The Discourses of Religious and Racial*

Difference in the Renaissance Empires. University of Chicago Press, Chicago.

Guernsey, Brenda

2008   Constructing the Wilderness and Clearing the Landscape: A Legacy of Colonialism in Northern British Columbia. In *Landscapes of Clearance: Archaeological and Anthropological Perspectives*, edited by Angèle Smith and Amy Gazin-Schwartz, pp. 112–23. Left Coast Press, Walnut Creek, CA.

Guglielmo, Thomas A.

2003   *White on Arrival: Italians, Race, Color, and Power in Chicago, 1890–1945.* Oxford University Press, New York.

Gunin, Joan

1979   Local "TV Stars" React to Hackett. *Orange Transcript* 81(49):1.

Gutman, Herbert

1977   *Work, Culture and Society in Industrializing America.* Vintage Books, New York.

Haber, Alejandro

2007   This Is Not an Answer to the Question "Who Is Indigenous?" *Archaeologies* 3(3):213–29.

Habu, Junko, Clare Fawcett, and John F. Matsunaga (editors)

2008   *Evaluating Multiple Narratives beyond Nationalist, Colonialist, Imperialist Archaeologies.* Springer, New York.

Hagan, Nicole A., Nicholas A. Robins, Ruben Dario Espinoza Gonzales, and Heileen Hsu-Kim

2015   Speciation and Bioaccessibility of Mercury in Adobe Bricks and Dirt Floors in Huancavelica, Peru. *Environmental Geochemistry and Health* 37(2):263–72.

Hagan, Nicole A., Nicholas A. Robins, Heileen Hsu-Kim, Susan Halabi, Ruben Dario Espinoza Gonzales, Daniel deB. Richter, and John Vandenberg

2013   Residential Mercury Contamination in Adobe Brick Homes in Huancavelica, Peru. *PLoS One* 8(9):e75179.

Hall, John C.

2014   Landscape Considerations for the Creek War in Alabama, 1811–1814. *Alabama Review* 67(3):219–32.

Hall, Martin, and Pia Bombardella

2007   Paths of Nostalgia and Desire through Heritage Destinations at the Cape of Good Hope. In *Desire Lines: Space, Memory and Identity in a Post-Apartheid City*, edited by Nick Shepherd, Noeleen Murray, and Martin Hall, pp. 245–58. Routledge, New York.

Hambidge, Jay

1898   An Artist's Impression of the Colliery Region. *Century* 55(6):822–28.

Hamilakis, Yannis

2018   *The New Nomadic Age: Archaeologies of Forced and Undocumented Migra-
        tion.* Equinox, Sheffield, UK.

Hamilakis, Yannis, Aris Anagnostopoulos, and Fotis Ifantidis

2009   Postcards from the Edge of Time: Archaeology, Photography, Archaeologi-
        cal Ethnography (A Photo-Essay). *Public Archaeology* 8(2–3):283–309.

Hanchett, Thomas W.

1998   *Sorting Out the New South City: Race, Class and Urban Development in
        Charlotte, 1875–1975.* University of North Carolina Press, Chapel Hill.

Hanke, Lewis

1971   A Modest Proposal for a Moratorium on Grand Generalizations: Some
        Thoughts on the Black Legend. *Hispanic American Historical Review*
        51(1):112–27.

Hanke, Lewis, and Celso Rodríguez

1978   *Los Virreyes españoles en América durante el gobierno de la Casa de
        Austria.* Ediciones Atlas, Madrid.

Hanks, William F.

2010   *Converting Words: Maya in the Age of the Cross.* University of California
        Press, Berkeley.

Hansen, Arthur A.

1985   Cultural Politics in the Gila River Relocation Center 1942–1943. *Arizona and
        the West* 27(4):327–62.

Harman, Chis

2009   *Zombie Capitalism.* Haymarket Books, Chicago.

Harvey, David

1985   *The Urbanization of Capital.* Basil Blackwell, Oxford.

1989   *The Condition of Postmodernity: An Enquiry into the Origins of Cultural
        Change.* Wiley, New York.

2009   *Cosmopolitanism and the Geographies of Freedom.* Columbia University
        Press, New York.

Hatch, Marion Popenoe de

2002   New Perspectives on Kaminaljuyu, Guatemala: Regional Interaction during
        the Preclassic and Classic Periods. In *Incidents of Archaeology in Central
        America and Yucatan: Studies in Honor of Edwin M. Shook,* edited by
        M. Love, Marion Popenoe de Hatch, and Hector Escobedo, pp. 35–50.
        University Press of America, Lanham, MD.

Hauser, Mark W., Whitney Battle-Baptiste, Koji Lau-Ozawa, Barbara L. Voss, Reinhard Bernbeck, Susan Pollock, Randall H. McGuire, Uzma Z. Rizvi, Christopher Hernandez, and Sonya Atalay

2018   Archaeology as Bearing Witness. *American Anthropologist* 120 (3):535–36.

Hawkey, Diane E., and Charles F. Merbs

1995   Activity-Induced Musculoskeletal Stress Markers (MSM) and Subsistence Strategy Changes among Ancient Hudson Bay Eskimos. *International Journal of Osteoarchaeology* 5(4):324–38.

Hayashi, Ken

2015   Interview by Koji Lau-Ozawa, November 15, Pasadena. Transcript in author's possession.

Heer, Hannes

2004   *Vom Verschwinden Der Täter. Der Vernichtungskrieg Fand Statt, Aber Keiner War Dabei.* Aufbau-Verlag, Berlin.

Held, Amy

2018   Denmark's Latest Stand against "Undesirable" Migrants: Ship Them to an Island. National Public Radio, December 4, https://www.npr.org/2018/12 /04/673240111/denmarks-latest-stand-against-undesirable-migrants-ship -them-to-an-island, accessed June 12, 2019.

Hemming, John

1970   *The Conquest of the Incas.* 2nd ed. Harcourt, New York.

Herring, Hubert, and Helen Baldwin Herring

1968   *History of Latin America from the Beginnings to the Present.* Knopf, New York.

Hervik, Peter

1998   The Mysterious Maya of National Geographic. *Journal of Latin American Anthropology* 4(1):166–97.

Hessel, Stéphane

2011   Time for Outrage! *Nation,* March 7–14, https://drive.google.com/file/d /1AySkVWjMiKSRWj1Lfm2jF7Dmmowg2sn8/view, accessed January 3, 2019.

Hilberg, Raul

2003   *The Destruction of the European Jews.* Yale University Press, New Haven, CT.

Hill, Robert

1989   Social Organization by Decree in Colonial Highland Guatemala. *Ethnohistory* 36(2):170–98.

1990   *Colonial Cakchiquels: Highland Maya Adaptation to Spanish Rule 1600–1700.* Harcourt, Brace, Jovanovich, Fort Worth.

1996   Eastern Chajoma (Cakchiquel) Political Geography: Ethnohistorical and Archaeological Contributions to the Study of a Late Postclassic Highland Maya Polity. *Ancient Mesoamerica* 7:63–87.

Hill, Robert M., and John Monaghan

1987   *Continuities in Highland Maya Social Organization: Ethnohistory in Sacapulas, Guatemala.* University of Pennsylvania Press, Philadelphia.

Hinton, Alexander L. (editor)

2002   *Annihilating Difference: The Anthropology of Genocide.* University of California Press, Berkeley.

Hirsch, Marianne

2012   *The Generation of Postmemory: Writing and Visual Culture after the Holocaust.* Columbia University Press, New York.

Hobbes, Thomas

2010 [1651] *Leviathan.* Rev. ed. Edited by A. P. Martinich and Brian Battiste. Broadview Press, Peterborough, ON.

Hodder, Ian

2003   *Archaeology beyond Dialogue.* University of Utah Press, Salt Lake City.

Hodges, Alison

2015   Resistance, the Church, and a Comparison of Ceramics from Sixteenth-Century Caluco, El Salvador. Master's thesis, Department of Sociology and Anthropology, Illinois State University, Normal.

Holloway, John

2010   *Crack Capitalism.* Pluto Press, London.

Honneth, Axel

2008   *Reification: A New Look at an Old Idea.* Edited by Martin Jay. Translated by Joseph Ganahl. Oxford University Press, New York.

Horkheimer, Max

2002   *Critical Theory: Selected Essays.* Translated by Matthew O'Connell. Continuum, New York.

House of Representatives

1901   *Papers Relating to the Foreign Relations of the United States, with the Annual Message of the President Transmitted to Congress December 5, 1898.* US Government Printing Office, Washington, DC.

Hrouda, Barthel

1965   *Die Kulturgeschichte Des Assyrischen Flachbildes.* Rudolf Habelt, Bonn.

Hudson, Charles M.

2005   *The Juan Pardo Expeditions: Explorations of the Carolinas and Tennessee, 1566–1568.* University of Alabama Press, Tuscaloosa.

Ichioka, Yuji

1988   *The Issei. The World of the First Generation Japanese Immigrants, 1885–1924.* Free Press, New York.

Imagire, Gloria Toshiko

2008   Gloria Toshiko Imagire Interview Segment. Densho Digital Repository, October 17, http://ddr.densho.org/ddr-manz-1-46/, accessed June 12, 2019.

Indiana State Board of Health

1917   *Thirty-Fifth Annual Report of the State Board of Health.* Indiana State Board of Health, Indianapolis.

Indianapolis Journal

1894   Several Park Sites. *Indianapolis Journal*, October 31.

Indianapolis News

1880a   Pollution. *Indianapolis News*, May 25.

1880b   The Death Rate, and Some Causes That Tend to Swell It. *Indianapolis News*, July 13.

1881   Typhoid Fever. *Indianapolis News*, November 11.

1887   New YMCA Home. *Indianapolis News*, September 2.

1890   In the Public Baths. *Indianapolis News*, June 28.

1894   Question of City Parks. *Indianapolis News*, November 15.

1896a   Parks for Indianapolis. *Indianapolis News*, January 9.

1896b   The Water of White River. *Indianapolis News*, May 23.

1897   Further about Parks. *Indianapolis News*, April 15.

1916   River Devoid of Natural Life. *Indianapolis News*, September 14.

1919a   Eighteen Swimming Pools Urged by Jarvis. *Indianapolis News*, July 3.

1919b   River and Creek May Be Freed from Sewage. *Indianapolis News*, July 9.

Indianapolis Recorder

1916   At Last a Summer Resort for Colored People. *Indianapolis Recorder*, March 18.

1926a   Idlewild of Indiana Advertisement. *Indianapolis Recorder*, July 3.

1926b   Deny Use of City Parks. *Indianapolis Recorder*, July 24.

1927a   Council May Annex Area of Casino G. *Indianapolis Recorder*, February 12.

1927b   New Opening Announced of Casino G. *Indianapolis Recorder*, February 19.

1927c   Casino Gardens Stand Reversed. *Indianapolis Recorder*, April 2.

1933   Eaglewood Beach Advertisement. *Indianapolis Recorder*, June 17.

1934   Body of Youthful Swimmer Recovered from Watery Grave in Fall Creek. *Indianapolis Recorder*, May 26.

1936   Formal Opening of New West Side Beach Saturday. *Indianapolis Recorder*, August 8.

1941a   Belmont Beach Draws Complaint on Health, Safe Swim Conditions. *Indianapolis Recorder*, June 28.

1941b   Suit Charges City Permits W'Side Menace. *Indianapolis Recorder*, July 5.

Indianapolis Star

1909   Parks Board Plans Indorsed by Club. *Indianapolis Star*, December 10.

1914a   Youthful Horde Enjoys Bathing at Playgrounds. *Indianapolis Star*, July 19.

1914b   Swimming Pool Is Opened for Colored Persons Only. *Indianapolis Star*, July 26.

1919   All Attendance Records Broken at Playgrounds. *Indianapolis Star*, July 6.

Ingold, Tim

1993   The Temporality of the Landscape. *World Archaeology* 25(2):152–74.

2000   *The Perception of the Environment: Essays on Livelihood, Dwelling and Skill.* Routledge, London.

Inomata, Takeshi

2006   Plazas, Performers, and Spectators: Political Theaters of the Classic Maya. *Current Anthropology* 47(5):805–42.

Inouye, Karen M.

2016   *The Long Afterlife of Nikkei Wartime Incarceration.* Stanford University Press, Stanford, CA.

Ishizuka, Karen L.

2006   *Lost and Found: Reclaiming the Japanese American Incarceration.* University of Illinois Press, Urbana.

Jackson, Kenneth T.

1985   *Crabgrass Frontier: The Suburbanization of the United States.* Oxford University Press, New York.

James, Susan E., Janice Johnson, Chitra Raghavan, Tessa Lemos, Michele Barakett, and Diana Woolis

2003   The Violent Matrix: A Study of Structural, Interpersonal, and Intrapersonal Violence among a Sample of Poor Women. *American Journal of Community Psychology* 31(1–2):129–41.

Jamieson, Ross

2002   *Domestic Architecture and Power.* Springer, Boston.

Jargowsky, Paul

2015   Architecture of Segregation: Civil Unrest, the Concentration of Poverty, and Public Policy. Century Foundation, https://tcf.org/content/report /architecture-of-segregation, accessed 14 June, 2019.

Jarvis, Walter

1923   Indianapolis Provides for Its Colored Citizens. *Playground* 16(10):541–42.

Jett, Jason

1986   Help Arrives for "DMZ" off Rt. 280: Residents Hope It's Not a Frail Gesture. *Star-Ledger*, August 31, p. 92.

Johnson, Bob

2010   "An Upthrust into Barbarism": Coal, Trauma, and Origins of the Modern Self, 1885–1951. *Journal of American Culture* 33:4:265–79.

Johnson, Lee

1934   Drowning Season Is On. *Indianapolis Recorder*, June 16.

Johnson, Matthew

2007   *Ideas of Landscape*. Blackwell, Oxford.

Johnson, Walter

2013   *River of Dark Dreams: Slavery and Empire in the Cotton Kingdom*. Harvard University Press, Cambridge, MA.

Jones, Elsie

1979   Double-Standard System. Letter to the editor, *Orange Transcript* 81(49):4.

Jones, Grant

1982   Agriculture and Trade in the Colonial Period Southern Maya Lowlands. In *Maya Subsistence: Studies in Memory of Dennis E. Puleston*, edited by Kent V. Flannery, pp. 275–93. Academic Press, New York.

Joyce, Rosemary

2004   Mesoamerica: A Working Model for Archaeology. In *Mesoamerican Archaeology: Theory and Practice*, edited by Julia A. Hendon and Rosemary Joyce, pp. 1–42. Blackwell, Malden, MA.

2005a Solid Histories for Fragile Nations: Archaeology as Cultural Patrimony. In *Embedding Ethics*, edited by Lynn Meskell and Peter Pels, pp. 253–73. Berg, Oxford.

2005b What Kind of Subject of Study Is "The Ancient Maya"? *Reviews in Anthropology* 34:295–311.

Joyce, Rosemary, and Russell Sheptak

2014   History Interrupted: Doing "Historical Archaeology" in Central America. In *The Death of Prehistory,* edited by Peter R. Schmidt and Stephen A. Mrozowski, pp. 161–82. Oxford University Press, New York.

Judd, Margaret A.

2002   One Accident Too Many. *British Museum Studies in Ancient Egypt and Sudan* 3:42–54.

Juderías, Julián

1960 [1914] *La leyenda negra; estudios acerca del concepto de España en el extranjero*. Editora Nacional, Madrid.

Jureit, Ulrike

2004   Zeigen Heißt Verschweigen. *Mittelweg* 36(1):3-27.

Kagan, Richard

2000   *Urban Images of the Hispanic World, 1493-1793.* Yale University Press, New Haven, CT.

2009   La policía y la plaza. In *El sueño de Eneas: Visiones utópicas de la ciudad*, edited by Víctor Mínguez, Inmaculada Rodríguez, and Vicent Zuriaga, pp. 121-31. Universitat Jaume, Castellón, Spain.

2016   Policía y la plaza: Útopia y dystopia en la ciudad colonial. *TEMPUS Revista en Historia General* 4:111-36.

Kamp-Whittaker, April

2010   Through the Eyes of a Child: The Archaeology of WWII Japanese Internment at Amache. Master's thesis, Department of Anthropology, University of Denver.

Keeley, Lawrence H.

1996   *War before Civilization: The Myth of the Peaceful Savage.* Oxford University Press, New York.

Keenan, Thomas, and Eyal Weizman

2012   *Mengele's Skull: The Advent of a Forensic Aesthetics.* Sternberg Press, Berlin.

Keen, Benjamin

1969   The Black Legend Revisited: Assumptions and Realities. *Hispanic American Historical Review* 49(4):703-19.

Kennedy, Robert F.

1968   Remarks to the Cleveland City Club, April 5, 1968. John F. Kennedy Presidential Library and Museum, https://www.jfklibrary.org/learn/about-jfk /the-kennedy-family/robert-f-kennedy/robert-f-kennedy-speeches/remarks -to-the-cleveland-city-club-april-5-1968, accessed January 3, 2019.

Kim, Yung Soo

2012   Photographers' Ethical Calls May Rest on "It Depends." *Newspaper Research Journal* 33(1):6-23.

Kimmerle, Erin H., and Jose Pablo Baraybar

2008   *Skeletal Trauma: Identification of Injuries Resulting from Human Rights Abuse and Armed Conflict.* CRC Press, Boca Raton.

Kizior, Liz

2013   Colonial Ethnic Identity, Urban Organization, and Ceramic Variability at Caluco, El Salvador. Master's thesis, Department of Sociology and Anthropology, Illinois State University, Normal.

Klaus, Haagen D.

2008   Out of Light Came Darkness: Bioarchaeology of Mortuary Ritual, Health,
        and Ethnogenesis in the Lambayeque Valley Complex, North Coast Peru
        (AD 900–1750). PhD dissertation, Department of Anthropology, Ohio State
        University, Columbus.

2012   The Bioarchaeology of Structural Violence: A Theoretical Model and
        Case Study. In *The Bioarchaeology of Violence*, edited by Debra L.
        Martin and Ryan P. Harrod, pp. 29–62. University Press of Florida,
        Gainesville.

Klaus, Haagen D., and Rosabella Alvarez-Calderón

2017   Escaping Conquest? A First Look at Regional Cultural and Biological Vari-
        ation in Postcontact Eten, Peru. In *Colonized Bodies, Worlds Transformed:
        Toward a Global Bioarchaeology of Contact and Colonialism*, edited by
        Melissa S. Murphy and Haagen D. Klaus, pp. 95–128. University Press of
        Florida, Gainesville.

Klaus, Haagen D., and Manuel E. Tam

2009   Contact in the Andes: Bioarchaeology of Systemic Stress in Colonial Mor-
        rope, Peru. *American Journal of Physical Anthropology* 138(3):356–68.

Knüsel, Christopher, and Martin Smith (editors)

2013   *The Routledge Handbook of the Bioarchaeology of Human Conflict*. Rout-
        ledge, New York.

Köhler, Gernot, and Norman Alcock

1976   An Empirical Table of Structural Violence. *Journal of Peace Research*
        13(4):343–56.

Komisaruk, Catherine

2010   Indigenous Labor as Family Labor: Tributes, Migration, and Hispaniciza-
        tion in Colonial Guatemala. *Labor: Studies in Working-Class History of the
        Americas* 6(4):41–66.

Kotek, Joël, and Pierre Rigoulet

2000   *Le Siècle des Camps: Détention, Concentration, Extermination, Cent ans de
        mal Radical.* JC Lattès, Paris.

Kunze, Max

1995   *Der Pergamonaltar: Seine Geschichte, Entdeckung und Rekonstruktion.*
        Philipp von Zabern, Mainz.

Kuramoto, Frances

2014   Interview by Koji Lau-Ozawa, December 28, Pasadena. Transcript in au-
        thor's possession.

Lachman, Joseph Shoji

2017　A Colorado Legislator Just Tried to Justify Japanese-American Incarceration. Let's All Tell Him He's Wrong. *Huffington Post*, March 23, http://www
.huffingtonpost.com/entry/a-colorado-state-rep-tried-to-justify-japanese
-american_us_58d34950e4b002482d6e6e66, accessed June 12, 2019.

Landon, David B.

2005　Zooarchaeology and Historical Archaeology: Progress and Prospects. *Journal of Archaeology Method and Theory* 12:1–36

Larsen, Clark Spencer

2015　*Bioarchaeology: Interpreting Behavior from the Human Skeleton.* Cambridge
University Press, New York.

Law Pezzarossi, Heather, and Russell Sheptak

2018　Introduction. In *Indigenous Persistence in the Colonized Americas: Material
and Documentary Perspectives on Entanglement*, edited by Heather Law
Pezzarossi and Russel Sheptak, pp. 1–18. University of New Mexico Press,
Albuquerque.

Lawler, Andrew

2012　The Battle Over Violence. *Science* 633:829–30.

Lave, Jean, and Etienne Wenger

1991　*Situated Learning: Legitimate Peripheral Participation.* Cambridge University Press, Cambridge.

Lefebvre, Henri

1991　*The Production of Space.* Blackwell Publishers, Oxford.

Leone, Mark P.

1995　A Historical Archaeology of Capitalism. *American Anthropologist*
97(2):251–68.

2010　*Critical Historical Archaeology.* Left Coast Press, Walnut Creek, CA.

Leone, Mark P., James M. Harmon, and Jessica Neuwirth

2005　Perspective and Surveillance in Eighteenth-Century Maryland Gardens,
Including William Paca's Garden on Wye Island. *Historical Archaeology*
39(4):138–58.

Levi, Primo

1998　The Grey Zone. In *Violence in War and Peace: An Anthology*, edited by
Nancy Scheper-Hughes and Philippe Bourgois, pp. 83–90. Blackwell, Malden, MA.

2007　*Survival in Auschwitz: If This Is a Man.* BN Publishing, Thousand Oaks,
CA.

Libro Viejo

1934   *Libro Viejo de la fundación de Guatemala, papeles relativos a D. Pedro de Alvarado.* Sociedad de Geografía e Historia, Guatemala City.

Liebmann, Matthew

2008   Postcolonial Cultural Affiliation: Essentialism, Hybridity and NAGPRA. In *Archaeology and the Postcolonial Critique*, edited by Matthew Liebmann and Uzma Z. Rizvi, pp. 73–90. AltaMira Press, Lanham, MD.

Liebmann, Matthew, and Melissa Murphy

2011   Rethinking the Archaeology of "Rebels, Backsliders, and Idolaters." In *Enduring Conquests: Rethinking the Archaeology of Resistance to Spanish Colonialism in the Americas*, edited by Matthew Liebmann and Melissa Murphy, pp. 3–18. SAR Press, Santa Fe, NM.

Liebmann, Matthew, and Melissa Murphy (editors)

2011   *Enduring Conquests: Rethinking the Archaeology of Resistance to Spanish Colonialism in the Americas.* SAR Press, Santa Fe, NM.

Lieverse, Angela R., Vladimir Ivanovich Bazaliiskii, Olga I. Goriunova, and Andrzej W. Weber

2013   Lower Limb Activity in the Cis-Baikal: Entheseal Changes among Middle Holocene Siberian Foragers. *American Journal of Physical Anthropology* 150(3):421–32.

Lightfoot, Kent G.

1995   Culture Contact Studies: Redefining the Relationship between Prehistoric and Historical Archaeology. *American Antiquity* 60(2):199–217.

Lillquist, Karl

2007   *Imprisoned in the Desert: The Geography of World War II-Era Japanese American Relocation Centers in the Western United States.* Central Washington University, Geography and Land Studies Department, Ellensburg.

Lock, Grahame

1996   Subject, Interpellation, and Ideology. In *Postmodern Materialism and the Future of Marxist Theory: Essays in the Althusserian Tradition*, edited by Antonio Callari and David F. Ruccio, pp. 69–90. University Press of New England, Hanover, NH.

Lockhart, James

1992   *Nahuas after the Conquest: A Social and Cultural History of the Indians of Central Mexico, Sixteenth through Eighteenth Centuries.* Stanford University Press, Stanford, CA.

Lohmann Villena, Guillermo

1949   *Las minas de Huancavelica* 2. Imprenta de la Escuela de Estudios His-
pano-Americanos, Sevilla.

Lombroso, Cesare

1896   Criminal Anthropology: Its Origin and Its Application. *Forum* 20:33–49.

Lotchin, Roger W.

2018   *Japanese American Relocation in World War II: A Reconsideration.* Cambridge University Press, New York.

Lovell, W. George

1992   Disease and Depopulation in Early Colonial Guatemala. In *"Secret Judge-
ments of God": Old World Disease in Colonial Spanish America,* edited by
Noble David Cook and W. George Lovell, pp. 49–83. University of Oklahoma Press, Norman.

2005   *Conquest and Survival in Colonial Guatemala: A Historical Geography of
the Cuchumatán Highlands, 1500–1821.* McGill-Queen's University Press,
Montreal.

Lovell, W. George, Christopher Lutz, Wendy Kramer, and William Swezey

2013   *Strange Lands and Different Peoples: Spaniards and Indians in Colonial
Guatemala.* University of Oklahoma Press, Norman.

Ludlow Collective

2001   Archaeology of the Colorado Coal Field War, 1913–1914. In *Archaeologies of
the Contemporary Past,* edited by Victor Buchli and Gavin Lucas,
pp. 94–107. Routledge, London.

Lukács, Georg

1971   *History and Class Consciousness: Studies in Marxist Dialectics.* MIT Press,
Cambridge, MA.

Lyon, Cherstin M.

2012   *Prisons and Patriots: Japanese American Wartime Citizenship, Civil Disobe-
dience, and Historical Memory.* Temple University Press, Philadelphia.

MacLeod, Murdo J.

1973   *Spanish Central America: A Socioeconomic History, 1520–1720.* University of
California Press, Berkeley.

Madden, Milton Thomas

1969   A Physical History of the Japanese Relocation Camp Located at Rivers, Arizona. Master's thesis, Department of History, University of Arizona, Tuscon.

Magen, Ursula

1986   *Assyrische Königsdarstellungen, Aspekte der Herrschaft: Eine Typologie.*
Philipp von Zabern, Mainz.

Malkin, Michelle

2004   *In Defense of Internment. The Case for "Racial Profiling" in World War II and the War on Terror.* Regnery, Washington, DC.

Mariotti, Valentina, Marco Milella, and Maria Belcastro

2009   Musculoskeletal Stress Markers (MSM): Methodological Reflections. Paper presented at the workshop Musculoskeletal Stress Markers (MSM): Limitations and Achievements in the Reconstruction of Past Activity Patterns, Coimbra, Portugal, July 2–3.

Martin, Debra L., Ryan P. Harrod, and Misty Fields

2010   Beaten Down and Worked to the Bone: Bioarchaeological Investigations of Women and Violence in the Ancient Southwest. *Landscapes of Violence* 1(1):1–19.

Martin, Debra L., Ryan P. Harrod, and Ventura R. Pérez (editors)

2013   *The Bioarchaeology of Violence.* University Press of Florida, Gainesville.

Marubayashi, Roy

1944   #30. Marubayashi, Roy (Royutaka). Online Archive of California, http://www.oac.cdlib.org/ark:/28722/bk0013c579m/?brand=oac4, accessed June 12, 2019.

Marx, Karl

1967   *Capital*, Vol. 1. International Publishers, New York.

1978   Grundrisse. In *The Marx-Engels Reader.* 2nd ed. W. W. Norton, New York.

2018   *Capital: A Critique of Political Economy*, Vol. 3. Edited by Friedrich Engels. Marxists Internet Archive, https://www.marxists.org/archive/marx/works/download/pdf/Capital-Volume-III.pdf, accessed November 25, 2018.

Massey, Douglas S., and Nancy A. Denton

1993   *American Apartheid: Segregation and the Making of the Underclass.* Harvard University Press, Cambridge, MA.

Matsumoto, Imiko

1943   #23. Masumoto, Imiko. Online Archive of California, http://www.oac.cdlib.org/ark:/28722/bk0013c5716/?brand=oac4, accessed June 12, 2019.

Mathiesen, Karl

2015   "Even God Can't Help You Here": Nauru Refugees Describe a Life Devoid of Hope. *Guardian*, March 19, https://www.theguardian.com/world/2015/mar/19/even-god-cant-help-you-here-nauru-refugees-describe-a-life-devoid-of-hope, accessed June 12, 2019.

Matthew, Laura E.

2012   *Memories of Conquest: Becoming Mexicano in Colonial Guatemala.* University of North Carolina Press, Chapel Hill.

Matthews, Christopher N.

2002   An Archaeology of History and Tradition: Annapolis and the Making of the
        Modern Landscape. Kluwer Academic/Plenum Press, New York.

2012a   Gilded Ages and Gilded Archaeologies of American Exceptionalism. *Inter-
        national Journal of Historical Archaeology* 16(4):717–44.

2012b   *The Archaeology of American Capitalism.* University Press of Florida,
        Gainesville.

Mauss, Marcel

2000   *The Gift: The Form and Reason for Exchange in Archaic Societies.* W. W.
        Norton, New York.

McAnany, Patricia A., and Tomás Gallareta Negrón

2010   Bellicose Rulers and Climatological Peril? Retrofitting Twenty-First Cen-
        tury Woes on Eighth-Century Maya Society. In *Questioning Collapse:
        Human Resilience, Ecological Vulnerability, and the Aftermath of Empire,*
        edited by Patricia A. McAnany and Norman Yoffee, pp. 142–75. Cambridge
        University Press, Cambridge.

McGuire, Randall H.

1992   Archeology and the First Americans. *American Anthropologist* 94(4):816–36.

McGuire, Randall, and Ruth Van Dyke

2008   Dismembering the Trope: Imagining Cannibalism in the Ancient Pueblo
        World. In *Social Violence in the Prehispanic American Southwest,* edited by
        Deborah L. Nichols and Patricia L. Crown, pp. 7–40. University of Arizona
        Press, Tucson.

McKeown, Adam M.

2008   *Melancholy Order: Asian Immigration and the Globalization of Borders.* Co-
        lumbia University Press, New York.

McNally, David

2011   *Global Slump.* PM Press, Oakland, CA.

McNiven, Ian J., and Lynette Russell

2005   *Appropriated Pasts: Indigenous Peoples and the Colonial Culture of Archae-
        ology.* AltaMira Press, Oxford.

Merleau-Ponty, Maurice

1968   *The Visible and the Invisible: Followed by Working Notes.* Translated by Al-
        phonso Lingis. Northwestern University Press, Evanston, IL.

Meskell, Lynn

1998   *Archaeology Under Fire: Nationalism, Politics and Heritage in the Eastern
        Mediterranean and Middle East.* Routledge, London.

2005   Archaeological Ethnography. *Archaeologies* 1:83–102.

Mignolo, Walter D.

2003   *The Darker Side of the Renaissance: Literacy, Territoriality, and Coloniza-
        tion.* 2nd ed. University of Michigan Press, Ann Arbor.

2007   What Does the Black Legend Have to Do With Race? In *Rereading the
        Black Legend: The Discourses of Religious and Racial Difference in the
        Renaissance Empires*, edited by M. R. Greer, W. D. Mignolo, and M. Quilli-
        gan, pp. 312–24. University of Chicago Press, Chicago.

Miller, Daniel, and Christopher Y. Tilley (editors)

1984   *Ideology, Power, and Prehistory.* Cambridge University Press, Cambridge.

Mills, Barbara J.

2016   Communities of Consumption: Cuisines as Networks of Situated Practice.
        In *Knowledge in Motion, Constellations of Learning across Time and Place*,
        edited by Andrew P. Roddick and Ann B. Stahl, pp. 248–70. University of
        Arizona Press, Tucson.

Milner, George R.

2005   *The Moundbuilders: Ancient Peoples of Eastern North America.* Thames &
        Hudson, New York.

Mintz, Sidney

1985   *Sweetness and Power: The Place of Sugar in Modern History.* Viking, New
        York.

Močnik, Rastko

1993   Ideology and Fantasy. In *The Althusserian Legacy*, edited by E. Ann Kaplan
        and Michael Sprinker, pp. 139–56. Verso, London.

1994   Das "Subjekt, dem unterstellt wird zu glauben" und die Nation als eine
        Null-Institution. In *Denk-Prozesse nach Althusser*, edited by Henning Böke,
        Jens C. Müller, and Sebastian Reinfeldt, pp. 225–74. Argument-Verlag,
        Hamburg.

Mohl, Raymond A.

2000   Planned Destruction: The Interstates and Central City Housing. In *From
        Tenements to Taylor Homes: In Search of an Urban Housing Policy*, edited
        by John F. Bauman, Roger Biles, and Kristen M. Szylvia, pp. 226–45. Penn-
        sylvania State University Press, University Park.

Montag, Warren

2013   *Althusser and His Contemporaries: Philosophy's Perpetual War.* Duke Uni-
        versity Press, Durham, NC.

Montejo, Victor D.

1999   Becoming Maya? Appropriation of the White Shaman. *Native Americas*
        16(1):58–60.

2005   *Maya Intellectual Renaissance: Identity, Representation, and Leadership.*
        University of Texas Press, Austin.

Moran, Dermot

2016   Lived Body, Intercorporeality, Intersubjectivity: The Body as a Phenomeno-
        logical Theme. In *Philosophy of Mind and Phenomenology: Conceptual and
        Empirical Approaches,* edited by Daniel O. Dahlstrom, Andreas Elpidorou,
        and Walter Hopp, pp. 57–78. Routledge, London.

Moreton-Robinson, Aileen

2016   *Critical Indigenous Studies: Engagements in First World Locations.* Univer-
        sity of Arizona Press, Tucson.

Morris, Ian

2014   *War! What Is It Good For? Conflict and the Progress of Civilization from
        Primates to Robots.* Farrar, Straus & Giroux, New York.

Moshenska, Gabriel

2015   Introduction: The Only Way Is Ethics. In *Ethics and the Archaeology of Vi-
        olence,* edited by A. González-Ruibal and G. Moshenska. pp. 1–17. Springer,
        New York.

Mrozowski, Stephen A.

2006   *The Archaeology of Class in Urban America.* Cambridge University Press,
        Cambridge, MA.

Mrozowski, Stephen A., Holly Herbster, David Brown, and Katherine L. Priddy

2009   Magunkaquog Materiality, Federal Recognition, and the Search for a
        Deeper History. *International Journal of Historical Archaeology* 13(4):430–63.

Mrozowski, Stephen A., Grace H. Ziesing, and Mary C. Beaudry

1996   *Living on the Boott: Historical Archaeology at the Boott Mills Boarding-
        houses, Lowell, Massachusetts.* University of Massachusetts Press, Amherst.

Muhammad, Khalil Gibran

2010   *The Condemnation of Blackness: Race, Crime, and the Making of Modern
        Urban America.* Harvard University Press, Cambridge, MA.

Mulrooney, Margaret

1989   *A Legacy of Coal: Historic American Buildings Survey/Historic American
        Engineering Record.* National Park Service, Washington, DC.

Mumford, Kevin

2007   *Newark: A History of Race, Rights, and Riots in America.* New York Univer-
        sity Press, New York.

Münkler, Herfried

2005   *The New Wars.* Polity Press, Cambridge.

Murillo, Dana Velasco

2009   The Creation of Indigenous Leadership in a Spanish Town: Zacatecas, Mexico, 1609-1752. *Ethnohistory* 56(4):669-98.

Murray, Alice Yang

2008   *Historical Memories of the Japanese American Internment and the Struggle for Redress.* Stanford University Press, Stanford, CA.

Myers, Adrian

2011   The Things of Auschwitz. In *Archaeologies of Internment*, edited by Adrian Myers and Gabriel Moshenska, pp. 75-88. Springer, New York.

Myers, Adrian, and Gabriel Moshenska (editors)

2011   *Archaeologies of Internment.* Springer, New York.

Mytum, Harold, and Gillian Carr (editors)

2013   *Prisoners of War: Archaeology, Memory, and Heritage of 19th- and 20th-Century Mass Internment.* Springer, New York.

Nakamura, Yosh

2015   Telephone interview by Koji Lau-Ozawa, December 17. Transcript in author's possession.

Nassaney, Michael S., and Marjorie R. Abel

2000   Urban Spaces, Labor Organization, and Social Control: Lessons from New England's Nineteenth-Century Cutlery Industry. In *Lines That Divide: Historical Archaeologies of Race, Class, and Gender*, edited by James A. Delle, Stephen A. Mrozowski, and Robert Paynter, pp. 239-75. University of Tennessee Press, Knoxville.

National Advisory Commission on Civil Disorders

1968   *The 1968 Report of the National Advisory Commission on Civil Disorders.* Pantheon Books, New York.

National Park Service (NPS)

2006   *Cultural Landscape Report: Manzanar National Historic Site.* National Park Service, US Department of the Interior, Pacific West Region, San Francisco.

Nelson, Diane M.

1996   Maya Hackers and the Cyberspatialized Nation-State: Modernity, Ethnostalgia, and a Lizard Queen in Guatemala. *Cultural Anthropology* 11(3):287-308.

Newman, Andy

1999   Police Officer in Orange, N.J., Is Shot to Death as She Confronts Robbery Suspect. *New York Times*, April 9, http://www.nytimes.com/1999/04/09

/nyregion/police-officer-in-orange-nj-is-shot-to-death-as-she-confronts
-robbery-suspect.html, accessed June 14, 2019.

Ng, Laura

2014   Altered Lives, Altered Environments: Creating Home at Manzanar Reloca-
        tion Center, 1942–1945. Master's thesis, Department of Anthropology, Uni-
        versity of Massachusetts, Boston.

Ng, Laura, and Stacey L. Camp

2015   Consumption in World War II Japanese American Incarceration Camps. In
        Historical Archaeologies of Capitalism, edited by Mark P. Leone and J. E.
        Knauf, pp. 149–80. Springer International, Cham, Switzerland.

Ngai, Mae

1999   The Architecture of Race in American Immigration Law: A Reexamination
        of the Immigration Act of 1924. *Journal of American History* 86(1):67–92.

2004a   Race, Nation, and Citizenship in Late Nineteenth Century America. In
        The Columbia Documentary History of Race and Ethnicity in America,
        edited by Ronald H. Bayor, pp. 309–36. Columbia University Press,
        New York.

2004b   *Impossible Subjects: Illegal Aliens and the Making of Modern America*.
        Princeton University Press, Princeton, NJ.

Nida, Brandon

2013   Demystifying the Hidden Hand: Capital and the State at Blair Mountain.
        Historical Archaeology 47(2):52–68.

Nixon, Rob

2011   *Slow Violence and the Environmentalism of the Poor*. Harvard University
        Press, New York.

Normark, Johan

2004   Discontinuous Maya Identities, Culture and Ethnicity in Mayanist Dis-
        course. In *Material Culture and Other Things: Post-Disciplinary Studies in
        the 21st Century*, edited by F. Fahlander and T. Oestigaard, pp. 109–60. Uni-
        versity of Gothenburg, Gothenburg, Sweden.

2006   Ethnicity and the Shared Quasi-Objects: Issues of Becoming Relating to
        Two Open-Fronted Structures at Nohcacab, Quintana Roo, Mexico. In
        *Maya Ethnicity: The Construction of Ethnic Identity from the Preclassic
        to Modern Times*, edited by F Sachse, pp. 61–81. Verlag Anton Saurwein,
        Markt Schwaben, Germany.

Novak, Michael

1996   *The Guns of Lattimer*. Transaction, New Brunswick, NJ.

Nystrom, K. C.

2014   The Bioarchaeology of Structural Violence and Dissection in the 19th-
Century United States. *American Anthropologist* 116(4):765–79.

Oland, Maxine, and Joel W Palka

2016   The Perduring Maya: New Archaeology on Early Colonial Transitions.
Antiquity 90(350):472–86.

Ollman, Bertell

2003   *Dance of the Dialectic: Steps in Marx's Method.* University of Illinois Press,
Urbana.

2014   Historical Archaeology, Dialectical Materialism, and "C.F.U.G. Studies."
International Journal of Historical Archaeology 18(2):361–73.

Orange Transcript

1979a   Instant Replay. Letter to the editor. *Orange Transcript* 81(47):21.

1979b   Police Arrest William Cook. *Orange Transcript* 81(46):15.

1980   Grand Jury. *Orange Transcript* 82(5):31.

Orser, Charles E., Jr.

1996   *A Historical Archaeology of the Modern World.* Plenum Press, New York.

2004   *Race and Practice in Archaeological Interpretation.* University of Pennsylvania Press, Philadelphia.

2005   Symbolic Violence, Resistance and the Vectors of Improvement in Early
Nineteenth-Century Ireland. *World Archaeology* 37(3):392–407.

2006   Symbolic Violence and Landscape Pedagogy: An Illustration from the Irish
Countryside. *Historical Archaeology* 40(2):28–44.

2007   *The Archaeology of Race and Racialization in Historic America.* University
Press of Florida, Gainesville.

2011   The Archaeology of Poverty and the Poverty of Archaeology. *International
Journal of Historical Archaeology* 15(4):533–43.

Ortner, Sherry

1972   Is Female to Male, as Nature is to Culture? *Feminist Studies* 1(2):5–31.

Orton, Clive, Paul Tyers, and Alan Vince

1993   *Pottery in Archaeology.* Cambridge University Press, Cambridge.

Ortiz, A., M. S. Murphy, J. Toohey, and C. M. Gaither

2017   Hybridity? Change? Continuity? Survival? Biodistance and the Identity of
Colonial Burials from Magdalena de Cao Viejo, Chicama Valley, Peru. In
*Colonized Bodies, Worlds Transformed: Toward a Global Bioarchaeology
of Contact and Colonialism,* edited by Melissa S. Murphy and Haagen D.
Klaus, pp. 375–410. University of Florida Press, Gainesville.

Oviedo y Valdés, Gonzalo Fernández de

1851   *Historia general y natural de las Indias, islas y tierre-firme del mar océano.*
        La Real Academia de la Historia, Madrid.

Ozawa, Koji

2016   The Archaeology of Gardens in Japanese American Incarceration Camps.
        Master's thesis, Department of Anthropology, San Francisco State Univer-
        sity, San Francisco.

Pagden, Anthony

1987   Identity Formation in the Spanish America. In *Colonial Identity in the At-
        lantic World, 1500-1800,* edited by Nicholas Canny and Anthony Pagden,
        pp. 51-94. Princeton University Press, Princeton, NJ.

Palka, Joel W.

2009   Historical Archaeology of Indigenous Culture Change in Mesoamerica.
        Journal of Archaeological Research 17:297-346.

Palmer, Jamie, and Kathleen Schmidt

2016   *Financial Needs for Water and Wastewater Infrastructure in Indiana
        (2015-2034).* Indiana Advisory Commission on Intergovernmental Relations,
        Indianapolis.

Panich, Lee M.

2013   Archaeologies of Persistence: Reconsidering the Legacies of Colonialism
        in Native North America. *American Antiquity* 78(1):105-22.

Paredes, Jose Hector, and Luis A. Romero

2008   La Ceramica Tipo Chinautla Del Convento de Santo Domingo. In *Investi-
        gaciones Arqueologicas En El Convento de Santo Domingo, Antigua Guate-
        mala,* Vol. 2, edited by Zoila Rodriguez Giron, pp. 81-90. Asociación Tikal,
        Guatemala City.

Paynter, Robert

1988   Steps to an Archaeology of Capitalism. In *The Recovery of Meaning: Histor-
        ical Archaeology in the United States,* edited by Mark Leone and Parker B.
        Potter, pp. 407-33. Smithsonian Institution Press, Washington, DC.

Pérez Campos, Elizabeth Mejía, and Alberto Juan Herrera Muñoz

2013   Minas y mineros: presencia de metales en sedimentos y restos humanos al sur
        de la Sierra Gorda de Querétaro en México. *Chungará (Arica)* 45(1):161-76.

Pezzarossi, Guido

2014   A New Materialist Archaeology of Antimarkets, Power and Capitalist
        Effects in Colonial Guatemala. PhD dissertation, Department of Anthro-
        pology, Stanford University, Stanford, CA.

2015   A Spectral Haunting of Society: Longue Duree Archaeologies of Capitalism and Antimarkets in Colonial Guatemala. In *Historical Archaeologies of Capitalism*, 2nd ed., edited by Mark P. Leone and Jocelyn Knauff., pp. 345–74. Springer, New York.

2017   "Confites, Melcochas Y Otras Golosinas . . . muy Danosas": Sugar, Alcohol and Biopolitics in Colonial Guatemala. In *Substance and Seduction*, edited by Stacey Schwartzkopf and Kathryn E. Sampeck, pp. 147–75. University of Texas Press, Austin.

Pezzarossi, Guido (editor)

2019   Introduction: Rethinking the Archaeology of Capitalism. Special issue, *Historical Archaeology* 53(3).

Phillippi, Bradley D.

2016   From Coercion to Compensation: Labor Systems and Spatial Practice on a Plural Farmstead, Long Island. PhD dissertation, Department of Anthropology, Northwestern University, Evanston, IL.

Picq, Manuela Lavinas

2018   *Vernacular Sovereignties: Indigenous Women Challenging World Politics.* University of Arizona Press, Tucson.

Pierce, Richard

2012   "Little Progress 'Happens'": Faburn E. DeFrantz and the Indianapolis Senate Avenue YMCA. *Indiana Magazine of History* 108(2):98–103.

Pike, Ruth

1967   Sevillian Society in the Sixteenth Century: Slaves and Freedmen. *Hispanic American Historical Review* 47(3):344–59.

Pinker, Steven

2011   *The Better Angels of Our Nature: Why Violence Has Declined.* Viking Press, New York.

Pinkowski, Edward

1950   *The Lattimer Massacre.* Sunshine, Philadelphia.

Polley, Claudia

1993   Segregation Creates Hidden Paradise. *Indiana Preservationist* 4:12–13.

Pollock, Susan

2013   Commensality, Public Spheres, and Handlungsräume in Ancient Mesopotamia. In *Big Histories, Human Lives. Tackling Problems of Scale in Archaeology*, edited by John Robb and Timothy R. Pauketat, pp. 145–70. School for Advanced Research Press, Santa Fe, NM.

2016   The Subject of Suffering. *American Anthropologist* 118(4):726–41.

Pollock, Susan, and Reinhard Bernbeck

2015   A Gate to a Darker World: Excavating at the Tempelhof Airport. In *Ethics and the Archaeology of Violence*, edited by Alfredo González-Ruibal and Gabriel Moshenska, pp. 137–52. Springer, New York.

2015   Wrestling with Truth: Possibilities and Peril in Alternative Narrative Forms. In *Subjects and Narratives in Archaeology*, edited by Ruth Van Dyke and Reinhard Bernbeck, pp. 277–86. University of Press of Colorado, Boulder.

Pope, Gregory A.

2001   The Watchungs: A Physical Presence in New Jersey's Natural and Human Landscape. In *From the Hudson to the Hamptons: Snapshots of the New York Metropolitan Area*, edited by Ines M. Miyares, Marianna Pavlovshaya, and Gregory A. Pope, pp. 126–33. American Association of Geographers, Washington, DC.

Porambo, Ron

1971   *No Cause for Indictment: An Autopsy of Newark*. Holt, Reinhart, and Winston, New York.

Portland Cement Association

2017   How Concrete Is Made. Portland Cement Association, http://www.cement .org/cement-concrete-basics/how-concrete-is-made, accessed April 24, 2020.

Powell, P. W.

2008 [1971]. *Tree of Hate: Propaganda and Prejudices Affecting United States Relations with the Hispanic World*. University of New Mexico Press, Albuquerque.

Prison Policy Initiative

2015   The Racial Geography of Mass Incarceration. Prison Policy Initiative, https://www.prisonpolicy.org/racialgeography/, accessed June 18, 2019.

Quijano, Aníbal

2000   Coloniality of Power and Eurocentrism in Latin America. *International Sociology* 15(2):215–32.

2007   Coloniality and Modernity/Rationality. *Cultural Studies* 21(2–3):168–78.

Ragland, David

2014   Michael Brown and America's Structural Violence Epidemic. Common Dreams, August 14, https://www.commondreams.org/views/2014/08/14 /michael-brown-and-americas-structural-violence-epidemic, accessed January 3, 2019.

Rahman, Atif, Premkumari Kumarathasan, and James Gomes

2016   Infant and Mother Related Outcomes from Exposure to Metals with Endo-
        crine Disrupting Properties during Pregnancy. *Science of the Total Environ-
        ment* 569:1022–31.

Raxche´

1996   Maya Culture and the Politics of Development. In *Maya Cultural Activism
        in Guatemala*, edited by Edward F. Fischer and R. McKenna Brown, pp.
        74–88. University of Texas Press, Austin.

Reckner, Paul E.

2009   Social Difference, Community-Building, and Material Social Practice: Sol-
        idarity and Diversity at the Ludlow Tent Colony, 1913–14. PhD dissertation,
        Department of Anthropology, State University of New York, Binghamton.

Redfield, Robert

1962   Maya Archaeology as the Maya See It. In *Human Nature and the Study of
        Society: The Papers of Robert Redfield*, edited by Margaret Park Redfield,
        pp. 152–60. University of Chicago Press, Chicago.

Reiter, Bernd, and Kimberly Eison Simmons (editors)

2012   *Afrodescendants, Identity, and the Struggle for Development in the Americas.*
        Michigan State University Press, East Lansing.

Renshaw, Layla

2011   *Exhuming Loss: Memory, Materiality and Mass Graves of the Spanish Civil
        War.* Left Coast Press, Walnut Creek, CA.

Restall, Matthew

2003   *Seven Myths of the Spanish Conquest.* Oxford University Press, New York.

2004   Maya Ethnogenesis. *Journal of Latin American Anthropology* 9(1):64–89.

Rice, Prudence M.

2013   *Space-Time Perspectives on Early Colonial Moquegua.* University Press of
        Colorado, Boulder.

Ricoeur, Paul

1994   Althusser's Theory of Ideology. In *Althusser: A Critical Reader*, edited by
        Gregory Elliott, pp. 44–72. Blackwell, Oxford.

Roberts, Peter

1901   *The Anthracite Coal Industry.* Macmillan, London.

Robins, Nicholas A.

2011   *Mercury, Mining, and Empire: The Human and Ecological Cost of Colonial
        Silver Mining in the Andes.* Indiana University Press, Bloomington.

Robins, Nicholas A., and Nicole A. Hagan

2012 Mercury Production and Use in Colonial Andean Silver Production: Emissions and Health Implications. *Environmental Health Perspectives* 120(5):627–31.

Robins, Nicholas A., Nicole A. Hagan, Susan Halabi, Heileen Hsu-Kim, Ruben Dario Espinoza Gonzales, M. Morris, G. Woodall, Daniel de B Richter, Paul Heine, Tong Zhang, Allan Bacon, and John Vandenberg

2012 Estimations of Historical Atmospheric Mercury Concentrations from Mercury Refining and Present-Day Soil Concentrations of Total Mercury in Huancavelica, Peru. *Science of the Total Environment* 426:146–54.

Robinson, Eugenia

1990 *Reconocimiento de Los Municipios de Alotenango Y Sumpango, Sacate-pequez.* CIRMA, La Antigua Guatemala.

1997 Proto-Historic to Colonial Settlement Transition in the Antigua Valley, Guatemala. In *Approaches to the Historical Archaeology of Mexico, Central and South America*, edited by Janine Gasco, Greg Charles Smith, and Patricia Fournier-Garcia, pp. 59–70. Institute of Archaeology, University of California, Los Angeles.

Robinson, Eugenia, Heather Wholey, and Hector Neff

1998 La Tradición Ceramica Flesh Ware En Las Tierras Altas Centrales y Costa Del Pacifico De Guatemala. In *XI Simposio de Investigaciones Arqueológicas En Guatemala*, edited by J. P. Laporte and Hector Escobedo, pp. 751–66. Museo Nacional de Arqueología y Etnología, Guatemala.

Robinson, Greg

2009 *A Tragedy of Democracy: Japanese Confinement in North America.* Columbia University Press, New York.

Roddick, Andrew, and Ann Stahl

2016 Introduction: Knowledge in Motion. In *Knowledge in Motion: Constellations of Learning across Time and Place*, edited by Andrew P. Roddick and Ann B. Stahl, pp. 248–70. University of Arizona Press and Amerind Foundation, Tucson.

Rodriguez Giron, Zoila

2008 *Investigaciones Arqueologicas En El Convento de Santo Domingo, Antigua Guatemala*, Vol. 2. Asociación Tikal, Guatemala City.

Roediger, David

2005 *Working Towards Whiteness.* Basic Books, New York.

2017 *Class, Race, and Marxism.* Verso, London.

Roller, Michael

2013   Rewriting Narratives of Labor Violence: A Transnational Perspective of the Lattimer Massacre. *Historical Archaeology* 47(3):109-23.

2015   Migration, Modernity and Memory: The Archaeology of the Twentieth Century in a Northeast Pennsylvania Coal Company Town, 1897-2014. PhD dissertation, Department of Anthropology, University of Maryland, College Park.

2018   *An Archaeology of Structural Violence: Life in a Twentieth Century Coal Town.* University Press of Florida, Gainesville.

2019a   The Archaeology of Machinic Consumerism: The Logistics of the Factory Floor in Everyday Life. *Historical Archaeology* 53(1):3-24.

2019b   Response to Forum Comments on "The Archaeology of Machinic Consumerism: The Logistics of the Factory Floor in Everyday Life." *Historical Archaeology* 53(1):35-40.

Rood, Henry

1898   A Pennsylvania Colliery Village: A Polyglot Community. *Century* 55(6):809-21.

Rose, Dan

1981   *Energy Transition and the Local Community.* University of Pennsylvania Press, Philadelphia.

Rose, Mark H., and Raymond A. Mohl

2012   *Interstate: Highway Politics and Policy since 1939.* University of Tennessee Press, Knoxville.

Runnels, Moses T.

1883   Impure Water and Its Dangers. *Public Health Papers and Reports* 7:283-90.

Rutgers Oral History Archives

2009   Alexander, II, Walter. Rutgers Oral History Archives, http://oralhistory .rutgers.edu/interviewees/30-interview-html-text/355-alexander-ii-walter, accessed June 14, 2019.

Said, Edward W.

1979   *Orientalism.* Vintage Books, New York.

Saignes, Thierry

1985   Notes on the Regional Contribution to the Mita in Potosí in the Early Seventeenth Century. *Bulletin of Latin American Research* 4(1):65-76.

Salinas y Córdoba, Buenaventura de

1957 [1653] *Memorial de las historias del nuevo mundo Pirú.* Universidad Nacional Mayor de San Marcos, Lima.

Sampeck, Kathryn E.

2007   Late Postclassic to Colonial Landscapes and Political Economy of the Iza-
        lcos Region, El Salvador. PhD dissertation, Department of Anthropology,
        Tulane University, New Orleans.

2010   Late Postclassic to Colonial Transformations of the Landscape in the Izal-
        cos Region of Western El Salvador. *Ancient Mesoamerica* 21(2):261–82.

2014a   Making the Municipio: Political Geographies in Colonial Guatemala. *Jour-
        nal of Latin American Geography* 13(2):153–79.

2014b   From Ancient Altepetl to Modern Municipio: Surveying as Power in
        Colonial Guatemala. *International Journal of Historical Archaeology*
        18(1):175–203.

2015   Chronology and Use of Guatemalan Maiolica: Ceramics as Reducción in
        the Izalcos Region of El Salvador. *Historical Archaeology* 49(2):18–49.

Sampeck, Kathryn, Jonathan Thayn, and Howard H. Earnest Jr.

2015   Geographic Information System Modeling of De Soto's Route from Joara to
        Chiaha: Archaeology and Anthropology of Southeastern Road Networks in
        the Sixteenth Century. *American Antiquity* 80(1):46–66.

Sampson, Robert J.

2013   *Great American City: Chicago and the Enduring Neighborhood Effect.* Uni-
        versity of Chicago Press, Chicago.

Sanders, Alison P., Heather H. Burris, Allan C. Just, Valeria Motta, Chitra Amara-
siriwardena, Katherine Svensson, Emily Oken, Maritsa Solano-Gonzalez, Adriana
Mercado-Garcia, Ivan Pantic, Joel Schwartz, Martha M. Tellez-Rojo, Andrea A.
Baccarelli, and Robert O. Wright

2015   Altered miRNA Expression in the Cervix during Pregnancy Associated with
        Lead and Mercury Exposure. *Epigenomics* 7(6):885–96.

Sato, Jack Kenzo

1944   #33. Sato[w], Jack Kenzo. Online Archive of California, http://www.oac
        .cdlib.org/ark:/28722/bk0013c5828/?brand=oac4, accessed June 12, 2019.

Saunders, Farid

1979   Application of Justice. Letter to the editor, *Orange Transcript* 81(49):6.

Sawyer-Lang, Monique

1989   *Recovery of Additional Information from the Gila River Farms Expansion
        Area: A Study of a Japanese-American Relocation Center.* Cultural
        Resources Report 53. Archaeological Consulting Services, Tempe.

Schele, Linda, and Mary Ellen Miller

1986   *The Blood of Kings: Dynasty and Ritual in Maya Art.* W. W. Norton, New York.

Scheper-Hughes, Nancy, and Philippe Bourgois (editors)

2003   *Violence in War and Peace: An Anthology*. Blackwell, Oxford.

Scheper-Hughes, Nancy, and Philippe Bourgois

2004   Introduction: Making Sense of Violence. In *Violence in War and Peace: An Anthology*, edited by Nancy Scheper-Hughes and Philippe Bourgois, pp. 1–31. Blackwell Publishers, Malden, MA.

Schmidt, Peter R., and Stephen A. Mrozowski (editors)

2014   *The Death of Prehistory*. Oxford University Press, Oxford.

Schmidt, Peter R., and Karega Munene

2010   An Africa-Informed View of Postcolonial Archaeologies. In *Handbook of Postcolonial Archaeology*, edited by Jane Lydon and Uzma Z. Rizvi, pp. 215–26. Left Coast Press, Walnut Creek, CA.

Schoettle, Anthony

2016   Could the White River Get a Beach Downtown? Maybe, Says Visit Indy. *Indianapolis Business Journal*, January 29, http://www.ibj.com /articles/56929-visit-indy-pursuing-development-of-white-rivers -downtown-shores, accessed June 16, 2019.

Scholz, Trevor

2017   *Uberworked and Underpaid. How Workers Are Disrupting the Digital Economy*. Polity Press, Cambridge.

Schroer, Markus

2000   Gewalt Ohne Gesicht. Zur Notwendigkeit Einer Umfassenden Gewaltanalyse. *Leviathan–Zeitschrift Für Sozialwissenschaft* 28(4): 434–51.

Schwartz, David

1997   *Culture and Power: The Sociology of Pierre Bourdieu*. University of Chicago Press, Chicago.

Scott, Doug

2011   *Analysis of Ammunition Components from the Lattimer Massacre Site*. Connor Consulting, Lincoln, NE.

Shackel, Paul A.

2018   *Remembering Lattimer: Labor, Migration, and Race in Pennsylvania Anthracite Country*. University Press of Illinois, Champaign.

Shackel, Paul A. (editor)

2001   *Myth, Memory and the Making of the American Landscape*. University of Florida Press, Gainesville.

Shackel, Paul, and Michael Roller

2012   The Gilded Age Wasn't So Gilded in the Anthracite Region of
        Pennsylvania. *International Journal of Historical Archaeology* 16(4):
        761–75.

Sharer, Robert J., and Loa P. Traxler

2006   *The Ancient Maya.* Stanford University Press, Palo Alto, CA.

Sharer, Robert, Wendy Ashmore, and Robert Hill

1970   *The Pottery of Antigua Guatemala.* Hispanic American Project, Guatemala
        City.

Shew, Dana Ogo

2010   Feminine Identity Confined: The Archaeology of Japanese Women
        at Amache, a WWII Internment Camp. Master's thesis, Department
        of Anthropology, University of Denver.

Silliman, Stephen W.

2009a   Blurring for Clarity: Archaeology as Hybrid Practice. In *Postcolonial Per-
        spectives in Archaeology*, edited by Peter Bikoulis, Dominic Lacroix, and
        Meaghan Peuramaki-Brown, pp. 15–25. Chacmool Archaeological Associa-
        tion, Calgary.

2009b   Change and Continuity, Practice and Memory: Native American
        Persistence in Colonial New England. *American Antiquity* 74(2):211–30.

Simpson, Audra

2014   *Mohawk Interruptus: Political Life across the Borders of Settler States.*
        Duke University Press, Durham, NC.

Singleton, Theresa A., and A. D. Bograd

1995   *The Archaeology of the African Diaspora in the Americas.* Society for Histor-
        ical Archaeology, Tucson.

Sivilich, Dan

2011   *Electronic Phase I Archaeological Survey Conducted at: Lattimer 1897
        Massacre Site, Lattimer Road, Lattimer, Luzerne County, Pennsylvania.*
        Report prepared for the Lattimer Massacre Project, College Park, Mary-
        land. Battlefield Restoration and Archaeological Volunteer Organization,
        Monmouth, NJ.

Skiles, Stephanie A., and Bonnie J. Clark

2010   When the Foreign Is Not Exotic: Ceramics at Colorado's WWII Japanese
        Internment Camp. In *Trade and Exchange: Archaeological Studies from
        History and Prehistory*, edited by Carolyn D. Dillian and Carolyn L. White,
        pp. 179–91. Springer, New York.

Slaughter, Michelle

2006   An Archaeological and Ethnographic Examination of the Presence, Acquisition, and Consumption of Sake at Camp Amache, a World War II Japanese Internment Camp. Master's thesis, Department of Anthropology, University of Colorado, Denver.

Smith, Adam T.

2004   The End of the Essential Archaeological Subject. *Archaeological Dialogues* 11(1):1–20.

Smith, Linda T.

1999   *Decolonizing Methodologies: Research and Indigenous Peoples.* Zed Books, London.

Smith, Page

1995   *Democracy on Trial: The Japanese American Evacuation and Relocation in World War II.* Simon & Schuster, New York.

Smith, Patrick

2001   Memory without History: Who Owns Guatemala's Past? *Washington Quarterly* 24:59–72.

Society for Historical Archaeology (SHA)

2014   Bottle Dating. SHA, http://www.sha.org/bottle/machinemadedating.htm, accessed June 19, 2019.

Sofsky, Wolfgang

1999   *The Order of Terror: The Concentration Camp.* Translated by William B. Templer. Princeton University Press, Princeton, NJ.

Sontag, Susan

1977   *On Photography.* Farrar, Strauss, Giroux, New York.

2003   *Regarding the Pain of Others.* Picador/Farrar, Straus and Giroux, New York.

Spencer, Robert F.

1942a   Recreational Activities. Online Archive of California, http://www.oac.cdlib.org/ark:/28722/bk0013c9536/?brand=oac4, accessed June 12, 2019.

1942b   Religious Life in the Gila Community. Online Archive of California, http://www.oac.cdlib.org/ark:/28722/bk0013c9559/?brand=oac4, accessed June 12, 2019.

1942c. Report #2 on Gila. Online Archive of California, http://oac.cdlib.org/ark:/28722/bk0013c939g/?brand=oac4, accessed June 12, 2019.

1942d   Social Groups in the Gila Community. Online Archive of California, http://www.oac.cdlib.org/ark:/28722/bk0013c956v/?brand=oac4, accessed June 12, 2019.

Spencer-Wood, Suzanne

2009   A Feminist Approach to European Ideologies of Poverty and the Institution-
        alization of the Poor in Falmouth, Massachusetts. In *The Archaeology of
        Institutional Life*, edited by April M. Biesaw and James G. Gibb, pp. 117-36.
        University of Alabama Press, Tuscaloosa.

Spencer-Wood, Suzanne M., and Christopher N. Matthews

2011   Impoverishment, Criminalization, and the Culture of Poverty. *Historical
        Archaeology* 45(3):1-10.

Spivak, Gayatri Chakravorty

1988   Can the Subaltern Speak? In *Marxism and the Interpretation of Culture*,
        edited by Cary Nelson and Lawrence Grossberg, pp. 271-313. University of
        Illinois Press, Urbana.

1990   Strategic Essentialism, Political Power, Strategy. In *The Post-Colonial
        Critic: Interviews, Strategies, Dialogues*, edited by Sarah Harasym, pp. 1-16.
        Routledge, New York.

Starzmann, Maria T.

2010   Structural Violence as Political Experience in Palestine: An Archaeology
        of the Past in the Present. *Present Pasts* 2(1):126-41.

2014   Excavating Tempelhof Airfield: Objects of Memory and the Politics of
        Absence. *Rethinking History: Journal of Theory and Practice* 18(2):211-29.

2015   The Materiality of Forced Labor: An Archaeological Exploration of Pun-
        ishment in Nazi Germany. *International Journal of Historical Archaeology*
        19(3):647-63.

Starzmann, Maria, Susan Pollock, and Reinhard Bernbeck (editors)

2008   Imperial Inspections: Archaeology, War and Violence. Special issue,
        Archaeologies 4(3).

Staudigl, Michael

2013   Towards a Relational Phenomenology of Violence. *Human Studies*
        36(1):43-66.

Stephens, Ronald J.

2013   *Idlewild: The Rise, Decline, and Rebirth of a Unique African American
        Resort*. University of Michigan Press, Ann Arbor.

Stern, Steve J.

1993   *Peru's Indian Peoples and the Challenge of Spanish Conquest: Huamanga to
        1640*. University of Wisconsin Press, Madison.

Stone, Pamela K.

2016   Biocultural Perspectives on Maternal Mortality and Obstetrical Death from the Past to the Present. *American Journal of Physical Anthropology* 159(S61):150–71.

Sullivan, Mary, Monique Sawyer-Lang, Richard W. Effland Jr., and Margerie Green

1987　*An Archaeological Survey of the Gila River Farms Expansion, Pinal County, Arizona.* Archaeological Consulting Services, Tempe.

Sussman, Robert W.

1997　Exploring Our Basic Human Nature: Are Humans Inherently Violent? *Anthro Notes* 19(3):1–6, 17–19, doi.org/10.5479/10088/22362, accessed January 3, 2019.

Tamir, Orit, Scott C. Russell, Karolyn Jackman Jensen, and Shereen Lerner

1993　*Return to Butte Camp: A Japanese-American World War II Relocation Center.* Cultural Resources Report 82. Archaeological Consulting Services, Tempe.

Tascón, Antonio Matilla

1958　*Historia de las minas de Almadén 2.* Minas de Almadén y Arrayanes, Madrid.

Taussig, Michael T.

1986　*Shamanism, Colonialism, and the Wild Man: A Study in Terror and Healing.* University of Chicago Press, Chicago.

Theune, Claudia

2014　*Archäologie an Tatorten des 20. Jahrhunderts.* Theiss, Stuttgart.

Thomas, Aline

2014　Bioarchaeology of the Middle Neolithic: Evidence for Archery among Early European Farmers. *American Journal of Physical Anthropology* 154(2):279–90.

Thomas, Julian

2012　Archaeologies of Place and Landscape. In *Archaeological Theory Today,* 2nd ed., edited by Ian Hodder, pp. 167–87. Polity Press, Cambridge.

Thomas, Nicholas

1991　*Entangled Objects: Exchange, Material Culture and Colonialism in the Pacific.* Harvard University Press, Cambridge, MA.

Thompson, Eric S.

1943　A Trial Survey of the Southern Maya Area. *American Antiquity* 9(1):106–34.

Thompson, Ernest, and Mindy Thompson

1976　*Homeboy Came to Orange: A Story of People's Power.* Authors Choice Press, New York.

Tilley, Christopher Y.

2010　*Interpreting Landscapes: Geologies, Topographies, Identities. Explorations in Landscape Phenomenology.* Left Coast Press, Walnut Creek, CA.

Tomasello, Michael

2009   *Why We Cooperate*. MIT Press, Cambridge, MA.

Tringham, Ruth

1991   Households with Faces: The Challenge of Gender in Prehistoric Architec-
        tural Remains. In *Engendering Archaeology: Women in Prehistory*, edited by
        Joan Gero and Margaret W. Conkey, pp. 93–131. Blackwell, Oxford.

Tsuchida, Nobuya

1984   Japanese Gardeners in Southern California, 1900–1941. In *Labor Immigra-
        tion Under Capitalism: Asian Workers in the United States Before WWII*,
        edited by Lucie Cheng and Edna Bonacich, pp. 439–69. University of Cali-
        fornia Press, Berkeley.

Tsukashima, Ronald Tadao

1991   Cultural Endowment, Disadvantaged Status and Economic Niche: The
        Development of an Ethnic Trade. *International Migration Review* 25(2):333.

2000   Politics of Maintenance Gardening and the Formation of the Southern
        California Gardener's Association. In *Greenmakers* = グリーンメーカーズ:
        Japanese American Gardeners in Southern California, edited by Naomi
        Hirahara, pp. 66–93. Southern California Gardeners' Federation,
        Los Angeles.

Tuan, Yi-fu

1977   *Space and Place: The Perspective of Experience*. University of Minnesota
        Press, Minneapolis.

Tung, Tiffiny A.

2012   *Violence, Ritual, and the Wari Empire: A Social Bioarchaeology of Imperial-
        ism in the Ancient Andes*. University Press of Florida, Gainesville.

Turner, George

1977   The Lattimer Massacre and Its Sources. *Slovakia* 27(50):9–43.

UPI

1986   CBS, Rather Cleared in Libel Case. UPI Archives, February 28, http://
        www.upi.com/Archives/1986/02/28/CBS-Rather-cleared-in-libel-case
        /1413509950800/, accessed June 14, 2019.

Urry, John

1973   Towards a Structural Theory of the Middle Class. *Acta Sociologica*
        16(3):175–87.

US Bureau of the Census

1952   *City and County Data Book*. US Government Printing Office, Washington,
        DC.

1962   *City and County Data Book*. US Government Printing Office,
        Washington, DC.

1967   *City and County Data Book*. US Government Printing Office,
        Washington, DC.

1972   *City and County Data Book*. US Government Printing Office,
        Washington, DC.

1977   *City and County Data Book*. US Government Printing Office,
         Washington, DC.

US Department of Justice, Federal Bureau of Investigation

2016   Uniform Crime Reporting Statistics. DOJ, http://www.ucrdatatool.gov/
        Search/Crime/Local/JurisbyJuris.cfm?CFID=125332219&CFTOKEN
        =302c08c32f312139-3168DF3F-0FB9-F440-2F9AF309B8F30047, accessed
        June 14, 2019.

Ussishkin, David

1980   *The Conquest of Lachish by Sennacherib*. Tel Aviv University, Tel Aviv.

Van Akkeren, Rudd

2005   Getting Acquainted with the Pipils of the South Coast of Guatemala: An
        Ethno-Historic Study of Indigenous Documents and of the General Archive
        of Central America. In *Symposium of Archaeological Investigations in Gua-
        temala*, edited by Juan Pedro LaPorte, Bárbara Arroyo, and Héctor E. Mejía.
        Foundation for the Advancement of Mesoamerican Studies, http://www
        .famsi.org/reports/03101/99ruud/99ruud.pdf, accessed June 18, 2019.

Van Bueren, Thad M.

2006   Between Vision and Practice: Archaeological Perspectives on the Llano
        Del Rio Cooperative. *Historical Archaeology* 40(1):133-51.

Van Dyke, Ruth

2015   The Chacoan Past: Creative Representations and Sensory Engagements. In
        Subjects and Narratives in Archaeology, edited by Ruth Van Dyke and Rein-
        hard Bernbeck, pp. 83-100. University Press of Colorado, Boulder.

Vargas, Iraida Arenas

2005   The Perception of History and Archaeology in Latin America: A Theoretical
        Approach. In *Making Alternative Histories: The Practice of Archaeology and
        History in Non-Western Settings*, edited by P. R Schmidt and T. C. Patter-
        son, pp. 47-68. School of American Research Press, Santa Fe, NM.

Vázquez, Francisco, and Lázaro Lamadrid

1944   *Crónica de La Provincia Del Santísimo Nombre de Jesús de Guatemala
        de La Orden de N. Seráfico Padre San Francisco En El Reino de La Nueva*

España de La Orden de N. Serafico Padre San Francisco En El Reino de La Nueva Espana, Vol. 2. Tipografía nacional, Guatemala City.

Vera Institute of Justice

2017   Incarceration Trends. Vera Institute of Justice, http://trends.vera.org /incarceration-rates?data=pretrial, accessed June 14, 2019.

Verhagen, Inez L.

1997   Caluco, El Salvador: The Archaeology of a Colonial Indian Town in Comparative Perspective. PhD dissertation, Department of Anthropology, Vanderbilt University, Nashville.

Vizenor, Gerald, and A. Robert Lee

2003   *Postindian Conversations*. University of Nebraska Press, Lincoln.

Voss, Barbara L.

2008   Gender, Race, and Labor in the Archaeology of the Spanish Colonial Americas. *Current Anthropology* 49(5):861-93.

2012   Sexual Effects: Postcolonial and Queer Perspectives on the Archaeology of Sexuality and Empire. In *The Archaeology of Colonialism: Intimate Encounters and Sexual Effects*, edited by Barbara L. Voss and Eleanor Conlin Casella, pp. 11-28. Cambridge University Press, New York.

2018   Archaeology Is Not Enough: Witnessing the Labor of Heritage Stakeholders. *American Anthropologist* 120(3):539-40.

Wacquant, Loïc

2004   The New "Peculiar Institution": On the Prison as Surrogate Ghetto. In *Violence in War and Peace: An Anthology*, edited by Nancy Scheper-Highes and Philippe Bourgois, pp. 318-23. Blackwell, New York.

Wäfler, Markus

1975   *Nicht-Assyrer Neuassyrischer Darstellungen*. Alter Orient und Altes Testament 26. Butzon & Bercker, Kevelaer, Germany.

Wainwright, Joel

2011   *Decolonizing Development: Colonial Power and the Maya*. Blackwell, Malden, MA.

Walker, Paul L.

2001   A Bioarchaeological Perspective on the History of Violence. *Annual Review of Anthropology* 30(1):573-96.

Wallace, Anthony F. C.

1987   *St. Clair: A Nineteenth-Century Coal Town's Experience with a Disaster-Prone Industry*. Cornell University Press, Ithaca.

Warren, Kay B.

1998   *Indigenous Movements and Their Critics: Pan-Maya Activism in Guatemala.* Princeton University Press, Princeton, NJ.

Watanabe, John M.

1995   Unimagining the Maya: Anthropologists, Others, and the Inescapable Hubris of Authorship. *Bulletin of Latin American Research* 14(1):25–45.

Wauchope, Robert

1970   Protohistoric Pottery of the Guatemala Highlands. In *Monographs and Papers in Maya Archaeology*, Vol. 61, edited by William R. Bullard Jr., pp. 89–245. Peabody Museum of Archaeology and Ethnology, Harvard University, Cambridge, MA.

Weber, Max

1978   *Economy and Society: An Outline of Interpretive Sociology.* Translated by Guenther Roth and Claus Wittich. University of California Press, Berkeley.

Webster, Andrew J.

2016   Ceramic Consumption in a Boston Immigrant Tenement. Master's thesis, Department of Anthropology, University of Massachusetts, Boston.

Weik, Terrance

2012   *The Archaeology of Antislavery Resistance.* University Press of Florida, Gainesville.

Weiss, Elizabeth, and Robert D. Jurmain

2007   Osteoarthritis Revisited: A Contemporary Review of Aetiology. *International Journal of Osteoarchaeology* 17(5):437–50.

Weiss, Peter

2005   *The Aesthetics of Resistance.* Translated by Joachim Neugroschel. Duke University Press, Durham, NC.

Weizman, Eyal

2014   Introduction: Forensis. In *Forensis: The Architecture of Public Truth*, edited by Forensic Architecture, pp. 9–32. Sternberg Press, Berlin.

Wenger, Etienne

1998   *Communities of Practice: Learning, Meaning, and Identity.* Cambridge University Press, New York.

Wernke, Steven A.

2013   *Negotiated Settlements: Andean Communities and Landscapes under Inka and Spanish Colonialism.* University Press of Florida, Gainesville.

West, Evan

2006   Pipe Dreams. *Indianapolis Monthly*, June, pp. 147–51, 285–87.

White, Tim D., Michael T. Black, and Pieter A. Folkens

2011   *Human Osteology.* 3rd ed. Academic Press, Cambridge.

White, William A.

2017   #metoo in Cultural Resource Management Archaeology. Succinct Re-
         search, November 10, http://www.succinctresearch.com/metoo-in-cultural
         -resource-management-archaeology/, accessed January 3, 2019.

Wiegel, Gerd

2002   Das Verschwinden der Bilder. Von der alten zur neuen "Wehrmachtsau-
         sstellung." *Informationen. Wissenschaftliche Zeitschrift des Studienkreises
         Deutscher Widerstand 1933–1945* 56:17–20.

Weiss, Elizabeth, and R. D. Jurmain

2007   Osteoarthritis Revisited: A Contemporary Review of Aetiology. *International
         Journal of Osteoarchaeology* 17(5):437–50.

Wilcox, Michael

2009a   *The Pueblo Revolt and the Mythology of Conquest: An Indigenous Archaeol-
         ogy of Contact.* University of California Press, Berkeley.

2009b   Marketing Conquest and the Vanishing Indian: An Indigenous Response
         to Jared Diamond's *Guns, Germs, and Steel* and *Collapse. Journal of Social
         Archaeology* 10(1):92–117.

Wilkie, Laurie

2001   Race, Identity and Habermas's Lifeworld. In *Race and the Archaeology
         of Identity*, edited by Chares Orser, pp. 108–24. University of Utah Press,
         Salt Lake City.

Wiltse, Jeff

2009   *Contested Waters: A Social History of Swimming Pools in America.* Univer-
         sity of North Carolina Press, Chapel Hill.

Wolcott, Victoria W.

2012   *Race, Riots, and Roller Coasters: The Struggle over Segregated Recreation
         in America.* University of Pennsylvania Press, Philadelphia.

Wolfe, Patrick

2006   Settler Colonialism and the Elimination of the Native. *Journal of Genocide
         Research* 8(4):387–409.

Wood, Denis

2010   *Rethinking the Power of Maps.* Guilford Press, New York.

Worth, John

2007   *The Struggle for the Georgia Coast.* University of Alabama Press, Tuscaloosa.

Wrangham, Richard, and Dale Peterson

1996   *Demonic Males: Apes and the Origins of Human Violence.* Houghton Mifflin, Boston.

Wright, David K.

2010   *Results of Survey and Monitoring for the Proposed GRIC-DPW Installation of a Water Tank and a Water Main from Butte Camp to Preschool Road, Pinal County, Gila River Indian Community, Arizona.* CRMP Technical Report 2010-14. Cultural Resource Management Program, Sacaton, AZ.

Yaeger, Jason, and Greg Borgstede

2004   Professional Archaeology and the Modern Maya: A Historical Sketch. In *Continuities and Change in Maya Archaeology: Perspectives at the Millennium,* edited by Charles Golden and Greg Borgstede, pp. 259-86. Routledge, New York.

Yanagisako, Sylvia, and Jane Fishburne Collier

1987   Toward a Unified Analysis of Gender and Kinship. In *Gender and Kinship: Toward a Unified Analysis,* edited by Jane Collier and Sylvia Yanagisako, pp. 14-52. Stanford University Press, Stanford, CA.

Ylimaunu, Timo, Sami Lakomäki, Titta Kallio-Seppä, Paul R. Mullins, Risto Nurmi, and Markku Kuorilehto

2014   Borderlands as Spaces: Creating Third Spaces and Fractured Landscapes in Medieval Northern Finland. *Journal of Social Archaeology* 14(2):244-67.

Yoshihashi, Tok

2015   Interview by Koji Lau-Ozawa, December 20, Los Angeles. Transcript in author's possession.

Zeeb-Lanz, Andrea, and Fabian Haack

2016   Diversity in Ritual Practice at the End of the LBK. In *Something Out of the Ordinary? Interpreting Diversity in the Early Neolithic Linearbandkeramik and Beyond,* edited by Luc Amkreutz, Fabian Haack, Daniela Hofmann, and Ivo Van Wijk, pp. 247-82. Cambridge Scholars Publishing, Newcastle upon Tyne.

Zeidel, Robert F.

2004   *Immigrants, Progressives, and Exclusion Politics: The Dillingham Commission, 1900-1927.* Northern Illinois University Press, DeKalb.

Žižek, Slavoj

2008   *Violence: Six Sideways Reflections.* Picador, New York.

CONTRIBUTORS

KYLE HUSKINS is a graduate student in the Department of Sociology at Indiana University–Purdue University, Indianapolis, where he is completing his thesis research on African American suburbanization in postwar Indianapolis.

SUSAN B. HYATT is a professor and chair in the Department of Anthropology at Indiana University–Purdue University, Indianapolis. Her academic interests include urban anthropology, service learning and ethnographic methods, social movements, the anthropology of policy, the anthropology of contemporary Europe and North America, and the impact of incarceration and reentry.

KOJI LAU-OZAWA is a PhD candidate in the Department of Anthropology at Stanford University. His work focuses on the archaeology of the Japanese diaspora and in particular the Gila River Incarceration Camp. He received his master's degree in anthropology from San Francisco State University and his undergraduate degree in archaeology and social anthropology from the University of Edinburgh.

CHRISTOPHER N. MATTHEWS is a professor in the Department of Anthropology at Montclair State University. He is the author of *An Archaeology of History and Tradition* (Plenum, 2002) and *The Archaeology of American Capitalism* (University Press of Florida, 2010). He is also the past editor of the journal *Historical Archaeology* as well as codirector of the A Long Time Coming project in Setauket, New York, and the Reverse Archaeology of I-280 project in Orange, New Jersey.

PAUL R. MULLINS is a professor in the Department of Anthropology at Indiana University–Purdue University, Indianapolis and a docent in American historical archaeology at the University of Oulu in Finland.

GUIDO PEZZAROSSI is an assistant professor in the Maxwell School at Syracuse University. His research on colonialism and capitalism spans English colonial contexts in Massachusetts, multiethnic colonial/imperial engagements in Wisconsin, and Spanish colonial contexts in Guatemala. His research focuses on postcolonial and indigenous approaches to the archaeology of colonial identities and difference, the archaeology of food, and the economic dynamics of colonization. His current research explores the intersection of postcolonial and new materialist perspectives to analyze the entanglements between capitalism and colonialism, via an analysis of how transformations in labor and economic practices in colonial Guatemala—catalyzed by the violence of colonization—affected the experience of daily life for Maya communities.

BRADLEY D. PHILLIPPI, assistant professor of anthropology and director of the Center for Public Archaeology at Hofstra University, received his PhD from Northwestern University in 2015. As a historical archaeologist of the modern world, he has special interest in issues of race, labor, and inequality in the eighteenth- and nineteenth-century Northeast. His most recent project investigated the material and spatial transition from enslaved to free labor on Long Island and its impact on social relations and daily practice. This work was funded by grants from the National Science Foundation and the Wenner-Gren Foundation.

TERREN K. PROCTOR is a graduate student currently pursuing her PhD in anthropology at Vanderbilt University. She received her bachelor of science degree in anthropology and biology from McGill University in 2014. Her doctoral research seeks to investigate the embodiment of structural violence, with a specific focus on the indigenous laborers of colonial Peru. In 2015 she joined the Proyecto de Investigación Histórico Arqueológico-Santa Bárbara as primary bioarchaeologist and as codirector with Douglas K. Smit. This project is an ongoing research program involving both American and Peruvian scholars looking at questions of indigenous labor at colonial Huancavelica in the central Peruvian Andes. She has also worked as a researcher on the Ayacucho Bioarchaeology Project directed by Tiffiny A. Tung, investigating intentional cranial modification as the embodiment of ethnic and social identities.

MICHAEL P. ROLLER graduated in the spring of 2015 with a PhD in anthropology and historical archaeology from the University of Maryland–College Park. His dissertation research, titled "Migration, Modernity and Memory: The

Archaeology of the Twentieth Century in a Northeast Pennsylvania Coal Company Town, 1897–2014," uses a combination of ethnographic approaches and historical archaeology to examine the materialist trajectory of everyday life in the anthracite coal region of Northeast Pennsylvania. At the center of the dissertation is the traumatic labor massacre of migrant workers in 1897 that took place in Lattimer. This moment of punctuated violence serves as a lens to examine the representational violence inflicted upon generations of racialized migrants to the region across the century. Currently, Roller works as an archaeologist for the National Park Service in the Archaeology Program, the National Historic Landmarks Program, and the National Register. He is developing his dissertation into a book to be published in the near future.

KATHRYN E. SAMPECK (BA, MA University of Chicago; PhD Tulane University) is an associate professor of anthropology at Illinois State University. Her writings on the archaeology and ethnohistory of Spanish colonialism have appeared in *American Antiquity*, *Ethnohistory*, *Historical Archaeology*, *International Journal of Historical Archaeology*, *Mesoamérica*, *Ancient Mesoamerica*, and *Journal of Latin American Geography*. She was guest editor for "Colonial Mesoamerican Literacy: Method, Form, and Consequence" (*Ethnohistory* 62[3]), published in cooperation with the John Carter Brown Library, Brown University. Sampeck is the 2015–2016 Central America Fellow at the David Rockefeller Center for Latin American Studies and the Afro-Latin American Research Institute at the Hutchins Center at Harvard University. She is an associate editor for the journal *Historical Archaeology* and is on the editorial board of *Ethnohistory*. Previous honors include fellowships from the John Carter Brown Library and Colonial Williamsburg and grants from the National Science Foundation, Wenner-Gren Foundation, Social Science Research Council, Fulbright program, and Cherokee Preservation Foundation.

DOUGLAS K. SMIT is a doctoral candidate currently finishing his PhD with the joint anthropology program between the University of Illinois at Chicago (UIC) and the Field Museum of Natural History. He received his BA in archaeology from the George Washington University in 2008 and his MA in anthropology from UIC in 2012. His doctoral research examines the relationship between states and markets, with a specific focus on the role of indigenous peoples in the political economies of colonial Latin America. Since 2013 he has directed the Proyecto de Investigación Histórico Arqueológico-Santa Bárbara. This collaborative research program between American and Peruvian scholars examines indigenous laborers of colonial Huancavelica, located in the central highlands of Peru and the largest mercury mine in the Americas from the sixteenth to the eighteenth century. This research has been funded by the National Science Foundation, the Wenner-Gren Foundation, and various other small external and internal research funds, and has been published in both Spanish and English.

LOUANN WURST received her PhD in anthropology from Binghamton University and is currently a professor of industrial archaeology at Michigan Technological University. Her research focuses on the historical archaeology of class, labor, ideology, and gender in the United States. She is currently working on two research projects. One focuses on capitalist transformations in agricultural production based on sites in the Finger Lakes National Forest in New York State, and the other examines workers' experiences in the northern forests of Michigan beginning with early twentieth-century lumber camps. She is the author of "Historical Archaeology of Capitalist Dispossession" (*Capital and Class*, 2015) and "Toward a Collective Historical Archaeology" (*Reviews in Anthropology*, 2015), and coeditor with Stephen Mrozowski of "Studying History Backward" (special issue, *International Journal of Historical Archaeology*, 2014).

INDEX

Page numbers in italic text indicate illustrations.

direct violence, 89, 97, 99–100, *100*

discipline: Foucault on power and, 68–73, 75; in Izalcos region, public, 75; place and, 64–65, 68–73

discursive violence, 207, 220; hate speech, 213–14; in Maya history, 39, 45–47, 60, 215–16; symbolic violence and, 211

dogs, eating of, 80–81

Dubofsky, Melvyn, 113

Du Bois, W. E. B., 6, 172

Dyson, Michael Eric, 169–70, 197–98

Earnshaw, Joseph, 160

earthenwares. *See* maiolica

economy, of violence, 18, 38n1

Elias, Norbert, 17, 67

Eliot, Charles, 160

El Salvador, 39, 62

Englert, George E., 186

environmental violence, 155–56

Essex County, New Jersey: African American community in, 187–88, *189*, 189–90, *190*, 191–92, 195–96, 200n3, 229; carceral landscape of, 12, 171, 175–76, 177, 178–79, 183, 187–88, *189*, 195–98, 203, 229–30; crime in, 178, 180, *181*, 182–83, 192–93, 196, 198; demographics of, changing, 178–79, *179*, 182, 195–96; factory closings in, 186–87; highway-scape of, 187, 192–94, 196; I-280 through, 12, 171, 176, *177*, 178, 182, 184, 187–88, *189*, 190–92, *193*, 193–98, 200n3, 211, 229; incarceration rates for, 183; Italian Americans in, 12, 187–88, 191–92, 195–96, 200n3, 229; motorist-scape of, 187, 193–95;

Newark, 12, 170, *171*, 180, *181*, 195–96; Newark Rebellion in, 172, 175–76, 182–85; Orange, 12, *171*, 175–76, *177*, 178, *179*, 180, *181*, 182, *193*, 193–94, 197–99; Orange, communities in, 187–88, *189*, 189–90, *190*, 191–92, 195–96, 200n3, 229; Orange, police violence protested in, 178, 183–87, 196; racialized police violence in, 172, 175–76, 178, 183–87, 196; reverse archaeology for, 198–99; segregation in, 170–71, 175, 178, 183, 188, 190–91, 195–99, 229; suburban, 170–71, *171*, 178–79, *179*, 180, *181*, 182–83, 194–98, 203, 229–30

excavations: photography of, 27–28; reification in, 38; symbolic violence of, 33, 38n4

Fabian, Johannes, 34, 36

Fanon, Frantz, 18

Farmer, Paul: on materiality, 5–6, 156–57; on structural violence, 1–2, 5, 76–77, 82, 156–57, 220, 227

Ferguson, Missouri, police shooting in, 3–4

Fleming, Henry, 164–65

La Florida, 62, 63, 74, 209, 224; food in, 77, 80–81; fort in, 73, 75, 75; Pardo in, 69, 74–75, 77, 84, 86; spatial violence in, 69–70, 73, 77, 84–85, 202; surveillance, panopticon in, 73–74, 75, 75; symbolic violence in, 84–86; as wilderness, 84, 202

Folkmar, Daniel, 127

food: ceramics for, 81, 205; in La Florida, 77, 80–81; in Izalcos region, 77–81; security and access to, 77–80, 205

forced resettlement. *See* congregación

fort, Spanish American, 73, 75, 75

Foucault, Michel, 70, 72, 75–76; on panopticon, 73, 77; on prison, 68–69, 174; on quarantine, 68–69, 71; on spatial violence, 61, 68–69, 83; on subjectivation, 21, 38n3

Franco, Francisco, 92

Frühsorge, Lars, 60

Gage, Thomas, 85

Galtung, Johan, 19, 94, 156

gardening, Japanese American: immigrant, 11, 150–52, 202–3; in incarceration camps, 11, 134, 140, 141, 142, 143–45, *145*, 147, *148*, 148–49, *151*, 151–52, 202–3, 205, 219–20

gardens, power in, 64, 68

Geertz, Clifford, 18

gender, 214–15

Germany: Nazi period in, 18–19, 23–27, 29, 30, 33–34, 204–5, 214; Syrian refugees in, 15–16

Gibson, Mel, 46

Giddens, Anthony, 212

Gila River Incarceration Camp, 209, 211; archaeological research on, 139, *140*, 141, 142, 143, 145–47, 152; Butte Camp in, *136*, 137, *138*, 141, 144, 147–48; Canal Camp in, 135, 137, 144; diversity in, 149, 152, 203, 220; gardens in, 11, 134, 140, 141, 142, 143–45, *145*, 147, *148*, 148–49, *151*, 151–52, 202–3, 205; Hayashi on, 133, 143–44; marginalized populations in, 149, 152, 220

Gila River Indian Community (GRIC): incarceration camps and, 11, 134–35,

146–47, 152–53, 202; sovereignty of, 11, 146–47, 152, 202

Gila River Indian Community Cultural Resource Management Program (GRIC-CRMP), 139, 141

Goldhagen, Daniel, 24

González-Ruibal, Alfredo, 207

Graeber, David, 223

Greene, Lynda Sheryl, 3

Greenough, Walter Sidney, 161

GRIC. *See* Gila River Indian Community

GRIC-CRMP. *See* Gila River Indian Community Cultural Resource Management Program

grid plan, 70–71, *71*, 72, *72*, 99

Guatemala, 9, 58, 80, 216; Antigua Valley, 40, 49–51, 54, 56; civil war in, Maya and, 46; colonial narratives in, undermining, 47–49, 60; food security and access in colonial, 78; as Indio, Maya in, 42; Ladino in, 43, 47; Maya archaeology in highland, 40–41, 49–53, *53*, 54, 54–56, 59, 201; Maya in, archaeological bias on, 40; mestizaje in, 8, 43–44, 47

Guzmán, Diego de, 78

habitus, 67

Hackett, Mims, 186

Hambidge, Jay, 125, 127

Hamburg Institute, 24–26

Hamilakis, Yannis, 213

Hamm, Daniel, 173

Hanks, William, 67

Harlem, New York, 172–73, 183, 196–97, 199n2

hate speech, 213–14

Hayashi, Ken, 133, 143–44

Heer, Hannes, 24–25

Herat, Afghanistan, 15–16

Hessel, Stéphane, 214

Hilberg, Raul, 24

Hitler's Willing Executioners (Goldhagen), 24

Hobbes, Thomas, 20

Hodder, Ian, 35

Hoffman, Paul, 194–95

Holocaust, 18–19, 23, 214; archaeology of, 33–34; photography and, 24–27

Honneth, Axel: on intersubjectivity, 8, 22–23, 26–27, 204; on recognition, 8, 22–23, 25–26, 29, 34, 203; on reification, 22–23, 26, 34, 203–4

Horkheimer, Max, 26, 36

Huancavelica, 205, 209, 225; Black Legend and, 9, 90–91, 202; direct violence in, 89, 97, 99–100, *100*; as *mina de la muerte*, 9, 90, 104; mitayos in, 9–10, 90, 96–97, 103–4, 106n10, 202, 224; structural violence in, 94–95, 101–4, 202

I-280. *See* Interstate 280

ideology, 20–21, 207

immigrants: in coal industry, 10, 107, 111–14, *119*, 120–21, 123–29, 131–32, 203, 205, 221; Japanese American, 11, 150–52, 202–3

imperialism, comparative, 215

Indianapolis, Indiana: African American country club blocked in, 12, 164–66; African American resorts outside, 166; Near Westside, African Americans in, 11, 158–62, 164, 166–67; pools in, segregation and, 11–12, 162–65, *165*, 202; segregation in, 11–12, 154–55, *156*, 157, 158, 158–59, 162–65, *165*, 166, 168, 202; urban renewal in, 162, 167

Indianapolis, Indiana, waterways in: aesthetics of, 160–62; African Americans and pollution of, 11, 154–55, 159–62, 164, 166–68, 202; beaches along, 154, *156*, 162, 166, 168, 202, 205; pollution of, 11–12, 154–57, 159–62, *163*, 163–64, 166–68, 202; proposals for, 12, 154, 160–62, 167–68, 202, 205; sewage problems of, 154–55, 159–60, 164, 167; structural violence and, 11–12, 155–57, 159, 168, 202

Indio, 39, 42–43

Ingold, Tim, 87

interpellation, 20–22, 32

Interstate 280 (I-280): through Essex County, 12, 171, 176, 177, 178, 182, 184, 187–88, *189*, 190–92, *193*, 193–98, 200n3, 211, 229; Newark and, 12, 171, 182, 195–96; Orange and, 12, 171, 176, 177, 178, 187–88, *189*, 190–92, *193*, 193–98, 200n3, 229

intersubjectivity, 18, 109; coevalness and, 34, 36; Honneth on, 8, 22–23, 26–27, 204; recognition and, 8, 22–24, 26–27, 203–4

Irish demesne, 82

Islamic State (IS), 15, 30

issei. *See* Japanese American immigrants

Italian Americans: in coal industry, 126–29; in Essex County, 12, 187–88, 191–92, 195–96, 200n3, 229

Italians, southern, racialization of, 127–29

Izalcos region, 62, 63, 209; Caluco, 71, 72, 73, 74, 79, 83, 85; ceramics in, 81, 205; congregación in, 69-71, 79; food in, 77-81, 205; grid plan in, 70-71, 72; public discipline in, 75; San Pedro y San Pablo church in, 73, 74; segregation in, 69-73; spatial violence in, 69-73, 77-79, 83, 202; symbolic violence in, 83, 85

Jackson, Jesse, 3
Japanese American immigrants, 11, 150-52, 202-3
Japanese American incarceration, World War II, 10, 204, 209, 211; archaeological research on, 138-39, 140, 141, 142, 143, 145-49, 152, 219; congressional commission on, 133; gardens in, 11, 134, 140, 141, 142, 143-45, 145, 147, 148, 148-49, 151, 151-52, 202-3, 205, 219-20; language of, 135; legacy of, 133-34, 220-21; Manzanar War Relocation Center, 138-39, 143, 149, 151, 219-20; marginalized populations in, 148-49, 152, 220; on Native American land, 11, 134-35, 146-47, 152-53, 202; oral histories of, 137, 139, 141, 143-45, 219-20; under WRA, 135, 146-47, 149. *See also* Gila River Incarceration Camp
Jarvis, R. Walter, 163-64
Johnson, Walter, 223-24
Joyce, Rosemary, 43
Juderías, Julian, 91

Kennedy, Robert, 2
Kessler, George, 161

King, Martin Luther, 2, 218
Klaus, Haagen, 94-95, 103, 209
Kooskia Internment Camp, 139
Kuramoto, Frances, 144-45
Kurosawa, Akira, 110

Ladino, 43, 47, 81
Landon, David B., 207
las Casas, Bartolomé de, 91-92
Lattimer, Pennsylvania: as company town, 108, 118, *119*, 119-20, 131; domesticity in, 107-9, 118, *119*, 119-22, 123, 123-26, 203, 205; Italian immigrants in, 126-27; Lattimer No. 1, 118-19, *119*, 120-22, 123, 123-24; Lattimer No. 2, 118, *119*, 120; middle class in, 110, 113, 115, 124-25, 131-32, 211, 221-23; New Immigrants in, 10, 107, 111, 113, *119*, 120-21, 123-29, 131-32, 203, 205, 221; Pardee family running, 108, 118-19; racialized immigrants in, 10, 107, 111, 113, *119*, 120, 123-27, 129, 132; systemic violence in, 10, 111, 123-24, 205
Lattimer Massacre, 209; archaeology of, 116-17, *117*, 118, 131; middle class and, 115, 211, 221-23; strikes and, 10, 107-8, 114-16, 131; subjective violence of, 10, 109, 111, 116, 129, 131, 203-4, 221; symbolic violence and, 10, 113, 118, 124-25; systemic violence and, 10, 111
law, violence and, 65-66
Law Pezzarossi, Heather, 58-59
Lefebvre, Henri, 64-65, 70
Levi, Primo, 23, 220
Leviathan (Hobbes), 20
Leyenda Negra. *See* Black Legend
liberation theology, 5-6

mounds, 84, *84*

mujahedin, Afghan, 15–16

Mulrooney, Margaret, 123–24

multivocality, 35–36, 204

Munene, Karega, 36

Münkler, Herfried, 38n1

Murphy, Ray, 190

Myers, Adrian, 33–34

Nahuat, 62

Nakamura, Yosh, 143

narrative: multivocality in, 35–36; violence and, 34–37

National Park Service (NPS), 138–39

Native Americans, 218; Ani-yunwiya, 62, *63*, 69–70, 84, 84–85; excavations resisted by, 38n4; GRIC, 11, 134–35, 146–47, 152–53, 202; incarceration camps and, 11, 134–35, 146–47, 153, 202; racialization of, 217; as wilderness, lands of, 82–84, 202. *See also* Izalcos region; Maya

Nazi Germany, 18–19, 23, 214; archaeology on, 33–34; photography of, 24–27, 29, 30, 204–5

Near Westside, Indianapolis: African American beach near, 166; African Americans settling in, 158; urban renewal in, 162; water pollution and, 11, 159–62, 164, 166–67

Negro problem, 172–73

Neolithic *Linearbandkeramik* sites, 17

Newark, New Jersey, 170; crime in, 180, *181*, 182–83; I-280 and, 12, *171*, 182, 195–96; Newark Rebellion, 172, 175–76, 182–85

new forensics, 213

Normark, Johan, 43–44

normativity, 110

NPS. *See* National Park Service

objectification, 8, 22–23, 28

objectivation, 26–27, 204

objective violence, 5, 210–11

Olmsted, Frederick Law, Jr., 160

Olmsted, John Charles, 160

On Photography (Sontag), 27

Orange, New Jersey, 175, *179*; African American community in, 187–88, *189*, 189–90, *190*, 191–92, 195–96, 200n3, 229; crime in, 180, *181*, 182–83; factory closings in, 186–87; I-280 through, 12, *171*, 176, 177, 178, 187–88, *189*, 190–92, *193*, 193–98, 200n3, 229; Italian American community in, 12, 187–88, 191–92, 195–96, 200n3, 229; police violence protested in, 178, 183–87, 196; reverse archaeology for, 198–99; segregation in, 188, 190; Shorty's barbershop in, 189–90, *190*; YMCA in, 188, *189*

Ordinary Men (Browning), 18–19

Orser, Charles, 82

osteoarthritis, 101–2

Palka, Joel W., 48–49

panopticon, 64; in American carceral landscape, 174; in La Florida, 73–75, *75*; Foucault on, 73, 77

Pardee family, 108, 118–19

Pardo, Juan, 69, 74–75, 77, 84, 86

Paris, France, 154

Pee Posh, 134, 146

Pennsylvania. *See* Lattimer Massacre

Pergamon Altar, 8, 31–32, *32*

reducción, 66, 76, 81; congregación and, 9, 67, 82; grid and, 70, 99; Maya and, 42; in Peru, 99; policía and, 9, 67–68, 84

reification, 216, 218; in anthropological writing, 34; capitalist violence and, 210–11; classification and, 207–8; Honneth on, 22–23, 26, 203–4; materiality and, 29–30, 36, 38; of Maya, analogy and, 44; objectification and, 22–23; objectivation and, 26–27, 204; in photography, 26–29; place in, 64; recognition contrasted with, 22–23, 203–4; scholarly, of violence, 8, 30–31, 38; in structural violence, 212–13; subjectivity and, 22–24, 26–27, 33, 203–4

relativism, cultural, 215–16

reverse archaeology, 198–99

ritualistic violence, 17

Robinson, Eugenia, 49–50, 56

Roediger, David, 210–11

Rood, Henry, 125, 127

Roosevelt, Franklin, 134–35

Runnels, Moses T., 159

Salinas y Córdoba, Buenaventura de, 89

San Pedro y San Pablo church, 73, 74

Santa Bárbara mining camp, 98; burial remains of, 99, 100, 100–103, 208; CCSB and, 97, 225–26

Saudi Arabia, 212

Scheper-Hughes, Nancy, 5, 14

Schmidt, Peter R., 36

scientific racism, 127–29

Scott, Doug, 116

segregation: contemporary, 169–70; in Essex County, 170–71, 175, 178, 183,

188, 190–91, 195–99, 229; in Indianapolis, 11–12, 154–55, 156, 157, 158, 158–59, 162–65, 165, 166, 168, 202; in Lattimer, 10, 107, 119, 120–21; pools and Indianapolis, 11–12, 162–65, 165, 202; in Spain, 72–73; in Spanish America, 69–73; structural violence and de facto, 172

sexuality, 215

Sheptak, Russell, 58–59

Silliman, Stephen, 35

silver mining: mita in, 90, 96–97, 105n1, 106n7; under Toledo, 90, 95, 106n6

Simpson, Audra, 66

slavery, 97, 106n7, 217, 223–24

Smith, Linda Tuhiwai, 37

Soaries, Buster, 184–86

social archaeology, 48

Society for Historical Archaeology, 4

Sofsky, Wolfgang, 19

Sontag, Susan, 27–28

Soto, Hernando de, 77, 80, 84

Southeast, US. See La Florida

Soviet Union, 24–26

Spain, 72–73

Spanish America, 85, 209, 218; Black Legend of, 9, 90–93, 104, 105n2, 105nn4–5, 202, 204; ceramics in, 41, 50, 52–53, 53, 54, 54–58, 81, 201, 205; Christianity under, 42; congregación in, 9, 50, 62, 66–67, 69–71, 79, 82; food in, 77–81, 205; fort in, 73, 75, 75; grid plan in, 70–71, 71, 72, 72, 99; as Indio, Native communities under, 39, 42–43; mestizaje in, 8, 43–44, 47; Native counterviolence in, 86, 86; panopticon of, 73–75, 75; place and violence in, 9, 61–62, 66–68, 84–87; policía in, 9, 66–68, 70–71, 71, 72, 72–73, 84; reducción in, 9, 42, 66–68, 70, 76, 81–82, 84, 99; slavery under, 97, 106n7; spatial segregation in, 69–73; structural violence in, 61–62, 66, 77, 80, 91, 93–95, 101–5, 202, 224–25; surveillance in, 73–74, 75, 75; symbolic violence in, 61–62, 82–87; violence, New World, and, 46; wilderness in, 82–84, 202. *See also* La Florida; Izalcos region; Maya; Peru, mining in

spatial violence, 66–67, 205–6; of congregación, 9, 62, 70–71, 82; discipline and punishment in, 64–65, 68–73, 75; in La Florida, 69–70, 73, 77, 84–85, 202; Foucault on, 61, 68–69, 83; in Izalcos region, 69–73, 77–79, 83, 202; law and, 65; policía and, 68; refuge from, 62, 76; symbolic, 82–87; wilderness and, 82–84. *See also* place

Spencer, Robert, 141, 144, 149

Spivak, Gayatri C., 35

The Stranger (Camus), 130

strikes: in coal industry, 10, 107–8, 113–16, 124, 131; Lattimer Massacre and, 10, 107–8, 114–16, 131

structural violence, 201, 226, 228–30; action and, 212–14; African Americans and, 3–4, 155–57, 159, 168, 172, 202; Black Legend obscuring, 91, 93, 104, 202; capitalism and, 210–11; class and, 207, 221; environmental, 155–56; Farmer on, 1–2, 5, 76–77, 82, 156–57, 220, 227; food and, 77; Galtung on, 19, 94, 156; in Huancavelica, 94–95, 101–4, 202; in Indianapolis, African

Americans and, 11–12, 155–57, 159, 168, 202; institutions in, 2–3; Klaus on, 94–95, 103, 209; in mining, Peruvian, 94–95, 101–4, 202; perpetrators of, 209–11; reification in, 212–13; in Spanish America, 61–62, 66, 77, 80, 91, 93–95, 101–5, 202, 224–25; studying, 5–7; subjective violence and, 203–5, 209–10; as term, 207; visibility of, 205–6, 209; Žižek on, 5, 8

structuration, 212–13

subjective violence: of Lattimer Massacre, 10, 109, 111, 116, 129, 131, 203–4, 221; structural violence and, 203–5, 209–10; symbolic violence and, 10, 110–11, 129–30; systemic violence and, 10, 110–11, 130. *See also* direct violence

subjectivity, 208; Althusser on, 20–22, 38n3; Assyrian war scenes and, 30–31; Foucault on, 21, 38n3; interpellation in, 20–22, 32; intersubjectivity, 8, 18, 22–24, 26–27, 34, 36, 109, 203–4; past, traces of, 33, 37–38; in photography, 25; reification and, 22–24, 26–27, 33, 203–4

surveillance, 73–74, 75, 75

symbolic violence, 37, 204; Bourdieu on, 7, 14n1, 19, 38n2, 82; discursive violence and, 211; of excavations, 33, 38n4; Lattimer Massacre and, 10, 113, 118, 124–25; Maya and, 42; misrecognition in, 7, 82; normativity in, 110; of photography, 26–28; racialized, in coal industry, 113, 129; in Spanish America, 61–62, 82–87; spatial, 82–87; subjective violence and, 10, 110–11, 129–30; systemic violence supported by, 110, 124, 129–31

Syrian refugees, 15–16
systemic violence: in Lattimer, 10, 111,
123–24, 205; subjective violence and,
10, 110–11, 130; symbolic violence
supporting, 110, 124, 129–31; Žižek on,
210–11

Taussig, Michael, 82–83
Te Punga Somerville, Alice, 84–85
terrorism, 16
Terry, Curtis, 167
thick description, 18–19, 25
Time and the Other (Fabian), 34
Tlaxcallans, 72–73
Toledo, Francisco, 90, 95, 106n6
Tomasello, Michael, 22
town house mounds, 84, 84
traza (central plaza), 70–71, 71, 72, 75
Turkey, 35

urban renewal, 162

Velasco, Luis de, 89
violence. See specific types of violence
visibility, theme of, 205–6, 209, 218, 227
Voss, Barbara, 215, 226

Wacquant, Loïc, 5, 14n1, 174
Walker, Darrell, 184–87, 196
war journalists, 38n4
War Relocation Authority (WRA), 135,
146–47, 149
Weber, Max, 20

Weiss, Peter, 8, 31–32
Weizman, Eyal, 27
Wenger, Etienne, 56
White, Russell, 184, 186
White Legend, 92
whiteness: binoculars of, 169–71, 175,
197–99, 205, 229; capitalism and, 210–
11; Dyson on, 169–70, 197–98; wages
of, Du Bois on, 6
white poverty, 170
White River, Indiana: in African American neighborhoods, 11–12, 154–55, 159,
161–62, 166; beaches along, 154, 156,
162, 168, 202, 205; pollution of, 11, 154–
55, 157, 159, 161, 163, 164, 166–68, 202;
proposals for, 12, 154, 160–62, 167–68,
202, 205; segregation and, 156, 157–58,
158, 162, 165–66
widowed landscapes, 9, 83–84
wilderness, 82–84, 202
witness, archaeology as, 13–14, 225
Wolfe, Patrick, 217
WRA. See War Relocation Authority

Yanagisako, Sylvia, 214
Yemen, conflict in, 212

Zille, Heinrich, 24
Žižek, Slavoj, 111, 205, 219; on structural
violence, 5, 8; on systemic, objective
violence, 5, 210–11; on violence, cold
analysis of, 13, 207, 218

CPSIA information can be obtained
at www.ICGtesting.com
Printed in the USA
LVHW112013271020
669966LV00004B/94